W9-CPO-898

TECHNIQUES OF MEDIATION

By

WALTER A. MAGGIOLO

OCEANA PUBLICATIONS, INC.
New York • London • Rome

Library of Congress Cataloging in Publication Data

Maggiolo, Walter A., 1908-
  Techniques of medition.

  Bibliography: p.
  Includes index.
  1. Mediation and conciliation, Industrial—United
States.   2. Mediation and conciliation, Industrial.
I. Title.
HD5504.A3M23   1985   331.89'142   85-13879
ISBN 0-379-20694-3
Second Revised Edition

Manufactured in the United States of America

To my late brother
COMMISSIONER HENRY L. MAGGIOLO
an outstanding mediator
and a constant source
of inspiration and encouragement.
His unselfish sacrifices
made all things possible.

TABLE OF CONTENTS

FOREWORD

Walter Maggiolo's excellent book warrants a wide audience, both lay and professional.

The author is a veteran mediator and an acknowledged authority on conflict resolution. While his prior book Techniques of Mediation in Labor Disputes was, as its title indicates, confined to mediation of labor disputes, the present volume has a broader sweep, demonstrating the value of mediation in many areas.

This is not a mere academic treatise. It reflects both the experience and the techniques which the author has gained and employed during his distinguished career of 35 years as a professional mediator.

It is almost conventional wisdom that the art of mediation cannot be taught; that it is an art--not a science.

Mr. Maggiolo convincingly argues a contrary view that there are techniques and guidelines which can be taught and learned in conflict resolution.

His book, therefore, is an important text for an age which has come to recognize that conflict resolution by mediation is preferable to imposed solutions.

It is must reading for those who are committed to the view that "jaw, jaw, jaw" is far more preferable than "war, war, war" in both foreign and domestic conflicts.

Arthur J. Goldberg
Former Justice of the Supreme
Court of the United States,
Secretary of Labor,
and Ambassador

PREFACE

Since the publication of the author's book, <u>Techniques of
Mediation in Labor Disputes</u>, in 1971, there has been an ever
increasing acceptance of the concept of mediation as the
most desirable method of resolving conflicts. This acceptance has engendered experimentation in and expansion of the
role of mediation far beyond its traditional use in labor-
management disputes. Disputants in controversies involving
other social, economic, and legal fields have turned to mediation. Mediation is being utilized in disputes involving
divorce, family, consumers, housing, age discrimination, environment, civil rights, prison, and landlord-tenant situations.

The recognition of the right of public employees to bargain
collectively has had the effect of opening new horizons on
the uses of mediation not only in its pure form but also
in combination with other recognized dispute resolution
procedures.

In view of these developments, readers of the prior volume
have urged that it be revised not only by expanding on some
of the suggested mediation techniques but also updating it
in the light of the current developments in the field.

In this volume, we have attempted to meet both objectives,
and in doing so have tried to continue to place the major
emphasis on the practical rather than the theoretical.

This volume is a distillation of the experiences and techniques which the author has used in his cases spanning over
33 years as a full-time professional mediator.

It is an attempt to assist not only those who contemplate
entering this most challenging and dynamic field but also
to articulate some of the approaches and techniques used
by many practitioners.

For a long time, many mediators have insisted that mediation was a pure art and, hence, could not be the subject
matter of analysis or definition. While mediation in many
senses is an art, nevertheless, the techniques used can be
described and discussed. The correct application of these
techniques to a given situation is the true art.

No guide or set of techniques can be a substitute for the mediator's judgment. His judgment must be based on the then status of negotiations, the personalities involved, and the issues in dispute. After carefully weighing all these factors, he--and he alone--should decide what of the suggested approaches and techniques, if any, may be applicable in a given situation.

ACKNOWLEDGMENTS

The author wishes to express his appreciation to Professor Jerome T. Barrett of the Northern Kentucky University and former Director of Technical Services of the Federal Mediation and Conciliation Service, who is the author of Chapters III, IV, V, XXVII, XXVIII, XXIX, and XXX, and compiled the Bibliography. Doctor Barrett also assisted in the editing of the manuscript and gave generously of his time in making suggestions for improvement.

We are also indebted to Mr. Joseph Swire, nationally recognized insurance and pension consultant, for his contribution of much of the material found in Chapter XXXII; and to Miss A. Lauretta Whitney who so patiently deciphered our handwriting and typed the manuscript.

Walter A. Maggiolo

1985

CHAPTER I
THE NATIONAL LABOR-MANAGEMENT DISPUTE POLICY

Philosophical Basis

In order to evaluate properly our national labor-management
dispute policy and the relationship of the mediation process
to it, the policy should be assessed in the light of some
of the basic concepts upon which our democratic society has
been founded.

Our society is fundamentally a "meeting-of-minds" civilization. Our whole way of life is predicated on the principle
that while the individual members of our society may have
varying economic, political, and social backgrounds and consequently divergent viewpoints, when occasion demands, they
can and must subordinate and accommodate their self-interest to the common good. As members of a democratic society,
each individual group, although starting from apparently
widely divergent positions, can by the process of reasoning,
utilization of the normal avenues of communication, discussion, judicious use of constructive compromise and recognition of human ideas, arrive at a "meeting of minds" and go
down the road together toward a common objective--the over-
riding public welfare. Conflict is thus supplanted by cooperation.

To many, the word "compromise" conjures up the concept of
"splitting the difference," regardless of the reason for
doing so. Constructive compromise is based on the recognition that others may have ideas which are equally valid
and which call for a modification of our ideas to accommodate theirs.

The notion that differences and difficulties between individuals and groups in our society are reconcilable is basic
to our democratic society. Our whole legislative process
is one of constructive compromise. Legislators seek out
the possible rather than insisting on the perfect which is
unattainable.

Our society is also predicated on the principles of voluntarism as opposed to compulsion. Duties as well as rights
flow out of the social relationship. The primary burden of

carrying out the purpose of the society properly is upon
the individual members or groups rather than the governing
power. To the extent that the component individuals voluntarily assume and exercise their individual responsibilities
as members of the society to resolve their own political,
economic, and social differences, a democracy is strength-
ened and flourishes.

Further, there is an inter-relationship between all group
economic actions and the common welfare. This relationship
is effectuated in our democratic society through a recognition that private economic rights may not be exercised in a
manner which will override the paramount public interest of
the society as a whole.

Consistent with these basic principles, we have evolved our
national policy by defining relative responsibilities for
maintaining industrial peace. Essentially, this national
policy charges both labor and management with the primary
responsibility of making collective bargaining work and,
through acceptance of this responsibility, to seek amicable
solutions to their labor disputes. In turn, the Government
has the responsibility of defining the base lines within
which justice demands that the parties confine themselves
and, as assistance to the parties, making available to them
full and adequate facilities for conciliation and mediation.

Legislative History of Policy

This policy is not new. Its roots may be found in legislation dealing with railroad disputes which preceded the creation of the Department of Labor. It is carried forward in
the Act establishing the United States Department of Labor,
the 1918 recommendations of the War Labor Conference Board,
the National War Labor Board of World War I, in Section 7(a)
of the National Labor Relations Act, and Section 502 of the
Defense Production Act. It is implied in the spirit and
letter of the Wagner Act and the Labor-Management Relations
Act, 1947. Each, legislatively and administratively, emphasized that the parties should voluntarily seek solutions to
their disputes utilizing the assistance provided by mediation and conciliation, if necessary.

This policy was re-emphasized by former President Eisenhower
who stated:

>   "Labor relations will be managed best when worked
>   out in honest negotiation between employers and

> unions, without Government's unwarranted inter-
> ference. This concept, relying as it does on
> collective bargaining, assumes that labor or-
> ganizations and management will both observe
> the highest standards of integrity, responsi-
> bility, and concern for the national welfare."

It is not the responsibility of the Government, except in
periods of emergency, to dictate to the parties the terms
of their collective bargaining contract.

A free industrial society demands that the members of that
society have full freedom of contract, provided that freedom is exercised consonant with the paramount public interest. The collective bargaining contract should be the result of earnest and intelligent efforts of both parties to
the agreement. It should be their own contract--to govern
their own relationships--for the stated term.

A labor contract imposed by Government fiat is as repugnant
to our moral and legal principles as a unilateral dictation
of the terms of the contract by labor or management, without due regard for the rights of the employees involved and
its impact on the public interest.

In our industrial society, no longer may either labor or
management regard their labor disputes as their private
property to be settled according to the dictates of their
own self interests and resort to the economic weapons of
the strike or lockout without regard to their impact on the
community. (Of course, the right to strike or lockout must
be preserved since often the effect of a threatened strike
or lockout is the sole motivation for compromise and settlement.)

If labor and management espouse the doctrine of free collective bargaining, they must adopt its corollary--collective
bargaining to be free must be responsible. Responsible to
the public welfare.

Relation Of Mediation To National Policy

The mediation process assumes the validity and force of the
basic concepts (outlined above)--namely, a meeting-of-minds
civilization, voluntarism, the reposing of responsibility
upon subsidiary groups, and the principle of the supremacy
of the public interest. In a word, the professional mediator facilitates the meeting-of-minds process and by volun-

tary means and methods re-emphasizes the prime responsibility of the disputant parties to seek their own solution compatible with the public interest. It is an entirely voluntary process which permits the parties to negotiate their own agreement free from Government compulsion or dictation.

As former Director William E. Simkin expressed it, "the core of mediation is the preservation of the fundamental right of the parties to say no without incurring legal sanctions for doing so." Mediation carries forward the concept of free and responsible collective bargaining as the optimum method of achieving industrial peace.

Paul Hanri Spaak, former Secretary General of the United States, stated:

> "Mediation and conciliation are playing a greater and greater role in relations between classes and nations. This is fortunate. It is a manifestation of a tendency in which one can fully rejoice. It is an expression of one of the highest virtues which can be practiced: the desire to understand and be just toward one another. Each time that one attempts to resolve a conflict without force one renders to men an enormous service in leading them in the path of wisdom and of respect for themselves and for each other."

In this book, an attempt will be made to evaluate and analyze mediation and its role as a dispute settling process.

CHAPTER II

DISPUTE RESOLUTION PROCEDURES— PRIVATE SECTOR

In the United States today, there are four basic procedures
used for the settlement of labor disputes--collective bargaining, arbitration, fact-finding, and mediation. The dispute resolution procedures of arbitration, fact-finding and
mediation have, in turn, a number of variations and combinations fashioned to meet the desires of the parties to the
dispute, or in implementation of an industrial relations
policy adopted by a legislature.

Collective Bargaining

Collective bargaining has been described as the process by
which representatives of an employer and representatives of
his employees meet to discuss and negotiate the various
phases of their relationship, which have been declared to
be proper subject matters of bargaining, with the objective
of arriving at a mutually acceptable labor agreement.

On the Federal level, such bargaining must take place within the peripheries established by Congress in various relevant statutes such as the Labor-Management Relations Act,
the Fair Labor Standards Act, and the like.

An agreement arrived at by successful collective bargaining
without the use of any substitute, aid, or adjunct is the
most desirable method of settlement of any labor dispute.

If the settlement is cast with a consciousness of the public
interest, an agreement arrived at through voluntary collective bargaining reflects the full assumption of the basic
responsibility for the maintenance of industrial peace by
the parties themselves.

Arbitration

Arbitration, in the context of labor disputes, is an adver-
sarily proceeding. It involves the submission of a dispute
to a neutral or a group of neutrals whose function it is to
conduct hearings, evaluate the evidence and testimony submitted, and render a judgment (termed an award) which is
binding upon the parties.

There are two broad categories of arbitration--rights arbitration and interest arbitration. By rights arbitration is meant the arbitration of grievances over the rights of the parties under a collective bargaining contract. By interest arbitration is meant the arbitration of terms and conditions to be incorporated in an initial or renewal of a collective bargaining agreement.

Arbitration can be either compulsory or voluntary. Arbitration is compulsory if the submission of the dispute to the neutral is based not on the consent, expressed or implied, of the parties but rather on administrative or legal compulsion or direction.

In the United States--on the Federal level--there is no compulsory arbitration. In the United States today, the only instances of compulsory arbitration are found in some State statutes relating to public utilities or "industries affected with a public interest. In such States,[1] the legislature having restricted or prohibited the right to strike realized the necessity for some machinery to adjust labor disputes arising in these industries. Compulsory arbitration was the selected process.

Arbitration is voluntary when the submission to the neutral is based on the consent, expressed or implied, of the parties. This is the most widely used arbitration method. It is most prevalent as the terminal point of the grievance procedure provisions of collective bargaining contracts.

Arbitration is termed by many as a substitute for collective bargaining. However, most professional arbitrators insist that it is merely an extension of collective bargaining.

Types of Arbitration

There are three basic types of arbitration: permanent or impartial chairman, tripartite, and ad hoc.

"Permanent" or Impartial Chairman

A number of collective bargaining contracts name one individual as the "permanent" or impartial chairman (also in some contracts termed "impartial umpire") who has been selected by the parties to act as arbitrator for all disputes arising under the existing contract. His term of office expires coincidental with the expiration of the contract.

Normally, his compensation is based on a retainer plus a
per diem which is shared by both parties.

Those who espouse this type of arbitration allege that such
a person will become thoroughly versed in the terms of the
collective bargaining contract and the application of those
provisions in the particular company involved and thus assure consistency and uniformity in the awards rendered on
the disputes which arise during the contract term. They
further state that this type of arbitration avoids necessity of "educating" an arbitrator each time a dispute arises
as to the collective bargaining contract provisions and
plant practices.

Those who refuse to accept this type of arbitration argue
that it may be fine if the "permanent" chairman's performance during the contract term is satisfactory to both parties. However, if the person selected is found by one
party to be unsatisfactory in the first few months or middle of the contract term, it would be difficult, and perhaps costly, to dispense with his services before the expiration of his term.

A variation of the "permanent" arbitrator type found in
some contracts is the naming of three or more arbitrators.
Such arbitrators serve on a rotating basis for the duration of the contract. If any of the arbitrators whose turn
it is are unavailable, the next arbitrator on the list is
selected. A few contracts provide for the establishment
of a roster of arbitrators to serve on a rotating basis
for the duration of the contract. The collective bargaining agreement also provides that during the contract term
the parties will review the roster periodically. During
such review period each party has the unchallenged right to
have any of the arbitrators striken from the roster.

Tripartite Arbitration

In the tripartite type, each party to the collective bargaining agreement selects his own representative on the
arbitration panel. The two so selected then pick the neutral chairman. The three then hear and determine disputes
arising under the contract as a panel. Normally, the vote
of the majority determines the disposition of the issue
presented.

The proponents of this type of arbitration allege that this method assures that each party's viewpoint will be considered not only at the hearing but also when the panel is deliberating its award in executive sessions.

If this method is chosen, care must be taken to make provision for the selection of the neutral in the event the two appointees are unable to agree. The most practical way of breaking such an impasse is to provide in the collective bargaining agreement that the two appointees must agree on the neutral within a limited time period. Upon failure to do so, provision should be made that such neutral will be selected by an outside agency--either the Federal Mediation and Conciliation Service, the American Arbitration Association, or the State Mediation Agency, if there is one.

Ad Hoc

Under the ad hoc type, the arbitrators are selected on a case-by-case basis. Generally speaking, the practice is to provide that if the parties fail to agree on an arbitrator within a prescribed time period, some agency that maintains an arbitration roster will be requested either to submit a panel or to make a direct appointment of a neutral.

Those who advocate this type of arbitration assert that it has a number of advantages over the permanent chairman and the tripartite types. They also urge that the ad hoc approach is more realistic than the tripartite type. They argue that the arbitrators nominated by each party must of necessity be partisan and consequently the real decision is made by the neutral. Ad hoc arbitration, they say, cuts through this sham and additionally assures more expeditious disposition of the grievance.

Last Offer Arbitration

In the public sector, some State statutes provide for the submission of the last offer of each party to an arbitrator who must select one or the other last offer. As will be described in Chapter IV, other statutes provide a number of variations; e.g., issue-by-issue, etc.

Expedited Arbitration

In relatively recent years, parties to collective bargaining contracts have decided that there are some grievances

which should be disposed of without the necessity of pre-
or post-hearing briefs, stenographic records, or formal
arbitrators' opinions. These grievances usually involved
disciplinary actions.

This procedure has been termed expedited arbitration. The
arbitrator hears the evidence, which often consists of an
agreed statement of facts, and issues an award without opinion. If the arbitrator feels it necessary, he may issue a
short explanatory comment. Under almost all expedited procedures, the award is not considered a precedent in future
grievances.

The value of expedited arbitration lies not only in the
avoidance of the cost and expense of a formal arbitration
proceeding but also in cutting down on the attendant delays.

Obtaining the Services of an Arbitrator

In addition to the Federal Mediation and Conciliation Service and the American Arbitration Association, there are
several State agencies which maintain a roster of people
who have been selected by the agency as being qualified to
handle the arbitration of labor disputes.

Many contracts provide that if the parties are unable to
agree on an arbitrator either may request one of the agencies mentioned above to provide them with a panel of available arbitrators. Upon receipt of such a request, unless
otherwise specified, the agency will send to each party a
panel of arbitrators. The Federal Mediation and Conciliation Service normally sends a panel of seven. The American
Arbitration Association's practice is to send panels containing nine to twelve names. Accompanying such panel is
usually a short biographical sketch of each name appearing
thereon. The parties then meet and usually by a system of
alternatively striking, arrive at a selection and then advise the agency of the name of the arbitrator selected.

Another practice followed by some is for each to independently indicate opposite the panel member's name their first,
second, and third choice. Each then transmits to the agency
his order of choice. The agency will then compare the two
transmissions and appoint as arbitrator the one upon whom
there is agreement, or absent an agreement, the arbitrator
standing the highest in the order of preference indicated
by both parties.

A problem arises where one or both parties reject the panel
of arbitrators submitted to them. Under the American Arbitration Association's "Voluntary Labor Arbitration Rules,"
if the parties fail to agree upon any of the persons named
on the list or if those named decline or are unable to act,
or if for any other reason the appointment cannot be made
from the submitted lists, the Administrator has the authority to make the appointment from other members of the panel
without the submission of any additional lists. No second
panel would be submitted unless, in exceptional cases, there
are special circumstances which would warrant a departure
from its general rule.

Under the procedures of the Federal Mediation and Conciliation Service, if one party requests the submission of a second panel, the Federal Mediation and Conciliation Service
will examine the collective bargaining agreement between the
parties to determine whether there is specific language permitting the submission of a second panel on such unilateral
request. If both parties request a second panel, the Federal Mediation and Conciliation Service will comply with
that request.

Upon notification of his appointment, the arbitrator has a
duty to contact promptly both parties to arrange for a date
for the hearing. The proceedings are then conducted under
the rules and regulations[2] prescribed by the appointing
agency.

It is important to note that at the point when the agency
appoints the arbitrator selected by the parties or, if desired, by direct designation, the arbitrator so selected or
designated is not an employee of the appointing agency but
an employee of the parties themselves. Consequently, the
questions of fee and its collection, dates of hearing, procedures, briefs, stenographic records and the like are matters to be decided between the parties and the arbitrator.
Similarly, the merits of the award, its modification or its
enforcement must be pursued by the parties. The appointing
agency has no authority to review, modify, or enforce the
arbitrator's award. The appointing agency does, however,
investigate complaints of excessive charges, improper conduct, and undue delays in either scheduling hearings or
rendition of awards.

Each arbitrator determines what his normal per diem fee is
and certifies it to the appointing agency. An arbitrator

may change his per diem fee at any time, but under the Federal Mediation and Conciliation Service rules must give at
least thirty days' notice of his intent to do so. The biographical sketch sent to the parties reflects each arbitrator's normal per diem charges.

Fact-Finding

In its original context, fact-finding was described as the
submission of a dispute to a neutral or group of neutrals
whose duty it is to conduct hearings, find the facts concerning the dispute, and make such findings public. Fact-
finding did not necessarily imply any duty of the fact-
finding body to make recommendations for the settlement of
the dispute.

The theory behind fact-finding was that once the neutral or
neutrals had found the facts and made them a matter of public knowledge there would be a marshalling of public opinion. The moral force of such marshalled public opinion would
persuade the disputants to change their prior positions and
make agreement possible. Whether there could a marshalling
of public opinion behind the public recommendations of a
fact-finding report depends on the impact of the dispute on
the public and the community. Prescinding from cases involving the national safety or health, unless there is a
strong underlying problem of public inconvenience (as in a
strike of the drivers of a major urban or inter-urban tran-
sit company) or a prolonged work stoppage at the plant of
the major employer in the community, there would be little
likelihood of a strong surge of public opinion, sparked by
the media, in support of the fact-finder's report.

Like arbitration, fact-finding can be either compulsory or
voluntary. An example of compulsory fact-finding is found
in Section 206 of the Labor-Management Relations Act, 1947,
as amended, relating to the appointment of boards of inquiry in emergency disputes. Voluntary fact-finding occurs
when the procedure is founded on the consent, expressed or
implied, of the parties to the disupte. It has been utilized in disputes involving initial contracts, contract re-
newals, and the adjustment of grievances, especially those
concerned with incentive or work-load problems.

One of the popular misconceptions about fact-finding is that
it necessarily involves the making of recommendations for
the settlement of the dispute. No fact-finding board has

the inherent right to make such recommendations. In its pure sense, fact-finding confines itself to a public finding of the facts. The power to go the further step of recommendation must be specifically granted to the board. It can be founded either on the consent of the parties or in the statute creating the board.

On analysis, fact-finding is a misnomer. The parties usually know what the facts are. The basic purpose of fact-finding is to facilitate a settlement not merely to produce a report. One of the proven functions of the selected neutral is to serve as a lightning rod. It is incumbent upon the fact-finder to fashion recommendations which the parties can use as a blueprint or at least as a guide for the settlement of outstanding issues between them. The real guide for a fact-finder is to seek out and determine what kind of recommendations the parties can ratify and live with comfortably.

"Advisory" arbitration is not a novel concept. For a long period of time, this dispute settling technique was utilized in the private sector, particularly in American Newspaper Guild contracts with the wire service companies such as Associated and United Press. "Advisory" arbitration is really a contradiction in terms since it lacks the finality of true arbitration. Finality is one of the distinguishing attributes between arbitration and fact-finding. "Advisory" arbitration is in reality fact-finding with authority to make recommendations.

The basic distinction between arbitration and fact-finding is that, in arbitration, the parties are bound to accept the arbitrator's award; whereas, in fact-finding, the parties are free to accept or reject the fact-finder's report.

Mediation and Conciliation

Generally speaking, mediation or conciliation of a labor dispute has been described as the intercession of a neutral third person in a dispute for the purpose of assisting the parties to resolve their differences voluntarily. The ultimate goal of mediation is to assist disputants to arrive at their own agreeement.

Mediation and conciliation have been used interchangeably. The name Federal Mediation and Conciliation Service was the result of a compromise reached in a conference committee of the Senate and House. The Senate wanted Federal Mediation; the House wanted Federal Conciliation. Some State statutes establishing a mediation agency will in the preamble or title speak of a Board of Mediation and in the body of the law refer to its employees as conciliators.

Even though the terms conciliation and mediation often are used interchangeably, there is at least a technical distinction between the process of conciliation and mediation.

Conciliation is the more passive role. As is indicated by its latin derivative, it is the act of "gaining good will; to render concordant; to mollify." It involves the bringing of disputing parties together, under circumstances and in an atmosphere most conducive to a discussion of the problem in an objective way for the purpose of seeking a solution to the issue or issues involved. It has been equated to the extension of the "good offices" concept of international law.

Mediation is the more active role. It goes beyond the simple catalytic agent stage. When occasion demands, a mediator interjects himself into the discussions and makes affirmative suggestions and recommendations for developing areas of possible agreement on the issues involved in the dispute.

Both Federal and State mediation statutes, often in the same context, use the two terms synonymously.

In actual practice, the professional mediator when handling a dispute case frequently alternates between the role of a conciliator and that of a mediator. When the discussions are following fruitful paths, he may well adopt the role of the passive chairman (conciliator). If discussions encounter an apparent roadblock or appear to wander into dead-end lanes, he will resume his role as mediator and by adroit questioning and suggestions either indicate the by-pass or point out the true road.

The concept of the use of mediation to reconcile conflicts is not new. One of the early legendary uses goes back to biblical times. According to the legend, a village shiek died leaving three sons. In his will, he left 1/2 of his herd of camels to his oldest son; 1/4 to his middle son and 1/5 to his youngest son. When the sons discovered that there were only 19 camels in the herd, a bitter quarrel

broke out as to the proper division. A wise old man with
only one camel was visiting in the village. When he heard
of the quarrel, he had the three sons to meet him at the
corral. When they had done so, he added his one camel to
the herd. He then directed the eldest son to take his half.
The son took 10 camels. He then directed the middle son to
take his fourth. That son led away five camels. The youngest then took his fifth or four camels. When all this was
accomplished, the old man took his one camel and slowly continued his journey.

Realistically, mediation by agencies of State or the Federal Government is not new. In 1878, Maryland passed an
arbitration and conciliation law. By 1900, the same type
of legislation was enacted in twenty-five States. On the
Federal level, Government mediation was first made available in railroad disputes. In 1913, Congress in creating
the United States Department of Labor authorized the Secretary of Labor to appoint commissioners of conciliation. In
1947, an independent agency--Federal Mediation and Conciliation Service--was established which assumed the functions
and personnel of the United States Conciliation Service.

Mediation is and should be purely a voluntary process. To
this end, the Federal Mediation and Conciliation Service
has consistently resisted any legislative attempt to grant
it subpoena powers. The Service has felt that if a party
is compelled to attend a mediation meeting scheduled by the
Service, the reluctant party may by its attitude make it
clear that its attendance is only because of the compulsion
and not for the purpose of resolving the dispute. It would
create an atmosphere which is not conducive to successful
mediation efforts. The Service perfers to rely on persuasion rather than compulsion.

Questions have been raised as to whether either party can
refuse with impunity to accept mediation proffered by the
Service in view of the provisions of Section 204(a)3 of the
Labor-Management Relations Act. That section reads:

> "...in case such dispute is not settled by con-
> ference, participate fully and promptly in such
> meetings as may be undertaken by the Service
> under this Act for the purpose of aiding in a
> settlement of the dispute."[3]

Somewhat similar language is contained in the Health Care Amendments--Section 8(d)(c) of the Labor-Management Relations Act, 1947.

The implication drawn from the statutory language is that the refusal of a party to "participate fully and promptly" in mediation meetings may be some evidence of a refusal to bargain in good faith. In view of the Service's policy of the voluntary nature of mediation, it is extremely doubtful if the Service would ever initiate or suggest any such charge. There has been no test of the enforceability of this section.

On the Federal level, there is one exception to the general rule of the voluntary nature of mediation. That exception is found in the provisions of the Railway Labor Act. If mediation is requested by either party or the Board, in the national interest, intercedes in a dispute on its own motion, the Act requires the parties to submit their dispute to mediation by the National Mediation Board. Such procedure has been termed "mandatory mediation."

Several State mediation agencies, including New York, have subpoena power but very rarely resort to it.

Mediation is inseparable from collective bargaining. It is an integral part of the dispute settlement process. It is not a substitution for collective bargaining but a supplement to it, or--as some writers have expressed--it is an extension of the collective bargaining process.

Mediators, unlike arbitrators, are concerned not with what they personally may deem to be a just settlement but rather what is acceptable to the parties. Also, unlike arbitration, the parties can freely, and without penalty, reject suggestions or recommendations made by mediators. To that extent, it partakes of some of the attributes of the modern fact-finding process. It, however, lacks the formalities surrounding fact-finding in that mediators do not issue reports or make recommendations except in a very limited type of case more fully described in Chapter XXII.

Med-Arb

Med-Arb is a dispute settlement technique fostered and promoted by Sam Kagel, a prominent arbitrator in the Bay area of California. It is now found mostly in the public sector.

It can be described as the dispute resolution process in which the parties select an individual with the understanding that he will first mediate the issues in dispute and all issues not settled through mediation will be disposed of by the same person acting as an arbitrator.

In the med-arb process, the mediator has much more authority than an individual acting solely as a mediator. Advocates of this approach contend that the possibility of an adverse award on issues unresolved by mediation places greater pressure on the parties to cooperate with the med-arb individual when he is acting as a mediator.[4]

NOTES

1.   Examples of such States are Florida, Indiana, Wisconsin, and Nebraska. cf Bus Employees v. Wisconsin Board, 340 U.S. 383; Amalgamated Association v. Missouri, 374 U.S. 74.

2.   For text of rules and regulations of the Federal Mediation and Conciliation Service and the American Arbitration Association cf Appendix.

3.   cf Appendix.

4.   cf Chapter III, page 24.

CHAPTER III

DISPUTE RESOLUTION PROCEDURES— FEDERAL SECTOR

Most writers trace the history of modern labor-management relations in the U.S. Government to the administration of John Kennedy. Prior to President Kennedy, there was little encouragement of unionization or collective bargaining for Federal employees. The Pendleton Act of 1883, for example, made clear that only the Congress could regulate Federal employees' wages and working conditions. The La Follette Act of 1912 opened the door only slightly by giving postal employees the right to join unions that did not assert the right to strike. That Act did not cover the majority of Federal employees, and it did not provide for collective bargaining even for postal employees.

Even the Roosevelt New Deal did not change the status of Federal employees. While extending revolutionary rights and protections to private sector employees with the 1935 Wagner Act, President Roosevelt continued the policies of the past for Federal workers.

The President Kennedy Executive Order

It was the issuance of Executive Order 10988 by President Kennedy in 1962 which started the movement toward rights for Federal employees to join unions and to engage in bargaining with their employer. The Executive Order provided a limited form of collective bargaining compared to the private sector. The scope of bargaining was limited to less consequential topics like rest periods, safety, bulletin boards, and jury duty. The more important topics such as wages and benefits were determined by the Congress. Also, by defining management rights very broadly, the Executive Order significantly limited the topics available for negotiations. In spite of the limitations of the Executive Order, thousands of Federal employees joined unions within the next few years. President John Griner of the American Federation of Government Employees was moved to characterize the Executive Order as the "magna charta" for Federal employees.

The Executive Order had a unique procedure for resolving bargaining impasses. If negotiations did not result in settlement, the union's only recourse, since strikes were strictly prohibited, was an appeal to the top management of the agency with which the union had the dispute. It was a system in which the referee was on the payroll of one of the parties.

While the Executive Order did not provide for the use of the Federal Mediation and Conciliation Service (Service) in Federal employee impasses, the Service did receive a number of requests for assistance from labor and management. To clarify the situation for Federal agencies, the Civil Service Commission (CSC) issued Bulletin 700-5 on April 30, 1962, stating that the Order gave the Service no authority to mediate in the Federal service. The Bulletin effectively stopped further requests for FMCS assistance during the next two years. The Service agreed with the effect of the Bulletin because budget and staffing limits made it convenient to do so.[1]

By 1965, as the number of Federal service impasses continued to grow, the Service initiated a series of discussions with the CSC, other Federal agencies, and unions of Federal employees. A concensus evolved that the use of mediation should be reconsidered. To do so, it was agreed that it would be helpful to have some information on actual mediation cases in the Federal service.[2]

In response, in 1965, the FMCS adopted an unpublicized policy and procedure for considering mediation requests in the Federal service. Among other things, this policy included the following provisions: (1) All requests for mediation had to be screened and decided upon at the National Office level in Washington, D.C. (2) No request would be considered unless made jointly by both parties and usually in writing. (3) No request would be considered unless, following genuine bargaining efforts, both parties agreed that an impasse had been reached. (4) In the event that a joint request was approved, the FMCS would select and assign the individual mediator. (5) The mediator assigned would be available only for a limited period of time or a limited number of joint meetings, as the situation dictated.[3]

During the next four years, 40 cases were mediated under this experimental policy. A number of the cases had been in negotiation for two and three years. In spite of these protracted periods of impasse and the limited circumstances under which mediation was made available, mediation was successful. As a Service official wrote about this project in May 1969, thirty-four cases were settled, four had not been settled, and six were still in mediation.[4]

The President Nixon Executive Order

The experience of the parties and several studies encouraged the Nixon administration to issue a new Executive Order effective in January 1970 (E.O. 11941) which corrected many of the shortcomings in the earlier Order. Provision was made for resolving bargaining unit questions; election procedures were established; binding arbitration of grievances was allowed with an expanded scope of grievances; management's right to exclude topics from negotiations by issuing rules and policy was significantly limited. But most significantly, for the first time, third-party neutrals were allowed in Federal employee impasses with the creation of the Federal Service Impasses Panel with authority to use the traditional methods of mediation, fact-finding, and arbitration.

While the Kennedy Order had not provided for the use of the Federal Mediation and Conciliation Service, the new Executive Order gave the Service a formal status in the procedure. Former FMCS coordinator of this program, Jerry Ross, discussed the program in the early 70's in this way:

"In most instances, mediators in Federal service negotiations confront factors not usually present in private sector disputes. The parties were usually inexperienced in contract negotiations. Many issues involved questions of negotiability under the management's rights clauses in the Executive Order, and many others concerned complex problems dealing with civil service personnel regulations not found in private sector labor relations. Further, several levels of management not represented at the bargaining table were involved in decisions which directly affected the negotiations, and the bureaucracy often was not responsive to the bargainers' needs for timely answers, nor were there any strong pressures on the parties to reach agreement as quickly as possible. Because of these factors, mediators often determined that mediation could be of no service to the parties and withdrew from negotiations. Union and agency bargainers usually remained at the negotiations table for many, many months before agreements were reached."[5]

A New FMCS Policy

In 1973, William Usery, newly appointed Director of FMCS, initiated a new policy in which the Service became an "active advocate" of collective bargaining in the Federal Government. The new policy was accompanied by organizational changes which made monitoring of Federal disputes more comprehensive and effective. In significant part, the policy said:

> "...we must recognize two important differences in the way mediators must work in Federal Government negotiations: (1) During negotiations more time must be devoted to patiently educating the parties to their roles and responsibilities, and (2) more time must be devoted to ascertaining, and dealing with, the real decision-makers, especially within agencies. Of course, these two considerations must be coupled with the same aggressive mediation style which contributes to producing hundreds of settlements in the private sector."[6]

The new policy resulted in an extensive increase in mediation assistance provided by the Service. Having handled less than 100 cases in 1973, during the Fiscal Years 1973-75, the Service mediated 959 cases, and provided technical assistance in 76 cases. This volume of mediation has continued. During a comparable period (Fiscal Years 1979-81), the Service mediated 1097 cases.[7]

Federal Service Impasses Panel

The Service has not been the only agency providing mediation assistance in the Federal service. In spite of objections by the Service, the Federal Service Impasses Panel mediates disputes. The Panel, created by the 1970 Executive Order, is to adjudicate impasses in the Federal service. Part of their procedure is to conduct fact-finding hearings on impasse cases after agreement has not been reached during mediation by the Service. Beginning informally in 1973, Panel staff scheduled pre-hearing conferences on the day before each fact-finding hearing at which time they offered their own mediation assistance. The practice continued to grow, and in spite of the objection of the Service, it continues today. The Service objects because it is confusing to the parties at best, and in the worst cases the parties

do not take the mediation efforts of the Service seriously
enough on the assumption that more mediation will follow
with the Panel.

Meetings between the two agencies following a critical report by the General Accounting Office resulted in an understanding that (1) if the Service requests the return of a
case from the Panel to allow further mediation by the Service, the case will be returned; (2) Panel staff will limit
their mediation effort to the pre-hearing meeting with the
parties. Neither agency is completely happy with this
arrangement.

Obviously, the problems in part involve the ego and reputation of the mediators and agencies. Mediators like to get
settlements; they do not enjoy others getting settlements
which they could have procured. The Panel staff has the
advantage of working full time on Federal sector problems,
and they have intimate knowledge of the voluminous rules
and regulations that impact these negotiations. They also
have the inherent power of a hearing officer who recommends
action to the Panel. But probably their greatest advantage
is timing; in a process that has almost no deadline pressures, they offer an opportunity for settlement on the eve
of the fact-finding hearing--they offer settlement on the
courthouse steps.

In contrast, the Service mediators spend most of their time
in other types of labor relations; therefore, they do not
have the intimate knowledge of the Federal sector. These
mediators also resent those parties who treat the mediation
process as an intermediate step before going to the Panel.

In spite of these problems, during the eight years under the
Nixon Executive Order, Service mediators totally settled 70%
of the cases, and significantly reduced the number of unresolved issues in the other 30%, most of which were then
certified to the Panel. The Panel reports a 50% settlement
rate for mediation at the pre-hearing meeting.

Civil Service Reform Act of 1978

During President Carter's administration, the Nixon Executive Order was replaced with a statute, Title VII of the
Civil Service Reform Act of 1978, which made further refinements and improvements in the labor relations process.[8] The
Act created the Federal Labor Relations Authority (FLRA) with

functions similar to the National Labor Relations Board in the private sector. The scope of bargaining was clarified by defining management rights, and expanding the issues subject to grievance arbitration.

The Federal Service Impasses Panel remains a part of the process under the new FLRA. The relationship discussed above between FMCS and the Panel remains the same as under the Executive Order. A study in 1980 recommended that the two agencies establish a staff exchange program as "a constructive effort in integrating these two agencies' separate yet interrelated functions, as well as producing a healthy dialogue on Federal sector dispute resolution techniques."[9]

The FMCS was directed by the new statute to continue to provide mediation services. Pursuant to the new law, the Service issued rules outlining how mediation would be made available. The rules provided greater discretion for the Service in making its services available, and the parties are required to give the Service 30 days' notice of a dispute, similar to the private sector.

Mediation/Arbitration Or Med-Arb

As labor relations have become more sophisticated, so have the negotiators and the third-party impasse procedures. In the last several years, the Federal service has used a new impasse process which combines mediation and arbitration.

> "The term med-arb refers to a process in which a neutral third party is empowered to render final and binding decisions, but which also allows for the application of less formal and flexible mediation techniques encouraging voluntary settlement prior to the need for the neutral to mandate the terms of the settlement."[10]

Sam Kagel, who is often credited with initiating med-arb, explained its advantages this way:

> "The parties for the first time really have to bare their souls, because if they are dishonest in the sense of holding back on a particular issue, they know the med-arbitrator is going to make the decision. It really does keep them honest, and that is the whole point in med-arb."[11]

The Federal Service Impasses Panel, which encourages the use of med-arb, estimates that med-arb has been used in twenty cases in the past few years. Since no exact figures are available, and the parties are free to agree upon their own impasse procedures, the use may be even greater. The lack of a terminal point in these negotiations and the large number of issues frequently reaching impasse are two reasons for using med-arb.

With the large number of issues, med-arb frequently requires many sessions with the neutral moving back and forth in the two roles. For example, the neutral may mediate on one issue or group of related issues for a time without achieving an agreement. He might then tell the parties, in general terms, how he might decide the issues, and then suggest to them that they meet for a period in direct negotiations on those issues. If the parties reach agreement, the neutral will mediate other issues in the next session. If the parties have not reached agreement, the neutral will make a decision before moving on to more mediation.

The advantage of this combined process is that issues are resolved as the process moves along, while also allowing and encouraging the parties to resolve issues on their terms.

Postal Reorganization Act

Postal employees have traditionally been the most highly unionized of all Federal employees. They have been credited with carrying the Federal workers' cause to the Congress and the Administration to such an extent that other Federal workers had not felt the need to unionize earlier. This changed in 1970 when the postal unions were allowed to go their own way.

In 1970, following a nationwide strike of postal employees, the Postal Reorganization Act created a quasi-governmental agency called the United States Postal Service, and made its labor relations subject, in most respects, to the private sector law administered by the National Labor Relations Board.[12] The exception for the Postal Service was on two key issues--the right to strike and the impasse procedures. Strikes remain strictly prohibited with very harsh penalties if the prohibition is violated.

Impasses not resolved in mediation provided by FMCS become involved with a fact-finding and arbitration process.

Conclusions

Federal sector negotiations have increased with the rise in
unionization of Federal workers, and the liberalization of
procedures allowing collective bargaining. The role of FMCS
in providing mediation and technical assistance has also
grown. Although the Service was reluctant to get involved
in the 1960's, today Federal sector cases constitute five
percent of the Service's annual caseload. The uniqueness
of this sector--no right to strike, protracted negotiations,
inexperienced bargainers, narrow scope of bargaining, numerous written rules and regulations--has made the transition
difficult for the Service and its mediators, who generally
prefer the more familiar private sector.

The mediators have had to add to their usual repertoire of
tactics great imagination, persistence, and some new techniques. The latter have included artificial deadlines,
withdrawal or the threat of withdrawal from negotiations,
and time limits on their availability.

NOTES

1. Willoughby Abner, "The FMCS and Dispute Mediation in the Federal Government," Monthly Labor Review, Vol. 92, No. 5, May 1969, p. 27.

2. Ibid., p. 27.

3. Ibid., p. 27.

4. Ibid., p. 28.

5. Jerome H. Ross, "Federal Mediation in the Public Sector," Monthly Labor Review, Vol. 99, No. 2, February 1976, pp. 41-42.

6. Ibid., p. 42.

7. FMCS Annual Reports, 1975 and 1981.

8. See Civil Service Reform Act of 1978 in Appendix.

9. Douglas M. McCabe, Mediation and Labor-Management Relations in the Federal Government. Funded by the U.S. Department of Labor, December 1980, p. 476.

10. Jerome H. Ross, "The Med-Arb Process in Labor Agreement Negotiations," Society of Professionals in Dispute Resolution, Occasional Paper No. 82-1, February 1982, pp. 1-10.

11. Sam Kagel, "Combining Mediation and Arbitration," Monthly Labor Review, Vol. 96, No. 9, September 1973, p. 62.

12. See Postal Reorganization Act of 1970 in Appendix.

CHAPTER IV

DISPUTE RESOLUTION PROCEDURES— PUBLIC SECTOR— STATE AND LOCAL LEVELS

Since the 1960's, government employment, as a part of the service sector of the economy, has grown more rapidly than the private sector, particularly manufacturing. Along with this shift from manufacturing to service in the post-war industrial society, State and local government employment has grown even faster than Federal employment. With this growth came an increasing awareness of the disparity between wages and benefits in the public and private sectors. This awareness and the increased number of employees presented an unprecedented opportunity for growth in unionization.

Traditional private sector unions began to organize government workers, while government employee associations, once considered social organizations, began to grow by adopting traditional union programs and characteristics. The American Federation of State, County and Municipal Employees, once a relatively small national union, has experienced phenomenal growth to become one of the largest affiliates of the AFL-CIO. The National Education Association, a professional association of teachers, has completely changed its image and tactics in the past 15 years to become the largest labor organization in the United States.

The Legal Framework

Since State and local government employees are specifically excluded from the protection of national labor policy in the National Labor Relations Act, State and local law provides the only framework for their protection and rights. Traditionally, the employment relationship of government employees was regulated by civil service and merit systems laws and procedures.

The civil service/merit system was basically a professionally run personnel office for the government entity. Since the system functioned as both a protector of employees and the employer representative, a union or employee association had little, if any, function. It was against this tradition that unions attempted to carve out a legitimate function.

The Executive Order of President John Kennedy in 1962, mentioned in the previous Chapter, gave encouragement to State
and local government unions to seek a new legal framework
for employee relations. The unions sought this new framework in a variety of forums: the courts, attorney generals'
opinions, local ordinances, State legislatures, executive
orders, and the voluntary acts of public officials. The
unions lobbied, supported political candidates, hired legal
counsel, and called strikes and boycotts to influence public
opinion and the political system. The result was a patchwork of arrangements that varied from State to State, and
even from city to city within the same State.

During the 1960's and early 1970's, several attempts were
made in the U.S. Congress to provide a national framework
for State and local government employee relations. But constitutional[1] and political[2] considerations made that impossible. Instead, the variety of arrangements in the various
States was spoken of as a "laboratory" in which experimentation was being used to discover the best arrangement for
handling the problem. The Secretary of Labor expressed it
this way:

> "I regard the whole field of public sector bargain-
> ing today as something of a gigantic research and
> development laboratory in which many experiments
> are being conducted...Out of this experimentation
> I think we can expect to find some "breakthroughs"
> which are worth pursuing."[3]

Experimentation By The States

The experimentation by the States did not deal with the single question of having unions or not but, rather, a variety
of secondary questions were encountered. The answers to
these questions provided even more variety. Some of these
questions included:

1. Which employees should be covered by the law--police
    and firefighters, teachers, blue and white collar,
    prison guards, etc.--and should they be covered by
    the same law?

2. Should employees be allowed to bargain with their
    employer, or merely to "meet and confer"? If they
    could bargain, what topics could they bargain about--
    wages, hours, and working conditions--or should bar-
    gaining be limited as it is with Federal employees?

3. Should employees be allowed to strike? Should some
    employees, such as the protective services, not be
    allowed, while other less essential employees are
    allowed to strike?

4. How should impasses in bargaining be resolved?
    Should the legislative body, which must appropri-
    ate funds, stand as the final decider? Should
    third-party procedures--such as mediation, fact-
    finding, or arbitration--be used? And if so, in
    which combination?

It is this latter question on impasse resolution with which
this Chapter is most concerned.

Impasse Procedures

The first State laws prohibited all employees from striking.
For this reason, they tended to provide elaborate impasse
procedures as a substitute for the right to strike. Wisconsin, New York, and Michigan were in this category.[4]

Some States that passed laws later, benefitting from the
experience of other States, allowed some employees to strike
after utilizing the impasse procedure. Employees covered by
this procedure were designated by the law as "non-essential."

For those employees not allowed to strike, a more compulsive
impasse procedure was provided, that is, one with finality,
such as arbitration. Employees covered by this procedure
were designated by the law as "essential" employees; typically, this covered police officers, firefighters, and prison guards. Pennsylvania, Minnesota, and Hawaii are in this
category. The statutes provided three usual forms of impasse processes--mediation, fact-finding, and arbitration--
some singly, others in combination.

Mediation

Mediation used in State and local government employee disputes does not differ essentially from the mediation described elsewhere in this book.[5] What is unique about this
mediation is its application in combination with fact-finding and arbitration. It is typically used before either
fact-finding and/or arbitration, but it can also be used
after either of them, particularly fact-finding. Almost

without exception, the individual who mediates does not perform fact-finding or arbitration on the same case.

Because most mediation in the public sector is conducted without the pressure of a strike deadline, mediators have created artificial deadlines to force finality on the parties. This is typically done by the mediator placing a deadline on his availability to mediate that particular case.

Mediation is the most utilized form of impasse resolution in the public sector. This is not surprising since it has been very successful. In Iowa over an eight year period, mediation has produced a settlement rate of 78%.[6] A six-State study of impasse procedures with mediation, fact-finding, and arbitration concluded: "The mediation stage of the impasse procedure stands out in our study as the critical period in the achievement of policy objectives."[7] An earlier study which surveyed the major writers in the field concluded the same.[8]

Fact-Finding

Where the State statute requires it or the parties agree to it, fact-finding may include the fact-finder's recommendations for settlement. These recommendations can provide public and political pressure for settlement. They may also provide one or both of the parties with the "face saver" needed for them to settle. On the other hand, the recommendations may only provide the basis for further negotiations and mediation.

Some statutes require the fact-finder to consider certain criteria in making recommendations, such as prevailing wages and conditions, ability to pay, and the public welfare. Some statutes provide no guidelines.

Arbitration

The arbitration process, unlike mediation and fact-finding, has finality. The decision of the arbitrator is binding on the parties to the impasse. Arbitration of bargaining impasses in the public sector on the State level can be voluntary--agreed to by the parties, or compulsory--required by statute. Most often, arbitration is used for employees in the protective service who are denied the right to strike,

but other groups of employees use it as well since 33 States
have laws providing it for some employees.

Two criticisms are made of compulsory arbitration by schol-
ars and practitioners--they are called the "chilling effect"
and the "narcotic effect." The chilling effect occurs

> "if either party anticipates that it will get more
> from the arbitrator than from a negotiated settle-
> ment, it will have an incentive to avoid the trade-
> offs of good faith bargaining and will cling to ex-
> cessive or unrealistic positions in the hope of tilt-
> ing the arbitration outcome in its favor. This lack
> of hard bargaining will occur because of a signifi-
> cant reduction in the costs of disagreement. Not
> only will there be no strike cost, the uncertainty
> associated with continued disagreement is reduced
> because of the usual compromise outcome: the arbi-
> trator gives less than the union has asked for and
> more than the employer has offered. In other words,
> since conventional arbitration imposes much smaller
> costs of disagreement than strikes, there is little
> incentive to avoid it."[9]

The narcotic effect occurs simply because the legal requirement for arbitrating an impasse provides an easy, habit-form-
ing release from the obligation to engage in hard bargaining.[10] The existence of the narcotic effect is supported by
studies.[11]

Both of these difficulties with arbitration present a challenge to the mediator to make the mediation process one
which is not just a pass-through on the way to arbitration,
but rather a serious effort by the bargainers to reach an
agreement.

Last Best Offer Arbitration

Further refinements have been made in the types of arbitration over the past few years. This has been motivated by
a desire to encourage the parties to settle their dispute
in negotiations and not rely on arbitration. These refinements are generally referred to as "last best offer" or
"final offer" arbitration. One authority explains the
theory for this new form of arbitration this way:

> "The theory which underlies final-offer arbitra-
> tion is quite simple. If the arbitrator was per-

mitted to select only one or the other of the
parties' final offers, with no power to make a
choice anywhere in between, it was expected that
the logic of the procedure would force negotiating parties to continue moving closer together
in search of a position that would be most likely
to receive neutral sympathy. Ultimately, so the
argument went, they would come so close together
that they would almost inevitably find their own
settlement. In short, final-offer arbitration
would obviate its own use, thus eliminating the
chilling effect of binding arbitration."[12]

A number of States have adopted some variation of this type
of arbitration. Wisconsin, Massachusetts, and Hawaii have
the pure or harsh form in which both parties submit a final
position on all unresolved issues. The arbitrator must
choose one or the other list in toto. Some critics of this
process feel that the arbitrator does not have the choice of
the best offer, but rather the least inequitable offer. But
it is also argued that the high risk for the parties does
discourage the use of arbitration.

Under the Iowa statute, the arbitrator is given a third
choice--the recommendations of the fact-finder which occurred before arbitration. The availability of this third
choice has tended to make the parties' final offers more
realistic.

The Connecticut and Michigan statutes allow the arbitrator
to choose on an "item-by-item" basis from the final offer
of each of the parties. Thus, the arbitrator can fashion
a final package by choosing the best from each party's
final position. Although this method does not discourage
arbitration as much as pure final-offer, it has been criti-
cized less for producing inequities.

With more than one half the States now allowing or requiring arbitration for some of their employees, the variations
in the process are great. One final variant is the timing
of the submission of the final offer. In Wisconsin, it
must be made five days before the hearing, and it may not
be changed. While in Michigan, the final offer is due before the end of the hearing. Further flexibility is provided in Michigan by a practice of recessing the hearing
to allow the parties more time to negotiate and/or design
their final offers.

Conclusion

In the early 1960's, when public sector labor relations was in its infancy, mediation was thought to be too weak or too mild a procedure to resolve disputes in a sector that prohibited strikes. The assumption was made that mediation worked in the private sector because the union had the "muscle" to strike. The experience gained from the State "laboratories" has proven this assumption wrong.

Today, mediation is the preferred impasse procedure in State and local public sector disputes. It has proven to be an effective process in the majority of cases without being intrusive upon the negotiations of the parties. Mediation has also afforded maximum flexibility and compatibility with other impasse procedures.

Fact-finding has provided a useful assist to the bargaining process, and a compatible complement to mediation. Arbitration has provided the needed finality when necessary, while at the same time, it has remained sufficiently unattractive to discourage its excessive use. The "last-offer" variety of arbitration has been an experiment that retains the finality feature of arbitration while introducing uncertainty to discourage its use.

NOTES

1. The constitutional question was in two parts:
(1) can the basic right of collective bargaining enjoyed in
the private sector be denied to public employees, or left to
the accident of which State the employee lives in; and (2)
whether States' rights or sovereignty precluded the Federal
Government from regulating such a basic State and local government concern as employee relations? Some observers
thought the latter question was resolved in 1967 when the
U.S. Supreme Court ruled that the extension of the Fair
Labor Standards Act was constitutional. Maryland vs. Wirtz,
389 U.S. 1031 (1967). For a good discussion of the issue,
see: Fred Heddinger, "Proposed Bargaining Legislation May
Violate States' Rights," Journal of Collective Negotiations,
Vol. 4, No. 4, 1975, pp. 329-339.

2. A keen observer of such matters, Abe Raskin, wrote
that too many work stoppages by public employees in the mid-
70's killed support in Congress for such national legislation for public employees. See A. H. Raskin, "The Current
Political Contest," Public Employee Unions: A Study of the
Crisis in Public Sector Labor Relations, Institute of Con-
temporary Studies, San Francisco, 1976.

3. James D. Hodgson, "Welcoming Address," Proceedings of the Secretary of Labor's Conference on State and
Local Government Labor Relations, November 21-22, 1971, p.3.

4. For an excellent summary of the State public employee laws, see: Summary of Public Sector Labor Relations
·Policies: Statutes, Attorney Generals' Opinions and Selected Court Decisions, U.S. Department of Labor, Labor-Management Services Administration, 1981.

5. One researcher has concluded that mediators in
the public sector spend time training the parties in addition to the usual mediation tasks. See: Peter A. Veglahn,
"Education by Third-Party Neutrals: Function, Methods, and
Extent," Labor Law Journal, Vol. 28, No. 1, January 1977,
pp. 20-29.

6. Ronald Hoh, "The Effectiveness of Mediation in
Public Sector Arbitration Systems: The Iowa Experience,"
Arbitration Journal, Vol. 39, No. 2, June 1984, p. 40.

7.   Paul Gerhart and John Drotning, A Six-State Study of Impasse Procedures in the Public Sector, U.S. Department of Labor, Labor-Management Services Administration, 1980, p. 185.

8.   Dispute Settlement in the Public Sector: The State of the Art, U.S. Department of Labor, 1972, p. 57.

9.   Peter Feuille, "Final Offer Arbitration and the Chill Effect," Industrial Relations, Vol. 14, October 1975, p. 304.

10.   Robert Howlett, "Arbitration in the Public Sector," Proceedings, Southern Legal Foundation, 15th Annual Institute of Labor Law, 1969, p. 234.

11.   Hoyt N. Wheeler, "Compulsory Arbitration: A Narcotic Effect," Industrial Relations, Vol. 14, October 1975, p. 316.

12.   Charles M. Rehmus, "Interest Arbitration," Portrait of the Process: Collective Negotiations in Public Employment, Robert D. Helsby, Editor, Labor Relations Press: Fort Washington, Pa., 1979.

CHAPTER V

FEDERAL INVOLVEMENT IN LABOR DISPUTES OF STATE AND MUNICIPAL EMPLOYEES

Although State and municipal employees are specifically excluded from the coverage of the National Labor Relations Act, the Federal Mediation and Conciliation Service has been involved in these disputes since, at least, the 1960's. With the growth of public employee collective bargaining, referred to in the previous Chapter, the involvement of the FMCS has continued to grow.

The apparent lack of FMCS legal jurisdiction in these matters has not been arbitrarily disregarded by the Service. It has been more a matter of the Service reluctantly evolving its policy because of public pressure. When the public is inconvenienced or threatened by a public employee dispute, and the Service is the only qualified source of assistance in the geographic area, it would not be acceptable for the Service to explain its reluctance to help on constitutional grounds. In addition to the public need for mediation assistance, "...the Service believes that it is operating within the mandate of existing legislative authority, and administrative and judicial accord."[1]

The Service Policy

Beginning in the early 1960's, some States passed legislation authorizing public employees to engage in collective bargaining. A few of these States provided staff to resolve the impasses that would arise under their new law. In some States where no law was passed, the employees attempted collective bargaining without a law. As disputes arose in States with a law but without staff mediators and in States with no law, the Service was asked to assist with mediation. Providing mediation in the absence of a law has presented special problems for the mediator.[2]

During most of the 1960's, the number of these requests for assistance was small enough that no policy decision was necessary. In some instances, if the local FMCS mediator had time and was willing, he handled the case informally. In other instances, the parties' request for assistance was denied. By 1969, the number of requests had become large enough that a formal policy was necessary.

The 1969 policy required that any request must be in writing and signed by both labor and management. And secondly, no assistance would be provided until it was authorized by the National Director of FMCS.[3] During the four years that this policy was in effect, the number of requests continued to increase. By 1973, with State and municipal collective bargaining continuing to expand, the Service broadened its policy. First, the new policy stated that the Service would actively assist any State which wanted to develop its own mediation function for these disputes. Secondly, the Service would proffer mediation services where no other mediation assistance was available.[4]

Helping The States

Several States took advantage of the Service's willingness to share its expertise. Some States sent their new mediators to workshops and seminars conducted by FMCS for its staff. Others requested the Service to provide expert testimony during the drafting of legislation. Two States, Florida and Iowa, received extensive assistance in the implementation of their new public employee collective bargaining laws. In 1976, these two States accounted for 49% of the mediation cases handled by the Service in the State and local public sector.

When Florida passed its public employee law in 1974, the newly appointed Chairman of the Public Employee Relations Board sought help from the Service. Subsequently, an FMCS mediator with special expertise was assigned full time to the Board to assist in the drafting of the rules and regulations for that body. Arrangements were then made for FMCS to handle the majority of the impasses that arose under the law.

When the Iowa public employee bargaining law became effective in 1975, the Service conducted a training program for their Public Employee Relations Board staff and their adjunct mediators. Although the training was successful, it was not sufficient to handle the volume of disputes needing mediation. The Iowa statute, like many others, links negotiations and the impasse procedures to the budget year of the government. With most local governments and school boards having the same budget year, the demand for mediation overwhelmed the staff and adjuncts.

The Service agreed to help during this high volume period by making all mediators stationed in Iowa available, and sending in mediators from surrounding States. During the first round of bargaining under the new law, FMCS handled 182 cases involving 600 joint meetings. The five mediators stationed in Iowa and two stationed in Nebraska handled much of the work. They were assisted by 29 other mediators from other stations.[5]

In the best spirit of State/Federal cooperation, the Service has continued to help Iowa with mediation under their statute. The purpose of the Service's intense effort in the first year was to convince the many parties, who were negotiating for the first time, that good quality mediation can be effective. If this fact could be learned in the first year, the statute would be started on the right track, and the parties would not feel compelled to use all of the other impasse procedures available to them. This strategy has proven successful since Iowa has a higher rate of settlements in mediation (78%) than other States with similar impasse procedures ending in arbitration.[6]

The Service also helped in several States with disputes not traditionally within the mediation sphere. Staff members were assigned to conduct fact-finding in a teachers dispute in Southern California and in a firefighters dispute in Kansas. Representation disputes were handled in a Maryland school district and the Police Department in Little Rock, Arkansas. In each of these cases, the objective of the Service was to resolve a difficult dispute, but also, to help the State or local government develop its capacity to handle future disputes.

Distribution of FMCS Participation

The table below, taken from the 1977 Annual Report of the Service, is a typical pattern of the case distribution during the past ten years:

State and Local Cases Closed by the Service in Fiscal Year 1977

State	No. Cases	Percentage
Illinois	139	20.3
Florida	138	20.2
Iowa	110	16.1

State	No. Cases	Percentage
Ohio	50	7.3
Alaska	26	3.8
Washington	23	3.4
Vermont	20	2.9
Kansas	17	2.5
New Hampshire	14	2.1
Tennessee	13	1.9
Kentucky	11	1.6
Texas	11	1.6
Colorado	10	1.5
Delaware	9	1.3
Idaho	9	1.3
Indiana	9	1.3
Missouri	8	1.2
Oklahoma	7	1.0
California	6	0.9
New Mexico	6	0.9
Arizona	5	0.7
Massachusetts	4	0.6
Pennsylvania	4	0.6
Washington, D.C.	3	0.4
Montana	3	0.4
Nebraska	3	0.4
New Jersey	3	0.4
7 States with	2	2.1
9 States with	1	1.3
Total	684	100.0

Source: FMCS Annual Report 1977, page 14.

The four States with the highest number of cases include two
States (Iowa and Florida) with public employee laws and two
States (Illinois and Ohio) without a public employee law.
In the case of Iowa and Florida, neither has provided for an
adequate mediation staff of their own; instead, they have
made arrangements with FMCS to handle much of their mediation work.

In 1983, both Illinois and Ohio passed legislation providing for public employee bargaining. Prior to 1983, these
two States had a great deal of collective bargaining occurring but no arrangements were made by the State to deal with
it. If the disputing parties wanted mediation, they dealt
directly with FMCS.

The States of Alaska, Vermont, and Washington have public
employee legislation but no staff to handle impasse disputes. The result is that FMCS is quite active in these
States.

The States of Minnesota, Wisconsin, Michigan, and New York
have public employee legislation and staff to handle impasse disputes. The FMCS policy is not to provide mediation
in States where the State agency provides it. There are a
few exceptions to this each year. California, Massachusetts,
Pennsylvania, and New Jersey, all have State mediation agencies, yet FMCS was involved in 17 cases in those States in
1977. In such cases, the FMCS mediator typically enters the
case with the approval of the State mediation agency and, in
some cases, works with a State mediator. This procedure is
consistent with the Code of Professional Conduct discussed
in Chapter XXIX.

Contrast of Federal and State Mediation

State mediation agencies have had to accommodate themselves
to the unique features of State and local bargaining. Some
State and local laws require that public business be conducted in public. These laws are generally referred to as
Sunshine Laws. Where such laws apply to negotiations and
mediation, mediators have accommodated their mediation style
and tactics to these requirements. In some cases, only joint
meetings are conducted in the sunshine and very little is
accomplished there. Caucuses and side-bars are used as
"executive" sessions excluded from the sunshine. Some laws
which do not allow even that much flexibility make the mediator's task very difficult.

The prohibition of strikes in most States and the multiple
impasse procedures present additional challenges to the mediator. The absence of a deadline and the need to work with
or even act as a fact-finder are contingencies not found in
the private sector. Since many State mediators work exclusively in the State and local sector, they have become accustomed to these unique features.

A recent study based on observations of State mediators
working in the public sector and Federal mediators working
in the private sector made a distinction between two groups.
The State mediators were said to be primarily "dealmakers"
who provide the parties will skills, suggestions, and ideas
that the negotiators often do not themselves possess and

without which they would be unable to settle their dispute.
These mediators see themselves as contributing to the sub-
stance of the negotiations.[7]

The Federal mediators were said to be primarily "orchestra-
tors of the process" who provide a forum for the parties to
come together to explore their differences, offering them
only intermittent suggestions, and then usually only when
requested.[8]

It is highly questionable whether the researcher found any
"real" differences. The research conclusions have not been
met with enthusiasm in the two camps. A researcher and former mediator questioned the conclusions based on his experience and research, but also as an over generalization from
too small a sample--one FMCS office and one State mediation
service.[9]

In part, the difficulty with the conclusions is with the
values that the mediators attach to them. Is an orchestrator
better than a dealmaker? It does sound better. But a dealmaker sounds so much more active, so much more involved and
relevant. Isn't that how mediators see themselves? The
truth is that mediators from both agencies and in both sectors are probably a little bit of each, depending on the
circumstances.

NOTES

1. Herbert Fishgold, "Dispute Resolution in the Public Sector: The Role of FMCS," Labor Law Journal, Vol. 27, No. 12, December 1976, p. 734.

2. John R. Stepp and Robert P. Baker, "The Art of Dispute Resolution - Mediation: The Mediator and Public Sector Bargaining Without A Statute," Proceedings of 5th Annual Meeting, Society of Professionals in Dispute Resolution, October 1977, pp. 18-28.

3. Twenty-First Annual Report of the Federal Mediation and Conciliation Service, 1968, p. 45.

4. W. J. Usery, "Bargaining in the Public Sector: Problems, Progress and Prospects," Oklahoma City University Law Review, Vol. 1, No. 1, Spring 1973, pp. 11-12.

5. The Mediator: FMCS Newsletter, Vol. 3, No. 4, June 1976, pp. 6-7.

6. Ronald Hoh, "The Effectiveness of Mediation in Public Sector Arbitration Systems: The Iowa Experience," Arbitration Journal, Vol. 39, No. 2, June 1984, p. 40.

7. Deborah M. Kolb, The Mediators, The MIT Press; Cambridge, Mass., 1983, p. 230; and Deborah M. Kolb, "Roles Mediators Play: State and Federal Practice," Industrial Relations, Vol. 20, No. 1, pp. 1-17.

8. Ibid.

9. Charles M. Rehmus, "Book Review of the Mediator," by Deborah M. Kolb, Industrial and Labor Relations Review, Vol. 38, No. 1, October 1984, pp. 121-122.

CHAPTER VI

JURISDICTION— FEDERAL, STATE, AND LOCAL MEDIATION AGENCIES— PRIVATE SECTOR

In at least eighteen States and Puerto Rico, both Federal and State mediation services are available to the parties. In eight other States, the Commissioner of Labor performs a limited amount of mediation. In addition, a few cities and communities, municipal, county, or quasi-public mediation facilities have been established. Typical of the latter are Toledo's Labor-Management Committee; Nassau County's Mediation Division; Wilkes-Barre Committee; and Louisville Labor-Management Committee.

Where more than one mediation facility is available, parties seeking mediation assistance may be in a quandry as to which mediation agency has jurisdiction in their particular dispute. There are no tailor-made, clearly defined jurisdictional lines between various mediation agencies. Practical as well as legal considerations inhibit any rigidity. The very voluntary nature of the mediation process negates the necessity of strict jurisdictional limitations.

An examination of State statutes dealing with the mediation of labor disputes discloses no limitations on their jurisdiction to the extent that they do not even draw a distinction between inter- and intra-State commerce. In a few States, the statutes set a minimum as to the amount of employees which must be involved before mediation facilities are made available. Illinois and Oklahoma require 25 or more. Montana sets the minimum at 20. Maine and New Hampshire require that there be 10 or more.

There are only two clearly defined jurisdictional boundaries between Federal and State agencies. The Railway Labor Act gives exclusive jurisdiction to the National Mediation Board over disputes involving railroads and airlines. By interpretation, the Labor-Management Relations Act grants exclusive jurisdiction to the States in disputes that are limited to intra-State commerce.

Statutory Authority Of Federal Mediation And Conciliation Service

On the Federal level, statutory language provides little

guidance. The Labor-Management Relations Act, 1947, as
amended, provides in part (Title II, Section 203(b)):[1]

> "The Service may proffer its services in any labor
> dispute in any industry affecting commerce...when-
> ever in its judgment such dispute threatens to
> cause a substantial interruption of commerce. The
> Director and the Service are directed to avoid at-
> tempting to mediate disputes which could have only
> a minor effect on interstate commerce if State or
> other conciliation services are available to the
> parties..."

> "Section 202(d): "Final adjustment by a method
> agreed upon by the parties is hereby declared to
> be the desirable method for settlement of griev-
> ance disputes arising over the application or in-
> terpretation of an existing collective bargaining
> agreement. The Service is directed to make its
> conciliation and mediation services available in
> the settlement of such grievance disputes only as
> a last resort and in exceptional cases."

As the statutory quotations indicate, some restrictions on
the Federal Mediation and Conciliation Service's assertion
of jurisdiction in disputes can be inferred. One restriction is where the statute speaks of a dispute which threatens to cause a "substantial" interruption of commerce. Another restriction can be found in the language which directs
the Service to avoid mediating disputes which have only a
minor effect on commerce. The final restriction is the admonition contained in Section 202(d) directing the Service
to make mediation available in grievance disputes only as
a "last resort and in exceptional cases."

The determination of what is "substantial" and "minor"
wisely is left to the judgment of the Service. It is not
difficult to imagine the confusion and conflicts which
would arise if the determination had been left to the
judgment of each State.

There has been no definition or establishment of any precise guidelines by the Federal Mediation and Conciliation
Service as to what constitutes a "minor" effect on commerce.
Perhaps the experience of the National Labor Relations Board
under Section 2(7) of the Labor-Management Relations Act, as
amended, and the Department of Labor in its administration

of the Fair Labor Standards Act in attempting to define even the broader concept of "commerce" under those respective Acts were deterrents from doing so.

In a memorandum issued in 1950, Director Cyrus Ching stated:

> "The Service believes that a proper interpretation of the Act calls for a statement of jurisdictional policy expressed in general terms, rather than in terms of precise and specific jurisdictional limitations. The Service believes that it may accomplish the legislative objective more effectively through a judicious application of the terms of the Act in the light of the general labor-management relations policy of the Government, rather than through a narrow, legal definition of jurisdiction or the establishment of specific formulae."

In the same memorandum, Director Ching outlined the general factors which would enter into the Service's consideration in determining whether a particular dispute would cause a substantial interruption of commerce. These factors were:

> The volume and dollar value of the product exported from or imported to the State;

> The nature of the industry or employer establishment and its importance in the industry or economy, local or national, with particular reference to:

>> the degree of integration in the industry and the degree of reliance upon the product or services affected;

>> the relationship of the dispute to negotiations involving other firms in the industry, other industries, or to the national bargaining policy of the union;

>> the existence of other sources of supply of the product or service;

> Number of employees.

Agreement With States

Under Section 10A of the Labor-Management Relations Act, the National Labor Relations Board is empowered to cede jurisdiction to State labor mediation agencies "even though such cases may involve labor disputes affecting commerce..." No such power of delegation is granted to the Federal Mediation and Conciliation Service.

The only legislative approach to delegation is found in Title II, Section 201(c) which provides:

> "The Director may establish suitable procedures for cooperation with State and local mediation agencies."

Soon after the establishment of the Federal Mediation and Conciliation Service as an independent agency, the Service undertook to implement the foregoing provisions of the Act. The first attempt was characterized by the negotiation of both formal and informal agreements with some of the existing State mediation agencies. As a result of such negotiations, written or oral agreements were consummated with New York, California, Connecticut, Michigan, North Carolina, Pennsylvania, and Washington.

The most detailed agreement was with the State of New York. In general, it reserved to the State Board the exclusive right to intercede in intra-State disputes. The State recognized that "it is normally preferable for the Federal Service to handle certain types of disputes of a national or multi-State character which threaten a grave and serious effect on inter-State commerce." In the more troublesome area of "minor" versus "major" effect on inter-State commerce, the agreement spelled out the primary responsibility of the Federal Service to make the initial determination. However, it further states "it is also recognized that the State agency has an interest in such decisions and that the standards used in making these decisions can be most satisfactorily applied through mutual understanding and consultation between the agencies." The agreement recognized that many disputes would fall into a gray area. In an attempt to set forth guidelines, it was provided that neither agency will attempt to intercede so long as direct negotiations were proceeding satisfactorily and when the services of a mediator were required, the preferences of the parties would be given the greatest weight in determining which agency would mediate.

The efforts of both the State and Federal mediation services to delineate their respective jurisdictions continued even after these foregoing formal and informal agreements through conferences and consultation between the agencies affected. These efforts culminated in the drafting of the Code of Professional Conduct for Labor Mediators.[2]

Code Of Professional Conduct

Director William Simkin finally took the initiative to try to find a solution to the problem of overlapping jurisdictions. In an address to the Association of Labor Mediation Agencies, in the fall of 1963, he suggested that the State and Federal mediation agencies jointly draft a code of professional ethics for all mediators, covering the most frequent points of possible conflicts between agencies. In 1964, a joint committee of the Service and the Association developed a Code of Professional Conduct. The Code contained a grievance procedure under which complaints by either State or Federal mediators concerning mediators of other agencies could be considered and appealed to higher levels within each group. The Code was approved by the Federal Mediation and Conciliation Service and ratified by all important State agencies. Section 2 of the Code provides in part:

> "A mediator should not enter any dispute which is being mediated by another mediator, without first conferring with the person or persons conducting such mediation. The mediator should not intercede in a dispute merely because another mediator may also be participating. Conversely, it should not be assumed that the lack of mediation participation by one mediator indicates a need for participation by another mediator..."

From an attempt to delineate sharply the jurisdictional boundaries of Federal and State mediation agencies by formally executed agreements to the Code provisions cited, there has been a devolution to a mere statement of a modus vivindum.

Under the statutory language, in a strict sense, any dispute which has more than a minor effect on inter-State commerce is within the exclusive responsibility of the Federal service. Support for this view can be found in several court cases which are founded on the general doctrine of preemption. The courts have said that Congress, by its legislation (NLRA, LMRA, etc.), has preempted the field of labor relations as regards inter-State commerce. On this

basis the Federal courts have enjoined intrusion by a State
board in negotiations between unions and employers engaged
in inter-State commerce as being in conflict with specific
terms or general policy fairly attributable to the Federal
legislation encouraging voluntary agreements arrived at by
free collective bargaining. The cases were not framed in
terms of FMCS versus the State Mediation Board. Rather,
they were simply brought because the employer objected to
the State Board's assertion of jurisdiction. However, by
overruling this State intervention, the courts implicitly
recognize FMCS jurisdiction (at least one might contend).
In one case, the court even noted the presence of FMCS mediators during all meetings prior to the attempted State
Board intervention.[3]

Despite the statutory language and court decisions, there
are a number of factors which militate against a clear demarcation of jurisdiction between the Federal and State
services. It is not very realistic to expect a State to
always divorce itself from the economic impact of labor disputes arising within its borders. If a plant of a multi-
plant, inter-State company is the major industry in a community or State and a stoppage occurs, the municipal or
State officials cannot ignore it by asserting that the matter is being handled by the Federal service. Political
considerations alone would dictate that they publicly demonstrate their concern for the community affected. If a
mediation service exists in that State, one of the ways in
which these officials can express their interest is by requesting or instructing their State agency to intercede and
to attempt to bring the dispute to an early termination.
Another alternative open is the personal intercession by
the mayor or governor, usually by inviting the parties to
appear before them. The difficulties are multiplied when
the dispute falls in the gray area of major or minor effect
on commerce.

Beyond the political considerations, at least one other factor militates against rigid jurisdictional lines of demarcation. One or both of the parties may prefer one service or
a particular mediator over the other. This is quite understandable since mediation is most successful when the parties have confidence in the mediator's neutrality and ability. Any attempt to interject the other agency in lieu of
the one desired by the parties would be either rejected out-
right or ignored by the parties.

Dual Mediation

There are cases where the dispute is of such a nature that joint efforts by Federal and State mediators could be justified. Disputes which threaten a power shutdown, cessation of food deliveries, and disruption of passenger transportation are examples. On the other extreme, a proliferation of mediators can be an unconscionable waste of tax payers' money. An example of such occurred in a dispute involving the milk industry whose drivers threatened to stop all milk deliveries in a metropolitan area which embraced three States and a large city. In addition to the Federal mediator, each State and the city assigned mediators, making a total of five. One byproduct occurred when two State mediators got into a sharp quarrel in front of several reporters who were covering the negotiations. The following day two of the newspapers carried the story under the headline of "Who Will Mediate The Mediators?"

In summary, there is little doubt that Congress has imposed an affirmative responsibility on the Federal Mediation and Conciliation Service to intercede and render mediation assistance in disputes having more than a minor effect on inter-State commerce. In the exercise of this exclusive jurisdiction, there must be a recognition that in specific cases, political and practical considerations may dictate joint or concurrent efforts on the part of State public officials or agencies.

Further, it is quite clear that Congress also intended the exclusive jurisdiciton of the State agencies in disputes of purely an intra-State character if a viable State mediation agency has been established.

In the gray area of disputes having only a minor effect on inter-State commerce, while the initial jurisdictional determination should be made by the Federal agency, the best approach appears to be an ad hoc one with the desires or preferences of the parties a weighty consideration in the final determination as to which agency can best assist the parties to resolve their dispute.

NOTES

1. cf Appendix.

2. cf Appendix.

3. Grand Rapids City Coach Lines v. Howlett et al, 137 F. Supp. 667; General Electric Co. v. Callahan, 294 F. 2d 60; Oil, Chemical and Atomic Workers International Union v. Arkansas Louisiana Gas Co. 332 F 2d 64.

CHAPTER VII

FEDERAL MEDIATION AND CONCILIATION SERVICE

Historical Background

State legislation authorizing mediation assistance preceded Federal entrance into this field by over 30 years.

In 1878, Maryland became the first State to pass a law providing for conciliation of labor disputes. In 1883, Pennsylvania instituted mediation. In 1886, New York set up the State Board of Arbitration. While the original act was silent as to mediation, an amendment was passed in 1887 empowering the Board to mediate and make investigations in certain cases. In 1886, Massachusetts passed a statute which authorized the State to provide mediation, arbitration and, under certain circumstances, investigation with a public report.

The first Federal intrusion into the collective bargaining process was in 1888 when Congress passed a law providing for voluntary arbitration under Government auspices and for the investigation of the cause of and means for the adjustment of specific controversies by a Board composed of the Commissioner of Labor and two presidential appointees. The law proved inadequate. The arbitration section was never invoked and the Board conducted only one investigation--the Pullman strike of 1894.

In 1898, the Erdman Act was passed which, with the added amendments of the Newlands Act of 1913, governed railway labor relations until World War I. The two Acts stressed mediation and, if mediation failed, voluntary arbitration. Both Acts applied only to operating employees of railways.

For forty years, the representatives of labor agitated for a separate department in the Federal Government, with a Secretary, who would be on a cabinet level, whose primary concern would be the welfare of wage earners. During this period of time, various pieces of legislation were enacted shuttling the labor functions of the Government from the Interior Department to the Commerce Department. In the majority of these Acts, the labor function was mainly confined to investigations into the causes of labor disputes and the compilation of statistical data with reference thereto.

All the agitation by the labor organizations and the inadequacies of the various Acts, culminated with the passage of the Organic Act of 1913 creating the Department of Labor administered by a Secetary of Labor who had Cabinet status. Section 8 of that Act provided:

> "That the Secretary of Labor shall have power to act as mediator and to appoint commissioners of conciliation in labor disputes whenever in his judgment the interests of industrial peace may require it to be done..."

Congress, however, failed to provide any funds for the organization within the Department of a bureau or division to administer the mediation function conferred on the Secretary by the statute. Nor were any funds provided for the hiring of a mediation staff. As a result, the Secretary was compelled to detail employees from bureaus within the Department organized for other purposes. In the first case, the chief statistician from the Bureau of Labor Statistics was designated as a Commissioner of Conciliation and assigned to mediate the dispute. In another dispute, the Assistant Secretary of Labor was detailed as a mediator. In a third, a member of the Immigration Service was detailed.

Since the Erdman Act exluded non-operating railway employees, their disputes fell within the jurisdiction of the Department of Labor. Of the first nine reported cases, in which employees of other bureaus were detailed to mediate, six involved non-operating employees of railroads.

In October 1913, a deficiency bill provided the first sums earmarked for the mediation function of the Department-- $5,000 for the expenses of those employees detailed to mediate disputes.

It was not until April 1914 that Congress appropriated $20,000 for the salary and expenses of the mediators. No provision had been made in the Organic Act for supervisory work. Provision for such was finally made in the passage of the Legislative, Executive, and Judicial Appropriations Act for the Fiscal Year 1915. The same Act extended the jurisdiction of the Commissioners of Conciliation to the District of Columbia and provided for payment of salaries for Commissioners as well as per diem.

United States Conciliation Service

In 1917, the United States Conciliation Service was established as a division in the Department of Labor. Hugh Kerwin was named Director by Secretary of Labor Wilson.

The choice of Kerwin has an interesting background. A favorite evening meeting place for the coal miners of Arnot, Pennsylvania, was the back room of the cobbler's shop owned by a man named Hugh Kerwin. Kerwin had a comparatively large collection of books and, in addition, he subscribed to several newspapers and the Congressional Record. At these gatherings, the miners indulged in lively debates about national and international affairs, theology, philosophy, and economics. Wilson's father took young Wilson to one of the meetings. Young Wilson was profoundly impressed by what he had heard and looked forward to attending future meetings. The cobbler noted the intense interest the boy took in the meetings and his interest in the cobbler's books. The cobbler lent young Wilson his books to take home and read. When Wilson had read and digested most of the cobbler's books, under Kerwin's guidance, a library society was formed and Wilson was elected librarian.

Wilson never forgot or ceased to be grateful to the teacher-shoemaker. Wilson attributed to Kerwin the start of his real education. Although the cobbler was dead for many years, Wilson's first official act after taking the oath of office as Secretary of Labor was to appoint the cobbler's son as his private secretary. When the United States Conciliation Service was established, Wilson appointed him as its first Director.[1]

Wilson thought so highly of the mediation function of the Department that he devoted much of his energy to its development and acceptance. In report after report, Secretary Wilson stated that first among the functions of the Department of Labor was the adjustment of industrial disputes. His opinion did not change even after eight years. In an official statement to the press on March 5, 1921, he said that the greatest problem facing the Department during the following twenty-five years would be the perfection of the conciliation work. There was nothing as important, he thought, as "the promotion of a better understanding between the man who works and the man he works for."

In the beginning, it looked as though Wilson's efforts to have the Department play a leading role in the settlement

of labor disputes was doomed to failure. From its inception to June 30, 1914, the Department handled only 33 cases.
Even after Congress recognized the need to allocate funds
for this function, neither labor nor management seemed interested in utilizing mediation in their labor disputes.
However, by the middle of 1915, the pace of requests for
assistance accelerated as the following chart indicates:

	1914	1915	1916	1917	1918	1919	1920	1921
Number of Cases	33	42	227	378	1217	1780	802	457
Adjusted	28	26	178	248	865	1223	596	338
Unable to Adjust	5	10	22	47	71	111	96	68
Pending	-	5	21	42	7	13	9	24
Unclassified*	-	1	6	41	66	214	101	37
Referred to War Labor Board	-	-	-	-	208	219	-	-

*Unclassified - Parties settled themselves; lost strikes;
 plant closings; method of settlement agreed upon before
 mediator entered; settled with aid of local authorities.

Several factors contributed to the greater acceptance of
mediation assistance. The problems of industrial peace and
stability of labor relations multiplied in the period starting with World War I.

Another factor which contributed to this acceptance was the
care with which the Secretary chose the mediators to be used
in specific disputes. He insisted on complete neutrality on
their part, and because mediation under the Department of
Labor was voluntary, the Commissioners of Conciliation were
instructed to act in a diplomatic capacity and not in a judicial one. Secretary Wilson regarded the administration of
this function "as contemplating a development of diplomatic
duties with reference to labor disputes analogous to those
of the Department of State with reference to international
controversies."

Hugh Kerwin became Director of the U.S. Conciliation Service at a crucial time. During his twenty-year (1917-1937)
administration, he had to cope with peaks and valleys of demands for mediation assistance. In the late 20's and during
the depression, the decline in business activity and in union membership and strength were reflected in the diminished
number of labor disputes into which the Service was requested
to intercede.

With the country's entry into World War I, the demand for
mediation assistance escalated rapidly. The Service was
both understaffed and underfinanced to meet the challenge.
There were no regional offices. Commissioners served out
of their homes and in the absence of regional boundaries
were subject to assignment anywhere in the United States.
Assignments were made from the Washington office and all
mediator reports were sent to it. In order to provide a
more equitable compensation for the mediators (a mediator
salary ranged from $2100 to $4000 per year) Commissioners
received per diem travel expense starting with the moment
they left their homes to go on an assignment. Until a regional office was established there, the mediators in New
York City used a mid-town hotel as their headquarters. The
hotel provided a free room equipped with a desk, typewriter,
telephone and a table. When meetings were scheduled at the
hotel, it got the benefit of the meals and refreshments purchased by the labor and management participants.

During the first half of the 1930's, the number of full-time
mediators held steady at about 40. With the passage of Section 7(a) of the National Industrial Recovery Act and the
Wagner Act in 1935, there was another surge in the caseload
which jumped from 1000 in 1935 to 4200 in 1938. In 1940,
there were 65 full-time mediators.

With the declaration of war in 1942, the demands on the Service far exceeded its available manpower and the Service embarked on a crash hiring program. The changes in the size
of the staff during this period of expansion are indicated
by the following:

1943.........343		1946.........488	
1944.........421		1947.........449	
1945.........416		1948.........442	

With the end of the war, the caseload declined from a war-
time peak of about 23,000 cases per year to about 18,800 in
1946. The post-war period of unstable labor relations was
marked by strikes, many of which were protracted. This led
to greater demands on the Service despite a falling caseload.

Kerwin died in 1937. He was succeeded by Dr. John R. Steelman. Steelman had taught at Alabama College. In 1934,
Steelman joined the Service as a mediator.

The tremendous increase in the number of mediators highlighted the need for greater supervision and coordination
of mediation activities. Steelman embarked on a program
designed to decentralize the Service. Chicago was the first
regional office to be established. New York, Cleveland,
Atlanta, and San Francisco soon followed. Within each region, field stations were set up. Each region was administered by a Regional Director. Assignments were no longer
made from Washington but from the Regional Office which also
received and processed the reports and expense vouchers of
the mediators in that region.

The advent of the National Defense Mediation Board and its
successor, the War Labor Board, created problems for the mediator. The agreed-upon procedure between the Service and
the Board called for mediation of disputes by the Service
in the first instance and if mediation failed to settle the
dispute, the Service would certify the case to the War Labor
Board. It soon developed that some of the parties to a dispute tried to use the mediator as a mere conduit and exerted
pressure on him to immediately certify the case to the Board.

The more capable mediators resisted such pressures, even when
there was a stoppage, and refused to certify the case until
the mediators were satisfied that the parties had really bargained in trying to reach agreement. Experience soon demonstrated that these mediators had the highest percentage of
cases settled without the need of certification. The less
capable often took the easy way out and confined their activities to one or two perfunctory meetings and then immediately certified the case to the Board.

Dr. Steelman resigned in 1944 and was succeeded by Howard
Colvin, the Southern Regional Director. Later Steelman was
appointed by President Truman as an Assistant to the President. Colvin served as Acting Director until 1945 when

Edgar Warren was appointed by Secretary of Labor Swellenbach. Warren served from 1945 to 1947.

Warren had been the head of the Regional War Labor Board in Chicago. Warren brought with him a number of former War Labor Board employees. In an unfortunate memorandum to the field mediators, Warren announced that these ex-War Labor Board employees were hired to "strengthen the Service." A deep-seated morale problem was created among the mediators who resented the implication that the Service was weak as well as their efforts and that these "outsiders" had been brought in to show them how to operate. To compound the problem, several of the ex-War Labor Board employees in the Washington staff indulged in what became known as "parachuting." In the middle of his efforts, and especially if the dispute had attracted the attention of the press, the mediator would be advised that one of the Washington staff would be joining the negotiations. In a few cases, the first the field mediator knew of the impending intrusion of the "parachutist" was an item in the local newspaper.

Warren was beset not only by personal problems but also by budgetary restrictions which necessitated lay-offs.

Federal Mediation and Conciliation Service

When Congress was considering the Labor-Management Relations Act (also known as the Taft-Hartley Act), some members felt that since the Department of Labor was created primarily to safeguard the interest of labor, the Service as a neutral was improperly housed in the Department as it would be if it was a bureau within the Department of Commerce. As a consequence, Congress in Title II of the Act removed the Service from the Department of Labor and established it as an independent agency. To make certain that it would be a total divorce, Congress in Section 202(d) of the Act stated:

> "The Director and the Service shall not be subject in any way to the jurisdiction or authority of the Secretary of Labor or any official or division of the Department of Labor."

The Act in the same section transferred all the mediation functions of the U.S. Conciliation Service and all its personnel to the new agency--the Federal Mediation and Conciliation Service. The combination of mediation and conciliation in its title was as a result of a compromise in joint congressional committee--one bill before it designated the new agency as the Federal Mediation Service--the other termed it the Federal Conciliation Service.

Cyrus Ching, a former Vice President of the U.S. Rubber Company, was appointed by President Truman in 1947 as the Director of the new agency. Unlike the directors of the U.S. Conciliation Service who were appointed by the Secretary of Labor, directors of FMCS are presidential appointees.

To Cyrus Ching fell the task of intermeshing the personnel and records of the United States Conciliation Service with the new Federal Mediation and Conciliation Service and setting up the new internal operating structure. New policies and procedures, in conformity with the limitations that the new Act imposed on the Service, had to be devised and promulgated.

Operating on the theory that the main work and heart of the Service was in the field, he decentralized the national office eliminating all personnel and functions except those essential for the purpose of formulating basic policy and coordinating field operations. The number of regional offices were increased from 8 to 12. A preventive program was inaugurated and training and study programs for mediators were instituted in all regions.

The most outstanding legacy Ching left the Service was his successful fight to establish the principle that all mediator appointments should be made on the basis of proven qualifications and not because of the applicant's political affiliation or sponsorship.

Cyrus Ching resigned in September 1952 and, on his recommendation, David L. Cole was appointed by President Truman as his successor. David Cole was a nationally known and respected arbitrator.

Cole's term of office was rather short from October 1952 to April 1953. Like Ching, Cole was a firm believer in the principle that mediation appointments must be non-political. He refused to accede to pressure exerted by a New Jersey senator who insisted that all contemplated appointments be first cleared with his party's national committee. Rather than to accede to this demand, Cole resigned.

Clyde Mills, the Assistant Director, then served as Acting Director. Mills transferred the administration of the

arbitration function of the Service from the office of the
Associate Director to the office of General Counsel.

In July 1953, Whitley P. McCoy was appointed Director by
President Eisenhower. McCoy, an arbitrator and law professor at the University of Alabama, was a self-proclaimed
"Eisenhower Democrat." Because of his arbitration background, McCoy stressed the arbitration function of the
Service. As one of the pioneers in the establishment of
the National Academy of Arbitrators, he insisted that, if
at all possible, members of the Academy be given first consideration in the selection of panels to be submitted to
the parties.

The number of regions was reduced from 12 to 8. The Regional Offices in Boston, District of Columbia, Detroit,
and Houston were eliminated.

McCoy resigned on November 30, 1954, and Joseph Finnegan,
a New York attorney, was appointed in February 1955 by
President Eisenhower on the recommendation of Secretary of
Labor Mitchell. Finnegan served as Director until 1961.

Under Director Finnegan, area offices with their Commissioners-In-Charge which existed within regions were eliminated. Audio-visual programs were developed for the training of labor and management. In addition, mock mediation,
both on film and live, was perfected. In the latter, mediators assumed the roles of labor and management representatives and demonstrated negotiations of typical labor-management problems during a mediation meeting. Both devices
proved to be not only very valuable tools for training representatives of labor and management but also as public relations methods of acquainting the labor-management community of the work of the Service. Finnegan eliminated the
Seattle Regional Office and assigned its jurisdiction to
the San Francisco Office.

Finnegan was succeeded by William E. Simkin, an arbitrator
and educator, who was appointed by President Kennedy and
confirmed by the Senate on March 31, 1961. Simkin served
as Director until 1969.

Missile Sites Labor Commission

Early in 1961, soon after the Kennedy Administration began,
major labor relations problems developed at missile sites.
To meet these problems, President Kennedy signed an Execu-

tive Order establishing the Missile Sites Labor Commission and provided for the formation of local Missile Site Labor Relations Committees at major missile sites throughout the Nation.

There were two basic steps which had to be undertaken. First, securing a no-strike/no-lockout pledge from many of the principal contractors and unions who were involved in missile site work. Many such pledges were obtained. The second was the creation of a tripartite dispute settlement authority. This, too, was accomplished. Secretary of Labor Arthur Goldberg was Chairman and Director Simkin became Vice Chairman.

In order to avoid delays and resolve certain types of disputes--mostly grievances--on the site, Missile Site Labor Relations Committees were established at each base. The size and format of each committee was left to the judgment of the people directly involved at the site. The only guideline was that each committee should include appropriate representatives of labor, management, and governmental procurement agencies actually working at the site. At each location, a mediator stationed near the site was named as chairman of the site committee.

The primary function of the site commiteee was to anticipate impending labor problems, discuss these problems and to arrange for their resolution. The local committee utilized fully all voluntary settlement procedures already in existence and encouraged the establishment of grievance and jurisdictional procedures if none existed.

For specific disputes, the mediator-chairman exercised his normal mediation functions in assisting the parties to resolve their differences. While most disputes were resolved at the site, if a particular dispute defied local efforts, it was referred to the Commission for resolution. In its six-year history, the Commission found it necessary to take formal action in only 32 disputes.

One unique aspect of the Commission's work was its jurisdiction over "uneconomical practices." This usually involved cutting back fringe pay provisions in existing contracts or practices, and the establishment of guidelines beyond which approval would not be granted. Having determined that a practice was non-economical, the Commission would advise the procurement agencies that reimbursement

by the Government beyond the limits set by the Commission
need not be allowed.

The Commission was dissolved by an Executive Order of President Johnson in 1967. The Order was largely motivated by
the gradual disintegration of the no-strike/no-lockout
pledges. These pledges were obtained when the missile program was critical. By 1967, the missile site construction
program had been substantially completed so that the foundation upon which the pledges were based had eroded.

During the Simkin administration, the preventive program of
the Service was revived. Mediators were advised that the
Service considered the preventive program on a par with
their dispute mediation activities. A national office staff
member was designated to monitor the program. Greater use
of audio-visual aids and mock mediation, both live and film,
was made.

In limited and carefully selected cases, mediators were encouraged to make recommendations of a basis for settlement
of the dispute. If circumstances warranted, mediators had
the authority to formalize such recommendations and make
them public.

The tier or escalation approach of supplemental assistance
to mediators was perfected and utilized in a significant
number of disputes which defied the efforts of the single
assigned mediator. In a few cases, the efforts of the members of the Service were supplemented by the ad hoc appointment of an outside person who had a national reputation in
labor-management relations.

The National Labor-Management Panel as authorized by Section 205 of the Labor-Management Relations Act, 1947, as
amended, was reactivated. The Act provides:

> "It shall be the duty of the Panel...to advise
> in the avoidance of industrial controversies,
> and the manner in which mediation and voluntary
> adjustment shall be administered, particularly
> with reference to controversies affecting the
> general welfare of the country."

Regional and field offices were updated or moved to larger
and more desirable spaces in newly constructed Federal
buildings. A joint committee of representatives of State

mediation agencies and the Federal Mediation and Conciliation Service drafted and adopted a Code of Professional Conduct which is still in use today.[2]

The eight-year term of Director Simkin was the longest any
Federal Mediation and Conciliation Service director served.
It was marked by a resurgence of the high morale of the
field staff.

William Simkin resigned and Curtis Counts was nominated in
1969 by President Nixon as his successor. Counts had been
a Vice President of McDonnell Douglas Corporation. Director Counts' administration was uneventful except for some
changes in the Service's top staff. He was replaced in
1973 by William Usery, a former Grand Lodge Representative
of the Machinists Union and an Assistant Secretary of Labor.
Usery subsequently became Secretary of Labor.

During Usery's tenure, the Administration imposed mandatory
wage and price controls as an anti-inflation measure. In
January 1973, these controls were replaced by a system of
voluntary restraints using the former ceilings as flexible
guidelines.

In 1974, the Health Care Act was passed. Under its provisions, the Service had the responsibility of providing mediation assistance and, under prescribed circumstances,
appointing Boards of Inquiry.

Because of the energy crisis, the President appointed
Director Usery as Special Assistant to the President for
Labor Relations. While he was directed to place special
emphasis on disputes involving the production and distribution of fuel and power, he was also authorized to intervene in other major disputes. As Special Assistant, he was
instrumental in assisting in the settlement of a threatened
strike of 600,000 postal employees and averting a nationwide strike by the Brotherhood of Railway Clerks.

Usery coined the term "aggressive mediation" which he defined as "alert and positive action in safeguarding the
public interest in the labor-management field." William
Usery was appointed Secretary of Labor in February 1976 and
was succeeded by James Scearce, his Deputy Director.

During Director Scearce's tenure (1976-1977) the Service
moved from the old Department of Labor Building to its own

building. Wayne Horvitz succeeded Scearce in 1977. During
his administration (1977-1980), the Emergency Provisions of
the Taft-Hartley Act were invoked in the bituminous coal
mine strike for the first time in six years.

With the election of President Regagn, Director Horvitz resigned and Kenneth Moffett, the Deputy Director, became
Acting Director in 1981. Moffett was soon actively involved in the baseball and air controllers' negotiations.

A severe budget problem brought about drastic changes in
the organization of the Service. Four regions were abol-
ished and, in lieu thereof, four larger regions were established, each headed by a Regional Director. In each new
region three district directors were appointed in former
regional and some field stations. Many of the functions
formerly performed by regional offices were centered in
the national office.

The majority of field office conference room spaces were
eliminated as part of the economy move. Only the District
Offices now have conference rooms. Only the district and
regional directors have clerical assistance. All mediators
answer their own phone and receive messages through answering machines. Reports and forms are hand-written by the
mediator and mailed to the district office.

The wisdom of these drastic changes has been seriously questioned. Every former Director recognized that the major
work of the Service was in the field and not in the national
office. Cyrus Ching, in his first report to Congress, emphasized the need to keep the national office staff at a
minimum "in order to make available to the field, where
the bulk of the service is performed, the maximum amount
of staff and funds."

The appointment of District Directors seemed to ignore the
lessons of the past. The Service had experimented with
Commissioners-in-Charge and Regional Representatives. Morale problems soon arose and what was at the beginning perceived to be clear demarcation of lines of authority soon
became sources of friction. Both the Commissioners-in-
Charge and Regional Representative concepts were soon dis-
carded.

The computerization of many of the Service's functions
raised the question whether it was needed. The Service,

in the scheme of the Federal bureaucracy, is one of the
smallest agencies. The overall permanent staff--national
and field, professional and clerical--is 352. Internal re-
forms of the reporting system, elimination of surplus regional staff personnel, and reassignment of some mediators
may have gone a long way to meet the budgetary requirements.

After a lapse of almost a year, President Reagan appointed
Kay McMurray in 1982, a former member of the National Mediation Board, as Director of the Federal Mediation and Conciliation Service.

Atomic Energy Labor-Management Relations Board

In March 1953, because of the criticality of the national
atomic energy problem and the need for uninterrupted production in that industry, President Eisenhower requested
that an Atomic Energy Labor-Management Relations Board be
established within the Federal Mediation and Conciliation
Service. His request was complied with and Cyrus Ching
was named Chairman.

Whenever a dispute involving the atomic energy program
proved not to be susceptible to mediation by the Service,
the dispute was referred to the Panel. The Panel had full
discretion to use any method of assisting the parties to
arrive at a settlement through voluntary methods. These
methods included returning the dispute to the parties for
further bargaining and mediation or for settlement under
existing procedures agreed to by the parties. The Panel
could also recommend to the parties a basis for the settlement of the dispute. Even though the recommendations of
the Panel were not binding on the parties, the Panel enjoyed a high degree of success. In 1956, the Panel was
transferred to the Atomic Energy Commission.

The National Mediation Board[3]

The National Mediation Board is the second and smaller mediation agency of the Federal Government. The Board was
established in its present form in 1934. It replaced the
United States Board of Mediation created in 1926. Its
original jurisdiction was over railroads and their employees. In 1936, its jurisdiction was extended to air carri-
ers and their employees. It is administered by a board of
three appointed by the President for three-year staggered

terms. Not more than two Board members can be of the same political party and Board members alternate as Chairman.

There are no educational requirements for mediator applicants. Applicants must take an examination which is conducted by the Board which also interviews them to assure their qualifications. Weight is given to subjective and personality characteristics. If the applicant is successful, he is placed on a roster. Appointments are made from the roster and on appointment the applicant is granted civil service status.

The principal function of the Board is to mediate disputes in the railroad and airline industry which arise over requests by either party for changes in wages, benefits, or rules. A distinction is made between disputes involving contract negotiations which are termed "major disputes" and grievances which are called "minor disputes."

Board members and its mediators do not handle "minor disputes." These are handled by the National Railroad Adjustment Board, a semi-independent agency created in 1934. The Adjustment Board is composed of equal representation of labor and management. If the Board cannot dispose of the dispute, it selects a neutral to break the deadlock on the Board.

In "major disuptes," if either party desires to change an existing collective bargaining contract, it must give the other party notice of its intention. After service of the notice, the two sides, within 10 days thereafter, must agree to confer. Such conference must be held within 30 days of the notice. During this period and for 10 days after the conference ends, both parties must maintain the status quo. If negotiations reach a statemate, either party may request the services of the Board. The Board on its own motion may intercede in the dispute if it decides it is in the national interest to do so. In either case, the status quo has to be maintained by the parties while the Board retains jurisdiction.

If the mediation efforts of the Board fail, the Board has the statutory duty to urge the parties to voluntarily submit the dispute to arbitration. If arbitration is rejected, the Board notifies both parties that for 30 days neither party can change any contract provisions unless in the intervening period an emergency board is created under the Act.

If during this 30-day status quo period the Board decides
that the dispute "should threaten substantially to interrupt
inter-State commerce to a degree such as to deprive any section of the country of essential transportation services, it
notifies the President. The President, in such cases, may
"create a board to investigate and report respecting such
dispute."

The Emergency Board has 30 days in which to investigate and
issue recommendations. Such recommendations are not binding and either party is free to reject them. If rejected,
neither party can change existing contract provisions for
30 more days. If at the end of the 60-day period no agreement has been reached, the parties are free to resort to
economic action.

NOTES

1. Roger W. Babson, <u>W. B. Wilson and the Department of Labor</u>, p. 33 at seq.

2. cf Appendix.

3. Forty-Eighth Annual Report of the National Mediation Board; The Railway Labor Act at Fifty, U.S. Government Printing Office.

CHAPTER VIII
ANATOMY OF A MEDIATOR

Former Federal Mediation and Conciliation Service Director William E. Simkin lists[1] sixteen combinations which a potential mediator ought to possess:

1. the patience of Job
2. the sincerity and bulldog characteristics of the English
3. the wit of the Irish
4. the physical endurance of the marathon runner
5. the broken field dodging abilities of a halfback
6. the guile of Michavelli
7. the personality-probing skills of a good psychiatrist
8. the confidence-retaining characteristic of a mute
9. the hide of a rhinoceros
10. the wisdom of Solomon
11. demonstrated integrity and impartiality
12. basic knowledge of and belief in the collective bargaining process
13. firm faith in voluntarism in contrast to dictation
14. fundamental belief in human values and potential, tempered by ability to assess personal weaknesses as well as strengths
15. hard-nosed ability to analyze what is available in contrast to what might be desirable
16. sufficient personal drive and ego, qualified by willingness to be self-effacing.

There is one characteristic, which may be implicit in some of the foregoing, which transcends all of those listed: he must be the master of the alternative. He should be capable of fashioning acceptable alternatives to the unobtainable positions of parties to a labor dispute.

Many of the listed qualities cannot be measured by the written word alone. Many are purely subjective, others can only be demonstrated by actual performance in the field of labor relations. As a consequence, the appointing agency should be granted great latitude in selecting acceptable candidates as mediators. Further, in exercising such discretion, the appointing agency should be able to base its judgment on merit and not on the political affiliations of the applicants.

The ideal method of recruiting potential mediators would appear to be to first establish general criteria as to required experience and educational equivalence for the purpose of screening out applicants who are obviously not qualified. Secondly, a field investigation in the labor-management community in which the applicant operated for the purpose of ascertaining his reputation for integrity, objectivity, ability, and acceptability. The field investigation should be supplemented by an in-depth interview by the chairman or director and top staff of the appointing agency. Such interview could be preceded by a written test, if legislation requires, but the real determining factor should be the interview.

Relying solely on a written test or making passing the written test a condition precedent to the interview is not a very satisfactory method of selection of potential mediators. A number of years ago, a test for mediator positions was given in a State which required passing the test as a condition to the interview. From the nature of the questions, it was apparent that it had been prepared by some professor at the State college. Most of the questions pertained to labor history, economics, and statistics. Any recent graduate with a major in industrial relations could have passed the test with ease. Most practitioners who might have had a limited educational background but unlimited experience and who had not refreshed their recollection on the subject matters of the test questions would have great difficulty attaining a passing grade. As a matter of fact, in this particular examination, three highly qualified experienced applicants left the room without completing the test.

On the Federal level, in recognition of their need for latitude in the selection and appointment of mediators, Congress incorporated in Title II of the Labor-Management Relations Act, Section 202(b):

> "The Director is authorized...without regard to the provisions of the civil service laws and the Classification Act of 1923, as amended, appoint and fix the compensation of such conciliators

and mediators as may be necessary to carry out
the functions of the Service..."

The Federal Mediation and Conciliation Service, because of
the above exemption, does not utilize any civil service ros-
ters as a source of potential mediators.

The Federal Mediation and Conciliation Service requires that
applicants have at least seven years of progressively responsible collective bargaining experience in the last twelve
years. Relevant educational background, such as degrees in
law, industrial relations, business administration, economics, and personnel management, may be substituted for some
of the experience requirements. In evaluating applications,
emphasis is placed on the quality of the experience; e.g.,
the chairman of either union or management bargaining team
will be rated higher than a grievance committee member.

If the application indicates that the applicant does meet
the criteria, a committee of mediators rate the applications
numerically and a cut-off point is established. Those applications which exceed the minimum are then scheduled for
an interview before another committee of mediators. Based
on such interviews, the committee makes recommendations to
the Director. Based on such recommendations, the Director
selects those to be appointed.

On the State level, the selection process differs among the
various States. Typical are the following:

In Pennsylvania, applicants must have a relevant college
degree and four years of labor relations experience. If
he meets these requirements, the applicant must pass a
written test as a condition for further consideration. If
he passes the test, he is interviewed by the Director and
other staff personnel. His name is then placed on a civil
service roster and appointments are made from such list.

In general, the same practice is followed in Illinois.

Minnesota requires that all applicants have at least five
years of practical and responsible experience in labor
relations. Selection is a two-step process--a written
test and an interview. Passing the test, however, is not
a condition precedent to the interview. Based on both,
applicants are assigned points on the basis of most qualified, qualified, and not qualified. The successful appli-

cants are placed on a civil service roster from which appointments are made.

Indiana requires four years of "full time paid experience
in labor or industrial relations, personnel management or
public administration." Accredited college training may be
substituted for three years of experience. Among the per-
missive substitutions are a major or minor in business administration, business law, economics, and labor relations.

Connecticut and Massachusetts mediators are selected by
direct appointment.

New York and California select their mediators by a combination of written test and interview and appointments are
made from a civil service roster developed thereby.

Background of Mediators

A comparison of the experience background of State mediators in a few typical State agencies and the Federal Mediation and Conciliation Service indicates that most recruit
potential mediators from the same sources--labor, management, and government.

Occupations of Mediators Prior to Being Hired

Agency	Labor	Management	Government	Mixed*
FMCS	117	83	16	43**
Connecticut	All	--	--	--
Pennsylvania	9	6	2	5
Minnesota	10	4	1	--
Massachusetts	5	1	1	4
California	9	2	--	--

* Mixed: These mediators had experience in two or more
            fields of labor, management, or government.
** Source: Federal Mediation and Conciliation Service
            personnel records as of 1984.

Prior Occupations Of Federal Mediators
Appointed Between 1945 And 1952

Labor	Management	Government	Academic
15	11	17	5

Source: FMCS personnel records

A Rutgers University Study, conducted in 1964, of the experience backgrounds of Federal mediators indicated that of 139 mediators with labor or management backgrounds, 52% were from the ranks of labor.

A review of the above studies indicates that the majority of appointments in the Federal Mediation and Conciliation Service since at least 1945 has been from the ranks of labor. One reason is that more applications have been received from persons with labor backgrounds than those with management. Many of the union applicants become disillusioned by the uncertainties of intra-union politics. Whenever there was a drastic change in the international leadership of a union, the Service would receive a great number of applications from international representatives who had had the misfortune to back the wrong slate of officers. Further, salaries and benefits in the Federal mediation service have been more attractive and it offered more stable employment.

Despite the disparity in applications received, the Service has managed to maintain an acceptable ratio between mediators with a labor and those with management backgrounds. The 1984 data shows a ratio of 117 labor to 83 management or 59% to 41%. The 1945-1952 appointments are 15 to 11 or 58% to 42%. The 1964 Rutgers' Study shows 72 to 53 or 58% to 42%.

Trying to attain an alleged ideal balance of 50% of each labor and management is debatable. The correct criteria in selecting potential mediators is not necessarily their past affiliation but the depth of their collective bargaining experience and the quality of their performance. Experience has shown that applicants who possess both have no difficulty in adapting themselves to their new role as neutrals when appointed to the mediation staff.

Educational Background Of Federal Mediators

A study by the Federal Mediation and Conciliation Service in 1953 of the educational background of mediators hired between 1945-1952 disclosed the following:

Grammar School	Some High School	High School	Some College	College	Some Graduate	Graduate
2	5	9	11	3	3	16*

* This was a period when, in the author's opinion, academic background was overemphasized.

The excellent Rutgers' Study of 1966 broke down the educational level on the basis of length of service in the Federal service:

	Length of Service In Present Agency			
	3 Years or Less	4 to 9 Years	10 to 15 Years	16 or More Years
Federal Mediators				
Education				
Some high school	2	7	10	15
Completed high school	21	5	7	15
Some college	30	33	32	35
Completed college	13	19	7	13
Some graduate school	16	16	12	8
Graduate degrees(s) completed	19	21	21	13

Simkin's survey of the educational background of mediators hired between 1961-1969 disclosed:

Some High School	High School	Some College	College Degree	Some Graduate Work	Graduate Degree
10	38	42	22	15	20

The 1984 personnel records of the Federal Mediation and Conciliation Service reveal the following:

Grammar School	High School	Some College	College Degree	Postgraduate
6	76	38	80	50

These studies indicate that the Federal mediation service--and undoubtedly most of the State mediation agencies--are attracting more candidates with college and graduate degrees than in the past. There are several possible reasons. The uplifting of the journeyman mediator's salary, pension, and the fringe benefits made mediator positions financially attractive. Further, many colleges and universities have recognized that the field of industrial relations is in itself a distinct academic discipline and have established courses of study leading to degrees in this field. It was not too long ago that a course in labor or industrial relations was a one-semester, often optional, class either in a personnel administration or economics program.

From these charts and studies emerges the typical successful candidate for the position of mediator. He usually has
had the minimum of a high school education and probably has
a college degree. He came from either the ranks of labor
or management--with a minimum of four or more years of progressively responsible collective bargaining experience. He
must be confident and self-reliant and have demonstrated
many of the qualities enumerated by former Director Simkin,
including the ability to fashion acceptable alternatives in
conflict situations.

Training

At the Federal level, the training of newly appointed mediators has followed a pattern. The new appointees are brought
into the national office for a week or two of orientation.
On completion, they are assigned either to a regional or district office where their field training is conducted by the
Regional or District Director. The new mediator sits in on
mediation sessions conducted by an experienced mediator.
After a period of time, he receives his solo case assignments which are gradually upgraded as he acquires mediation
skills.

From time to time, as budget permits, seminars and workshops
are conducted either on a regional, multi-regional, or national basis. These are designed not only to update the
attendees on the latest developments in collective bargaining but also to sharpen their skills by the cross fertiliza-
tion of ideas from mediators operating in various sections
of the country.

Evaluating A Mediator's Performance
Federal Mediation and Conciliation Service
System of Mediator Rating

In order to meet the specifications required by Chapter 431
of the Federal Personnel Manual, the Service adopted a new
approach to its method of evaluating mediator performance.[2]
It is essentially a numerical value system.

Three "critical" areas were established--dispute mediation,
technical assistance and public information, and professional responsibility. Each "critical" area is evaluated and
the mediator is rated in one of five levels:

1. Outstanding.

2. Exceeds Fully Successful.

3. Fully Successful.

4. Minimally Successful.

5. Unacceptable.

The final rating is determined by adding the numerical values assigned to each level of rating in each element. The
numerical values are:

	Dispute Mediation	TA & PI	Professional Responsibility
Outstanding	8	4	4
Exceeds Fully Successful	6	3	3
Fully Successful	4	2	2
Minimally Successful	2	1	1

No value is assigned to a rating of "Unacceptable." By
regulation, an Unacceptable rating on any critical element
requires a summary rating of Unacceptable.

The ratings are done by the District Director who must
first discuss the intended ratings with the Regional Director before issuing them to the mediators.

The following data is the basis on which ratings are made:

--Statistics including number of active cases
   and number of joint meetings, strikes prior
   to activation, percentage of activation, and
   other measures of the amount of dispute activity consistent with the work available.

--The mediator's acceptability and effectiveness
   in the labor-management community.

--Assessment of a mediator's attitude toward his
   supervisor, other employees, and/or the parties.

--Reports of T.A & P.I. activities--both from the
   mediator and parties.

Mediators dissatisfied with the rating may not grieve it
or appeal it. The only recourse is to request a review by
the Regional Director.

In the case of an unacceptable rating, three District Directors from other regions will be asked to review the documen-
tation by the rating official. If they are unable to agree,
the case will be reviewed by the Deputy Director.

While this rating plan is an improvement over the number of
active cases system, there are several areas which deserve
reconsideration. The most inequitable is the denial of the
right of a mediator to grieve if he is dissatisfied with
the rating he has received. His only recourse is to appeal
to the very same Regional Director who had already approved
the rating.

Secondly, the data which forms the basis of the District
Director's judgment is still based on the number of cases
and joint meetings. If the number of meetings held is
merely one of many factors to be considered, then it is
an acceptable ingredient in the formation of the District
Director's judgment. If it is of major importance, then
it is open to serious question. An effective mediator times
his entrance into a dispute when he believes he can make
the most contribution. A poor mediator has a tendency to
interject himself into the negotiations prematurely and as
a consequence his statistical record will show a greater
number of meetings than the effective mediator. One of the
best tests is personal observation by a mediator's supervisor. By attending a cross section of meetings conducted
by the mediator, the supervisor can observe and evaluate
the conduct of the meeting and the mediator's contribution
to the solution of the problems raised at the bargaining
table.

Another factor to be weighed is the reactions of and responses given by mediators at meaningful seminars. By
meaningful seminars we mean those where the participants
are confronted with real, down-to-earth problems faced by
mediators and not some esoterical, theoretical, nonsensical problem replete with "interfaces," "acclimatization,"
and "interpersonal relations." The criteria to be used in
rating under this factor should be "what solutions did he
advance"--"what alternative approaches did he suggest?"

Mediator Attitude
And Affirmative Philosophy

The day of the mediator who merely acts as the complacent chairman is long past. Parties to a labor dispute expect and generally want the mediator, at appropriate times, to come forward with suggestions for some fresh approach to the problems under discussion. As a well-known union attorney said in a talk before a seminar of mediators, "all disputes are eventually settled; we will settle the dispute with your help or despite it."

In the past, one Federal Mediation Director urged the mediators to be "aggressive." This may be misconstrued. "Aggressive" conjures up a picture of a mediator thrusting himself into negotiations, whether needed or not, and starting to dictate to the parties.

At the other end of the scale is the mediator who avoids meetings until "the parties are ready to settle." Translated, this means until the parties have hurt each other economically so badly that they are motivated to reach agreement. If we wait until the "parties are ready" to settle, do they need us then? Is it not meddling rather than mediation? Each dispute has a key to its solution. If a meeting is held by a mediator and it fails to achieve a settlement, then it is because the mediator as yet has not found that key.

One of the characteristics of a top-flight mediator is that he does not stop thinking about his case when he adjourns the meeting. Such a mediator takes time when he returns to his office or home to mentally review the various moves which have occurred during the meeting. He analyzes his efforts and keeps asking himself--what else could I have done to help the parties reach agreement? Was there something I did or failed to do which I should have done? What is the key to the problem?

An effective mediator must have an abiding faith in the collective bargaining process for the resolution of labor disputes.

His approach to each dispute is not whether agreement is possible, but rather how can agreement be achieved.

He should proceed during his mediation efforts on these
basic assumptions:

    a.   there is no issue or dispute that cannot
        be resolved.

    b.   that basically the parties want to reach
        agreement.

    c.   that despite the threats hurled at the bar-
        gaining table, neither side really wants a
        stoppage--certainly not a protracted one.

    d.   that despite the repeated statements by the
        parties, during negotiations, that they have
        gone as far as they can go, there is always
        some "elbow room" which can lead to compro-
        mise.

He should accept the idea that he is expendable and that,
as a mediator, he is there to assist the parties and not
to supplant them. It is the parties who settle the dispute and not the mediator.

NOTES

1. William E. Simkin, Mediation and the Dynamics of Collective Bargaining, Bureau of National Affairs, 1971.

2. cf Appendix.

CHAPTER IX

TYPES OF MEDIATION

Mediation agencies, particularly the Federal Mediation and Conciliation Service, use several different approaches in seeking to assist the parties to resolve their differences thorugh mediation. Among these are solo mediators, industry mediators, panels, teams, and the tier approach, also known as the escalation approach. Which approach is utilized depends on a number of factors including manpower availability and the nature, duration, and impact of a particular dispute.

Solo Mediation

The vast majority of cases, in both the Federal and State levels, are handled by a single mediator without supplementation or substitution by his agency. It has been estimated that 97% of all cases are mediated by one mediator. The solo mediator is fully responsible for the case assigned to him and he conducts his meetings with literally no supervision except for a review of his reports. Such reports normally contain the names of the parties, the issues involved, the progress of negotiations, and his future plans.

Which mediator should be assigned to a particular case is a matter of judgment for his immediate supervisor. Such judgment is normally based on the location of the dispute, the mediator's caseload and the mediator's experience, if any, in handling prior disputes between the same parties. If both parties request a particular mediator, the agency usually will try to acommodate them depending on the availability of the requested mediator.

Industry Mediators

The idea of "industry mediators" has been tested in a number of situations. The United States Conciliation Service (the predecessor agency of the Federal Mediation and Conciliation Service) experimented with the industry approach. In 1939-40, as part of its cooperative program with the Advisory Council on National Defense, the U.S. Conciliation Service selected seven of its commissioners to work with what was then considered key defense industries--oil, aviation, manufacturing, machine tools, rubber and chemicals, building construction, shipbuilding, and steel. In 1940-41, this was expanded to nineteen mediators.

After a few years' experience, a number of weaknesses became apparent. While certain peripheral benefits were derived from the prolonged exposure to the problems of a particular industry, the industry mediator's effectiveness began to deteriorate for perfectly understandable reasons. Experience has taught that when a mediator is too readily accessible to the parties, there is a tendency on the part of one side or the other to rely on him without any sincere attempt to resolve the dispute by themselves. In addition, there is a serious question as to whether such an industry mediator becomes less forceful and persuasive because of this more intimate relationship with the parties. Somewhat parallel with this situation is the experience of so-called "permanent arbitrators" or "impartial chairmen."

One form of industry mediator in the 1960's was the missile site mediator designated by the Director of the Federal Mediation and Conciliation Service. His responsibility was not only to chair and guide the Missile Site Labor Relations Committee but also to mediate specific disputes at the assigned site.

The concept of industry mediators has lost most of its acceptability by mediation agencies. It is seldom, if ever, used today by either State or Federal mediation agencies. The last vestige is the designation in the national office of the Federal Mediation and Conciliation Service of national office representatives as coordinators of mediation activities in specific areas such as construction, public sector, health care industry, and technical assistance.

Mediation Panels

Occasionally, parties to a labor dispute find that a "panel" or "team" of mediators has been assigned to their dispute. In mediation parlance, a "panel" is composed of three mediators while a "team" usually denotes two mediators. It is rather interesting to trace the evolution of the panel approach to mediation.

For a number of years, especially during World War II, the Federal Mediation and Conciliation Service and its predecessor agency, United States Conciliation Service, made exten-

sive use of the panel approach to the more significant disputes. At one point in time, panels were instituted on a
rather rigid, formalistic basis. The panel consisted of
three mediators--one was designated as chairman, another as
associate, and the third, usually the junior in seniority
of the three, was designated the Secretary of the panel.
The mediator designated as Secretary performed no mediation
functions but had the sole responsibility to keep the minutes of the meeting and write the report to be sent to
Washington.

The conference conducted by such panels also followed a formal approach with opening statements by the parties and discussions. Indeed, there was one mediator who was often
designated Chairman of panels who insisted that the parties
rise when the panel entered the meeting room and that all
other panel members and the parties address him as Mr.
Chairman. A midwestern mediator who claimed to have been
a member of the judiciary somewhere in his career insisted
that the parties and his colleagues address him as "judge."
There were no regional boundaries and the panels travelled
through the length and breadth of this land.

The formal panel approach may sound rather cumbersome and
indeed almost ridiculous in the light of present-day negotiations and mediation. But strange as it may now seem,
such panels in that day and in the degree of sophistication
then prevalent, were highly successful. Formality was expected. It may be of interest that at that time all correspondence to mediators was addressed as to the Honorable
John Smith, United States Commissioner.

As time passed and negotiators became more mature in their
relationship with each other, the formal trappings of the
early panels gradually disappeared. Several concepts did,
however, remain--(a) the designation by the Washington office or Regional Director of a chairman, (b) the assignment
of the other members by such superiors, and (c) the thought
that a panel meant three members (no more, no less).

Subsequently, when regional offices were established, such
panels were regionally appointed and operated within the
region. Occasionally, a field mediator from another region
would be designated by the national office as a special representative of the Director.

Mediation by a panel is still an effective technique in a
limited amount of cases.

Team Mediation

In the mid-50's, the concept of a "team" in lieu of a panel evolved. There was a realization that there was really no magic in a three-man panel. Increasing regional caseloads with its attendant limitations on manpower led to a gradual acceptance of the team concept.

While each technique has merit in specific and selected cases, from a mediation viewpoint, the team concept appears to be the most desirable. Often in a panel situation, the members will caucus by themselves to try to arrive at a meeting of minds on the overall strategy to be employed. Difference of opinions as to the most effective approach inevitably arises. This often leads to an abandonment of a bolder or more affirmative approach in order to achieve an accommodation of the varying panel members' viewpoints. Time is consumed to arrive at a consensus. The members of a team have greater flexibility since an agreement on the techniques to be employed in the particular disputes usually can be arrived at more expeditiously.

Then, too, in a panel the scheduling of off-record meetings becomes awkward. Normally the off-record meeting is attended by one representative of each party. If the three panel members attend their number alone would overwhelm the representatives and hamper free exchange of ideas the meeting was intended to engender. If only one or two members of the panel attend, the problem then arises as to the identity of the one or two. If no agreement can be reached as to the panel attendees, ill feeling may be created if one insists that he alone attend.

Whether mediation intercession takes the form of a panel or team, the basic function is the same--to assist the parties to reach agreement. Such panels or teams exercise no greater or lesser responsibility than a single mediator. Generally speaking, the cases where panels or teams of mediators are used are those of more than local significance.

Tier (Escalation) Approach

The tier or escalation approach is not a new technique. It has been tried, at least in the Federal service, at various times since about 1942. It reached its most successful application during the administration of Director William E. Simkin of the Federal Mediation and Conciliation Service.

Under this approach, in selected cases, mediation efforts
are first conducted by the originally assigned mediator.
If he cannot successfully bring the parties to agreement
within a reasonable time, another mediator is assigned to
assist him. If their efforts fail, a headquarters mediator
who bears an official title other than a mediator joins the
panel of mediators. The basic approach is supplementation
of the efforts of the originally assigned mediator and not
a substitution for them.

It proved to be a most effective approach. Often the originally assigned mediator exhausted his effectiveness. This
was not by any means due to his lack of ability but often
related to the point of time in the negotiations when he
interceded. The interjection of a new face and perhaps new
suggested alternatives often is helpful in bringing about
agreement. If the intercession of a headquarters' trouble
shooter called a National Office Representative became necessary, it could be used as a device to forestall a strike
or lock-out until his advent. The trouble shooter had several advantages. First, time--he entered at a point where
there had been a complete exploration of the issues (hope-
fully a narrowing of the areas of conflict) and at a time
when the parties were faced with hard decisions. Over and
beyond these advantages, he could adopt bolder approaches
which the local or originally assigned mediator could not
utilize because of his frequent association with the parties in other disputes.

To be successful, the escalation technique must be founded
on three basic premises. First, the adoption by all mediators of the philosophy that a dispute case is not their private property but is the concern of the agency as a whole.
Second, that the important goal is not the self-glorifica-
tion of the individual but the resolution of the dispute.
As former Director Cyrus Ching put it--"There is no limit
to the amount of good you can do if you don't worry about
who gets credit." Third, that the supplemental mediators
be always conscious of or sensitive to the need to preserve
the integrity and future acceptability of the originally
assigned mediator. In order to preserve the status of the
local mediator, all press releases, to the extent possible,
should be issued in his name. Further, when the decision
has been made to use the tier approach in a particular case,
the local mediator should advise the parties that he has
initiated the addition of another mediator on the basis of
"two heads are better than one."

In determining if a dispute should be subject to the tier
approach, there are a number of considerations. It should
be used only in cases having more than a normal impact on
the economy of a community, State, or nation. It should
not be automatic but decided on a case-by-case basis. Care
must be taken to avoid what became known as "parachuting"
which took place in the United States Conciliation Service
under Director Warren. Often, without prior notification
to the originally assigned mediator, a national office representative would appear at the scene of the negotiations
and, amid attendant publicity, announce that he was joining
in the mediation efforts.

"Parachuting" can be avoided by carefully selecting the
cases which potentially may call for the tier approach.
Having done so, then it is incumbent on the national office
to have a running consultation with the local mediator and
his immediate supervisor as to the status of negotiations
and their prognosis as to the possibility of a settlement
in the immediate future. If they both feel that there is
a possibility of agreement in the near future, the national
office should defer all plans to intercede and confine its
activities to monitoring the progress being made. If there
appears to be little, if any, possibility of a settlement,
after fully advising both the mediator and his supervisor
of the plans to intervene, the national office representative should direct the local mediator to schedule the meeting in which he would participate.

A possible variation of the intra-agency tier approach, in
the Federal sector, is the addition of a private mediator
to the panel either in lieu of a national office representative or with such representative. At times, an entirely
new mediation panel composed of all private mediators has
been appointed. Whether it is a full panel of all private
mediators or the addition of one mediator, both are under
the jurisdiction of and responsible to the Director of the
Federal Mediation and Conciliation Service.

There has been and is a small group of private mediators
who have demonstrated outstanding ability as mediators.
Among these, are David Cole, George Taylor, Saul Wallen,
James Healy, John Dunlop, Leo Brown, Judge Maguire, and
Theodore Kheel.

Experience has shown that as between a full private panel
and addition of a private mediator to a mediation panel,
the latter is the more desirable and effective.

CHAPTER X
FUNDAMENTALS OF EFFECTIVE MEDIATION

A critical analysis of the mediation process reveals that effective mediation is based on four fundamental principles:

1. Understanding and appreciation of the problems confronting the parties.

2. Imparting to the parties the fact that the mediator knows and appreciates their problems.

3. Creating doubts in their minds as to the validity of the positions they have assumed with respect to such problems.

4. Suggesting alternative approaches which may facilitate agreement.

1. Understanding the Problems

The first principle involves a thorough knowledge of the field of labor and industrial relations, awareness of trends and patterns, a working concept of the economics of the industry and particularly of the employer involved, and an appreciation of any human relations problems which might have precipitated the dispute.

Equally important, the mediator must have a thorough knowledge of the issues which are the immediate causes of the existing impasse, an appreciation of the complexities and dimensions of such problems, and the personalities involved. If the mediator does not possess this arsenal of knowledge, his efforts to assist the parties would be ineffective and may even hamper the efforts of the parties to resolve their dispute.

2. Letting the Parties Know
That He Understands the Problems

As for the second principle, it is not enough for effective mediation that the mediator have knowledge and appreciation of the problems. It is equally important that the parties are made aware of the fact that he does have this knowledge and appreciation. Until this is conveyed to the parties, they will have doubts as to whether he can contribute to the solution of the dispute.

Conversely, if the mediator did not anticipate a problem and, consequently, did not have the opportunity to prepare himself, he should avoid conveying to the parties his lack of understanding. Rather, he should remain silent until, by careful listening and by adroit probing questions, he acquires an understanding of the dimensions of the issues being negotiated.

Not many years ago, a mediator, who came from an industrial area where hourly rates were the rule and incentive systems almost nonexistent, was assigned to a dispute in an area where incentives--both individual and group--were the general rule. At first, as the joint meeting progressed, conscious of his lack of knowledge of incentives, he remained the silent chairman. However, after awhile, feeling that he should say something to justify his presence, the mediator suggested what he thought might be a compromise to an aspect of the group incentive problem under discussion. Unfortunately, his suggestion disclosed his total ignorance of even the fundamentals of group incentive systems. As he later described the events that followed:

> "Both parties stopped talking and looked down the
> table at me in amazement. Thereafter, they com-
> pletely ignored me except to tell me when they
> were going to lunch and when they decided to ad-
> journ for the day. I learned my lesson to do my
> homework before the meeting. If I did not, then
> at least to keep my mouth shut until I understood
> the problems. To paraphrase the old admonition--
> "where ignorance is bliss, it is folly to be vocal."

3. Creating Doubts in the Parties' Minds

The third principle is also essential. Normally, mediation is not utilized until the parties have made good-faith attempts to resolve the dispute without mediation. The fact that the dispute continues is a clear indication that the position one or the other has assumed on a particular issue or issues is a roadblock to agreement. If such position is persisted in, the conflict has little chance of early solution. A mediator's task is then to create doubts as to the

validity of that position. The mere intercession of a mediator of itself often expedites the agreement-making process. He is the neutral representing the underlying broad
public interest. Both parties seek to impress him with the
validity of their position, cognizant that their expositions
must be stripped of partisan trappings. Their appeal to him
must at the very least appear logical rather than emotional.
Explanations under such circumstances often create doubt in
the minds of the parties as to the positions they have
assumed.

Beyond the fact of the intercession, the mediator can create
doubts by questioning in depth, by bringing into play the
broad experience he has acquired, and by assisting the parties in evaluating the road ahead in terms of the resultant
economic impact.

The late Dr. George W. Taylor--one of the outstanding students of mediation--related how he and a number of his colleagues met with mediators from the United Nations in an
effort to analyze the mediation process. All agreed that
this third fundamental principle was one of the keystones
for successful mediation. As stated by Dr. Taylor:

> "How can you get parties who are wide apart to an
> agreement? They, or one of them, obviously must
> voluntarily recede from an extreme position. One
> way of facilitating this process is to raise legiti-
> mate doubts in their minds about positions firmly
> held. Everyone has his own ways of raising legiti-
> mate doubts. I have found it helpful to say 'You
> are certainly right on the basis of the facts you
> have used, but did you realize this new fact which
> has just been brought out? This fact is certainly
> new to me, how does it fit in with your analysis?'"

4. Proposing an Alternative Solution

The fourth principle involves the art of the alternative.
Having created such doubts, the mediator must then be prepared to move forward and offer an alternative approach to
the problem which may lead to a viable accommodation of the
viewpoints of the parties. To do so effectively, the mediator should not only be knowledgeable but also innovative,
imaginative, and resourceful. Since a professional mediator's experience in the specific field of collective bargaining is of greater depth than most if not all negotiators

for labor or management, he can direct the parties' attention to successful methods for resolution which have been
adopted by others. The alternative suggested by the mediator may not be the one finally agreed to by the parties but
his suggestion is often designed to open up an approach which
can lead to the structuring of the final settlement.

The ideal alternate solution by a mediator is one which is
not attributed to the mediator but emerges later as the parties own approach to the resolution of the dispute. In such
situations, the mediator plants the seed and lets it germi-
nate in the minds of the parties until it blossoms forth as
their solution. One approach, used by experienced mediators,
to accomplishing this ideal alternate solution is for the
mediator to advance some thoughts in a deprecating manner.
Illustratively, when the mediator is persuaded that he has
created doubts in the minds of the parties, he can speculate
that X might be a possible approach but he is sure that the
parties have already thought of it, simultaneously asserting
that it probably wouldn't work anyhow.

To the extent that a mediator becomes a master of the art
of the alternative to that extent will his mediatory efforts
prove successful.

CHAPTER XI

CONTRIBUTIONS A MEDIATOR CAN MAKE WHEN IMPASSE OCCURS

When various writers seek to describe the role of a mediator in a labor dispute, they generally resort to generalities such as "He is a catalytic agent," or "He serves as a
conduit for channeling information." The difficulty with
such broad statements is that they have a negative connota-
tion. If the parties properly utilize the services of a
mediator, he can make an affirmative contribution to the
resolution of the labor dispute.

Most labor disputes present a variety of problems which increase in their complexity in almost direct relationship to
the real or assumed economic strength of each party. Attitudes, economic drives and patterns, emotions, breakdown of
communications, human relations problems, intra-company and
union politics, public relations postures, premature rigidity of positions, personalities--all become enmeshed in the
dispute. All too often these obscure the fundamental issues
which gave rise to the dispute.

This is not the uncommon picture which often confronts a
mediator when he is called upon to intercede in a labor dispute. He must approach the task before him objectively,
calmly, and sympathetically. He must be prepared to facilitate change in the parties' positions by utilizing the pressures inherent in all labor disputes. He must seek to induce the parties to change their perception of the issues
and the personalities involved. His objective should be to
start the process of change, keep it moving, and constantly
directing it along the path leading to the ultimate goal--
agreement by the parties.

In his mediation efforts, he constantly seeks to provide the
atmosphere which will be most conducive for the creation of
proper attitudes for a peaceful adjustment of the dispute
by the parties themselves. This was well stated by Truslow
Adams, President of the then Curb Exchange, in a letter
thanking a mediator for his efforts which brought about the
termination of a long and costly strike by Curb Exchange
employees. The letter stated "thank you for creating the
atmosphere which made settlement of the dispute possible."

An immediate prerequisite to his success is the mutual desire of the parties involved to reach agreement. Absent
such a desire, no mediator on earth can assist them. This
desire to reach agreement must be a desire to arrive at an
equitable accommodation of the conflicting viewpoints of the
parties. Each must be willing to be convinced and must be
ready to yield to a more reasonable view advanced by the
other. A state of mind must exist which has been aptly described as a willingness to accept the less perfect which
will lead to agreement and to abandon the perfect which can
lead only to continued conflict.

There are a number of specific areas in which a mediator
can make an affirmative contribution to success of the negotiations.

Mere Intervention of Mediator Contributes

The mere intervention of a mediator into a labor dispute of
itself often expedites the agreement-making process. He is
the neutral representing the underlying broad public interest. Both parties seek to impress him with the validity
of their position cognizant that their explanations must be
stripped of propagandistic trappings. Their appeal to him
must at the very least appear logical rather than emotional.
Explanation under such circumstances often creates doubts
in the minds of the opposing parties as to the position they
have assumed. Further, the presence of the mediator is an
effective reminder to the parties that this dispute concerns
the public interest.

Utilizing The Mediator's Training And Experience

All applicants for the Federal Mediation and Conciliation
Service must have had seven years of full-time progressively
responsible and successful experience in collective bargaining or in other closely allied fields of labor-management
relations before they are seriously considered. After appointment, the mediator's skills are constantly updated by
workshops and self-improvement devices. Applicants are recruited from the ranks of both labor and management.

The average Federal mediator handles 37 cases a year and
actively participates in over 118 joint collective bargaining meetings. The experience he acquires in conducting collective bargaining conferences far exceeds the experience
acquired by most representatives of management or labor.

This experience provides him with a reservoir of knowledge not only as to the techniques of bargaining but also, and equally important, the knowledge of how other parties have resolved specific issues. This experience will equip him to formulate alternatives which may enable the parties to accommodate their conflicting viewpoints.

A Mediator Can Advise And Counsel As To The Timing Of Offers And Counterproposals

Often the key to an agreement is the timing of an offer or counterproposal. Because of the mediator's neutrality, he is in the best position to assess the receptivity for a proposal or counterproposal. All too often, an offer or counterproposal which would otherwise be acceptable is rejected out of hand because it was made prematurely. If made too late, the climate of agreement has passed and the offer is no longer palatable. The mediator can judge better than a partisan when his counterpart is conditioned to accept the less perfect solution and when the offer or counterproposal may be timely. During the course of his mediation efforts, he has conferred separately with each party and engaged them in candid discussions about their positions and needs. As a result of these meetings, he is able to assess the mood of the parties and the pressures upon them.

The Training And Experience Of A Mediator Have Equipped Him To Be A Master Of The Alternative

From his experience in varied disputes, the mediator may be able to suggest compromises that the parties can accept. This is not to imply that mediators are more astute than the parties, but merely that since they bring experience and a fresh viewpoint to the issues, they may discern solutions which were overlooked by the parties. Further, parties will reject an alternative approach to solving the problem if it is advanced by their counterpart but will accept the same alternative if suggested by the mediator.

All too often, parties can only visualize the problem in their own frame of reference. They become so engrossed in their own positions that they fail to see the different approaches to the solution of the problem which is creating the impasse. An experienced mediator has encountered many similar situations and knows how other negotiators have solved the same problem without the necessity of total capitulation. As a result, he can suggest these alternative solutions to the parties and guide the discussions at the bargaining table so that the pathway to solution becomes viable to each party.

An illustrative situation occurred not many years ago. A mediator was called into a dispute involving a protracted strike. The union had continued negotiations for one month beyond the expiration date of the contract before striking. After a number of joint and separate meetings, the mediator was able to assist the parties in resolving all of the issues except retroactivity. The company insisted that it never granted retroactivity in any of its prior negotiations and would not depart from that principle. The union was equally adamant and insisted that no settlement was possible unless it provided for retroactivity. By careful probing, the mediator became aware that the company feared that many of its highly skilled employees had obtained other employment during the strike and that there existed some doubt as to whether such employees would return to work at the conclusion of the strike. Based on his experience in prior cases, the mediator suggested that an amount closely approximating the lump sum which would have been due each employee if retroactivity had been granted be set aside as a financial inducement for employees to return to work. He further suggested that this sum be paid to employees who returned to work within three days of the setetlement and remained on the job for 30 days after such return. This suggested alternative approach provided the basis for the resolution of the dispute.

A Mediator Can Assist In Modifying Rigid Positions

If a mediator is confronted with rigidity of positions, and is persuaded that adherence to such positions is either unrealistic or potentially unfruitful, he will seek to raise doubts in the minds of the parties as to the soundness of their position. He knows that, as previously stated, one of the requisites of the agreement-making process is acceptance by the disputants of the frequent necessity to forego the more perfect, but unacceptable, idea in exchange for the less perfect idea which is acceptable and hence has greater force and validity in creating agreement. Closely related to this technique is that which seeks to establish what has been so aptly termed as the "consent to lose" attitude. It is a recognition that it is not possible to achieve all the goals that the parties had hoped to accomplish in the negotiations. Many times this attitude is developed by a medi-

ator's skillful use of the alternate-solution technique,
discussed previously.

A Mediator Can Forestall Premature End Positions

It is axiomatic in collective bargaining that whenever emotions supplant reasoning, agreement is impossible. All too
often when emotions are high, parties in the heat of the
argument may take an end position prematurely. Having done
so, it may be difficult for them to gracefully retreat from
it when a later accommodation is advanced. A mediator is
ever alert to this danger and can avoid an emotional crisis
by the judicious use of the caucus device or by asserting
his chairmanship and directing the discussions to a less
emotional issue.

A Mediator Can Assist The Parties
To Explore Avenues Of Accommodation

Perhaps one of the major functions performed by the mediator
relates to exploration of offers. Often one party may want
to gauge the receptivity of an approach to a problem without
formalizing it into an offer and thus destroy or jeopardize
a bargaining posture. If the mediator is apprised of this
desire, he can put forth the approach to the other party in
a separate meeting, as the mediator's suggestion.

He can approach the other side by stating that he has given
considerable thought to their position and he wondered if X
would meet their problem and resolve the issue but he would
not try to get it out of their counterparts unless it would
settle the issue.

If the suggestion is rejected, the bargaining position of
the first party is preserved. If the suggestion is acceptable, the first party can formalize it into an offer.

A Mediator May Initiate A Desired Meeting

Often when meetings have been recessed and especially where
they have been subject to call, one of the parties may desire a meeting but fear that if they request the meeting it
may be construed prematurely as a change in their bargaining position or as a signal of capitulation. If the mediator is advised of the problem, he may initiate the call of
the meeting based on his appraisal of the necessity and thus
take the onus of its call upon his shoulders. The party who

desired the meeting then can reluctantly accept without running the risk of endangering their bargaining posture at the
outset of the scheduled meeting.

If they had not utilized the assistance of the mediator and
let the other party know of their desire to meet, they may
very well have faced the situation of being met at the opening of the meeting by a demand, such as "you wanted this
meeting--now what have you to offer?" This would put them
in an almost untenable position.

A Mediator Can Assist The Parties In Formulating And Structuring Their Offers Or Counterproposals

There are well-accepted devices for assuring the maximum
saleability of an offer. A mediator can assist the parties
to formulate their offers or counterproposals in such a way
as to assure that they will have a high degree of receptivity. Many times this is as simple as couching the offer in
affirmative terms and avoiding a negative introduction.

As an illustration, one of the issues in a dispute may involve the question of stewards leaving their workbench to
process a grievance and the necessity of obtaining the foreman's permission to do so. Expressing the offer as "no steward shall leave his work area without the permission of the
foreman" is almost certain to create resentment and quick
rejection. If the same offer was stated in the affirmative
such as "stewards shall have the right to leave their work
areas with the permission" a different reaction could be
expected.

In the final hours of most negotiations the issues remaining
in dispute become narrowed to four or five. At this point,
most practitioners start the process of packaging offers and
counterproposals. In such "packages," the thrust is to treat
it as a totality and not permit the other party to pick and
choose among the various items which comprise the package.
Illustrative of this technique of bargaining would be an
offer whereby one party suggests that if the other party
would withdraw its demands on issues 1, 3, and 5, it would
be willing to accede to demands 2 and 4. Theoretically, the
demanding party cannot counter by saying it accepts the concession on 2 and 4 and in addition wants demands 1 and 5.
The concession on 2 and 4 was made contingent on withdrawal
of 1, 3, and 5, and would not have been made unless withdrawal was acceptable.

The timing and structuring of such packages are often crucial. Here, too, the mediator can make a positive contribution to the final settlement. Such packages are often rejected because of the order in which issues are presented.
A negative reaction can well be anticipated if in the presentation of the package at the very outset mention is made
of the items which must be withdrawn before mention is made
of the items on which there are concessions.

A much more desirable method would be to outline first the
concessions and then the withdrawals on which they are predicated. Even in presenting the concessions, the better
practice is to choose as the lead-off item the concession
on the issue in which the other party has indicated the
greatest interest.

A Mediator Can Ferret Out
Underlying Motives For A Demand

In a number of situations, mediators have found that formidable, sweeping demands arise out of small grievances. It
has been further found that by exposing the reasons behind
such a demand, it can be put into a much narrower context
and thus be easier to address and explore possible solutions. Because of his neutral position, the mediator can
in the separate meetings probe into the reasons behind the
demand or position and bring to light the true basis or
cause. This is particularly true in the areas of application of the seniority provisions of the contract.

A Mediator Is Alert To The Interplay
Of Intra-Company And Union Politics

Since labor organizations are economic institutions operating
in a political environment, the crosscurrents of political
aspirations may well dictate the union's posture at the bargaining table. Similarly, internal company politics often
lead the negotiator to be overcautious in his approaches.
He becomes quite sensitive to the possibility of second-
guessing with its job security threat. Under such circumstances, the company negotiator will seek to spread the
decision making responsibility to avoid subsequent criticism. The bargaining table flexibility so essential to
agreement is thereby impaired. These factors cannot be ignored at the bargaining table since their presence will impede settlement. A mediator is alert to these overtones
and very often can take on the burden of urging or advoca-

ting solutions to the issues so that each party can avoid
the necessity of being the initiator.

In the proper case, the mediator can incorporate his suggestions in a formal or informal recommendation to the parties with the possibility of making such recommendations
public. Here, too, the parties are relieved of the responsibility of identification with the accommodations necessary for agreement. At times this may not involve the substantive issues but questions of procedure.

Illustratively, a problem may arise with the union negotiating committee as to conveying back an offer with a committee recommendation to the membership. While the individual
members of the committee may be persuaded that it is a fair
and equitable offer, the politics of the situation may dictate that they do not become too closely associated with
it. In such situations, the mediator can suggest that the
offer be submitted to the membership and that the vote be
taken by secret ballot. In support of his suggestion, he
can direct the parties' attention to Section 203(c) of the
Labor-Management Relations Act[1] which authorizes him to
make such suggestions.

A Mediator Can Assist In Minimizing
Possibilities Of Rejections Of Tentative Agreements

There are situations where tentative agreements arrived at
at the bargaining table are rejected by the union membership. This interjects an instability into the collective
bargaining relationships which can be destructive of the
whole collective bargaining process. There are a number of
techniques which a mediator can suggest which will minimize
the possibility of a rejection. These will be more fully
described in the chapter specifically dealing with minimizing rejections.

In summary, when the mediator intercedes, his approach is
based not on whether settlement is possible but rather on
how a settlement can be achieved. He will seek to instill
into the parties this affirmative philosophy. From his
wealth of experience and training, he can stimulate bargaining, analyze issues, factually evaluate positions, balance
equities, suggest alternate approaches and solutions to problems, and assist the parties to seek out areas of agreement.
He brings to the dispute the impartial and objective viewpoint which often has been lost sight of by the disputants

because of their individual partisan interests. By joint
and separate conferences, by directing discussion, by tact,
persuasion and objectivity, the mediator strives to create
the atmosphere which makes agreement possible. All of his
efforts are directed at one goal--an agreement acceptable to
both parties.

NOTES

1. cf Appendix.

CHAPTER XII
CONFIDENTIALITY

Confidentiality refers to the issue of whether statements made by the participants during a mediation session can be used as evidence in a subsequent administrative or legal proceeding. It also involves the degree to which mediation notes, reports, or other memoranda are open to public inspection and thus available to subsequent litigants.

As previously mentioned, the policy of the United States, and of most States, is to rely on collective bargaining and mediation as the principal means of resolving industrial conflicts. To effectuate that policy, mediators must not only be neutral but must be considered so by both parties to a labor dispute. In addition, the parties must be free to talk without risking subsequent disclosure of their confidence. Such confidence and disclosures are wholly voluntary and cannot be compelled by a mediator, but without them mediation would cease to be effective in settling labor disputes.

Some examples of the kinds of disclosures made to mediators are personal idiosyncrasies of representatives of labor and management, financial condition of the company or union, competitive problems, internal frictions, facts contained in the confidential records and files of both parties, inability to take a prolonged interruption of production, plans for future relocation, and end positions which may be premature if advanced at the bargaining table at the time the dislcosure is made.

Recognizing the need of confidentiality if mediation is to be effective, the Federal and many State Governments, by either administrative ruling or legislation, have adopted provisions shielding from disclosure any statements made during the course of a mediation effort.

On the Federal level, Congress in providing an exemption to the disclosure requirement of the Freedom of Information Act[1] for confidential commercial or financial information, explicitly included within that exemption information and materials acquired by the Government in the course of mediating labor-management disputes.[2]

General Order

Even prior to the Congressional action, the Federal Mediation and Conciliation Service adopted General Order 1 which
prohibited any disclosure by any employee of the Service of
information, oral or written, received by them in the course
of their official activities without prior approval of the
Director of the Service. These regulations are now contained in Title 29, Chapter XII, Code of Federal Regulations.[3]

Section 1401.2 of Chapter XII provides:

> "Public policy and the successful effectuation of
> the Federal Mediation and Conciliation Service's
> mission require that commissioners and employees
> maintain a reputation for impartiality and integ-
> rity. Labor and management or other interested
> parties participating in mediation efforts must
> have the assurance and confidence that information
> disclosed to commissioners and other employees of
> the Service will not subsequently be divulged,
> voluntarily or because of compulsion, unless
> authorized by the Director."

Opinions Of Courts And
National Labor Relations Board

Both the courts and administrative tribunals have respected
the rules of confidentiality as set forth in the Federal
Mediation and Conciliation Service's regulation cited above.
The inherent powers of the executive branch of the Government to refuse to disclose evidence contrary to the best
interest of the Government has been recognized since
Marbury vs. Madison.[4]

Since 1947, the National Labor Relations Board has held
that the public interest in maintaining the neutrality and
effectiveness of the mediator outweighs the parties' interest in obtaining his testimony.

In Tomlinson of High Point, Inc.,[5] in a proceeding before
the National Labor Relations Board, one of the parties attempted to subpoena a mediator in order to establish by
his testimony that bona fide collective bargaining had
taken place. The Board upheld the mediator's claim of
confidentiality. As stated by the Board:

"However useful the testimony of a conciliator
might be...to execute successfully their function of assisting in the settlement of labor
disputes, the conciliators must maintain a
reputation for impartiality, and the parties
to the conciliation conferences must feel free
to talk without any fear that the conciliator
may subsequently make disclosures as a witness
in some other proceeding, to the disadvantage
of a party to the conference...The inevitable
result would be that the usefulness of the
Conciliation Service in the settlement of future disputes would be seriously impaired, if
not destroyed. The resultant injury to the
public interest would clearly outweigh the
benefit to be derived from making their testimony available in particular cases."

This has been the consistent position of the National Labor
Relations Board.[6]

The courts also have recognized the need for confidentiality. One of the leading cases is NLRB vs. Macaluso.[7] In
that case, the union and the company enlisted the aid of a
mediator after several months of unsuccessful negotiations.
In a subsequent proceeding initiated by the union before
the National Labor Relations Board, the union contended that
an agreement had been reached during the negotiations. The
company denied that such was the case, insisting that the
negotiating sessions were "stridently divisive." The company subpoenaed the mediator seeking to prove by his testimony that no agreement had been reached.

The National Labor Relations Board, having quashed the subpoena, found that an agreement had been reached and ordered
the company to execute the contract. When the company resisted, the Board sought enforcement of its order in the
Circuit Court of Appeals.

The central issues before the Court were the power of the
Board to revoke the subpoena and the right of a party to
compel a mediator to provide information on purely objective, factual matters critical to the resolution of a factual dispute.

The Court found that under Section II(1) of the National
Labor Relations Act, 1947, as amended, the Board had the
statutory authority to revoke the subpoena. The Court

stated that there was a sufficient justification to exclude the mediator's testimony because "the public interest in maintaining the perceived and actual impartiality of Federal mediators outweighs the benefits derivable from (their) testimony."

It also rejected the contention that at least the mediator should be permitted to testify to objective factual matter. The court based its rejection on two grounds. First, the perception of partiality created by such testimony. Second, such testimony would create an insurmountable problem for the trier of the facts on where to draw a line between what is or is not an objective fact.

In Pipefitters Local Union No. 208 vs. Mechanical Contractors Association of Colorado,[8] in refusing to permit the mediator to testify, the court stated:

> "The congressionally created Freedom of Information Act exemption of information acquired by Government in the course of mediation, coupled with the creation of the FMCS for the express purpose of facilitating private dispute resolution and industrial peace, suggest a congressional policy against disclosure even by deposition. Effective mediation hinges upon whether labor and management negotiators feel free to advance tentative proposals and pursue possible solutions that later may prove unsatisfactory to one side or the other. Such uninhibited interaction may be impaired absent the assurance that mediation proceedings will remain confidential."

State Statutes And Regulations

A number of States, either by statute or regulations, have provisions similar to that of the Federal Mediation and Conciliation Service. Notable among these are Connecticut, Maine, Wisconsin, Indiana, Michigan, New Hampshire, New York, and North Carolina. There are some significant differences in some of these statutes. In the Federal Mediation and Conciliation Service regulations the only person who can waive the privilege is the Director of the Service. The waiver of the privilege by either or both parties is not determinative of the question whether the privilege should be waived. The theory of the Service is predicated on public policy.

In Connecticut the privilege of non-disclosure can be waived by the party who supplied the information.[9]

The New Hampshire statute[10] provides:

> "Neither the proceedings or any part thereof, before the labor commissioner by virtue of the foregoing provisions of this subdivision shall be received in evidence for any purpose in any judicial proceeding before any other court or tribunal."

Under the foregoing provision, there is a question whether a disclosure can be compelled before a non-judicial tribunal such as a legislative committee.

The New York, Florida, Oklahoma, and North Carolina statutes[11] specifically foreclose the possibility of a forced disclosure before an administrative as well as a judicial body.

In several States an exception is made to the rules of confidentiality as to criminal acts which might have occurred during the mediation sessions. It is not clear, however, who will determine criminality.

Problems Involving Confidentiality

There have been a number of questions raised, both on a Federal and State level, as to what statements made during a mediation session are actually privileged. Clearly those made to the mediator by one party during a separate meeting are privileged. Questions have been raised as to whether statements made at a joint meeting with the mediator and both parties should also be considered confidential. Whatever doubts existed about the latter were laid to rest by the court in the Macaluso case which held that statements made in the presence of both parties were part of the mediation process and therefore entitled to the cloak of confidentiality.

While a mediator's reports to his agency are clearly privileged, questions were raised as to his personal notes taken during the mediation efforts. The argument made was that such notes were not part of the "official record" of the agency but the personal property of the mediator and hence properly subject to being subpoenaed. However, since the

mediator's notes are the basis of his report, such notes
are entitled to the protection of the privilege.

At times attempts are made to circumvent the rule of confidentiality and obtain the privileged information by indirec-
tion. One example was the action of the Chairman of a Subcommittee of the House Operations Committee. The Chairman
subpoenaed the mediator's official expense vouchers. A
witness, who had participated in a mediation effort, testi-
fied before the Committee that the mediator had made a number of long distance calls to him suggesting that certain
concessions could be obtained from the party if the witness
withdrew some of his demands. The Chairman hoped that by
questioning the mediator as to the nature of each long distance call appearing on the expense voucher he could sub-
stantiate the claims of the witness (incidentally, a con-
stituent of the Chairman) and provide the basis of a law
suit. The agency resisted the subpoena duces tecum. The
question was never resolved because the Subcommittee was
dissolved shortly thereafter.

A troublesome situation arose when a mediator, with the
apparent approval of his supervisor, permitted an outside
observer to attend the mediation sessions conducted by the
mediator. During the course of the meetings, the observer
took copious notes on what transpired in both the joint and
separate sessions. In a subsequent proceeding before an
administrative body, one of the participants in the mediation effort announced that he might subpoena the observer's
notes. When the observer learned of the plan, he tore up
his notes.

This incident raises several serious questions apart from
the wisdom of permitting observers to attend mediation sessions. If the subpoena had been issued prior to the de-
struction of the notes, might not the observer be subject
to contempt citation? Even if such observer tears up his
notes prior to the issuance of a subpoena, is he not still
subject to being compelled to testify as to his recollection as to what transpired during the mediation sessions?
It is difficult to understand how the privilege of confidentiality can be applied to the observer's notes and testimony, since he is neither a mediator nor employee of the
mediation agency and has no official standing in the mediation process.

In summary, acceptability of a mediator and his effectiveness in a given dispute is directly related to the confi-

dence both parites have in his professional abilities and
his maintenance of confidences disclosed to him in the performance of his official duties. If mediation is to be effective, the privilege of non-disclosure should be an absolute one. It should be the privilege of a public officer
(such as the mediator) and not the privilege of the parties
to the dispute.

NOTES

1. 5 U.S.C. 522, as amended 88 Stat. 1561.

2. cf H.R. Regs. No. 1487, 89th Congress, 2nd Session, p. 10 (19660.

3. cf Appendix.

4. 1 Cranch 37.

5. 75 N.L.R.B. 681.

6. American Laundry Machine Co., 76 N.L.R.B. 981; New Britain Machine Company, 105 N.L.R.B. 646; International Furniture, 106 N.L.R.B. 127; Herman Bros. Pet Supply, Inc., 150 N.L.R.B. 1419.

7. 618 Fed. 51.

8. No. 79c 1382 D. Col. 1980.

9. Connecticut General Statutes Annotated, Title 31, Section 100.

10. Chapter 210, Section 18.

11. New York Labor Laws Article 21, Chapter 31, Section 754(3); Florida, Chapter 57-306 of Laws of 1957; Oklahoma, Dispute Resolution Act, Oklahoma Stat. Title 12, Sections 1801-1806; North Carolina, Chapter 95, Article 1, Section 36.

CHAPTER XIII

OBTAINING THE SERVICES OF A FEDERAL OR STATE MEDIATOR

On the Federal level, the statutory authority for the intercession of a Federal mediator in a labor dispute is found in
Section 8(d) and Section 203(b) of the Labor Management Relations Act. The relevant provisions are:

Section 8(d) (in part):

"That where there is in effect a collective bargaining contract covering employees in an industry
affecting commerce, the duty to bargain collectively
shall also mean that no party to such contract shall
terminate or modify such contract unless the party
desiring such termination and modification--

(1) serves a written notice upon the other party
...of the proposed termination or modification
sixty days prior to the expiration date...

(3) notifies the Federal Mediation and Conciliation Service within 30 days after such notice of
the existence of a dispute and simultaneously
therewith notifies any State or Territorial agency established to mediate and conciliate disputes
within the State or Territory where the dispute
occurred, provided no agreement has been reached
by that time..."

If the collective bargaining contract involves employees of
a health care institution, the party desiring to modify or
terminate the contract must give 90 days notice to the other
party (instead of 60 days). Notice to the Federal Mediation
and Conciliation Service and appropriate State agencies must
be given 60 days after the first notice.

Section 203(b) provides in part:

"The Service may proffer its services in any
labor dispute in any industry affecting commerce, either upon its own motion or upon request of one or more of the parties to a dispute..."[1]

These statutory provisions spell out the three ways in which the Federal Mediation and Conciliation Service is authorized to intercede in a labor dispute.

The first method is "upon its own motion." Normally this method of intercession is confined to disputes arising over the negotiations of a new contract. In such cases no 30-day notice is required by Section 8(d) quoted above since that section relates to disputes over the termination or modification of an existing collective bargaining contract.

Federal labor-management disputes have notice requirements similar to the private sector. Such notice requirements are set forth in the Civil Service Reform Act (cf Chapter III). State and local mediation cases handled by the Federal Service have no notice requirements (Chapters IV and V).

In the health care industry, however, in the cases of an initial agreement notice to the Federal Mediation and Conciliation Service and to appropriate State agencies is required. The unique notice in cases involving health care institutions is discussed in Chapter XXVII.

Section 8(d)B provides:

> "Where the bargaining is for an initial agreement following certification or recognition, at least thirty days notice of the existence of a dispute shall be given by the labor organization to the agencies set forth in Section 8(d)3."

In rare cases, the Federal Mediation and Conciliation Service will enter a dispute on its own motion at the request of some Federal, State, or local governmental agency if notified by such agencies that the dispute is having an impact on the economic well-being of the community or State.

The second method which will evoke the intercession of a Federal mediator is a request for assistance made by either management or labor. It need not be a joint request. It can be a unilateral one. Further, the request need not be in writing, an oral request is sufficient.

The third and more common method for the intercession of a Federal mediator is as a result of compliance by the parties with Section 8(d)3 of the Act--the 30-day notice requirement.

The Federal Mediation and Conciliation Service has prepared for the convenience of the parties a Notice Form.[2] While there is no statutory requirement that this particular form be used, the information elicited by the form assures an orderly processing of the case by the agency. For the convenience of the filing party, the Notice Form provided by the Service has copies attached for filing with the appropriate State or Territorial agency, for service on the opposite party, and the last copy for retention by the filer.

In all cases, except those involving health care institutions, compliance with the notice requirements of Section 8(d)3 is not considered by the Federal Mediation and Conciliation Service as a request for mediation assistance, nor does it commit the Service to assign a mediator. Whether a mediator will be assigned depends on the Service's determination as to whether the dispute meets the jurisdictional guides of the Act and its evaluation whether the status of negotiations demonstrates a need for mediation assistance.

In disputes involving employees of a health care institution, the filing of notice in compliance with Section 8(d)C mandates the Service to assign a mediator. The Act states that, after notice is given to the Service, it "shall promptly communicate with the parties and use its best efforts, by mediation and conciliation, to bring them to agreement."

Compliance with the provisions of Sections 8(d)3 and 8(d)A is utilized more frequently as a basis of intercession than a direct request because quite often the requesting party would fear that seeking mediation may be construed by the other party as a sign of weakness in its bargaining position.

The failure to file the statutory notice with the Service or State or Territorial agency, may expose the party seeking modification to legal penalties. The Act, in referring to the duty to bargain, states that parties to a collective bargaining contract may not terminate or modify the agreement unless notice is given and further in Section 8(d)4:

> "...continues in full force and effect, without resorting to strike or lockout, all the terms and conditions of the existing contract for a period of sixty days after such notice is given or until the expiration date of such contract, whichever occurs later."

(In the case of a contract involving a health care institution, the period is 90 days). The Act further provides that
an employee who engages in a strike within any notice period loses his status as an employee unless he is reemployed
by the employer. In health care cases, the notice refers
not only to the 60- and 90-day period but also to the 10-
day notice of intent to strike (Section 8g).

The failure to file the statutory notice to the Federal Mediation and Conciliation Service and, where appropriate, to
State and Territorial agency, may expose not only the employees but also the party seeking modification or termination to legal penalties. It has been held that if the union fails to file the required notice, a strike called to
compel modification or termination of a contract is illegal
and the employees engaging in the stoppage lose their status as "employees" protected by the Labor-Management Relations Act.[3] A similar ruling was applied to an employer
who invoked a lockout without notifying the Federal Mediation and Conciliation Service and terminated the contract.[4]
If the notice to the conciliation agencies is late, the union must wait until 30 days have expired after the actual
filing of the notice before calling a strike.[5]

The Federal Mediation and Conciliation Service's notice
form should be sent to the Notice Processing Unit in the
Washington office. The unit summarizes the information contained in the notice and transmits it to the District Director whose territory covers the situs of the dispute. Based
on the information received, the District Director determines whether a mediator should be assigned to assist the
parties if need arises. If the District Director feels he
has insufficient information to form a judgment, he may
assign a mediator to investigate to ascertain whether the
dispute meets the Service's jurisdictional requirements.
If, however, the dispute involves a health care institution,
the Area Manager immediately assigns a mediator to the case.

If a mediator is assigned, it is his responsibility to keep
himself fully advised of the progress of the negotiations
and intercede if the need for mediation assistance arises.

Subpoena Powers

The Federal Mediation and Conciliation Service does not have
authority to issue subpoenas to compel attendance at meetings scheduled by its mediators. Parenthetically, the Boards

of Inquiry appointed in health care institutions pursuant
to Section 206 of the Labor-Mangement Relations Act have
been specifically authorized to issue subpoenas in national
emergency cases.

From time to time, some mediators frustrated by this inability to persuade one or both parties to attend a scheduled mediation meeting will decry their inability to compel
attendance by subpoena. Such mediators argue that if the
Service had such power there would be little occasion to
resort to it since the mere threat of a subpoena would be
sufficient to induce the recalcitrant party to attend.

There are at least two inherent difficulties with the suggestion. First and foremost it contravenes one of the basic
principles upon which effective mediation is founded, viz.
voluntarism. The mediation process should be a voluntary
process. Secondly, while most parties would respond to
either the subpoena or the threat of one, their resentful
attitude at the meeting would negate any possibility by the
mediator to create the atmosphere which would be most conducive to a resolution of the dispute.

State Mediation Services

The requirements for obtaining the services of a State
mediator vary in the various States which have a viable
mediation agency. There are also some variations as to
subpoena powers among the States in connection with their
mediation efforts. Typically are the following:

The New York State Mediation Board may enter "an existing,
imminent or threatened labor dispute" on its own motion.
If so directed by the governor, the Board must intervene
in such dispute. The Labor Law of the State grants the
Board subpoena powers.

In Pennsylvania, Minnesota, and Connecticut, a mediator
will be assigned to a dispute either on a unilateral or
joint request of the parties.

The Pennsylvania Bureau of Mediation will not intervene in
a labor dispute on its own motion. The Bureau does not
have the authority to issue subpoenas.

The Minnesota Bureau of Mediation Services will intervene
on its own motion if it deems necessary. It does not have

subpoena powers with respect to mediation (and/or negotiation matters).

The Connecticut State Board of Mediation will intervene on
its own motion. The Board does have subpoena powers.

Illinois Conciliation and Mediation Division will only
assign a mediator if it receives a joint request from the
parties.

Even in those States where their mediation agencies have
been granted the authority to issue subpoenas, the power
is seldom exercised in connection with their mediation
efforts in a labor dispute.

NOTES

1. cf Appendix.

2. cf Appendix.

3. J. C. Penny, 109 N.L.R.B. 754; IAM and International Continental Engine, 177 N.L.R.B. #60; Porto Rico Jr. College, 265 N.L.R.B. #3, 111 LRRM 1499, 1503.

4. Bakers Council of Greater New York, 174 N.L.R.B.

5. Retail Clerks vs. N.L.R.B., 264 F2d, 814.

CHAPTER XIV

INTERVENTION BY MEDIATOR— TIMING

Premature Entry

One of the more troublesome questions in mediation relates
to the proper time for a mediator to intercede in a labor
dispute. There are two schools of thought on the subject.
Some have urged that the mediator should be invited to sit
in with the parties in the early stages of the negotiations
even before an impasse is reached. They claim that this
would enable the mediator to become thoroughly acquainted
with the issues and personalities involved and thus, when
roadblocks are reached in their discussions, be in a better
position to assist them to hurdle them.

Early intercession presents several disadvantages. it is
difficult to spell out what role, if any, the mediator
should play if he enters negotiations prior to the existence of an impasse. As a practical matter, it would be
difficult, if not impossible, for a mediator in such circumstances to long avoid being propelled into the early
discussions dealing with minor issues, which, incidentally,
the parties could have settled themselves, the mediator dissipates his persuasiveness to the point that he loses his
effectiveness when he is needed to resolve the more basic
issues. Further, since he entered the dispute when there
really was no need for mediation assistance, the mediator
does nothing of import and he soon becomes part of the furniture. In effect, he has become a meddler rather than a
mediator.

The inherent dangers of premature participation by a mediator was revealed in a dispute in a non-ferrous manufacturing
company. When Whitley P. McCoy was Director of the Federal
Mediation and Conciliation Service, he gave a talk before
a midwestern seminar attended by representatives of labor
and management. During the course of his remarks, he urged
those present to seek the assistance of the Service at the
very inception of their negotiations. The theme presented
was that by such early entry, the mediator could become
thoroughly versed in their problems and be in a better
position to assist in the resolution of the dispute.

Soon thereafter, a union representative, who had attended the meeting, advised the Service that he had scheduled a first negotiating meeting with a company and requested that a mediator be assigned. When contacted, the company, while expressing some doubt, consented. A mediator was assigned. Very early in the negotiations, the parties found themselves in disagreement on a number of very minor contract changes. None of these issues were serious enough to be the basis for a strike or lock-out. Nevertheless, despite his desires, the mediator was placed in a position of suggesting and urging the parties to accept alternative approaches. As the deadline approached and the parties addressed themselves to the more serious issues, the mediator found that his suggestions were falling on deaf ears. He had become too identified with the problems and lost the effectiveness which a fresh approach engenders. Another mediator was assigned to assist the original mediator and a settlement was arrived at, based in large measure on the new mediator's suggestions.

The idea of the efficacy of early entrance by the Service was thereafter discouraged.

A more disturbing objection to the early entry concept is that it ignores the basic philosophy on which the entire structure of the Federal policy, with reference to labor relations, is grounded. As stated before, this policy is that the basic responsibility for the maintenance of industrial peace is on the parties and not on the Government. Parties to a labor dispute should be given the opportunity and indeed urged to exercise this responsibility. It is only when they fail to do so that the Government has a role to play--mediation in the average case and invocation of the emergency provisions of the Taft-Hartley Act where the dispute endangers the public health or safety.

The other school of thought would delay entry of the mediator until almost the deadline date. The rationale behind the theory is that only when the parties have completely exhausted their own efforts and are face-to-face with a potential stoppage can the mediator be most effective and his suggestions welcomed.

The difficulty with this view is that to await until the last moment before inviting the participation of a mediator and expect him, by some miraculous power, to breathe life into the corpse in which rigor mortis has already set in, is to seek the impossible. This has been illustrated by those cases where the parties have delayed until a few hours before the deadline and then sent out an alarm for a mediator. The mediator, in such cases, finds himself propelled into a situation where the parties have assumed fixed positions on often quite involved and complex issues. He has no opportunity to acquaint himself with the personalities involved, the political interplays, or the nature and scope of the issues still in dispute. In the emotionally-charged atmosphere normally characteristic of this situation, it is unrealistic and unjust to expect him in the few remaining hours to conjure up through some sort of Divine revelation a "magic formula" which will bring peace and tranquility. A more practical and better approach would appear to lie somewhere between the two views expressed.

To be most effective, a mediator must have a reasonable time to absorb, evaluate, and analyze the issues properly, to appraise the impact of personalities, and to explore areas of possible accommodations. It is only after he has had an opportunity to balance all these factors that a mediator can make an effective contribution to the negotiations.

To assure that the mediator's intercession is timely, both parties should keep the assigned mediator fully apprised of the progress (or lack of it) of the negotiations. In addition, they should acquaint him with the dimensions of the major issues. Armed with this information, he should be able to evaluate the status of the negotiations and make a valued judgment as to the best time to intercede. Because of the depth of his experience in this field, great reliance should be placed in him by the parties. The mediator should base his decision of active participation on the information he obtains in his contacts with the parties--contacts which accelerate as the contract expiration approaches. Choosing the "right" time to enter is a question of informed mediator judgment.

Since entry is based upon a judgment factor, there will be occasions when, usually either because of misinformation received or political pressure brought to bear on his supervisor, a mediator may find that he has joined the negotiations prematurely. If he cannot immediately withdraw gracefully, his only alternative is to minimize the impact of his intercesssion. One method of doing so is to limit his involvement to procedural matters. By identifying and breaking down the issues, he can try to persuade the parties to

set up several subcommittees and to assign to each several
of the open issues. If he is successful, he then can withdraw advising the parties that if any of the subcommittees
run into a roadblock, he would be available to re-enter
immediately and assist.

A few unions[1] have adopted internal procedures which assure
that their local unions will utilize the assistance of a
Federal mediator before resorting to economic action. These
internal procedures are usually incorporated either in the
International Union by-laws or procedures which must be ad-
hered to by the local union before the International will
authorize strike action and make strike benefits available.
The effectiveness of the procedure depends on the control
the International has on the strike funds.

As a general rule, these procedures require the local unions
to demonstrate that they have sought and, if available, utilized the services of a Federal mediator prior to strike action. Such procedures have a dual advantage. From the International's viewpoint, they guard against precipitous
strike action by a local before the possibility of settlement through mediation has been explored. Equally important,
it buys the time necessary for a representative of the International Union to investigate the dispute and participate in
the negotiations before any stoppage takes place. From the
mediator's viewpoint, it enables him to enter the dispute
before economic action has taken place and before the many
new issues, which usually grow out of strike activities, are
raised. Further, he is in a position to forestall strike
action by seeking an extension if agreement before the deadline does not appear possible.

NOTES

1. International Association of Machinists; Oil, Chemical and Atomic Workers International Union; American Federation of Technical Engineers.

CHAPTER XV
SCHEDULING AND PREPARATION FOR FIRST MEETING

Separate vs. Joint Meeting

Having determined that the time has come for his active participation in the negotiations, the mediator must decide where and with whom he shall first meet. One of the first decisions he has to make is whether initially to have a separate meeting with each party or to schedule a joint meeting in the first instance.

The traditional practice is for the mediator to first meet separately with each party. Those who espouse this viewpoint insist that this procedure not only serves the purpose of making the mediator aware of the issues with which he will be confronted in his subsequent mediation efforts, but also enables him to get acquainted with the personalities who will be participating in the ensuing negotiations. It is also suggested that such separate meetings present an excellent opportunity for the mediator to "sell" himself and the mediation process.

Many experienced mediators do not subscribe to this traditional approach. They feel that when meeting with each party separately, all the time is spent in the party's trying to convince the mediator of their sincerity and resolve, the righteousness of their cause, and the fairness of their proposals. These mediators state that such separate meetings are merely propagandistic and do not serve any constructive purpose--"a waste of time." As far as obtaining information as to the issues, such information can be obtained either by a few telephone calls or at the first joint meeting. As a matter of fact, they assert that a recitation of the issues at the first joint meeting tends to be more realistic because of the presence of the other party. As far as personalities are concerned, if the parties had used mediation before, an evaluation of the principal negotiators can be obtained by contacting the previous mediator, or it can be accomplished in a subsequent meeting.

There are several exceptions to using an initial joint meeting and where a separate meeting may be more desirable.

One exception is the case of a wildcat strike where, for precedent reasons, management will not meet officially with the union. In such cases, the mediator may have to conduct not only the initial meeting but all subsequent meetings separately with each party.

Another exception is a strike situation especially where mediation assistance has not been sought until after the occurrence of the strike. The animosity between the parties, engendered by the stoppage, may require an initial separate meeting to enable the mediator to defuse the situation and create the proper atmosphere for a constructive subsequent joint meeting.

Further, a mediator may encounter undisguised hostility to his intervention on the part of one of the parties. Often this is expressed rather bluntly--"what can you do"--"we made them our rock bottom offer, there is no more, so we see no sense in wasting time in another meeting"--"they know what we want and unless they are ready to meet it, we don't see any need to meet." Under these circumstances, the mediator may want to meet separately with the party resisting mediation to explain his role and urge that it may be worthwhile to give it another try under his auspices.

Location of Meeting

If the mediator follows the traditional approach of an initial separate meeting, he normally will meet first with the party who requested his services. This is usually the union. If he cannot persuade that party to hold the meeting at his office or some other neutral location, he will meet at their office. He then will meet with the other side.

If the mediator decides that the initial meeting should be joint, there are a number of alternatives open to him. If the parties are located in the same geographical area as his office, then the meeting will normally be scheduled at his office. This is the most desirable meeting place from the mediation standpoint. If unavailable, then in some governmental office. Holding the meeting at his office or other governmental office has a number of advangages. It establishes that the meeting is his meeting, facilitates his control of the discussion, and makes the parties aware that a new dimension has been added to the dispute--the public interest in its resolution.

If the parties reside in an area where mediation or other public offices are not available or there are objections (normally based on inconvenience), there are several other meeting places open to the mediator:

1. Meet with the parties at a location they have customarily used either in the past or in the current negotiations.

2. Meet at the company facilities. The advantages are the ready availability of the company negotiator's supervisor for consultation and decision and the ready access to resource material. (The latter is especially advantageous in the Federal sector where there is need to refer to the Personnel Manual, pertinent statutes, memoranda, and the like.) The disadvantage is the uneasiness of many union committee members who are suspicious of "bugs" and monitoring of their telephone calls. Even though such suspicions are usually unfounded, such uneasiness inhibits open and frank discussion necessary if agreement is to be reached.

3. Meet at the union office. This is seldom an acceptable choice since companies will normally object to it.

4. Meet at a neutral place. As a rule there is seldom any serious objection to it. Interruptions, such as telephone calls and visitors, are kept at a minimum. It has the further advantage of physically establishing the mediator as the chairman of the meeting since he can control the seating arrangements.

If the meeting is held in a non-public facility, the usual practice is for the parties to defray the charges for the meeting rooms.

Physical Set-Up of Meeting Rooms

Having chosen the location of the meeting, the physical set-up of the meeting rooms becomes important. In addition to a meeting for joint meetings, there should be another room available for use as a "caucus" room. The "caucus" room is used for separate meetings either with the mediator or by a negotiating committee alone. This caucus room should be far enough removed from the joint meeting room so that discussion within it cannot be heard from the outside.

In very rare cases, having the "caucus" room adjoining the
joint meeting room can be an advantage.

One old timer in the Federal Mediation and Conciliation
Service tells of one of his experiences where it turned out
to be an advantage. Two rooms were engaged at a small hotel.
The only room available for a "caucus" room was next door
to the joint meeting room. The wall between was rather thin
and if voices were raised in the "caucus" room, they could
be easily heard in the joint meeting room.

At a crucial point in the negotiations, in a separate meeting, the union advised the mediator that if he could persuade the company to agree to issue "X," it would be willing to drop many of the remaining issues. "X" had been a
thorny issue and had up to that point defied all the union's
and mediator's efforts to obtain it. Even though he felt it
would be an exercise in futility, because of the union's insistence, the mediator reluctantly agreed to give it "one
more try."

The mediator then met with the company in the caucus room.
To his utter astonishment, the company readily agreed to
grant X. The mediator knew that if he immediately brought
this concession back to the union, it might have second
thoughts about dropping the other issues since X apparently
came so easy. In a sotto voce, he outlined a plan with the
company negotiator and then proceeded to play gin rummy with
him. Ever so often, the mediator would raise his voice insisting that the company had to reconsider the negative
position on X if it wanted a settlement. The company chief
negotiator would respond in an equally loud voice vehement-
ly opposing it. After a lapse of one hour, punctured by
similar outbursts at appropriate intervals, the mediator
returned to the union to advise them that he had persuaded
the company to concede X. The union committee was profuse
in its praise of the mediator telling him that the committee had heard how he had "taken on" the company. Shortly
thereafter, an agreement was reached on all issues.

Having arranged for two rooms, attention should be paid to
the seating and table arrangements in the joint meeting
room. Two tables or a single wide one should be arranged
so that the mediator's chair is at the head of the table
or tables. The spokesmen for each party should be requested to occupy chairs opposite each other and at the end of
the table nearest the mediator. The table arrangements can

be either a "T" or an inverted "U" arrangement. If the "T"
arrangement is used, the tables should be wide enough to
permit the parties to take notes and have whispered consul-
tations with their colleagues without having their counterpart "breathing down their throats."

Preparatory Material

Most experienced mediators do not take very much material
into the first joint meeting. If it is known that the cost
of living may be an issue, it may be helpful if the mediator has with him the latest Consumer Price Index published
by the United States Department of Labor--both national and,
if available, local.

If there have been other settlements in the industry or in
plants in the same area, the terms of such settlements may
be available either through the Bureau of Labor Statistics
of the U.S. Department of Labor or through the Bureau of
National Affairs who periodically publish surveys.

Apart from the foregoing, there is little need for additional material. If other material becomes relevant during
negotiations, the parties usually provide copies.

For note taking during the meeting, a spiral stenographer's
pad is helpful. It is small enough to fit into the average
brief case. It lies flat on the table. Since most of these
pads have a middle dividing line on each page, many mediators write their notes on the union demands on one side of
the line and the company response on the other.

Right To Attend Meeting

Normally, the mediator will invite the parties to the collective bargaining agreement to attend the meeting.

Occasionally, a dissident group within the union may insist
that they should attend any meeting called by the mediator.
Unless both parties agree to their presence, which is highly unlikely, they should not be invited. The basic principle which should guide the mediator is that if he has scheduled the meeting, it is his meeting and not that of the
parties.

Coordinated bargaining, whether on an industry- or company-
wide basis, presents sticky problems for the mediator both

in scheduling a meeting and in conducting a meeting where the company objects to any form of coordinated bargaining.

If he limits his invitation to the committee from one plant, the union will strongly object on the basis that the mediator is playing into the company's hand and undermining the union's bargaining strategy. If the mediator schedules a company-wide meeting, the company will insist that the mediator is in the union's pocket and is trying to foist on the company a bargaining procedure which it has refused to accept. The mediator is placed in the position of being damned if he does and damned if he doesn't.

The mediator can only attempt to persuade the parties that so long as they maintain their positions no agreement is possible and hope that economic pressures on the parties will compel them to accept the bargaining pattern he has selected.

The difficulties attendant upon scheduling a meeting in coordinated bargaining are compounded when the meeting is finally scheduled.

In multi-plant operations, because of the chronology of organization, separate certifications may exist for the individual plants and result in separate contracts. Generally speaking, most companies prefer to negotiate each contract separately. Again generally, labor organizations prefer to negotiate on a company-wide basis leading to a master agreement. When the companies resist the demand for company-wide bargaining, unions may resort to having representatives of the other plants either as members of the negotiating committee or as "observers." In this way, unions feel that they can assure uniformity and condition the company representatives to accept the concept of company-wide bargaining in the future.

The insistence of the union to have representatives of the other plants at the bargaining table often presents nice problems for the mediator. When the company observes the presence of these "outsiders," it reacts rather violently such as threatening to walk out of the meeting or refusing to go forward with negotiations unless the "outsiders" are excluded from the meeting room.

The Labor-Management Relations Act, 1947, provides:

"Employees shall have the right to self organization, to form, join or assist labor organizations,
to bargain collectively through representatives of
their own choosing..."

It is therefore quite clear that the employees have a statutory right to select anyone they desire to act as their representative or spokesman. There is also a correlative right
of management to select whomever it chooses to act as its
representative. While this is not an absolute right, the
Board and the Courts are reluctant to deny it except in
very extreme cases.

Consequently, if the "outsiders" have been designated as
part of the negotiating committee of the particular plant
involved, they have a legal right to attend and participate
in the negotiating session. If the company refuses to meet
under these circumstances, it may be risking an unfair labor practice charge.

The difficulty lies in circumstances in which the "outsiders" are attending as observers. The constitution of
the American Newspaper Guild expressly provided that all
union members in the bargaining unit had a right to attend
bargaining conferences as observers. If the number of members in the unit is 150, the two or three management representatives may be faced with a rather formidable array
across the table.

Another approach that may be used is to carry forward with
the meeting by having the parties in separate meeting rooms
with no joint meetings and the mediator shuttling back and
forth between them. Normally, this is an awkward and unproductive method of operation but in the situation outlined
above, it may be the only device open to the mediator to
get by the roadblock.

A final note of caution in scheduling the first and, indeed, subsequent meetings--do not accept a suggestion by
the parties to sit in on a conference scheduled by the
parties. As was stated very well by one writer, "the parties to a dispute should be your invited guests and not
you theirs."

Overcoming Reluctancy To
Attend Meeting

A situation may arise where, in an attempt to schedule a
joint meeting, the mediator finds that one party is not
only willing but anxious to meet but the other party is
reluctant to do so.

Some experienced mediators overcome this reluctancy by first
contacting the willing party and obtaining its agreement as
to a tentative date, place, and time for the proposed meeting. Thereafter, the mediator gets in touch with the reluctant party for the purpose of obtaining its approval of the
tentative arrangements made. If the reluctant party persists in its refusal to meet jointly, the mediator will inquire as to what he should communicate to the other party
in explanation of the reluctant party's reason for failing
to meet. In doing so, he should speculate as to the actions
the other party may take on receipt of the refusal, such as
publicity, filing a refusal to bargain charge with the National Labor Relations Board, handbills to the employees involved, letters to public officials and Government procurement agencies (if relevant), as well as the fact that if the
media contacts the mediator, he would have to confirm the
refusal to meet.

Often the realization of the possible consequence of its
refusal to meet induces the reluctant party to change its
position and agree to attend the scheduled mediation meeting.

CHAPTER XVI
CONDUCTING FIRST JOINT MEETING

After a meeting place has been agreed to by both parties, the mediator is then confronted with the problem of conducting the joint conference in such a manner as will ease tensions, create an atmosphere which will lead to fruitful discussion, and enable him to make the most effective mediation contribution to the dispute.

Presence Of A Stenographer
Or Tape Recorder

Occasionally when the mediator enters the joint meeting room, he will become aware of the presence of a stenographer or some type of recording device. Experience has taught that the presence of a stenographer or tape recorder does inhibit free collective bargaining. Both sides talk for the record and not for the purpose of advancing negotiations toward eventual settlement. Each becomes over-conscious of the recording of his remarks. The ease of expression so necessary to proper exposition of problems is hampered. The discussion generally becomes stultified.

If the past bargaining practice of the parties is to conduct their negotiations in the presence of a tape recorder or stenographer, there is little the mediator can do to exclude them. Similarly, if there is no past practice and both parties consent, the mediator must, in the main, adapt himself to the bargaining pattern which both parties urge.

Even where both parties consent, the mediator should advise both parties of the roadblocks to free discussion occasioned by a recording. Further, he should point out that the confidentiality which surrounds mediation meetings is jeopardized. Under the rules, either statutory or administrative, of most mediation agencies, a mediator may not disclose what is conveyed to him during the course of his mediation efforts, or at least not without the consent of the head of his agency. Because of the public policy considerations, such consent is rarely granted. A stenographic or tape recording of a mediation conference can be produced by either party at a judicial or administrative hearing without the safeguards of prior consent of the

mediation agency. Under these circumstances, a mediator
can be less effective.

Where there is an objection by one of the parties to the
presence of the stenographer or to the recording device,
the insistence on their continued presence by the other
party often creates issues extraneous to the real issues
in dispute. The party objecting may insist on a copy.
The other may either refuse to provide it or agree to
furnish it on the condition that the objector pay for it.

Under these circumstances, the mediator should meet separately with the chief negotiator of the party insisting on
having these recording devices and seek to persuade him to
dispense with them during the mediation sessions. In addition to raising the problem of confidentiality, the thrust
of his arguments could be that the object of the meeting
is to attempt to resolve the issues in dispute and insistence on such devices will only block or delay a resolution
of those issues. Further, the mediator can assure him that
he will see to it that there will be no backtracking on
issues that have been dropped or resolved during negotiations.

If all such arguments fail, the mediator can nullify the
presence of the recording devices by conducting a very
brief and formal joint meeting and thereafter hold separate meetings with the parties in most, if not all, of
the subesqeunt sessions. Since the conversations in such
separate meetings are confidential, he can exclude the
stenographer and/or the recording devices. Quite often,
after several such separate meetings, the party who brought
the recording devices will realize the futility of their
continued presence and dispense with them at that meeting
or subsequent ones.

Introduction And Appearances

While the mediator may be acquainted with the principal
spokesmen for each party, he is seldom familiar with the
individual committee members.

The management team may be composed of three or more people
in addition to the spokesman. They are selected by the company because of their familiarity with production problems,
the financial status of the employer, or with the various
grievance disputes which have arisen during the contract
term.

The union negotiating committee generally is composed of
the business agent or international representative, some
if not all of the local union officers, and committeemen.
The latter are usually elected from among the shop employees and these individuals may vary from contract year to
contract year.

The mediator should introduce himself to all present and
not merely to the principal spokesmen for each side. To
many of those serving on negotiating teams there is a matter of pride--especially on the union's side. Often, many
are undergoing their first experience as negotiators. They
have been singled out by their fellow workers to represent
them and justly feel a sense of urgent responsibility.
They are at once proud of their status and suspicious of
an "outsider." A warm and informal introduction may do
much to abate some of the suspicions and fears.

After the introduction, the appearances of those present
should be recorded. This can be done rather informally.
Many experienced mediators use the device of passing out
two sheets of paper--one to each side--each containing two
columns. One column is headed "Name," the other column
"Position and Title." Both sides are requested to fill in
the called for information and return it to the mediator.
The appearance sheets provide not only a record of who is
present but also gets the parties started on the habit of
following the mediator's procedural suggestions.

Upon receipt of the list, a good mediator will endeavor to
familiarize himself with the listed names and to identify
the individuals present with their names without appearing
to do so. He will particularly try to fix first names in
his mind. While he should avoid addressing people by their
first names at a joint conference, it is invaluable to use
first names when talking to each side during a caucus. Use
of first names during separate conferences often breaks
through the barrier of formality and establishes a camara-
derie which leads to freer and franker discussion of the
issues.

The use of first names has, of course, its limitations.
There are some people who resent being addressed by their
first names. This is particularly true on management's
side. Whether they are motivated by a feeling of superior-
ity, or the need of maintaining dignity or status in the
eyes of their subordinates is of little importance. The

good mediator should be quick to sense this feeling and respect it if he is to succeed in assisting the parties to
arrive at an agreement.

Explanation of Mediation Process
and Neutrality of Mediator

Some commentators on mediation techniques advocate that
after the mediator has introduced himself to the parties,
he should spend some time explaining the nature of the
mediation process and his exact function with particular
emphasis on his neutral role. Some also suggest that, in
addition, he should advise the parties that ultimately they
will have to sit down and reach agreement--"so why not get
started now and avoid hardships and uncertainty"--"eventually, why not now."

In the vast majority of cases, many mediators do not indulge in such opening remarks. The competency and neutrality of the mediator are not proven by his speech on
mediation or his protestations of neutrality but by his
attitudes and deeds. Further, since in the vast majority
of private sector disputes, mediation assistance is sought
by unions, the union representative generally briefs his
committee on the nature of mediation before the mediation
session.

Management representatives, in most cases, are fully aware
of the mediator's role in the negotiations.

There may be some situations, particularly in small establishments or owner-operated business, where parties do not
have professional guidance available to brief them on the
mediation process. This lack of knowledge is usually detected during the telephone call scheduling the meeting,
and an explanation by the mediator is appropriate.

One mediator recalls an illustrative case involving a small
owner-operated shop. He called the proprietor to advise
him that he was scheduling a mediation session with the
union and the proprietor. The proprietor responded "so
what is mediation?" After listening to a very profound
explanation by the mediator of the mediation process, the
proprietor said "the union wants 25¢ an hour--I can't
afford it--so what do I want mediation for." A personal
visit to the proprietor at his shop was immediately arranged by the mediator. During this one-on-one personal

conversation, the mediator was able to give the owner the necessary assurance which persuaded him to attend the mediation meeting.

There is also a possible exception to the "no speech" rule in public sector disputes. Because of the inexperience of some representatives and their committees, there may be some justification for the preliminary explanation of the mediation process. However, with the increased exposure to collective bargaining and the increased sophistication which follows from it, there is a better understanding of the mediator's role so that the need for an explanation becomes less and less.

Statement of the Issues

After the introduction and appearance taking, the mediator is prepared to go forward with the conference. Except in cases involving the negotiation of an initial contract, the mediator should request a copy of the existing or expired collective bargaining agreement which is the subject matter of the negotiations. This will enable him to follow subsequent discussions, particularly as they relate to requested modifications of contract provisions.

Generally, the next order of business is a statement of issues still remaining unresolved. Emphasis should be placed on a discussion of only the unresolved issues. It must be borne in mind that before the advent of mediation, the parties undoubtedly must have been meeting by themselves and, in most cases, have reached tentative agreement on a number of issues.

Experience teaches that to ask the parties to review issues already tentatively resolved hampers progress in negotiations and may open up a Pandora's box. Normally, the party making the demands is requested to start the recitation of the unresolved issues. Since generally it is the union which is seeking to modify the existing collective bargaining agreement, it is the proper party to make the first presentation. The mediator should permit the union spokesman to present the issues in his own way. He should not attempt to advise the union representative what issues he should address himself to first.

While the presentation of the demands should not be in too great a depth, it should be sufficient enough to give the

mediator a good grasp of the scope and complexity of the
problems he is facing. Often a mediator is confronted with
a presentation so sketchy that it is impossible for him to
intelligently appraise the dispute. Some business agents
will state: "We have five demands--union security, vacations, holidays, wages, and seniority," and then sit back
expecting the mediator by some Divine revelation to know
exactly what the problem may be. If such a presentation
is made, the mediator should draw out a fuller picture by
adroit questioning such as:

What form of union security is requested?

What form of union security did the expired or
expiring contract provide?

What modifications or additions in the holiday
and vacation program are being sought?

What were the provisions of the old contract?

Seniority, for example, is a multifaceted problem. Inquiry
must be made to ascertian the general areas of seniority
which the union is seeking to modify.

The questioning at this stage must be so worded as not to
place the union representative in a position of justifying
or defending its demands. The purpose of the questioning at
the first joint meeting is to elicit information and not to
persuade or change any party's position.

During the recitation of the issues, the mediator should
not display his reactions to the union demands even though
some may appear to be completely unrealistic. Nor should
he be surprised or overawed by the multiplicity of the union proposals. Union demands sometimes are the product of
membership meetings called for the purpose of formulating
such demands. At other times, a committee of employees is
appointed to draw up the demands. Frequently, but not necessarily, such committee becomes the negotiating committee.

All too often, the negotiating committee, for understandable
political reasons, cannot either refuse to accept or to present demands insisted on by individuals or a group of members even though the committee may well realize that some
are totally unrealistic or unobtainable. This often results
in a "laundry list" being presented at the first meeting.

By presenting these demands at the bargaining table and, as
expected, being promptly rejected by the company, the onus
is on the company and not the committee. It can then report back to the membership that despite its best efforts,
the company was adamant and refused to entertain the proposals.

After the union has presented its demands, the company is
then called upon to respond and to present such counter-
proposals as it may desire. Not too many years ago, management confined its remarks to a rebuttal of the union's
requests. However, the collective bargaining picture has
changed. Management is now interposing meaningful demands
and has a right to present them at the bargaining table.
Many of these demands are attempts by management to recap-
ture so-called management prerogatives lost in prior bargaining or through loose management practices at plant
levels.

Art of Listening

One of the principal keys to successful mediation efforts
used by the mediator is the art of listening--nor merely
hearing. The development and application of this art enables a mediator to sense the areas of possible agreement,
not only during the first statement of the issues, but also
during the course of future joint and separate conferences.

The emphasis or lack of emphasis placed by the parties on
particular issues, the use of negotiating language, "smoke
signals" indulged in--all when properly evaluated may point
out approaches to the final resolution of the dispute.

A company in resisting a wage demand may argue that the demand is unrealistic in view of the settlements the union
made in competitive companies in the industry. This would
indicate to the mediator that a wage increase at least comparable to the industry pattern may be attainable as negotiations progress.

Not many years ago, a large West Coast manufacturer was the
target of the first strike called by its union in its entire industrial history. The reason for the strike was evident. A rival union had successfully negotiated a settlement at a competitive company. The same rival union was
raiding the other union. To stave off further inroads on
its membership, the union had to be able to produce a set-

tlement which exceeded that obtained by the raiding union.
The manufacturer, not only for competitive reasons, but
also as a member of an industry association, was committed
not to exceed the pattern established by the competing company. When the company refused to exceed the pattern, the
union for its own survival had to resort to strike. Mediation was requested.

At the first meeting, in its rebuttal to the union's request
for improvements in the health and welfare provisions of the
old contract the company stated that it could find no basis
for the demand since it prided itself in being the leader of
the industry in this specific field. This remark was the
key to the solution of a costly strike. The mediator, exercising his art of listening, made a mental note of the
company's statement. During the course of the subsequent
discussions, he was able to develop that the competitor had
so improved his health and welfare contract provisions that
it equalled that of the struck employer. As a result, it
was no longer the leader. When the parties were conditioned
for a mediator's suggestion, he persuaded the company to revise its health and welfare offer so that it would retain
its leadership status. In terms of benefits, the union
could properly go before its membership and present a better package to them than obtained by the raiding union. A
strike was settled because the mediator exercised the art
of listening.

Most settlements arrived at during the mediation process
are reached not because the mediator at the crucial moment
had an extraterrestrial revelation and advanced the solution
which had not occurred to anyone but because the parties,
who fundamentally want a peaceful solution of the dispute,
have indicated by their statements, directly or indirectly,
where the final solution lies. The mediator, by careful
listening and constant evaluation of the positions taken
by the parties, translates their thoughts into suggestions
and advances them at the appropriate moment when each party
is prepared to accept them.

Note Taking

The mediator should not attempt to take detailed notes at
the meeting. The mediator's notes are to jog his memory
and not an exact recording of what has transpired. Some
mediators by use of symbols or arrows indicate issues which
may be coupled and those which one party or the other has
emphasized.

As a general rule, the mediator should not take notes during
a separate meeting. Separate meetings are for the purpose
of eliciting confidential, frank discussion of the issues.
Taking notes arouses suspicion and stifles meaningful talks.

There is an exception to note taking in a separate meeting.
If, as a result of the meeting, an offer is formulated to
be transmitted to the other party by the mediator, he may
jot it down in his notebook. Having done so, the mediator
should then read it out loud to make sure that what he has
written correctly states the offer.

<u>Representation And Unfair</u>
<u>Labor Practices Problems</u>

Either prior to his intercession, or shortly thereafter, the
mediator may be confronted by several problems--a challenge
to the majority status of the union, an assertion of jurisdiction by a competing union, or pending unfair labor practice charges. In each of these cases, the mediator is faced
with the problem of whether he should continue his mediation
efforts or withdraw from the case.

The company may assert that, from the information it has
received, it believes that the union no longer represents
the majority of its employees and consequently is reluctant to attend or proceed with the mediator's scheduled
meeting. If the mediator is persuaded that the company's
attack on the union's majority status is merely a bargaining strategy, he should insist on going forward with the
meeting. Normally, when the company's challenge is merely
a bargaining pressure, it is, in effect, stating that if it
can obtain a favorable agreement, it would seriously consider withdrawing its objections to the union's status. If it
encounters difficulties in the negotiations, it will vigorously pursue the challenge. It hopes that dangling this
sword of Damocles over the heads of the union negotiating
committee, they will be more tractable rather than risk decertification.

If, however, the company follows through on its challenge
by filing a decertification petition with the National Labor Relations Board, the mediator can assume that the company is serious and is not interjecting the issue for bargaining purposes. In such cases, the mediator should withdraw until the matter is resolved by the NLRB.

A somewhat similar situation can arise when the company, believing that the NLRB erred either in its determination of the appropriate unit or in its certification of the bargaining representative, refuses to bargain. If the union files an unfair labor practice charge alleging the refusal to bargain, the mediator should withdraw pending the resolution of the question either by the NLRB or the courts.

In some cases, a competing union may, either orally or by letter, advise the mediator that it is now the representative of a majority of employees in the unit. In such cases, the mediator should continue his efforts until and unless the competing union files a petition with the NLRB. If it files, the mediator should withdraw from the case.

If, in the course of his mediation efforts, the mediator finds that the only issues are those which are the subject matter of an unfair labor practice charge pending before the NLRB, he should withdraw unless both parties urge him to continue in an effort to resolve the issues through negotiations. If there are issues other than those which are the subject matter of the pending charge, the mediator should assist the parties to resolve such other issues.

Often charges are filed merely as a bargaining maneuver. Typically is a refusal to bargain charge filed by the union. If agreement is reached on all issues, the parties frequently will make part of the agreement a provision that all charges pending before the NLRB will be withdrawn. If such is the understanding, the mediator should remind the parties that an unfair labor practice charge involves a public law and, consequently, the parties should seek NLRB approval for such withdrawal.

CHAPTER XVII
JOINT MEETINGS

Control of Meetings

A mediator is neither the agent nor the broker of management or labor. He represents in a large measure the public
interest and is carrying out a statutory responsibility. A
mediation meeting is his meeting and not that of the parties.
The final determination should lie with him as to when a recess, caucus, or adjournment is to be called. To achieve
this control over the meeting, it is necessary for him to
establish the fact of his chairmanship at the very outset
of the meeting. He can do so physically by occupying the
chair at the head of the conference table between the parties.

A good mediator should never permit himself to be relegated
to the role of an observer. By the same token, the mediator should not become the autocrat of the conference table.
He can readily accede to the desires of the parties for recesses and adjournments, but in doing so he should make it
clear that requests should be addressed to him and that he
consents to them.

Since it is his meeting, he should insist that the parties
carry on their discussions in a dignified manner. There
should at the same time be a realization that negotiating
meetings are not prayer meetings--that the language indulged in is many times more forceful and picturesque than
that use in family living rooms. Many times bargaining
postures dictate role playing by the representatives of
the parties. Real or assumed indignation, shock, surprise,
impatience, threats of economic reprisals, humor--in fact,
a display of the whole range of human emotions--are all
part and parcel of the collective bargaining process.

The repeated use of bucolic or profane language should be
discouraged as much as possible. To permit it to run rampant seriously impairs the effectiveness of the mediator and
the success of the negotiations. Despite the facade of
being "tough" or thick-skinned, most people are normally
offended when exposed to profane diatribes. They impress
no thinking person and lower the dignity of the entire
meeting.

Similarly, it is inimical to agreement-making to permit parties to indulge in personal abuse or attack. The objective
of a negotiating session is to attempt to compose the differences between the parties so that agreement can be achieved.
Personality clashes have no place at the bargaining table.
At the best, they are roadblocks to agreement. A personal
attack almost always gives rise to a reply in kind. Tempers are substituted for reason. Areas of disagreement are
widened and often positions are taken in the heat of argument from which graceful retreat becomes impossible.

In the heat of negotiations, several parties very often try
to speak at the same time. The conference then becomes a
series of conferences without a common objective. Such
"cross fire" can quickly destroy any progress being made in
the negotiations. Collective arguing supplants collective
bargaining. "Cross fire" is normally born of a desire to
"get into the act" or of a committee member's feelings of
frustration when he feels he is being ignored. Nothing can
be achieved unless the chairman quickly discourages the
cross fire and insists that the meeting proceed through one
spokesman at a time. Most spokesmen will readily assist
the mediator to bring cross fire under control since it
also impinges on their prerogatives. Beyond causing the
meeting to deteriorate to a vocal brawl, cross fire often
reveals weaknesses in bargaining positions which may jeopardize the successful achievement of one or the other party's objectives.

Evaluation of Issues

During the course of the presentation and discussion of the
issues, a mediator should make an evaluation of the issues.
Such an evaluation can not only provide him with a better
perspective of the dispute, but often enables him to know
where the emphasis of his mediation efforts should be placed
as negotiations progress.

Issues can be first segregated into economic and non-economic. There are some items which have a direct cost impact such as wages, holidays, vacations, shift premiums,
and the like. There are other items which are clearly non-
cost items such as union security, some aspects of seniority, and grievance procedure. Other items fall into a gray
area--work rules and seniority areas are examples which
have an indirect cost impact and may be difficult to clas-
sify. The grouping of issues on economic and non-economic

issues assists the mediator when costs are being discussed.
The company negotiators will certainly consider the cost
impact of all the economic items as a package.

Issues can be further separated into strike and non-strike
issues. Wages and issues affecting job security are normally strike issues. Union security, unless coupled with
a job security or wage issue, is not an issue which normally will support a prolonged stoppage. Disputes relating to
grievance procedures, super seniority, leaves of absence,
and the like are not normally issues upon which a union
would engage in a strike.

Issues also can be grouped into (a) union institutional
issues (check-off/union security), (b) rank and file issues (job security/wages), and (c) matters of corporate
policy.

An evaluation of the issues also permits the mediator to
gauge the possibility of one or more demands being withdrawn if one with a higher priority (such as an economic
improvement) is granted.

Coupling of Issues

During the presentation and discussion of the outstanding
issues, and often aided by the evaluations suggested above,
the mediator can mentally couple interdependent or related
issues and thus plan his approach to the solution of some
of the issues.

To illustrate coupling of issues--a union may be seeking
to strengthen the union security provisions of an expiring
contract. It may also be demanding automatic progressions
in the rate ranges to the maximum where the contract provided for automatic progressions only to the midpoint with
merit thereafter. The reason behind the union request for
automatic progression to the maximum may be its fear that
a merit band in a rate range is or could be used to discriminate against employees active in the union. A strengthen-
ing of the union security provisions would dispel this fear
and remove the necessity for management to make concessions
in the rate range provisions.

As negotiations progress, the exercise of the art of successful coupling can materially narrow the issues and lead
to a logical packaging of the last remaining issues.

Packaging Issues

Closely allied to coupling of issues is "packaging" of issues. Packaging is most effective when the issues have been
reduced to six or seven. Also, it is best utilized when the
mediator is conducting separate meetings with the parties.

The mediator can suggest to the company that it review the
remaining issues and make up a "package," e.g., if the union will drop issues A, C, and D, the company will go along
with B and E. The propoal is normally given to the mediator as a proposal to be accepted in its entirety. On its
face, the condition is that if the union accepts B and E and
agrees to withdraw A but refuses to drop C and D, there is
no offer and the package is deemed withdrawn.

Inevitably, when the mediator presents it to the union, it
picks and chooses despite the condition imposed. It may
agree to withdraw A and D in return for the concession on
B and E but refuse to drop C. Even though this does not
meet the condition placed upon the package, it does convey
to the mediator that accommodations exist on issues A, B,
D, and E and that there is only one real issue separating
the parties--C. He then can concentrate his efforts on C
and inform the parties that C is really the only issue
separating them from agreement. If the parties are reluctant to package the remaining issues, the mediator can
initiate the approaches when he detects that one of the
parties may be willing to compromise one or two of the remaining issues. For example, he can state to the union,
"If I can persuade the company to concede D and E, would
you be willing to drop A, B, and C?" The fact that each
imposed a condition that the package must be accepted exactly as proposed should not deter the mediator. Even
though the condition of treating the package in its totality is present, the parties generally do not expect that
it will be treated as such but anticipates the possibility
that the other party will accept part and reject part.

Packaging is a useful tool in narrowing the issues and
advancing negotiations. When the real issue is segregated, the parties will realize that it alone stands between them and settlement and redouble their efforts to
reach an accommodation.

Stipulation of Total Agreement

Often during the course of a conference, a mediator discovers that one party or the other appears reluctant to
modify its position on a particular issue or to withdraw
a proposal or counterproposal because of the fear that in
doing so its position on that issue would be irretrievably
gone or that it would imply weakness. If this situation
is permitted to continue, little, if any, progress can be
made in the negotiations. This is particularly true if
there is a multiplicity of issues. To achieve settlement,
issues must be discussed, explored, and disposed of, either
by agreement or withdrawal. To pass them and leave them in
limbo can, at the very least, unduly prolong the dispute.

Under such circumstances, mediators often have utilized the
stipulation of a total agreement. In essence, the parties
in the joint meeting are requested to stipulate that "any
concession, modification, or withdrawal of any particular
issue made by any of the parties is for the purpose of arriving at a full agreement--if no agreement is reached,
either or both parties are free to revert to any position
they deem advisable on all the issues."

Experience teaches that this is usually readily adopted by
the parties. It protects their respective bargaining postures and at the same time permits the tentative disposition of issues so that the negotiations can go forward.

Developing a Habit of Agreement

In many cases, the mediator is confronted with a large
number of unresolved issues. The problem then arises as
to what specific issues or groups of issues should be discussed first. A guiding principle is to discuss first
those issues which appear the most susceptible of solution. The purpose of this approach is to establish a
habit of agreement. If agreement can be achieved on some
of the easier issues, hostility is dispelled, the parties
are made to realize that there are some common grounds between them, and a positive attitude is engendered toward
the mediation process. The momentum of the agreement on
some of these issues may carry over to the more difficult
unresolved issues.

If no issue or issues appear easier of solution, then
generally it is wise to leave the economic issues to the

last. The purchasing power of an additional percentage
point cannot be underrated. Often bitterly urged non-economic demands dissipate with an additional monetary offer.
The prospect of economic gains exerts pressure for resolution of the non-economic issues.

If the situation is reversed, the parties may find themselves in a position of having reached a tentative understanding on money matters still far from agreement because
of an emotionally charged non-economic issue.

CHAPTER XVIII
CAUCUS— SEPARATE MEETINGS

When Caucus Should Be Called

In the mediation process, the most effective reconciliation
of differences occurs during the separate meetings or caucuses of the parties with the mediator. In a caucus, the
mediator need not be as sensitive to the preservation of a
bargaining position as in a joint conference. The parties
are freer to talk in a caucus where their adversaries are
not present.

The joint meeting is designed primarily to structure the
situation in a manner conducive to compromise. During a
joint meeting, the parties often assume negotiating postures designed to impress their counterparts of the stead-
fastness of their positions. Seldom are approaches to an
accommodation advanced lest they be considered a sign of
weakness.

When the joint conference should be abandoned temporarily
in favor of continuing bargaining through caucuses or separate conferences does at times pose problems. A number
of general rules can be evolved as to when a request for a
caucus should be made:

1.   When the discussions at the joint conference
     become so heated that emotions are supplant-
     ing reason and a continuation may cause par-
     ticipants to take extreme positions from which
     retreat would be difficult, a caucus called at
     this point can provide a needed cooling off
     period.

2.   When the joint discussions have reached a
     stage where no further progress is being made
     and the parties are becoming merely repetitive,
     the mediator must not permit the joint meeting
     to continue since the positions of the parties
     may harden.

3.   Where one of the parties in the joint discus-
     sions has indicated a possible area of compro-

mise, the mediator should explore whether the
statements made at the joint meeting were
really meant to open the possibility of a
compromise. If so, a caucus at this point
will give the mediator an opportunity to
develop an area of agreement. In such an
event, the first caucus should be held with
the party who indicated the possible area of
compromise.

4. If neither side has indicated any flexibility
    in their bargaining position, the first caucus
    should be held with the party appearing most
    inflexible. In such situations, some movement
    is necessary if negotiations are to proceed
    along fruitful lines. Under these circum-
    stances, the mediator, by probing during the
    caucus, should attempt to review with the in-
    transigent party the consequences of its con-
    tinued adherence to its position--no agreement--
    possible economic dislocation.

5. The mediator should be alert to forestall one
    party from taking an end position prematurely.
    Many times in the heat of joint discussions,
    one party or the other may take a final posi-
    tion on an issue. Having taken such a posi-
    tion in the presence of the other side, pride
    dictates that that position be adhered to re-
    gardless of the change in bargaining climate.
    Compromise or withdrawal becomes difficult.
    Often, too, an expressed rigidity on one issue
    prematurely will prevent any progress on other
    pending issues. Effective mediation requires
    fluidity. An alert mediator who can anticipate
    that one party is about to take an end position
    prematurely at the joint bargaining session can
    do much to further advance bargaining by request-
    ing a caucus.

Exploration of Positions in Depth

As pointed out before, the separate conference or caucus
gives the mediator greater latitude in exploring issues
than a joint conference. A mediator should utilize the
separate conference to explore the issues in depth. Very
often demands are generalities. They represent an attempt

to formulate in general terms a number of related or un-
related grievances which have arisen during the contract
term.

By exploring the reasons which gave rise to a demand, a
mediator often finds that the real area of disagreement is
much narrower than the general demand indicates. This is
particularly true with respect to demands involving seniority, shift assignment, and distribution of overtime. Often
these are based on specific grievances--usually involving
a breakdown of communications. By addressing the discussion to the specific grievances rather than to the formalized demand, agreement becomes possible. The exploration
of positions, while a time consuming process, cannot be
rushed. Members of the same committee will have differing
perceptions of the problem and the solution. They must
have time to spell out their thoughts and to listen under
the guidance of the mediator.

Exploration vs. Offers

Very often during the course of a caucus, based on the
suggestions of either the mediator or the party, a possible area of agreement is developed which should be conveyed to the other party. The manner in which such possibility is conveyed to the other party then becomes important. Many times the party who accepts the suggestion or
initiates it may desire to preserve his bargaining position if the possibility is unattractive to the other party. In such cases, the mediator must be quite circumspect
as to the manner in which he discusses the problem with the
other party. If he unwittingly conveys it as an offer, he
destroys the bargaining position of the party. He should
and must convey it either as his suggestion or as an approach which might be fruitful if in the judgment of his
listener it has possibilities of leading to a solution.

If the party with whom he first confers decides to make
it a formal offer, the mediator should so convey it,
either alone at a separate conference with the other
party or else suggest that it be communicated directly
at a joint conference. Sometimes an allegedly sharp negotiator will attempt to get the mediator to convey to
the other party as the mediator's suggestion a completely
irresponsible offer or approach. The mediator is under
no obligation to do so. Throughout the negotiations, the
mediator must so conduct himself as to evoke the respect

and confidence of both parties. If he were to lend himself
to any such maneuver, he would destroy his effectiveness.
Under such circumstances, the mediator should refuse to convey the offer as his suggestion and insist that it be conveyed by the party directly to the other side.

Length Of The Caucus

The caucus should continue until the mediator feels that
the purpose for which it was called has been satisfied or
that the deadlock has been broken so that further progress
can be made by joint discussions.

There are times when one of the parties may adhere tena-
ciously to a bargaining goal which the mediator feels is
unrealistic or impossible to achieve. The mediator may be
further persuaded that unless the party abandons or substantially modifies his position, further progress will be im-
peded. Under such circumstances, despite the persuasiveness used by the mediator, that party, relying on some
statement out of context, lack of emphasis placed on an
issue during negotiations, or rumor, may persist in his
position. In such situations the mediator may recess the
caucus and have the parties meet jointly so that the hope-
lessness of the position can be exposed firsthand.

Further, if a caucus fails to produce movement, the mediator should terminate the caucus and reconvene the joint
meeting to see if discussion there generates new ideas and
approaches to a solution of the dispute.

There are situations where the mediator must be forceful
with a committee who stubbornly adheres to an unrealistic
position during a caucus. Before reconvening the joint
meeting, he may in a short speech want to castigate the
committee for its shortsightedness in insisting on their
position. After he has done so, he might leave the room
in feigned anger before the thrust of his remarks is di-
luted by the committee's response. As a caveat, before
indulging in this technique, he should be certain in his
own mind that he can get back into the negotiations without too much difficulty.

Several years ago, an international representative of a
union advised the mediator, just prior to attending a
joint meeting, that he intended to "take on" the company
and possibly stalk out of the meeting. When the mediator

expressed concern that his actions might "blow the meeting sky high," the representative stated "don't worry, I will slam the door so hard that it will spring open again." This should be the guiding rule when a mediator decides to "take on" a recalcitrant committee.

Conferring With The Other Side
Before And After A Caucus

Before recessing a joint meeting for the purpose of caucussing with the other side, the mediator should advise what he plans to do. He can do so by announcing "as a result of our joint discussions, I have some ideas which I would like to explore with the other side." He then can, before leaving the room, point out where the facilities, such as rest rooms, telephones, and refreshments, are located.

Whenever a mediator decides that he should terminate a caucus with one party and resume joint discussions, he should make it a point first to confer briefly and separately with the other party. There is an understandable curiosity on the part of the party who has been caucused as to what is transpiring while the mediator confers with the other. Further, the waiting party has a right to know what is the next step. If the mediator does not satisfy both desires, his next step will be viewed with suspicion and distrust.

Separate Meetings

For the purpose of clarity, a distinction is made between a caucus and a separate meeting. A caucus is a meeting attended by the negotiating committee of one party and the mediator. A separate meeting is a meeting with one or both principals without their committees. The mediator may or may not be present. This has been termed by some mediators as a "side bar" meeting.

In a separate meeting, the principals frequently take on an entirely new role quite different from that which they assumed in the joint meeting or caucus with the negotiating committee present. There is no need for them to maintain their bargaining table facade. Normally their discussion is quite frank about their mutual problems and possible accommodations. When across-the-table bargaining, even when interspersed with caucuses, fails to produce movement on basic issues, a separate conference arranged by the mediator often provides the key to a final solution of the dispute.

Political Problems In
Separate Conferences

At times, it may appear advantageous to have a separate
meeting with only the principal without his committee.

Before such a meeting is attempted, the mediator must first
ascertain if such principal is at liberty to do so. There
are some union negotiating committees who object to their
spokesman conferring alone with the other side or even with
a mediator. Even though this attitude is both shortsighted
and nonsensical, it is nevertheless a reality which must be
faced. In such instances, the mediator would create unnecessary barriers to an agreement if he insists upon meeting
with the principal alone. The principal would be placed in
a politically dangerous position if he accepts and an embarrassing one if he refuses to so meet.

While the problem is normally encountered with union committees, it also occurs, though with less frequency, with
management groups, especially if there is an outside attorney or consultant with whom the mediator desires to meet
alone. The "resident" labor relations man is apt to feel
that he is being bypassed and may refuse to accede to a
compromise, not because of its merits but because he wants
to demonstrate his importance in the scheme of things.

In one eastern State, a signal was developed between several union representatives and the mediator as to the existence of political problems to a separate meeting. If,
during the course of the mediation conference, the representative referred to the mediator by his formal title--
Commissioner or Mr. Mediator--it was an indication that
they could not meet alone with the mediator at that time.
If, however, they called the mediator by his first name, it
was a signal that there were no political obstacles to such
a meeting.

If there appears to be a political problem present, the
mediator should not abandon the separate conference idea.
After the meeting with the negotiating committee has been
adjourned, a telephone call often can arrange an off-record
meeting with one or both principals at a mutually convenient place--usually a hotel.

Separate Meetings Arranged
By The Mediator

During the course of his mediation efforts, the mediator ˙
may not wish to limit a planned separate meeting to one
principal alone but to have both principals present.

While the mediator may arrange for the two principals to
meet without him, experience dictates that the preferable
procedure is for the mediator to be present. The reason
is that if, as a result of the meeting, understandings--
procedural or substantive--are reached, the mediator is
in a better position to implement them at the ensuing meeting with the full negotiating committee.

If accommodations are reached in a meeting without the
mediator being present, he should be completely briefed
before the next meeting of the full committee. If he is
not made aware of it, he may be working at cross purposes
and make the implementation of the agreement difficult.
Even where the mediator is present, understandings arrived
by the principals away from the mediator's presence should
be conveyed to him.

Not too many years ago, during a long and bitter stike in
a basic industry, in an attempt to break the deadlock, the
Federal Mediation and Conciliation Service invited the
president of the company and the international president
of the union to a separate meeting in Washington, D.C.
Each appeared with their bargaining table spokesman and
economists. During the course of the cordial but incon-
clusive talks, the international president of the union
indicated that he would like the opportunity to meet alone
with the company president. Both then retired to another
room. After a lapse of three quarters of an hour, both
emerged smiling and announced that their respective bargaining committees should resume their meetings in a western city and that "there should not be any further difficulties." A meeting was arranged by the mediator. When
the parties faced each other across the bargaining table,
a deadly silence descended on the gathering. After awhile
each urged the other to "kick it off." Each in turn declined to do so. It then developed that each thought the
other had been briefed by their respective presidents on
what transpired in the separate meeting as to the procedures to be followed. Both then admitted that they had
not been informed what, if anything, were the understand-

ings reached by the two presidents. Neither had the mediator. Apparently, all the two presidents had done was to
exchange platitudes about the need of each to live together
and the hardship the lengthy strike had inflicted on both
sides without any understanding as to possible approaches
to solve the dispute.

When a separate meeting is arranged by the mediator, he
should at the very outset announce the conditions under
which the meeting is being held. The conditions are that
whatever is discussed at the meeting is "off the record"
and will not be used by either party in any subsequent
meeting of the full committee unless an area of accommodation is worked out as a result of the discussions. These
conditions usually are readily accepted.

During the meeting, the mediator should take an active part
and not hesitate to interject hypothetical questions such
as, "assuming for the purpose of our meeting that the union
pulls off issue X what can the company do about issue Y."
In these meetings, the mediator is much freer in his discussions and suggestions since he is not concerned about
the reaction of a committee and the preservation of its
bargaining position.

The efficacy of the separate meeting technique is proven by
the many cases in which the understandings reached during
such a meeting, when presented at the bargaining table,
have resulted in a final resolution of the dispute.

CHAPTER XIX
MEDIATION TECHNIQUES IN MEETINGS

All of the following and previously mentioned techniques
and suggestions are based on the presumption that the mediator will use common sense in deciding which to adopt in a
given situation. One or more may be applicable or none may
be relevant. The mediator's final judgment must be the result of his evaluation of the status of negotiations, the
personalities involved, the complexity of the outstanding
issues, and timing.

Timing

One of the keystones of successful mediation is timing. It
is a crucial element in the mediation process. Timing escapes definition. It can only be acquired. It cannot be
taught by rote, but only by experience. It becomes a sort
of sixth sense which a good mediator consciously or unconsciously develops.

It can be described broadly as a sense a mediator develops
as to when to urge a particular solution or approach which
would have a maximum impact on negotiations and be most effective and acceptable. If a suggestion is made too soon,
it may be rejected out of hand. If too late, it may be
disregarded. The mediator, to be effective, must be prepared "to seize the moment."

One of the mistakes most often committed by the inexperienced mediator is in this area. After a few meetings, such
a mediator may discern a logical solution to a particular
issue or a series of issues. His impatience, born often of
immaturity in the field, will prompt him to urge its adoption vigorously. He is then a very disappointed young man
when the parties summarily dismiss his brainchild.

In order for a mediator's suggestion to have the greatest
weight, it must be made at a time when the parties have
reached a stage in their negotiations at which they will
be most receptive. One of the prerequisites to receptivity
is that the parties must have been conditioned to accept
the less perfect because it may lead to an agreement, rather than to insist on the perfect which only continues the

impasse. This phase also has been characterized as the development of the consent to lose, as mentioned earlier.

A true union committee reflects the hopes of the entire membership. Many times it is charged with the responsibility of vigorously bargaining for demands which many of the negotiating committeemen know are impractical to achieve. Often a vociferous group representing a small segment of the employees will succeed in incorporating as a "must" some demand which reflects solely its special interests, regardless of its impact on the majority. For a union officer or a committee to refuse to carry such demands to the bargaining table would jeopardize their political position and, indeed, may endanger the union's representation status. Consequently, the committee cannot abandon the issue until it has made strenuous efforts to obtain it. After the committee has pressed for it without success, the membership may then realize that concessions affecting the majority are being denied because of the presence of these special interest issues. At that point, they are receptive to a mediation suggestion.

Other times, based on some information or rumor, the union or the management may feel that if a certain bargaining strategy is followed, its aims can be achieved. Until they have pursued this strategy and found it futile, any suggestion will fall on deaf ears. Each side must have its run--until economic pressures and realism take hold.

In some negotiations, company negotiators will receive reports from their foremen and some employees that the company's last offer is a reasonable and fair one and if submitted to the union membership it would be overwhelmingly accepted. As a result, the company will remain firm in its offer despite the insistence of the union negotiating committee that it would be rejected by the rank and file. Until the company's offer is submitted to the membership for acceptance or rejection, any mediator's suggested modification of the company's position will fall on deaf ears.

In such cases, the best mediation strategy is to urge the union to submit the company's offer to the membership as quickly as possible.

In a few instances, the union may decide to invoke a boycott. It probably convinced itself that the economic losses occasioned by the boycott would compel the company to capitulate to its demands. Until it has done so and gauged its impact, there will be no desire on its part to scale down its demands.

Some companies participate in industry "strike insurance" plans. Under such plans, struck companies are reimbursed, for a limited time, for loss of profits. Unions, who represent the employees in such companies, may feel that until the expiration of the insurance reimbursement approaches no "realistic" offer would be forthcoming from the company. In these cases, the union would not be receptive to any suggested accommodation by the mediator until the target date approaches.

Backtracking

In cases where there is a multiplicity of issues and protracted negotiations, there may arise serious questions between the parties as to whether an issue or series of issues have been withdrawn or tentatively settled. If tentatively settled, the question may further arise as to what disposition was made of such issue or issues. Resort to notes may not prove helpful because under the normal tensions of collective bargaining conferences, notes are often inadequate, sketchy, or contradictory.

Where this situation arises, backtracking becomes inevitable, which can only prolong and worsen the dispute. Equally disrupting are the emotional reactions evoked since questions of veracity come to the fore. There are a number of devices which a mediator can suggest which are calculated to avoid or minimize the problem of backtracking.

Whenever a meeting is about to adjourn, if there have been some tentative agreements reached, ideally the parties should reduce such agreements to writing. Such memoranda should set forth in simplified general terms the agreements reached. No attempt should be made to draft precise contract language. If it is impractical to reduce the agreed items to writing at the end of each session, the parties should orally summarize at a joint meeting the general nature of the tentative agreement or agreements. If there are any misunderstandings, they can be quickly resolved, since the matters are still fresh in the minds of the participants.

If the parties do not initiate the summarization of the tentative agreements, the mediator should do so. He can state that it is his understanding the parties have reached tentative agreement on vacations, for example--three weeks after fifteen years and holidays--one additional--Veterans' Day. He then should call upon the parties to affirm the correctness of his recapitulation.

Sometimes because of the lateness of the hour and the consequent impatience of the parties, none of the foregoing suggestions are practical. In such event, the mediator should start the next session with a joint meeting where he can recapitulate his understanding of the tentative agreements reached at the prior meeting.

While not directly related to mediation, it might be profitable to mention a device used in some sections of the United States to avoid misunderstandings of the application of formal contract language. It is the practice of explanatory addenda to the agreement. The addenda is cast in the form of a series of examples of the application of a particular section or subsection of the agreement. It is particularly applicable to sections relating to distribution of overtime, work overlapping regularly scheduled shifts, reporting pay, bumping sequence in seniority provisions, and the like. A typical example of this approach would be a contract providing the employees required to work prior to their regularly scheduled shift shall receive time-and-a-half for all hours worked prior thereto and also provided for shift differentials for the second and third shifts. The addendum would set forth an example as follows:

> If Employee A, receiving a rate of $6.00 per hour, is regularly scheduled on the first shift and is called in one hour before the start of the first shift and works through the first shift, he shall receive:

> 1 hour at $9.00 ($6.00 plus 1½ times) = $ 9.00
> 8 hours at $6.00   =   48.00
>   Total Pay $57.00

Withholding Offers

There are occasions during mediation efforts when, because of undisclosed economic pressure or inexperience, one party may indicate a willingness, in the early stages of negotia-

tions, to make a series of substantial concessions. If concessions come too quickly, the other party may be led to believe that its counterpart is ready to capitulate. As a
result, it may miscalculate and harden its position on a
number of issues even though it had been prepared to withdraw some at an appropriate time.

This creates a problem for the mediator. He must disclose
some of the concessions in order to indicate progress and
at the same time avoid giving the other party the impression
that more are immediately forthcoming if it hangs tough on
the remaining issues. In such circumstances, if he is convinced that disclosure of all the concessions would lead to
a hardening of positions, prolong negotiations, and make
settlement difficult, the mediator may well consider with-
holding temporarily some of the concessions. As one writer
aptly put it:

> "Where a mediator may perceive the settlement
> early, he will regulate progress toward that
> goal to a pace which the parties can tolerate;
> giving them time along the way to adjust to a
> lower level of aspiration; or a higher level
> of expense."

The risk to which the mediator, who withheld offers, is
exposed is if during a post negotiation conversation between the negotiators it is disclosed that the mediator
knew very early in the negotiations the available concessions.

A rather embarrassing situation arose during a non-ferrous
negotiation when a company decided to withhold an improved
offer from a minority union. Normally, in the non-ferrous
industry, the employees are represented by eight or nine
unions--one industrial and the balance craft. Following the
usual pattern, the company conducted separate but almost
simultaneous negotiations with each union. However, the
emphasis was on the industrial union since it represented
the majority of the employees. When agreement was reached
with the industrial union, the terms were offered to the
minority unions with some variations for their particular
problems.

Negotiations with the industrial union became protracted
and the minority unions were growing impatient. To buy
the time necessary for the continuation of the main nego-

tiations, the company decided to quiet the minority unions
by offering them an intermediate package substantially less
than the expected majority union settlement. The strategy
was to make the offer, have it rejected, and the company
then plead for time to reconsider its position.

To the company's consternation, two of the minority unions
accepted the intermediate offer. The company negotiators
realized that if they permitted the acceptance to stand and
the two minority unions subsequently learned that other unions had a better settlement, they would shut down the mines
immediately and prevent a return to work by the other employees. A hasty sub rosa meeting with the international
officers of the two unions resulted in a reversal of their
acceptance.

The Hypothetical Question

One of the better techniques adopted by experienced mediators is the use of the hypothetical question. The hypothetical question makes an assumption and then postulates a
possible alternative based on the validity of the assumption.

While the hypothetical question can be used in a joint
meeting, its greatest value is in a separate meeting. It
enables the mediator to probe for a possible area of accommodation without endangering either party's bargaining
posture. It also is quite useful in framing a package proposal, after there has been a reduction of the issues in
dispute. In such circumstances, the mediator by using hypothetical questions can "try on for size" several alternative packages until he finds the key acceptable grouping
which leads to the settlement of the dispute.

A typical example of a hypothetical question can be best
illustrated by the following question by the mediator to
one of the parties: "Assume for the moment that I am able
to persuade the other side to drop issue X, would you be
willing to change your position on issues Y and Z?"

Changing Location of Meeting

Often agreement is facilitated, after several mediation
meetings have failed to produce a settlement, by changing
the locale of the meeting place.

There are situations where the efforts of the main negotiating team are being hampered by constant inquiries by members of the bargaining unit as to what has occurred at the bargaining table. Pledges of secrecy while made in good faith seldom can be kept when close buddies buttonhole a committeeman for inside information. As a result of the consequent leaks, rumors become rampant and compromise by the negotiators becomes almost impossible.

Similarly, company negotiators may be the target of intra-company second guesses. In both cases, the mediator may well suggest a change of locale to permit the parties to get away from these local pressures.

In other situations, the mediator may feel that the intervention of a representative from a higher echelon of management and/or a union international representative could make a major contribution to the settlement of a dispute. Changing the locale of the meeting may be a convenient vehicle for introducing such representatives at the bargaining table without unduly upsetting the original negotiators who are normally jealous of their prerogatives and status.

The Federal Mediation and Conciliation Service utilized the change of locale technique in selected cases to try to facilitate agreements. Some meetings were moved to the regional offices. If the dispute affected a whole industry or was having a serious impact on the economy of a State or nation, the parties were invited to the national offices in Washington, D.C. Experience has indicated whether the case was removed to the regional or national offices, in most cases the prospect for a settlement of the dispute was greatly enhanced.

In speaking of meetings being removed to Washington, a pattern developed particularly if the union negotiating committee was from the midwest or far west.

No discernible progress was possible in the first two days of meetings. Committee members usually were more interested in sightseeing and kicking their heels in their new found freedom from the daily routine of back home. However, about the third or fourth day, attitudes changed. Mother and the kids were missed and the new found freedom became less and less attractive. As a result, the desire to reach agreement became heightened and both parties settled down to good faith bargaining which in almost all cases led to agreement.

Transmission of Final Offer

The proper transmission of the employer's final offer, especially if it culminates in agreement, is quite important to a mediator. The cardinal principle is that no mediator should convey a final offer if he has been shuttling between the parties during separate conferences unless he reconvenes the parties in a joint meeting and repeats the offer in the presence of both.

This procedure eliminates any possibility of misunderstanding. If there is any doubt as to the meaning or import of the offer, it can be clarified then and there. Neither party can thereafter raise a question that the mediator did not properly transmit the offer.

In an important case, the failure of a mediator to present the final offer in a joint meeting led to the prolongation of a strike, litigation, and left the mediator in an embarrassing position which threatened to undermine his future acceptability.

In mediating a strike situation involving a public utility in the midwest, the mediator conducted separate meetings throughout the day. Finally, when he thought that there was a meeting of minds, he so informed each party in separate meetings. The meetings had lasted all day and well into the night. Both parties were tired and anxious to get to their homes. Due to the lateness of the hour and the condition of the negotiators, the mediator decided to forego a joint meeting and dismissed the parties.

The union presented the "agreement" to the membership who ratified by a substantial majority. The following day, the five hundred and fifty striking employees reported for work. The company refused them admission insisting that as an essential part of the "agreement" was the understanding that the work force would be called back on a staggered basis as the plant was ready to absorb it. The union insisted that no such condition was attached to the company's last offer and it accused the company of bad faith and reneging on the agreement.

When the mediator's opinion was sought, in an attempt to avoid antagonizing either party, he stated he did not remember. Litigation followed.

All could have been avoided if he had insisted that the parties meet jointly before dismissal and review the terms of the "agreement."

Length of Meeting

How long the mediator should continue the mediation meeting generally follows the guidelines previously suggested as to when a caucus should be called by the mediator. Normally, if progress is being made in the negotiations, the mediator should be most persuasive in insisting that the parties continue their discussions past the normal adjournment time. If there is any possibility of an agreement, or even a partial one, a premature adjournment may lose the momentum he has crafted throughout the day.

If, however, the parties have exhausted the possibility of further movement, then, if not suggested by the parties, the mediator should adjourn the meeting. To allow it to continue is to increase the risk of tempers becoming short and statements being made which may make it difficult for the parties to retreat gracefully from positions taken in the heat of the moment. If an adjournment becomes necessary, before the parties leave, the mediator should urge them to review the outstanding issues and reevaluate their positions on each one to determine if any area of accommodation is possible.

A common picture often painted by lay writers is that of the mediator locking both parties in a room and keeping them there until, in a state of complete physical and mental exhaustion, they will agree to most anything in order to obtain their release. This is one of the most nonsensical and vicious myths ever perpetuated on the general public. It visualizes a mediator who has no home, no need for normal rest or recreation, a physical specimen who can out-endure men often 10 or 15 years his junior, and capable of physically and legally preventing the participants from breaking off negotiations whenever they desire to do so.

Mediators in the main are middle-aged or older with all the concomitant physical disabilities. They are normal individuals who enjoy their homes and families. They seek normal eating periods. They require reasonable rest and recreation. They certainly would enjoy a quiet evening at home much more than listening to parties repeat their positions ad nauseam, usually in a hot and eye-smarting, smoke-filled room.

The truth of the matter is that in almost all incidents of all-night or marathon continuous bargaining sessions, the mediator has had to adapt himself to a bargaining pattern followed by the parties for many a year. Traditionally and historically, many parties feel that no agreement is possible unless and until they have indulged in at least one of such sessions. Perhaps political considerations dictate such a course of conduct but seldom, if ever, is it inspired by the mediator.

A typical example comes to mind. In the New York area, year after year, the mediators assigned to a dispute found that the bargaining session on the eve of the termination of the contract would inevitably last from 10:00 a.m. to 6:30 a.m. the next morning. A pattern emerged--the company would withhold its final offer until 11:50 p.m. On the receipt of the offer, the union would call for a caucus agreeing that for deadline purposes, the clock was stopped as long as negotiations were continuous. Inevitably the union caucus continued until 6:00 a.m. at which time the union would announce acceptance of the offer with very inconsequential modifications. A half-hour joint conference would quickly dispose of these requested changes. The usual handshaking and self-pitying remarks would follow.

After several mediators had been subjected to this type of bargaining and had compared notes, it was discovered that the only reason why the union committee kept its caucus in session until 6:00 a.m. was the belief on its part that the only way the union membership would accept the offer and re-elect them was for the committee to appear at the plant at 8:00 a.m., when the first shift reported, with bloodshot eyes, bewhiskered chins, rumpled collars, and tousled hair. They could then loudly proclaim how they worked all night-- as evidenced by their physical appearance--to obtain the contract improvements for the rank and file. The time between 6:30 a.m. and 8:00 a.m. was to permit the committee members to eat hearty breakfasts (at union expense) and travel to the plant.

Parenthetically, after this discovery, the mediator's no-sleep problem was practically solved by the mediator designating an office with a couch as the mediator's conference room.

CHAPTER XX
AIDS TO REACHING AGREEMENT

One of the main functions of a mediator is to bring about movement in the positions of the parties, when they are apparently stalemated, and by doing so bring them closer to a resolution of the issues separating them. Quite often, during the course of his mediation efforts, he encounters an intransigent position by one or both parties on a particular issue. Such intransigency creates a "roadblock" to agreement, preventing further desired movement.

Some of the approaches mediators, as well as negotiators, have utilized successfully in overcoming or bypassing these "roadblocks" have been discussed in prior chapters dealing with the conduct of joint and separate meetings.

In this chapter, we will examine several approaches to overcoming other "roadblocks" to agreement.

Retroactivity - Attendance Bonus

There are situations where the parties have continued their negotiations beyond the expiration date of the collective bargaining agreement, without a formal extension. If they then fail to reach agreement, a strike may occur. If the stoppage is a prolonged one, the union will demand that any settlement must be made retroactive to the expiration of the old contract. Management representatives almost always will resist such a demand feeling that it would create a dangerous precedent in future negotiations. They may well argue that the granting of retroactivity will unduly prolong negotiations since it would destroy any incentive union committees might have to reach agreement before the contract expiration date.

Unless this issue of retroactivity is resolved, it becomes a roadblock to any agreement and could lead to a prolongation of the stoppage. In any protracted strike, it is axiomatic that the skilled workers will seek and often readily find other employment. The unskilled and semi-skilled have a much more difficult time to obtain employment and most remain unemployed for the duration of the strike.

When the strike is finally settled, the unskilled and semi-skilled workers usually are readily available. However, if the company desires to quickly resume its pre-strike efficiency and productivity, it must be in a position to lure back its experienced skilled employees, especially those who have found employment elsewhere.

One of the approaches to a resolution of this issue, utilized by mediators, is to convert the amount which would have been due to each employee if retroactivity had been granted into a lump sum as an "attendance" bonus. This "attendance" bonus would be offered to all employees who, after ratification, report back to work and remain in the company's employ for a period of time--usually not less than 30 days.

Such a suggestion has a number of advantages. The prospect of an immediate lump sum payment is particularly attractive to strikers who have suffered economic hardship because of the length of the strike. Consequently, it is an inducement for them to ratify the tentative settlement. Further, there is seldom any objection from the union. From its viewpoint, a "rose by any other name smells as sweet"-- especially if the amount of the bonus roughly equates the amount each employee would have received if retroactivity as such had been granted.

From the company's viewpoint, it has preserved its opposition to the concept of retroactivity as a matter of principle. The bonus would serve as a carrot to attract many of the skilled employees to return to their former employment.

The requirement of a time period in which the returning employees must remain in the company's employment before receiving the "attendance bonus" is to assure that the employees will sever their ties with their other employer and not merely take a few days off, collect the bonus, and return to their new employer.

"No" - "Why"

Many times during negotiations, a mediator's suggestion or transmittal of an offer is met with an unequivocal flat rejection--expressed by a simple "no." It is axiomatic that there cannot be any hope of changing the inflexibility of a flat "no." It seems to preclude any further discussion. However, if the party urging that "no" can be persuaded to state the reasons which led to his negative conclusion, persuasion and flexibility may be restored. An alert mediator would therefore seek out the reasons and then analyze and examine them in the light of the problem under discussion. By such exposure, the soundness of the flat conclusion may be reappraised. If the reasons fail to sustain the ultimate negative, the negative itself may become untenable and the roadblock to further progress overcome.

Frozen Money Positions

There are times when a company may refuse to make either an initial or improved wage offer unless and until the union becomes more "realistic" in its wage demands. The union, when faced with such a company position, may refuse to scale down its demands until the company makes a "realistic" offer on wages. As long as both parties maintain their positions, there is a roadblock to eventual agreement. Consequently, here too, the mediator must design an approach which will produce movement if he hopes to assist the parties resolve their dispute.

One of the methods used by some mediators who are confronted with this problem is to meet separately with the union and to persuade it to give him a commitment that there is some flexibility in its position without naming a specific figure. Usually, the union committee will insist that while there is flexibility, the mediator must understand that there is mighty little. These statements are part of the posturing indulged in during negotiations by both parties and are designed to impress the mediator and the other party how "tough" they are.

Having obtained a commitment of flexibility, the mediator can meet with the company separately to advise them of the commitment he has obtained and urge them to make a new wage offer, no matter how small, to "test out the good faith of the union committee." The important element in this approach is to induce the company to abandon its former position and to make a specific wage offer. The amount of such offer, at this stage of the mediation effort, is not too important. Having obtained this movement, the mediator can then approach the union committee and challenge them to live up to their flexibility commitment by naming a specific figure lower than that previously demanded.

If the mediator succeeds in this approach, a situation is created where the gap in the parties' positions is no longer between two intangible negatives but between two concrete offers. By shuttling back and forth in separate meetings, and--when the conditions are ripe--in joint meetings, the mediator has the opportunity to exploit the opening and narrow the gap between both positions and eventually an agreement can emerge.

Splitting The Wage Offer

Quite often, after some hard bargaining, the union committee will arrive at a wage figure from which it will not retreat. It becomes a "magic" figure in the minds of the committee and often in the membership. The company may resist the demand on the basis of cost.

The mediator, in this situation, is faced with the problem of preserving the "magic" figure for the union and at the same time to ameliorate the cost impact on the company. One approach is to suggest splitting the wage package.

Illustratively, if the union demand is for a 30¢ general wage increase, the mediator can suggest that 15¢ be put into effect when the contract is ratified and the additional 15¢ six months thereafter. This approach has advantages for both parties. The company's cost as compared with an immediate 30¢ wage increase is substantially less. As far as the union is concerned, it preserves the magic figure of 30¢ and in the next round of negotiations, the union is in a position to bargain from the plateau of a wage base which incorporates the 30¢ increase.

In select cases, the cost impact on a company can be lessened by an extension of the term of the collective bargaining agreement several months beyond the normal expiration date.

"You"

It is an old sales principle that you buy an article not because someone is selling it but rather because you feel, rightly or wrongly, that you need it. A good salesman always seeks to instill into the prospect this sense of need. Once established, the sale can be readily made.

The same basic technique applies to collective bargaining.
If the offer or counterproposal is presented not as a demand but rather as a solution to a need, it becomes more
readily susceptible of acceptance. Good collective bargaining is basically a solving of problems of mutual interest. If an offer or counterproposal appears to solve
a problem of one of the parties, he is much more amenable.

The value of the "you" approach was clearly illustrated in
a Teamster negotiations that occurred several years ago on
the Eastern seaboard. One of the chief objectives of the
union was the establishment of a pension plan. If the union presented it as a bargaining "must," it would have been
quickly rejected. The chief union negotiator, however,
pointed to the low productivity record of the large number
of superannuated employees in the industry and the need for
the industry to achieve greater productivity if it desired
to maintain its financial and competitive position. Younger employees were needed. At the same time, simple justice
required recognition of the long and faithful service rendered the industry by the old timers. After vividly paint-
ing the picture and conditioning the industry to the problem
it faced, the union suggested as a possible solution of the
industry's problem a pension plan. It argued that it would
solve the problem of productivity by permitting the company
to introduce younger workers in the industry as replacements
for the "old timers" who could be retired with dignity and
financial security. This approach led to the establishment
of the pension program.

"Representative Cloak"

Many of us will seek shelter behind our title or position
when we desire to divorce our decison-making from our individual feelings and thinking. We often hear the remark
that as an individual the suggested course of action appears
just, but as the vice president of the company or the business representative of the union it cannot be adopted. In
effect, the speaker has thrown about him his representative
cloak and speaks not as an individual but as a representative of another self-interest.

Mediators often experience this phenomenon during the
course of negotiations. Even though the proposal being
considered would tend to correct an injustice, the responsibility of being in a representative capacity will compel
the other party to reject it. To achieve agreement, the

mediator, or negotiator, must pierce the representative
cloak and reach the individual behind it.

A fair illustration would be a situation involving a request
for call-in pay. The company representative as such representative may resist the demand because of the increase in
costs which its granting may entail. In a desire to keep
costs at a minimum, such a representative may overlook the
human relations injustices which may be inherent in the denial of the request. By suggesting that he place himself
in the shoes of the individual employee who leaves his home
expecting work and who undergoes the inconvenience and expense of travel only to be told that, through no fault of
his own, and not because of any Act of God, there is no work
for him, the problem is brought home to that representative
not as a representative but as an individual human being.
As an individual he certainly would resent the injustice of
it.

Story Telling

During the course of negotiations, parties, having exhausted
their arguments, just sit and stare at each other. The silence is ominous and if permitted to continue could result
in a flareup and a breakup of the meeting. The mediator
should be alert to the situation and be prepared to defuse
the tension. One method of doing so is by the judicious
use of humor.

In using humor, the mediator should be aware of certain basic guidelines. Stories which denigrate an ethnic or religious group should be avoided. A story which requires
the use of obscene language, while it may evoke an immediate guffaw, lowers the professional status of the mediator.
Many times, the point of the story can be made without the
use of the offensive language. Mediators should also be
aware of regional idiosyncrasies. In certain sections of
the South, stories replete with bucolic expressions are
acceptable to many negotiators so long as the name of the
Lord is not used.

The Recalcitrant Committeeman

Several years ago, in a midwest aerospace negotiation, because of the multiplicity of issues and the imminency of
the contract expiration date, the mediator decided that the
most expeditious approach was to utilize a subcommittee.

With the consent of the parties, such a subcommittee was
established and two issues were divorced from the main
table and placed in the jurisdiction of the selected subcommittee. When the union subcommittee subsequently reported the progress it was making, one member of the union
bargaining committee, who had not been selected to serve on
the subcommittee, vigorously opposed any of the subcommittee's suggested concessions. Time and again, each time the
subcommittee reported, the same individual succeeded in
thwarting a possible compromise which would have led to a
disposition of the issue entrusted to the subcommittee.

Faced with this roadblock to the progress of the negotiations, the mediator resorted to the technique which is
founded on the pedestrian advice--"if you can't lick them,
join them." He suggested that the subcommittee be expanded
by one member from each side and, with the assistance of the
chief union negotiator, made certain that the recalcitrant
committeeman was one of those selected.

After this move, the negotiating climate changed dramati-
cally. During the subcommittee's deliberations, the recalcitrant was most conciliatory and was in the forefront of
those suggesting accommodations which led to the disposition of the issue.

Often, failure to include a certain union committeeman in
the across-the-table dialogue or on subcommittees may prove
to be the obstacle to agreement. It is human to desire
recognition. This becomes especially true as far as members of the negotiating committee are concerned. Such committeemen are proud of the fact that their fellow workers
have elected or selected them over all others as their
spokesman. If during the course of the negotiations they
are led to believe that they and their opinions are being
ignored by the other committeemen, they become resentful.
The only outlet available to them to demonstrate their
frustration is to force recognition by opposing what their
colleagues are doing.

If such a situation is presented, mediators may do well to
consider the possible advantage of having the recalcitrant
more closely identified with the dialogue and the structuring of the final settlement.

One Issue Must Be Settled First

In some negotiations, one party may take the position that issue X must be settled first before it will agree to address itself to any of the other open issues. If this position is maintained a deadlock will soon ensue and negotiations will be stalemated.

In such cases, the mediator must try to convince the party insisting on the "one issue first" procedure to lay it aside temporarily and negotiate the other issues. The thrust of his argument should be that when that issue is the only thing standing between the parties and settlement there will be a greater probability that an accommodation can be reached. When the union membership becomes aware that the issue is the only thing standing between them and a contract or getting back on the job, they will soon bring pressure to bear on the committee to dispose of it.

Similarly, there will be economic pressure on the company which will motivate it to resolve the issue so that production will not be interrupted or, in the event of a strike, to resume operations.

Joint Study Committees

During the course of negotiations, one or two issues may appear insoluble within the time frame remaining in the crisis bargaining. Yet until and unless some disposition is made of these issues no agreement is possible.

The union negotiating committee, because of political or other pressures with the rank and file, may not be in a position to withdraw the issue. The company may not be able to retreat gracefully from its position, especially if it has carried the issue to the public through the media. In such circumstances, both sides may indicate that agreement is possible if some device is found which will keep the issue alive and not entail a surrender of their respective positions.

In order to break the impasse, the mediator could suggest that the issue or issues be withdrawn from the bargaining table and relegated to a joint study committee which would be able to examine in depth the problems inherent in the referred issues in a calmer, non-crisis atmosphere. Such joint study committees normally are composed of an equal number of union and management representatives. Such representatives are persons with expertise and special interest in the topics being studied.

Depending on the desires of the parties, there are two types of committees the mediator can suggest. Under one type, and the more common, the committee would be given the responsibility to meet periodically during the contract term and examine into the problems and report back its non-binding recommendations to the parties so that they can be discussed during the next negotiations.

The other type is a joint committee also charged with the responsibility of meeting during the contract term. If, as a result of its deliberations, it reaches agreement on some or all of the problems entrusted to it, such agreement or agreements would automatically become part of the collective bargaining contract between the parties.

An example of a joint study committee occurred a number of years ago in the steel industry. During negotiations, the union insisted on the preservation of the past practice provision in the expiring contract. The industry vigorously and publicly objected to its inclusion in the new contract on the ground that perpetuated wasteful and costly practices had led to local plant inefficiency. A bitter strike followed when an impasse was reached mainly on this issue.

Finally, it was decided to relegate the problem to a joint committee of representatives from the higher echelon of both parties. The committee had the responsibility to visit each plant during the term of the new contract, meet with local management and union representatives, study the questioned local past practices, and reach understandings on their retention of modifications. This agreement led to a settlement of the protracted strike.

There are times when both parties desire to bypass an issue but again for political or public relations considerations cannot appear to have abandoned it. In such cases, they may "sweep the issue under the rug" by allegedly submitting it to a joint committee with little expectation that anything will be accomplished by it if indeed the committee meets at all.

Agreements Not Incorporated In Contract

On occasions, one of the parties, in a multi-plant situation, may refuse to incorporate a possible solution of an
issue into the master contract. The situation arises where
a local plant practice is more favorable to the employees
and differs from the provisions of the master contract covering the same practice in the other plants of the company.
If the local practice is a long-standing one and has created no major production problems, the company may decide
that the risk of a stoppage, if it insists on conformance
with the other plants, is not economically wise. However,
the company may be reluctant to spell out the practice as
an exception in the master contract lest the local union
negotiators at the other plants in the future demand that
they be accorded the benefits of the same practice.

In these circumstances, the roadblock may be solved by a
mediator's suggestion that the understanding as to the local practice be incorporated in a letter of intent and not
be mentioned in the master contract. The letter of intent
may be accomplished by an exchange of correspondence by the
parties or, in some cases, by agreeing that the letter of
intent be kept by the mediator in his files and if any question arises in the future as to its terms, the mediator be
authorized to produce it in the presence of both parties.

CHAPTER XXI
PITFALLS AND CAUTIONS FOR MEDIATORS

There are a number of situations to which a new mediator
may be subjected which, if not properly met, may cause difficulties in his attempts to effectively assist the parties
to a dispute. These have been termed "pitfalls."

Fair Offer

Quite often during the course of a joint meeting, a company
or union representative, after extolling the justness and
fairness of his proposal, will state: "I will leave it to
the mediator's judgment whether or not it is a fair and
good proposal." A silence follows as both sides gaze down
to the head of the table awaiting anxiously the mediator's
reply.

In such situations, if the mediator responds in either the
affirmative or negative he is tarnishing his image as the
neutral. Yet a response is expected. At this moment, the
real question is not what is a fair, just, or equitable
offer but rather what is an acceptable offer. The mediator's evaluation as to the merits of the offer is really
immaterial. Consequently, the mediator should refuse to
give his own appraisal of the offer at the joint conference
and indicate to the inquirer that the determinative opinion
as to fairness and justness is not the mediator's but that
of the other party.

When conducting separate conferences, however, the mediator
may and often does express his opinion as to the relative
merits of an offer or counterproposal in light of other
area and industry settlements. In doing so, he should not
pass judgment as to the fairness of the proposed offer or
counterproposal. He can raise questions as to its acceptability in the light of better industry or area settlements.

Conditional Meetings

Quite often when a mediation meeting has in the judgment of
one party been particularly unproductive, the disappointed
party may insist that the mediator not schedule any further
meetings unless he has prior assurance that the other party

is ready to change its position. In a few instances, the
condition imposed on further meetings is that the other
party be prepared to meet the last stated position.

To permit either party to impose preconditions on further
meetings is to thwart any possibility of a settlement.
Even though, because of economic pressures or other circumstances, one party may be placed in the position of having
to accede to the other's demands, it would be bargaining
folly to attend a meeting with a pre-conference commitment
of surrender. Such a posture not only invites the interjection of new issues but is also destructive of future
bargaining relationships. A surrender to such ultimata in
the present negotiations will encourage similar threats in
the future.

Even though one party has requested a meeting, in most
cases, the mediator, after so advising the requesting party, should convert the request into a meeting called by
the mediator. If he discloses that the meeting is at a
party's request, it may be construed as a sign of weakness
and encourage the other party to hold tight to its bargaining position.

Mediators should remember that a conference scheduled and
conducted by a mediator is his conference and not that of
the parties. Further, the mediator is carrying forward a
statutory responsibility in the public interest. Consequently, neither party has a right to dictate preconditions
to the scheduling of any mediation conference.

Faced with preconditions, the mediator should reject the
suggestion and advise the parties that, in fulfillment of
his statutory responsibility, he and he alone will determine when and under what conditions a further meeting will
be scheduled. The onus of refusing to attend with its consequent effect on that party's constituency and public relations posture is placed upon the party insisting on the
preconditions.

Overlapping Offers

Overlapping offers occurs when a mediator is advised confidentially by each party separately of its willingness, at
the appropriate time, to make an acceptable offer which exceeds the expectations of the other party. Overlapping
offers are not a common occurrence in mediation meetings,
but certainly are not rarities.

Typical of overlapping offers is a situation where a company's bargaining table offer is a 5% wage increase but it advises the mediator confidentially that, to avoid a strike, it will increase its offer to 7½% when timely. In the same situation, the union's bargaining table demand is a 10% wage increase but it has advised the mediator, confidentially, that it will accept a 7% increase if necessary to achieve a settlement.

Obviously, at this point, the mediator knows that there is a settlement but the problem is how to achieve it without breaking confidentiality. He is faced with a dilemma. If he advises the union that 7½% is obtainable or the company that the dispute can be settled for 7%, he runs the risk of destroying his future acceptability if it should ever be disclosed that he breached confidentiality. Such disclosure is almost inevitable. When the dust and heat of negotiations have settled, a union committeeman, in a conversation with a company negotiator, either in the plant or over a drink at a neighborhood tavern, may boast how his committee outsmarted the company which could have settled for the 7% figure as they had advised the mediator. Conversely, the company negotiator, in kidding his counterpart, may disclose that he had told the mediator that the company was prepared to go 7½%. It is easy to see that the scapegoat in this situation would be the mediator and not the negotiators.

After the mediator has acquired the confidential positions of the parties, he has two approaches available to him depending on the status of the negotiations. If there are outstanding issues in addition to wages, he can try to dispose of them by using some of the potential increase but being careful to always leave a negotiable gap between the two ultimate figures. Having reduced or disposed of the issues, he can then proceed in accordance with the following suggestion.

If all issues except wages have been settled, the mediator should convene the parties in a joint meeting and advise them that as a result of his explorations in his separate meetings with the parties, he is persuaded that both are in an area of settlement. He then should adopt the role of a passive chairman and permit the parties through across-the-table bargaining to find an acceptable figure by themselves. By either procedure, he preserves his position if there is a subsequent disclosure of his confidential knowledge.

Legal Opinions

Many mediators either have a background in law, or were
formerly associated with a State or Federal regulatory
agency concerned with wages and hours, labor relations,
minimum wages, and such like.

During the course of some negotiations, a question of the
legality of a demand or offer may arise. If the parties
have knowledge of the mediator's background or prior affiliations, they may solicit his opinion. Unless the inquiry is directly related to the mediation statute or regulation under which the mediator is functioning, it is
imprudent for him to give an opinion on the legality of
the matter before the parties. Even though the mediator
thinks he knows the answer, he is treading on dangerous
ground. Statutes are subject to amendment and rules and
regulations issued thereunder are subject to change. Unless one specializes in a particular subject as part of
his daily duties, it is almost impossible to keep abreast
of the recurring changes in the Act or interpretations
thereof. The advice given may well be outdated.

Further, parties normally have ready access to legal counsel. It is the responsibility of such counsel and not of
the mediator to properly advise his client.

If the mediator believes that a demand, offer, or suggested compromise may be of doubtful legality, he has a duty to
raise the question and to suggest that before the parties
proceed on that issue they seek legal counsel. If despite
his admonition the parties desire to go forward without obtaining the suggested advice, the mediator should not deter
them.

If the parties plan to incorporate into their collective
bargaining contract a provision which is not only illegal
but snocks the public conscience, there is a division of
opinion as to the position the mediator should take. Typical of such provision would be a seniority clause which,
when implemented, would discriminate against minority employees. If despite questions raised by the mediator as
to its illegality, the parties insist on going forward,
some writers insist that, in such cases, it is the duty of
the mediator to report it to the enforcing agency having
jurisdiction.

Most meditors do not subscribe to this viewpoint. It is
their position that even though the proposed action out-
rages their conscience, it is not compatible with their
role as mediators to act as informants, and the policing
is the responsibility of the agency specifically entrusted
with that duty. If a mediator feels that his continuing
presence at the bargaining table could be construed as con-
doning or sanctioning the unlawful act, he should withdraw.

Bargaining In Good Faith

In circumstances quite similar to that described in "fair
offer," a mediator may be confronted at a joint meeting by
a demand that he pass judgment on the good faith bargaining
of one side or the other. This demand is usually preceded
by across-the-table accusation of bad faith.

Whether a party is or is not bargaining in good faith is
not a matter for a determination of the mediator. His sole
responsibility is to assist the parties to resolve the issues separating them. The meeting he has scheduled is designed to accomplish that purpose and not be a judicial or
quasi-judicial forum for determining the bona fides of one
party or the other. Usually, the question is a rhetorical
one. No direct answer is expected. The better practice
would be for the mediator to ignore the question and suggest that the parties pass on to another issue.

If the inquirer is persistent and presses for an answer,
then the mediator should advise him of the purpose for
which the meeting was called. He should also advise that,
if the inquirer desires to pursue his accusation, there is
another forum (either the National or State Labor Relations
Board) to which he has recourse for a determination.

Job Content vs. Job Title

During the course of negotiations, a company negotiator for
Plant X may insist that, as far as wage rates are concerned,
his offer equals or exceeds the wage rates paid for similar
jobs in the area. To prove his point, he may produce a
wage survey which indicates, for example, that the highest
area rate for assembler B is paid by Y company and his offer for assembler B exceeds Y's rate.

If the mediator blindly accepts X company's assertion as a
fact and uses it as a basis for his arguments with the union

committee, his statements may be challenged and disproved to his chagrin.

Before accepting X's assertion as a fact, the mediator should request (or procure it himself) the job descriptions for both jobs. In examininig both, he will often find that while job titles may be the same, the job content may be significantly different. Assembler B in X company may be performing the same tasks as assembler A in plant Y. As a result, the proper comparison is between the wage rate of assembler A in Plant Y and assembler B in Plant X. Care should be taken that only jobs having the same content are equated.

Instructed Committee

There will be occasions where a mediator will be confront-ed with an alleged instructed committee. Illustrative of such a situation is the case where the mediator has sched-uled a conference. Prior to jointly convening the parties, the union committee advises the mediator that at a member-ship meeting held a few days previously the union member-ship mandated the committee to settle for 6% an hour in-crease and, therefore, unless the employer is prepared to meet that exact figure, there will be no point to continu-ing the mediation meeting.

Obviously, if the union committee maintains this posture, meaningful negotiations are impossible. There are several approaches which have been utilized by mediators to avoid the consequences of a committee maintaining this position.

The first approach is an appeal to the pride of the individ-ual committee members. The mediator can point out that the membership apparently has no faith in the judgment of the negotiating committee or else they would have placed some discretion in them. Further, he can stress that the union membership should not have bothered even going through the charade of electing or selecting a negotiating committee when a messenger boy could have served the function the committee was asked to perform.

If the appeal to pride does not break down the mandated posture, then a mediator may try the technique of the "false crisis." This is accomplished by first highlight-ing the position of the committee. It has been done by the following dialogue:

Mediator - "Let me understand your position quite
clearly. You say that the membership
has mandated you to get 6% an hour?"

Committee Chairman - "That is correct."

Mediator - "In a word that means that even if the
employer was to offer you 5.9%, you
would reject it because of your mandate?"

Often the mediator need not go further. The exposure of
the ridiculousness of the union's position leads to a union
caucus and an abandonment of their mandated position.

If, however, the committee adheres to its position, the mediator can state that there is really no point to prolonging
the proceedings and suggest that the parties immediately
meet jointly so that the employer can hear directly from
the committee as to the mandate. The mediator also announces that if the employer rejects the demand, he will
adjourn the meeting without date and see if he can fit in
the next meeting in two or three weeks.

This technique often creates a "crisis." The union committee now realizes that it can expect a resounding "no" from
the employer's representatives and that the joint meeting
would be of only a few minutes duration with the prospects
of a further meeting two or three weeks away. Their report
to the membership becomes a weighty responsibility. Despite
their selection as the negotiators for the membership, they
are faced with the prospect of having nothing to report except a demand and an out-of-hand rejection. They are not
in a position to report explorations, counteroffers, or
arguments.

In almost every case, the union committee caucuses and then
authorizes the mediator to proceed in the normal manner.

Contract Drafting and Signing

The normal practice after a tentative agreement has been
ratified is for the company representative or attorney to
draft tne new contract. When the draft has been prepared,
the parties often meet jointly to go over the proposed language and, if satisfactory, to sign the contract.

Most mediators will avoid attending such meetings. Quite
often, when the parties are discussing the draft language,
questions arise as to whether the proposed language correctly reflects the understandings reached at the bargaining
table. Most of the objections raised are of a minor nature
and are quickly resolved by the parties themselves.

Where there is a disagreement, experience has taught if the
parties are left alone they usually work out the problem.
The settlement has been ratified by the membership. The
union normally has no desire to reconvene the membership
and try to explain to them that instead of an understanding
there was a misunderstanding. If there has been a strike,
the union would be reluctant to ask the membership to return to the picket line when all were anticipating a return
to work. The company has started to gear up for a resump-
tion of production and perhaps called back its maintenance
and start-up employees. In addition, it most probably has
notified its customers of the settlement of the dispute.
The company has no desire to reopen the entire bargaining
process. There are both overwhelming political and economic pressures on both parties to solve the problems themselves.

If a mediator attends such a meeting, the parties may use
him as a crutch and the issues raised devolve into a question of credibility. The mediator is then placed in a
position of an arbiter of truth or falsity. As a result,
his future acceptability may be injured.

Occasionally one of the parties may request, or demand by
subpoena, that the mediator produce his notes on the subject matter in dispute. Many mediators destroy their notes
after they have been advised that the settlement has been
ratified. If later, they are requested to produce their
notes, they can advise that they no longer have them. Insofar as subpoenas for notes are concerned, such attempts
have been successfully resisted because of their confidential nature.

In the normal case, the mediator's responsibility should
terminate when the tentative agreement has been ratified.
The drafting and execution of the formal contract is the
responsibility of the parties. It is their duty to reflect correctly the understandings and to couch them in
language which makes their day-to-day application practical.

Of course, if the issue is crucial and there is a strong possibility that the entire settlement would be jeopardized if the dispute is not resolved, then the mediator, if he can recall what the agreement was, should assist the parties. This is best done by meeting separately with the party who is in error. At the meeting, the mediator can advise him what his notes disclose and persuade him to withdraw his request for mediator intervention and accept the version espoused by the other party. The separate meeting avoids embarrassing the party in error if the mediator were to correct him at a joint meeting.

Attendance At Union Membership Meetings

Mediators, on occasion, have been invited to attend ratification meetings. Usually, they are urged to do so on the basis of assisting the negotiating committee to explain and "sell" the package which has been tentatively agreed to by the committee.

Except in an exceptional case, mediators decline such invitations. The reason is that the ratification process is normally an internal union affair into which the mediator should not physically intrude. Over and beyond this basic reason is the question of responsibility. The basic responsibility for "selling" the package belongs to the committee, not the mediator. They, and not he, were selected by their fellow members to represent them and to bring back any agreement reached with their comments.

There are, however, times when circumstances dictate the mediator's presence at the meeting. In such circumstances, there are two cautions which should be observed:

A. <u>Never be the first speaker</u>. This caution is born of bitter experience. There have been instances in which the mediator permitted himself to be called on first to extol the virtues of the tentative agreement. At the conclusion of his remarks, a dissident minority registered its disapproval by shouts and stamping of feet. Fearing similar treatment, each following speaker refused to carry out his commitment to recommend the settlement or else did so in a most unenthusiastic manner. The mediator was left alone in an embarrassing position and his future usefulness in that dispute seriously impaired.

The mediator should insist that the negotiating committee
take the platform first. If they fail to endorse the tentative agreement, he should decline to speak.

B. Never characterize the offer as to its fairness
and justness. Since the acceptance or rejection of the
offer is dependent on its acceptability, the mediator
should not impose upon the membership his own judgment as
to its fairness or justness. The mediator should confine
his remarks to explaining the offer, to paying tribute to
the integrity and hard work of the negotiating committee,
and to indicating that the offer was the best that could
be obtained at that time, and if appropriate, without a
lengthy and costly stoppage.

If the mediator goes beyond the suggested limitations, he
will, in the event of a rejection, be hard put to justify
his actions in trying to get an improvement in an offer
which he has publicly stated is fair and just.

Even when treading on dangerous ground by attending a union
ratification meeting, a mediator's ingenuity may make all
cautions academic. An example of such ingenuity occurred
several years ago in Western New York. After hard bargaining, a long strike at a hand tool factory was tentatively
settled. Because he had fashioned the first package which
brought about the settlement, the mediator was prevailed
upon to attend the ratification meeting.

After the local union president outlined the basic terms of
the settlement, he called for a voice vote on approval or
rejection. The leatherlung boys, well spaced throughout
the auditorium, took over and outshouted everyone with their
nays.

From his prior conversation with the members of the union
negotiating team and some employees, the mediator felt that
the shouts were really a minority and that the majority
would accept. He brothered the president, who gave "brother" mediator the floor. The mediator stated that it was
not his intention to intrude in the meeting but he felt
sure that brother president, because of the pressure of
the meeting, had forgotten Article 23, Section 3(c) of the
International Constitution which provides that whenever
there had been a strike, any tentative settlement must be
voted on by secret ballot. An International Representative
who was attending the meeting immediately rose to the occa-

sion. He stated that he wished to thank "brother" mediator
because he too was about to call brother president's attention to the requirements of the International Constitution.
The local union president then conducted a secret ballot
vote. The tentative agreement was ratified by a 5 to 1
margin.

After the meeting, over a drink at a local tavern, both the
mediator and the international representative wondered whether there was an Article 23, Section 3(c) in the International Constitution.

Cautions For Mediators

There are a number of cautions of which mediators should
be aware.

Change of Position

When resuming a mediation conference in a joint session,
the mediator should never start by inquiring of one or both
parties if they have changed their position since the last
meeting. If the mediator does ask the question, both parties' response almost always has to be in the negative.
Even though one of the parties has decided to change its
position on some or all the outstanding issues, from a negotiating viewpoint, it would be the height of folly to ad-
mit it at the start of the meeting. If a party plans to
offer a compromise or make a concession, it usually will
make it only after an in-depth discussion and appear to
compromise or concede reluctantly. To do otherwise would
be an almost fatal display of weakness.

In view of the negative responses to the mediator's question, he is placed in an almost untenable position. One
party may insist that there is no point in continuing the
meeting in view of the other party's position of no change.

The joint meeting would be much more productive if the mediator would start the meeting by reciting his understanding of what issues have been settled at prior meetings and
the position of the parties on the remaining unresolved
issues.

The question about change of position should be reserved
for the separate meetings with the parties.

Criticism Of Other Mediators

A mediator should not permit either party to indulge in
criticism of another mediator, be he Federal or State. The
criticism states only one side of what occurred. There may
have been a very good reason for the mediator's action which
the critic fails to disclose. The same critic will be the
first to condemn the mediator in the instant case if he
fails to persuade the other party to accept the critic's
proposal.

Very often the attack on a previous mediator is prefaced by
flattering remarks about the present mediator's performance.
"You really know your business. Gosh, it is a welcomed re-
lief to have someone like you assigned to our dispute. What
a difference between the way you handle negotiations and
Mediator Jones. He didn't seem to know..."

There may be a tendency by some mediators to permit the criticism to go on not only because it is human to revel in
praise but also because they may feel that by listening
they may ingratiate themselves with the critic. It is a
mistake to permit the critic to continue. Any criticism
of another mediator is ultimately directed at the mediation
process and all its practitioners.

One of the most effective ways of stifling such criticism
is for the mediator, when he first detects that one party
is about to embark on such remarks, to interrupt and state,
"oh yes--Mediator Jones--one of the top notch mediators and
a good friend of mine," even though he never met Mediator
Jones. This usually silences any further derogatory remarks about Mediator Jones.

Unrealistic Offers Or Counterproposals

If an offer or counterproposal is unrealistic, in the light
of the status of negotiations, the mediator should not hesitate to so advise the party making the proposal. This
should be done in a separate session only. To do otherwise
may raise false hopes as to its acceptability. If despite
the mediator's advice, the party insists on making the proposal, the mediator should not hinder him from doing so.
At this juncture, until the offer or counterproposal is rejected, the proposer will not change his position on the
issue.

The mediator should not convey the proposal to the other party. He should convene a joint meeting and let the proposer present the offer or counterproposal to the other party. It is only when he hears the objections to it first hand will he reconsider his position.

If the mediator had undertaken to convey it to the other party, after trying to dissuade the proposer, and it, as expected, was rejected, the proposer might well feel that the mediator may have presented it in such a negative way that it invited the rejection. Further, he may cling to the belief that had the mediator presented it properly it would have been seriously considered by the other party.

The Clause With A "Hooker"

A somewhat similar situation as that mentioned above is the situation where one party desires to take advantage of the inexperience of his counterpart. For example, one party might suggest a contract clause whose deceptive language distorts the understanding the other party had when it agreed to the proposal the proffered clause is supposed to embody. In the vernacular of the trade, it is known as a "clause with a hooker."

Here, too, the mediator should attempt to persaude the party not to offer it to the other side. If he fails to dissuade him, the mediator should not present it himself. He should convene both parties in a joint meeting and let the proposer present the provision to the other party. If the mediator believes that the other party does not grasp the significance of the proffered provision, he should assume the behavior of the obtuse "country cousin." By asking a series of exploratory questions--under the guise of trying to understand the proposal--he should try to expose the true intent and meaning of the provision. If, after such exposure, the other party still is willing to accept it, there is nothing further the mediator can do.

Taking On The Mediator

There are times when one of the parties may decide to "take on the mediator" by making snide remarks about the manner in which the mediator is handling the dispute. Many times the remarks are couched in four-letter words and are quite irritating. In many of these incidents, the true motivation for the remarks is jealousy on the part of the offender.

Many times it becomes manifest when he feels that his committee members are no longer listening to him but are paying attention to the mediator's suggestions.

Normally, the mediator has to be thick skinned about such
remarks and to resist the temptation to respond in kind.
Frequently, ignoring the remarks brings about a cessation.
If, however, the remarks become personal and reflect on the
mediator's integrity, there is no reason why a mediator
should remain silent. This is especially true if such remarks are made in the presence of one or both negotiating
committees. In such cases, the mediator's reply should be
worded in a manner which makes the dispute a personal one
between the mediator and the maker of the remarks and should
not involve any member of his committee. The desired effect
is to isolate him, and to avoid encouraging anyone to defend
him.

Misleading The Mediator

There is one situation to which there is no easy solution,
if indeed, there is any solution. Illustratively, a union
negotiator may deliberately indicate to a mediator that if
the company was to offer a 20¢ increase, the union would
seriously consider withdrawing some of the remaining demands.
Relying on the good faith of the union negotiator, the mediator may persuade the company to offer the increase on
the basis of the mediator's statement that he feels confident that it would result in a withdrawal of some of the
outstanding demands.

When the mediator conveys to the union that the company
has agreed to the 20¢ increase, and requests the union to
indicate which demands it will withdraw, the union negotiator then takes the position that the mediator must have mis-
understood. The union will insist that all that had been
indicated, without any commitment, was that the union would
consider withdrawing some of the other demands. The union
also states that it has reviewed all of the outstanding demands and they all are "musts."

Here, the mediator has been deliberately misled. His effectiveness is completely destroyed. If he confesses to the
other side that he has been misled, the criticism is not
directed against the union but against the mediator for permitting himself to be used.

There is no answer to this. Such deceitful negotiators soon become known to the mediation community. If a mediator does not know the participants in a mediation case to which he is assigned it would be wise for him to consult his colleagues and get the benefit of their experiences with the parties.

Rings, Insignia, Pins

The wearing of rings, pins, or other insignia should be avoided especially if they may be controversial. Falling in the latter category are campaign buttons usually distributed by candidates for public office. Whether controversial or not, most experienced mediators avoid wearing any rings (except wedding rings), pins, or other insignia to avoid the appearance of using them as a crutch in their mediation efforts. There are times when the mediator will permit the parties to use his office either to make calls or as a caucus room. If such is the case, he should remove any plaques or other matter of a partisan or controversial nature from the top of his desk. It does not speak highly of a mediator's ability if he has to rely on his social, political, fraternal, or religious affiliation to obtain a settlement of a dispute.

In the same category, any mediator who has to rely on his ethnic background to further his mediation efforts does a disservice to the high ethical standards of the profession.

Relations With The Parties

The mediator should be friendly, but not be overly familiar with either party. There should be a line in the mediator's relationship which he should not permit others to cross by getting too close, especially to his personal life.

As a general rule, mediators, during the course of their mediation efforts, should not fraternize with either side during or after a meeting. Quite often, when a luncheon break is called, the company representative may invite the mediator to join them for lunch. While it should be avoided if possible, if however the mediator feels that it may present the opportunity in the informal atmosphere to have some off-record, frank discussions about some of the outstanding issues, he should accept. Before accepting the

invitation, he should advise the other party of his intention. Failure to do so may arouse suspicions and give rise
to insinuations that the mediator is in the other party's
"pocket." Some mediators handle the notification by announcing to the union committee, in a joking fashion, that
he has done better than they have since, at least, he has
been able to negotiate a free lunch from the company. Then,
in a serious vein, tell the committee that it may give him
the opportunity to explore some of the company's positions
on their demands if they have no objection to his acceptance of the company's invitation.

Denigrating Representatives

Mediators should avoid denigrating a negotiator in front
of his committee by backing him in a corner from which
there is no escape or by ridiculing his statements. This
is especially true of union representatives. Most have
attained their position through the election process and
consequently have a political position to protect. They
must look good in the eyes of their constituents.

Ultimatums - Threats

Mediators should not take ultimatums and stike or lockout
threats too seriously especially in the early stages of
negotiations. Threats and the like are part and parcel
of the posturing which negotiators indulge in trying to
impress the other party with the seriousness and firmness
of their position. As negotiations progress and agreement
becomes a possibility, such threats will soon vanish.

Mediator As An Observer

Mediators should not accept a request to sit in on a negotiating conference as observers. This is especially
true if the parties have scheduled the meeting. To do so
is demeaning to the status of the mediator. Many times,
the invitation is extended on the basis that it would give
the mediator the opportunity to get acquainted with the
parties and the issues so that if his services are required later, he will not have to be educated on the positions of the parties on the unresolved issues. This, they
insist, will save precious time.

As far as the need for getting acquainted with the parties and the issues, any experienced mediator can elicit

the same information by telephone calls prior to his entrance into the negotiations. If there are still gaps in the needed information, he can fill them in at the first joint meeting he schedules.

When an invitation is extended, the mediator should plead a heavy meeting schedule and advise the parties that, when his services are required, the parties can contact him at his office and he would schedule a meeting to see if he can be of assistance.

Crossing Picket Lines

There are occasions, during a strike situation, where the mediator may find it desirable to confer separately with the company's chief negotiator or his superior. When trying to arrange such meeting, the mediator may be advised that because of the increased duties, occasioned by the strike, such representative would prefer not to be absent from the plant.

The normal practice is for the mediator to avoid crossing the picket line in a dispute he is attempting to mediate. Consequently, his first step is to try to persaude such representative to meet away from the plant. If such persuasion is ineffectual, the mediator may have no alternative except to hold the separate meeting at the plant.

Before proceeding, the mediator should advise the union representative of the necessity of conferring with the company representative and the problem he has encountered in trying to arrange a meeting away from the plant. There are two methods of crossing the picket line. The first method is by "pulling" the pickets. When he is ready to enter the plant, the union pulls the pickets away from the company gate which the mediator intends to use. When the mediator has entered the building, the pickets resume their prior positions. When the mediator is about to leave the plant, he sends word to the picket captain by either security or management personnel. The pickets are then again pulled away from the gate until the mediator leaves the plant. This is the most desirable method.

The second method is that the mediator should insist that the strike captain or a local union officer accompany him while he crosses the picket line. When doing so, the mediator should carry on an obvious conversation with the picket captain.

These methods have two advantages. They obviate any possibility of bodily harm as a result of a misunderstanding of
his mission by an overzealous picket. Further, they foreclose the need for explanation later. A few years ago, a
mediator crossed a picket line with permission of the local
union. As he did so, someone took a picture of the incident.
Several years later, the picture surfaced and he was accused
of anti-union conduct. This put the mediator on the defen-
sive and compelled an explanation.

Ignoring Dropped Issues

In some negotiations, issues are raised by the parties, usually at the beginning of the mediation sessions, and when
final agreement is reached they ignore such issues without
any explanation or mention of them and without attempting
to resolve them. In such situations, the mediator should
accommodate himself to this bargaining pattern of the parties and not resurrect such issues by calling the parties'
attention to them.

Not too many years ago, in garment industry negotiations in
New York City, the union at the first mediation session outlined about fifteen demands. In the subsequent meetings, no
mention was made about eight of the demands and hard bargaining concentrated on the remaining seven. A newly appointed
mediator, as part of his training, was assigned to sit in
with a veteran mediator. Throughout the meetings, the new
mediator kept copious notes and remained silent. When the
parties had reached an accommodation on all seven and were
about to shake hands, the new mediator, after consulting his
notes, asked the parties "what about these other issues?".
A dead silence followed and the veteran mediator excused
himself and, in the corridor outside, proceeded to lecture
the new mediator on the realities of bargaining patterns.

CHAPTER XXII

RECOMMENDATIONS BY MEDIATORS

History

Closely akin to offers and explorations is the problem of recommendations made by mediators at a joint meeting.

For a long time, it was a cardinal principle of good mediation that the only proper place for suggesting an alternative or compromise solution to an issue or issues in dispute was in a separate meeting. It was only in rare cases where the mediator departed from this rule.

Such suggestions or compromises were informal and made orally. No thought was ever given to formalizing such suggestions in writing. The publicizing of such suggestions was never even considered. Many mediators felt that if a suggestion was formalized and publicized, it was stating in effect that in the mediator's opinion the suggestion represented his judgment as to what would be a fair and equitable solution to the dispute. If the suggestion was rejected by one or both parties, he would have lost his effectiveness thereafter. Further, if rejected, it ill behooved him a few days later to formalize another and different suggestion as to what would be a fair and equitable solution of the dispute.

While William E. Simkin was Director of the Federal Mediation and Conciliation Service, a number of disputes involving extended work stoppages dictated the need for a reexamination of the prior aversion to mediators' recommendations. A study of some of these cases revealed that the issues remaining in dispute did not warrant prolongation of the stoppage with its attendant impact on the employees, company, and the economic welfare of the community. Yet either because of prior positions taken by the parties or because of political interplays, the parties were reluctant to change their bargaining posture. In other cases, each party felt that if it came forward with a compromise of its prior position on an issue, the move would be construed as a sign of weakness on its part. If so misconstrued, the other party, instead of responding with a change of position, would firm up and demand not compromise but surrender.

In still other cases, the criticality to the national defense effort of the products produced was such that a stoppage of production was intolerable. In all such cases and
in similar cases, it appeared that it would be totally irresponsible to permit the dispute to continue without some
affirmative action by the mediator beyond his traditional
utilization of persuasion and separate meeting suggestions.
The public interest demanded a review of the traditional
mediation policy and called for experimentation. Experimentation was undertaken in highly selective cases in the
private sector.

In treating of a mediator's recommendations in this chapter,
we are not speaking of those situations where, because of
political or economic considerations, the parties want a
"settlement" to be imposed by the mediator by way of formal
recommendations. In such cases, the parties often assist
in the structuring and drafting of the recommendations. By
this device, one or both parties hope to be in a position
to throw the onus on the mediator. The union can go before
the membership and loudly proclaim that it could not achieve
a cherished bargaining goal (which was unobtainable by negotiations) because the mediator by his recommendations had
irretrievably damaged the union's bargaining position.
Management, especially in industries requiring governmental
approval of a rate or price increase, can maintain that it
resisted the union demands which would increase costs but
that it had no alternative when the mediator imposed his
recommendation on it.

Conditions Precedent

It was recognized that the indiscriminate use of mediators'
recommendations would be self-destructive. To avoid such
use, certain criteria were established before a mediator
was authorized to make recommendations. These criteria
were conditions precedent and are valid today.

The determination of what is a proper case for recommendations depends on whether the case meets the following
tests:

1. A threatened strike or the prolongation of
    an existing strike is having a major impact
    on the community involved, or the defense
    effort, or it has been attended by violence.

2. The parties are deadlocked and no negotiated
    solution appears possible in the immediate
    future.

3. The parties have rejected alternative methods
    of solving the issues; e.g., arbitration and
    fact-finding.

4. The mediator has a thorough knowledge of
    the issues in dispute.

5. The mediator has, by judicious explorations
    in joint or separate conferences, obtained
    a "feeling" for the issues and believes an
    acceptable middle ground exists if articu-
    lated by a neutral.

If a particular disupte meets these tests, the mediator
can go forward and make a suggestion or even a recommendation at the joint meeting specifically setting forth the
possible solutions to the outstanding issues. Before such
presentation, the mediator should advise the parties that
unless they are able to find a solution themselves by a
fixed time, he will have to give serious consideration to
the making of recommendations.

In some cases, the very existence of a threat of possible
recommendations has been sufficient to inspire agreement.

Format of Recommendations

In appropriate cases, the recommendations or suggestions
can be reduced to writing and handed to the parties in
each other's presence.

Generally, the written recommendations are prefaced by:

(a) Recitation of the importance and impact
     of the dispute.

(b) Recitation of the number of meetings held
     by the mediator in an attempt to help the
     parties resolve the dispute.

(c) The futility of such meetings.

(d)   A statement that as long as the parties
      adhere to their present positions, no
      agreement appears possible in the imme-
      diate future.

(e)   That in light of these factors, he is
      proposing "at this time" the following
      solutions.

One of the key phrases in the prefatory statements is "at
this time." Mediator recommendations should be designed
to respond to the bargaining situation at the time they
are made. If, in the future, there is a significant change
in the status of the negotiations due to the political and
economic pressures which have arisen since the recommendations, there should be nothing to deter the mediator from
making further suggestions--not necessarily in the form of
formal recommendations, but in the course of his renewed
mediation efforts.

Further, when recommendations are made, the parties should
be advised that they are offered as a basis for further
negotiations. This leaves the door open for the parties
to negotiate changes within the framework of the recommendations.

After the parties have received the copies of the document,
the mediator should not permit any discussion as to the
merits of the recommendations at that time but merely entertain questions relating solely to clarification. If no
such questions are asked, he should request the parties to
study the recommendations in separate caucuses and advise
him at a prescribed time of their acceptance or rejection.

Public vs. Private

If the making of recommendations is the course that the
mediator decides to pursue, the question then arises as to
whether he should make the recommendations public knowledge.

Each party to a labor contract negotiation is keenly conscious of its public relations positon. Each is seeking
to elicit public support for the alleged fairness and
reasonableness of its offer or demand. At the minimum,
each seeks sympathetic neutrality of the public; at the
maximum, each seeks the exertion of public pressure which
will impel the other party to either accept the offer or
demand or to modify its position.

Normally, neither party desires to have a public exposure by a neutral of the true differences between them. Nor, generally speaking, do they desire to have the public know that the neutral suggested a solution and they have rejected it.

Recognizing these facts, when mediators do make recommendations, in most cases, they will reserve the right to make such recommendations public. Experience indicates that the mere threat to do so at a later day compels each party seriously to consider the recommendations and, if unacceptable in whole or in part, to reevaluate their positions and find a new approach to the solution of the unresolved issues.

An examination of the disputes in which mediators have made recommendations shows that it has seldom been necessary to make the recommendations public. Apparently, they stimulated further thinking which led to a breaking of the log jam in the negotiations. If the parties do accept the mediator's recommendations, the preferable practice is to announce publicly that recommendations have been made but not to disclose the specific terms pending the ratification meeting.

Evaluation

Experience has taught that in the selected cases where the technique of recommendations was properly utilized, it proved highly effective in bringing about a settlement of the dispute. In 95% of the cases, both parties accepted the mediator's recommendations. In 3% of the cases, the recommendations were accepted by one party but rejected by the other. In the remainder of the cases, both parties rejected. As an interesting sidelight, a comparison of the terms of the final settlement and the recommendations in those cases where either or both parties rejected reveals that there were few, if any, variations.

It is unfortunate that the technique of recommendations has been all but abandoned by not only the Federal Mediation and Conciliation Service but also by many State agencies in the private sector. Much of the objections to recommendations stems from a puzzling reluctance to occasionally abandon traditional techniques and to experiment with new approaches to dispute resolution in the private sector. When public sector bargaining was recognized, not being bound by the straight jacket of private sector mediation, experimentation led to the fashioning of new dispute resolution approaches.

Again, a word of caution. Mediators should be highly selective in the type of cases in which they should utilize the
device of recommendations. For mediators to rush forth with
recommendations just because the case to which they were
assigned proves difficult of solution would be destructive,
not only of the efficiency of recommendations in future cases, but also of the mediation process. It would create the
somewhat analogous situation which occurred during World War
II with some mediators employed by the United States Conciliation Service. Whenever these mediators had a dispute which
did not respond readily to normal mediation efforts, they
would immediately recommend that the case be certified to
the War Labor Board for resolution rather than insisting
that the parties engage in hard, good faith bargaining before any certification would be considered.

CHAPTER XXIII

TECHNIQUES FOR MINIMIZING MEMBERSHIP REJECTIONS OF RECOMMENDED TENTATIVE AGREEMENTS

One of the more disturbing problems negotiators encounter in bargaining is the rejection of recommended tentative agreements by the union membership. The situation referred to is one in which the duly elected or selected union negotiating committee and the representatives of the employer have reached an understanding across the bargaining table, and the union committee has stated that it would recommend it to the membership for acceptance. The union committee honestly and sincerely carries out its commitment at the membership meeting and, despite its action, the membership rejects the settlement.

This type situation first came to the attention of the Federal Mediation and Conciliation Service in 1964 when it noticed that in 8.7% of the cases in which it was involved, tentative agreements were rejected by the membership. The rate of rejections reached a peak in 1967 when over 14% of all recommended tentative agreements were rejected by the membership.

The 1967 study of the Federal Mediation and Conciliation Service was confined to the approximately 7,500 cases in which the Service participated. It did not include disputes which were handled exclusively by State and local mediation agencies. Further, it did not include multiple rejections. The latter type of rejection involves situations where in the same set of negotiations the union membership rejects the recommended settlement two or more times. In the area of multiple rejections, the Service conducted a limited survey of 1,563 cases and found that in 21% of these cases, tentative agreements had been rejected two or more times before the agreement was ratified.

If nothing is done to minimize the chances of a rejection, it will not only lead to an unhealthy instability in negotiations but it is also destructive of the unity and leadership which makes a union an effective and respected spokesman for the betterment of the economic conditions of the rank and file members.

Causes

When a union submits a set of demands to an employer, that employer has a right to feel that those demands reflect the desires of his employees. He also has the right to believe that if he meets some or all of those demands, either by concession or compromise, and obtains the agreement of the selected or elected union bargaining committee, he has an agreement. If the membership rejects it, he has every right to question seriously whether the union spokesman or his committee really do represent his employees. Equally disturbing is the fact that his faith in the leadership abilities of the union representative will be destroyed.

There have been many theories advanced as to the causes of such rejections. One of the earliest theories was that the union leadership image was destroyed by the disclosures of the various congressional investigations and prosecution of corruption in unions. This theory does not appear very tenable. While the derelictions of some union leaders and their reckless disregard for their responsibilities to the rank and file were publicly exposed and did shake the confidence of some union members in their elected officials, it is also evident that the malfeasances and misfeasances are confined to a very insignificant minority of union leaders.

When union leaders are questioned as to the cause, many point to the impact of the Landrum-Griffin Act. They allege that the control which they could exercise over dissident groups has been greatly weakened by the Act and that any attempt by the International to exercise sanctions, such as trusteeship and the like, are fraught with legal technicalities and the possibilities of damage suits under Section 301 of the Labor-Management Relations Act of 1947, as amended.

Failure of union leaders to evaluate properly the desires and aspirations of the rank and file members is also cited as a cause. For a long period of time, negotiators on both sides of the table have become so engrossed in the main issues that they have swept aside, without resolution, so-called peripheral local issues. They have often described these local issues as nuisances which could be withdrawn or submerged by the size of the economic pie being offered. What they apparently fail to realize is that a grievance (and many of the so-called local issues are really that),

which is not corrected, can fester and grow out of all proportion to the original complaint. Local issues are close
to the rank and file member. Generally, they involve his
day-to-day working relationship and are directly and personally related to him. Pensions and health and welfare improvements are appreciated by an employee but usually only
when circumstances compel him to resort to them. Normally
there is no immediacy to them. Violations, real or fancied, of his seniority rights, unsettled grievances, improper classifications, the over-aggressive foreman who
insists on a too rigid compliance with the labor agreement,
are problems which confront him daily. They are constant
irritants.

Another theory that has been advanced as a probable reason
for the high rate of rejections is the failure of labor
leaders to exercise the responsibility which enures to their
position as leaders. Those who espouse this theory state
that positions in International Unions have become so desirable both from a monetary and status viewpoint that the in-
cumbents have become too job-security conscious. They allege that the average labor leader will avoid a conflict
with local leaders or rank and file in order to assure his
political future, even though the local leadership or a particular rank and file group seek goals which may be detrimen-
tal to the economic existence of the industry or company
involved. It is much easier for such leaders to follow than
to take a strong position.

Some commentators in the academic field point to the upward
trend in the educational level of the average American worker which impels him to question more closely the judgment
of his representatives. The median educational level of
the American worker is 12.7 years of school. Completing
of high school is 12. Those who espouse this theory point
out that many times in the past, the rank and file member
might defer because of his lack of education to the recommendations of his local business representative or International officer. Now he feels that such representatives no
longer have a corner on wisdom--he feels they are at least
equals.

Another reason advanced for the high rate of rejections is
the unsatisfactory and inadequate communications. It is a
typical practice to keep the results of negotiations secret
until the union leader and the committee make their report
to the membership. As a result, there may be too great a

gap between the members' expectations and the final settlement. Somehow or other union leadership must bridge the
gap between publicly stated objectives and the settlement
and the vote on ratification. The period may be too short
if it provides an inadequate opportunity to persuade the
membership to accept; it may be too long if it permits intra-union politics to become operative.

Whether this phenomena can be attributed to one of these
causes or a combination of two or more could be the subject
of an interesting academic exercise. To the practitioner,
however, the more important consideration is what techniques
to employ to minimize the possibility of a rejection.

There are a number of techniques that can be suggested
which, if properly utilized in appropriate cases, can go
a long way toward narrowing the possibility of a rejection.

Union's Avoidance Of
Announced Fixed Goals

Generally speaking, experience has demonstrated that union
negotiators should avoid announcing a fixed bargaining goal
either before or during early negotiations. This is particularly true in the wage area. If the committee announces
a fixed wage increase goal, it may become a magic figure in
the minds of the rank and file. If negotiators produce a
smaller figure, the disappointment of the membership is
heightened, and the possibility of a rejection increased.

Many union negotiators are keenly aware of this danger.
They try to set a flexible goal, usually couched in terms
of a "substantial increase." This permits the committee
either to stress the magnitude of the wage increase obtained
or the size of the total package, whichever is greater, at
the membership meeting, and avoid the psychological block
of a fixed wage goal.

Greater Use of Subcommittees in Bargaining

The possibility of rejection can be minimized by greater
utilization of subcommittees in the bargaining process. All
too often one or two of the principals go off by themselves
and negotiate out the proposed agreement. In such situations, the balance of the committees usually sit in another
room doing nothing. If there is ever a situation which can
engender suspicion and distrust, this is certainly it.

Some may argue that this is not a very realistic approach. Any experienced negotiator knows progress cannot be made where there are large committees present, since everybody is talking for the record. They won't let their hair down and really come to grips with the problems raised in the negotiations.

I am not advocating the abolishment of this time-proven agreement-making device. In fact, experience is that the vast majority of contracts have been reached through such an approach.

The subcommittee approach is something over and beyond the top level off-record meeting. During the course of most negotiations, issues arise which can be more expeditiously handled by divorcing them from the main bargaining table and permitting a subcommittee to explore possible solutions. Seniority, insurance, pensions, and the like are usually fruitful issues for the subcommittee approach. Wages, vacations, holidays, and other like issues usually are not as susceptible to the subcommittee approach.

How can this device minimize the possibility of a rejection? It does so by assuring that each member of the negotiating committee participate in the structuring of the final settlement. It is only human for someone who has been singled out by his union brothers to want, to use the parlance of the day, "a piece of the action." If he is given the opportunity to become actively engaged in the across-the-table give and take, there is every assurance he will support the tentative agreement which is eventually arrived at by the parties.

Making Final Offer Contingent
On A Recommendation

In presenting a final offer, management representatives should make it contingent on a recommendation of acceptance. This normally involves the company final offer being put before the committee on a basis that it must be recommended by the committee unanimously or else there is no offer before it. All too often mediators have witnessed company representatives who have been deluded into thinking that, if an offer is brought before the membership on either a split committee recommendation or presented without recommendation for or against, it will be accepted by the membership.

Experience has taught us that acceptance under these circumstances is a rare and unusual occurrence and that the
possibilities of rejection are greatly increased when the
final offer is presented by a split committee or without
any recommendation whatsoever.

Converting Last Offer to Union Offer

Wherever possible, convert the employer's last offer to a
union offer. If negotiations can be so guided that the union negotiating committee is placed in the position of making
a final offer and the company accepting it, a deterrent to
a rejection can be provided. Under such circumstances, the
onus is on the union committee to persuade the membership to
buy the package since it was the union's package to which
the company acceded.

This technique can be more easily employed if the services
of a mediator are utilized. The mediator, having advanced
knowledge of the company's last offer, can, without disclos-
ing it, indicate to the union commiteee that if they recast
their demands in the framework of what he knows to be the
company's last offer, he will try to persuade the company
to accede to it.

Polling The Committee

Entire Union Committee Should Make Commitment

This problem arises when it becomes apparent that one or
more members of the union committee are political fence
straddlers. During the course of negotiations, they studi-
ously avoid vocalizing their feelings. When the committee
is planning its strategy, they neither agree nor disagree.
When a tentative agreement is reached, they are noncomittal.
When the membership meeting is called, they sniff the political winds. If they feel that ratification is doubtful,
they will loudly proclaim that they had nothing to do with
the tentative agreement; in fact, they were opposed to it.
If the membership appears to be satisfied with the terms
of the tentative agreement, they will insist that they were
the only members of the negotiating committee who were solely responsible for the "goodies" in the package.

There is an effective way of dealing with this situation.
Each and every member of the committee should be polled to
ascertain whether they will join with the others in recom-

mending the agreement. While this will not preclude individuals from taking a contrary position at the membership
meeting, it will make it more difficult for them to do so
and subject them to accusations of bad faith. At the very
least, they cannot state that they did not agree with the
settlement and had no part of it.

If it can be prearranged, the most desirable method is to
have the poll conducted by the union spokesman; however,
there appears to be no great obstacle to having the mediator or company representative doing it.

In conducting the poll, the union committee members who
have openly stated their support of the tentative agreement
should be polled first and those who the negotiators feel
are the "fence straddlers" last. If a majority of the committee have openly indicated their support, there is a
psychological pressure on the remaining members to join
with that majority.

Reduction Of Tentative Agreement to Writing

When oral agreement has been reached at the bargaining
table, it should if possible be reduced to writing. This
does not mean that it should be done with the drafting pre-
cision of final contract language, but it should outline
the general terms of understanding. After the agreement
has been drafted, each member of the union committee should
be requested to initial the instrument. In such as agreement there should be a sentence that the undersigned members of the union committee agree unanimously to recommend
acceptance. (Such agreements should, of course, provide
that they are being executed subject to ratification.)
Again, this device will minimize the possibilities of one
or two members of the committee denying before a membership
body that they have agreed to the tentative agreement.

Use of Press Statements

There are occasions when after an exhausting negotiating
session the parties have neither the patience nor the time
to await the reduction of the tentative agreement to writing. Under such circumstances, the parties should consider
the use of a joint press statement as a deterrent device to
a possible rejection.

While, normally,such a release would not disclose the precise terms of the tentative agreement, it would announce

the conclusion that a tentative agreement had been reached.
It then should be followed by a statement, if such was the
fact, that "the agreement will be unanimously recommended
by the union negotiating committee consisting of (names of
each member of the committee)." Any member of that committee who decides to backtrack would be embarrassed to do so
at the membership meeting.

Committee Authorized To Make Final Agreement

One of the often-heard suggestions is predicated on having
the union negotiating team fully authorized to conclude an
agreement, and thus obviating the necessity for a ratification meeting. The argument for this position is that, in
the normal case, the management team comes to the bargaining table fully authorized to make a binding agreement, and
its counterpart should have equal authority.

This suggestion presents several difficulties. First, in
many unions this flies in the teeth of union constitutions
and by-laws which spell out the requirement of a ratification meeting. Secondly, even in those cases where there is
no union constitutional prohibition, it will violate long-
established tradition, which would be destructive of the
bargaining relationship. Lastly, it will deny the sense
of participation by the rank and file in the decision-
making process and may very well lead to their dissatisfaction with the terms of the new contract.

Perhaps a more palatable approach would be to have an official grouping larger than the negotiating committee but
substantially smaller than the membership. This larger
group would ratify or reject, and no further membership
meeting would be required. This technique has been used
rather successfully in multi-plant and multi-company bargaining. Query: could it be adaptable to a one-plant or
one-company situation?

Contract Expiration Dates and Union Elections

Burton Zorn, who was one of the prominent employer attor-
neys, in a speech made at the Human Relations and Industry
Conference, suggested that "Employers should try to set
contract expiration dates (if other economic factors permit) at some reasonable time subsequent to the date of the
local union election. It is true that competing candidates
will out-promise each other, but this is a lesser evil than

an expiration date before a union election, when the opposition candidates just will not agree on a reasonable settlement, or will continue a strike until the election has been held." This idea has merit.

Mediator's Involvement In Ratification Process

Trade unions have been described as economic institutions operating in a political environment. Ratification meetings are an aspect of the latter. Such meetings as a political process have voting blocks, special interest groups, constituencies, and demogoguery, all of which contribute to an unfavorable climate for a dispassionate analysis and discussion of the terms of a proposed settlement.

For a long number of years, the Federal Mediation and Conciliation Service, as well as management, adopted the policy that the mechanics of the union ratification process were purely an internal union affair and consequently the Service should play a minimal role, if any.[1]

A trend toward a comparatively high incidence of rejections compelled the Service to reassess its position. Specifically, the Service urged its mediators to become more involved in the ratification process. Mediators were urged to counsel and advise union representatives in matters such as manner of presentation of a tentative agreement, the planning and conduct of the membership meeting, and the voting procedure to be utilized. Among the suggestions a mediator can present for consideration by the parties are the following:

1. Affirmative Presentation Of Tentative Agreement

The chairman and committee should make an affirmative presentation of the contractual gains, rather than emphasize that which could not be achieved at the bargaining table. All too often, mediators have witnessed equitable settlements rejected because of the inept presentation of the terms before the membership meeting by local officials. It weakens any presentation to remind the members of a bargaining goal which had to be compromised. In a word, there should be an accentuation of the positive.

In drafting or outlining the report to the membership, management representatives can be of material assistance to the

union officials charged with this responsibility. Employers
often have more sophisticated and extensive communication
techniques than those available to most local union leaders.
There is no reason why this employer expertise should not
be made available to the union leaders for use in "selling"
the tentative agreement.

2.   Advising Membership of Settlement Terms In Advance of Meeting

There are advantages and disadvantages in informing the union membership in advance of the meeting of the basic terms
of the tentative agreement.

The traditional practice has been not to disclose the terms
of the settlement prior to the membership meeting. There
have been two main reasons for the adoption of this procedure. First, it assures the maximum attendance at the membership meeting. People will be motivated to attend because
of a quite natural curiosity as to the nature of the new
benefits which they will receive under the new contract. A
prior disclosure destroys the motivation to attend by those
who are in basic agreement with the new contract and brings
to the meeting only those who are dissatisfied. Second,
non-disclosure prevents political opponents from disparag-
ing the terms of the new agreement and marshalling opposition to it.

In light of the complexity of some modern settlements, union representatives should perhaps reevaluate the traditional procedure. When settlements include items relating to
changes in wage structure, pensions, insurance, and health
and welfare benefits, it is difficult for the rank and file
member to digest the details in an oral presentation.

If it is decided to inform the membership of the terms of
the settlement before the ratification meeting, the better
practice is to provide each member with a summary or digest
of the gains made rather than presenting the members with
a copy of the proposed contract. The very bulk of the proposed contract may discourage members from reading it and
thus defeat the very purpose of the strategy of informing
the membership in advance of the ratification meeting.

In keeping with the necessity of an affirmative presentation,
it is suggested that the summary outline the prior contract

provision and immediately opposite it a recitation of the improvement achieved by the committee as a result of their efforts.

Type And Timing of Ratification Meeting

Value Of A Quick Meeting
Versus A Delayed Meeting

Whether the union should schedule a membership meeting promptly after the tentative agreement or delay doing so is a matter which deserves more careful consideration than is normally given to it.

A quick meeting often has value in that it prevents distorted versions of the tentative agreement from running rampant among the rank and file. All too often, despite a pledge of secrecy, when there is a delay, bits and pieces of the final package leak out and the dissident group can capitalize on the information.

In some cases, however, a quick membership meeting may not be desirable. This is particularly true when the union officers need time properly to organize the material and strategy for the meeting. This situation may well arise when opposition by a dissident group is anticipated.

Stop-Work Versus Off-Premises Meeting

One of the bitterest complaints mediators often hear from union representatives is the lack of attendance at ratification meetings. The apathy of the average union member in union affairs often creates the climate conducive to a domination of the meeting by dissident elements.

The primary object of a union membership meeting, including the ratification meeting, is to assure the maximum attendance and, ideally, participation of a substantial majority of the members. It is only when there is such attendance that the actions taken can truly be said to reflect the desires of the employees in the bargaining unit.

A stop-work meeting is one conducted during the normal work hours on or adjacent to the plant affected. These are normally held at the beginning or end of a shift. The holding of a stop-work ratification meeting has proved to be quite effective in foreclosing the possibility of rejection by a

minority since it assures maximum attendance. The objections to such a meeting are that it disrupts production and
may create the impression of company domination of the union. Assuming that the union has operated through the contract year as an aggressive representative of the employees,
the latter objection appears to have little validity. While
the fact that a stop-work meeting does interrupt production
cannot be denied, the consideration should be the weighing
of the loss of a few hours against the possibility of a complete shutdown if the tentative agreement is rejected.

The stop-work meeting in some cases does have the disadvantage in that it may not give the union officials the opportunity to create the proper climate for acceptance. However,
stop-work meetings are deserving of serious consideration,
as is true of all the suggestions made in this chapter, only
if there is a possibility of a rejection.

In considering the place of the ratification meeting, union
representatives should be alert to the proximity of a bar
or cocktail lounge. If one is at or close, some members
may stop there on the way to the meeting. Unfortunately,
a few drinks in some individuals give them a false sense
of courage and often belligerency, which can be disruptive
of the meeting.

To every rule there seems to be an exception. In one case,
a round of beer precipitated a settlement. Traditionally,
when a tentative agreement was reached, the company representatives, who always conducted negotiations at a hotel,
always ordered a round of beer for all participants. On
this occasion, after the chairman of the union committee
had indicated that the company's last offer was acceptable,
the company ordered up a round of beer. While awaiting the
advent of the beer, two union committeemen resurrected several demands that the company had been led to believe had
been withdrawn. In the midst of the acrimonious exchanges
that followed, the beer arrived. The company chairman told
the bellboy to take it back. Immediately, the two committeemen protested and demanded that the beer be brought back
since they were dropping their objections to the settlement.

Pre-Vote Meeting

Where there is an organized dissident group, the ratification meeting may be a stormy one. Those opposed to the
tentative agreement are usually vociferous in highlighting

its deficiencies. Their technique is one of disruption.
They will often shout down the report of the negotiating
committee and effectively block any attempt to have either
a secret ballot or show of hand vote, in favor of a voice
vote. Those who would vote to ratify the settlement are
often intimidated by these tactics. Often those in favor
will remain silent or else be carried away by the loudness
of the protest, hesitating to oppose it lest they be deemed
weaklings. There is a human tendency to demonstrate that
one is as "tough" as his fellowman.

A technique adopted by several unions is to have a reporting
meeting on one day, followed by a secret ballot vote a day
or two later. This has proven to be quite successful in a
number of cases. Under this approach, a membership meeting
is called at which the union negotiating committee presents
the terms of the proposed settlement. The committee gives
a detailed explanation and then the proposal is open for
floor discussion. No matter what the membership's oral reaction is, no vote is taken at this meeting. On the following or within a very few days thereafter, a secret ballot
vote is conducted to determine acceptance or rejection.

The basic value of this technique is that it provides the
opportunity for the dissident group to shout and rant without permitting its outcries to affect the judgment of those
who would vote approval of the settlement. It tends to
foreclose the possibility of emotions supplanting reasoning
and assures that the decision of the membership will be free
of the coercive effect of the pressures exerted by the vocal minority.

Time And Place Of Ratification Meeting

The time and place of the ratification meeting are often
quite important in dealing with the problem of rejections.
The probability of an acceptance is enhanced if maximum
membership attendance can be achieved.

In our modern society, there is no longer a void in leisure
time entertainment. Television, plays, motion pictures,
sporting events, family outings, and the like are so readily
available that the interest in attending union meetings has
diminished sharply. The scheduling of a membership meeting
on a pay day or on an extended weekend should be avoided.
Similarly, scheduling a meeting for a time which conflicts
with a broadcast of a major sporting event cuts down on anticipated attendance.

If meetings are scheduled at such times, the dissidents will attend while those who might have supported the recommendations absent themselves and a rejection which could have been avoided may take place.

The selection of a meeting site also plays a part. If the meeting place is not readily accessible or is too small to accommodate the expected attendance, problems will be created which could discourage maximum attendance. If the acoustics in the meeting hall are marginal, arrangements for amplification should be made so that the report of the Chairman of the Negotiating Committee will be heard clearly throughout the hall.

Attendance of Union International Representative

Often, even though the Union International Representative has been involved in the negotiations, the demands on his time will induce him to leave the scene once a tentative agreement has been reached. In some cases, the presence of the International Representatives at the membership meeting may be highly desirable.

The International Representative is at least one step removed from the interplay of local union politics. His economic future is not normally dependent on the goodwill of a particular rank and file local membership. As a consequence, he is able to advocate a position before the membership which would be fraught with political pitfalls if assumed by a local union officer.

Further, the International Representative has a much broader exposure to collective bargaining trends and settlements than the local officers. He is in a much better position to counsel and advise the membership and appraise the fairness and comparability of the settlement terms with those achieved in other area or industry negotiations.

If there is a possibility of a rejection, the International Representative should be urged to attend the membership meeting so that at least by his physical presence he can support the recommendations of the bargaining committee. If for some reason, the International Representative is reluctant to attend the meeting, the mediator should enlist the support of his supervisor. Quite often a telephone call by the mediator's supervisor to the International President of the Union will overcome the hesitancy. However, this call should not be made by the mediator, especially if he expects to have occasion to work with the representative in the future.

There are, however, some cases where the presence of the International Representative at the membership meeting would be a hindrance to ratification. These cases are those in which there is a strong feeling of autonomy on the part of the local. In such cases the local wants to reach its own decisions without any alleged interference by "outsiders." Mediators know of some cases where locals have warned International Representatives to stay away from the bargaining table. Indeed, there are cases where the International Representative has been told to leave town.

Obviously in these types of cases, the International Representative's presence at the meeting would only enhance the chances of a rejection.

Type of Vote

Many persons who should have some expertise in the field of collective bargaining have long harbored the notion that ratification meetings and the type of membership vote required are mandated by the provisions of union constitutions. A study conducted by Herbert J. Lahne of the United States Department of Labor has proven that the assumption is unwarranted.[2] The vast majority of union constitutions make no specific provision for the type of vote required to approve a tentative agreement. Indeed in most constitutions there is no provision making even the ratification meeting necessary.

On the other hand, despite the absence of constitutional requirements, local unions have adopted practices concerning ratification meetings and types of vote necessary to approve an agreement which have become, because of the passage of time, unwritten law.

While the necessity for conducting a ratification meeting has a bearing on the problem, the type of membership vote has more relevancy. In most cases, a secret ballot vote is more valuable than a voice or show of hands vote. As mentioned above, a militant organized minority can dominate a meeting by heckling and shouting. Often, unfortunately, the average union member hesitates to give voice to his

disapproval of such tactics. As a result, the loudness of
the "no" vote offsets the weaker "yes" response. Under such
circumstances, a secret ballot vote would be a fairer approach to ascertaining the true desires of the membership.

A few unions traditionally have ratification votes by referendum. A number of other unions are experimenting with this
approach as an answer to the rejection problem. Certainly,
it has the advantage of secrecy. It also provides the member time to evaluate the settlement proposal dispassionately.
The disadvantage is the time lag necessary for the mechanics
of checking names and addresses against union records, mailing, return of ballots, examination of ballots which may be
subject to subsequent challenge, and sorting. This time
factor is particularly critical in those cases involving
multi-plant negotiation and a geographical spread of union
members.

Despite these handicaps, if a secret ballot is not possible
or desirable, the feasibility of a referendum ballot is
worth exploring.

NOTES

1. cf Chapter XXI, <u>Pitfalls and Cautions for Media-tors</u>.

2. Herbert J. Lahne, <u>Union Constitutions and Collective Bargaining Procedures</u>.

CHAPTER XXIV
EVE OF STRIKE AND STRIKE SITUATIONS

Necessity For Meeting On Deadline Date

There is little, if any, excuse to justify a mediator's
failure to schedule a meeting on the deadline date. (The
deadline date is the date on which the collective bargaining agreement is due to expire and/or the date on which the
union indicates an intention to strike if agreement is not
reached.) Everything is riding in favor of the mediator.
The economic pressures reach a crescendo on that day. The
moment of truth has arrived for both parties.

The union representatives have to face up to a number of
potential problems arising out of a strike situation. If
they call the strike, will all the unit employees respond
or will many continue to work crossing the picket line and
thus weaken, if not destroy, the solidarity needed for vic-
tory? How much financial support will be available from
other unions? From the International? Will other intra-
plant and outside unions respect the picket line? If the
strike is prolonged will the economic pinch on the workers
cause a return to work movement? Will the strike be effective or will the union representatives have to follow the
workers into the plant instead of leading them back to work?
Is the difference between the union's declared minimum pos-
tion and the company's offer worth the risks inherent in a
strike?

So, too, the company must seriously consider the potential
impact of a stoppage on its relations with its customers
and employees. Is the inventory large enough to anticipate
all customer requirements if there is a prolonged stoppage?
Will the company's customers remain loyal and agree to a
delay in getting their orders or will they seek what they
need from competitive companies? Is the company's credit
and cash position sound enough to meet its financial obligations despite the loss of income? Is the cost difference
between the two positions worth the potential loss due to
the interruption of production?

Mediators, by scheduling a meeting on the deadline date,
can take full advantage of the presence of these pressures
to effectuate a settlement of the dispute.

Some mediators may conclude, from the wide differences between the parties, that a strike is inevitable and not schedule a meeting on the expiration date. Even though there are cases where despite all efforts of the mediator a stoppage takes place, for a mediator to surrender to the apparent inevitability is to adopt a defeatist attitude which is the very antithesis of what a mediator's philosophy ought to be.

Even though one or both parties, being resigned to the inevitability of a strike, resist a deadline date meeting on the ground that they need the time for strike preparations, nevertheless, the mediator should insist that the meeting take place. Being conscious of their public relations position, the parties invariably attend despite their protestations.

Postponing Strike

Even though the parties seem too far apart for agreement, there are a number of devices which are available to the mediator designed to avoid or at least postpone the threatened stoppage. Postponing a threatened stoppage dissipates the strike fever which has been built up and buys time for the mediator to more fully explore alternatives in a calmer atmoshpere.

Extensions

One of the several devices for postponing a threatened strike is a request for an extension of the expiring collective bargaining contract. There are several types of extensions.

a. Fixed Term

This usually takes the form of extending all the terms and conditions of the expiring contract for a fixed period of time; e.g., 10, 20, or 30 days. A fixed term extension has both advantages and disadvantages to the parties. The company is assured of no disruption of production during the period and it presents an opportunity to plan for an orderly shutdown during the extended period.

If the union's strike threat was pure negotiating strategy, it can save face by reluctantly agreeing to the requested extension. Further, the membership will "cool off" and give their negotiating team more time to find accommodations on the still unresolved issues.

The disadvantage is that the parties, being relieved of the pressure of an immediate deadline, instead of intensifying their efforts to reach agreement, tend to relax until the eve of the expiration of the extension period. In effect, the crisis of a new deadline has been established.

b. Day-To-Day With Notice

A day-to-day extension with notice provides that the expiring contract be deemed extended unless and until either party gives X number of hours or days notice that it desires to terminate the extension.

This has a limited advantage to the company in that it will not be faced with an immediate stoppage and thus have an opportunity to prepare for an orderly shutdown. While the union, by agreeing to this type of extension, risks the loss of the strike momentum it has built up in the membership, it has the advantage of buying time for the resolution of the remaining issues.

c. Day-To-Day Without Notice

This is usually termed "stopping the clock." In this type of extension, the parties agree that as long as progress is being made in the negotiations, the terms and conditions of the expiring contract would be deemed extended.

The advantage to the company is that is gives it a little breathing space for a continuation of its efforts to reach agreement. The disadvantage is that a veritable sword of Damocles is hanging over its head. The advantage to the union is that it keeps the pressure on the company to make further concessions to avoid a possible walkout without the necessity for the union to issue an immediate strike call.

This type of extension is normally suggested by the mediator when, in his judgment, a settlement is imminently possible but the time remaining is too short for its effectuation.

There was at least one case where the mediator almost regretted suggesting a "stop the clock" extension. A number of years ago, the Teamsters threatened to shut down milk suppliers in Metropolitan New York. The mass media predicted dire consequences to the health of infants in the area. The City Fathers hastily passed resolutions decrying

the threatened stoppage and started emergency planning to
assure milk supplies to hospitals. The mediator detected
a split in the ranks of the members of the industry association. The larger companies appeared ready to accede to the
union's request for a pension plan while the smaller companies opposed it. He extracted a promise from the Teamsters that, as long as he kept round-the-clock negotiations
going, there would be no strike. Seventy-two hours later,
the press announcement of the settlement was accompanied by
a front page picture of the exhausted mediator seated next
to a two-foot stack of empty coffee cups.

Which of the foregoing types of an extension should be suggested by the mediator is a matter of his judgment based on
his appraisal of the status of the negotiations and his
knowledge of the prior practice of the parties.

There are a number of approaches which a mediator can utilize which may assist him in persuading the parties to grant
an extension:

(a)   If the mediator has been called into the negotiations
      at the very last moment, he can urge the parties that,
      in all fairness, he needs more time to see if he can
      help them reach agreement.

(b)   Obtain a commitment from the company on retroactivity
      as a quid pro quo for the extension.

(c)   Request the need for more time so that he can arrange
      to have another mediator join with him--using the old
      cliche "two heads are better than one."

(d)   Request more time to enable him to move the situs of
      negotiations to the main mediation office. In the
      Federal service, either the regional or national of-
      fice. This is often triggered by a prearranged wire
      to both parties from the head of the mediation agency
      or some other responsible public official such as a
      mayor or governor.

(e)   Attempt to get some movement, no matter how slight, on
      some key issue to demonstrate the hope of progress if
      more time was made available.

(f)   If no staff or International Union Representative is
      at the bargaining table, request the International to

request an extension in order to enable one to join
in the negotiations. This has a greater chance of
success if a commitment is obtained from the company
that if such International Representative is made
available, a representative from a higher echelon
of management would also be available.

One word of caution in the wording of any extension request.
Use of the term "status quo" in an extension request may be
dangerous. This is particularly true where there has been
some hiatus in the term of the contract. For example, a
contract containing maintenance of membership expires. The
parties continue to negotiate for a few days. During this
period, a number of employees escape from the union. A
strike is then threatened and the mediator requests the union to maintain the "status quo." Does the maintenance of
the "status quo" carry forward union security provisions of
the old contract so as to nullify the escape of the employees who chose to do so?

Alternatives To Strike

We have been exploring the "buying of time" through the device of an extension in order to enable the mediator to continue his efforts to assist the parties to reach agreement.
If the mediator believes that no extension is possible or
that even if a short extension were granted the parties
would not be able to reach agreement, the mediator in the
Federal service has a statutory duty to suggest alternate
means of resolving the dispute. These alternate means are
last offer ballot, arbitration, and fact-finding.

Section 203(c) of the Labor-Management Relations Act, as
amended, provides:

> "If the Director is not able to bring the parties
> to agreement by conciliation within a reasonable
> time, he shall seek to induce the parties volun-
> tarily to seek other means of settling the dis-
> pute without resort to strike, lock-out, or other
> coercion, including submission to the employees
> in the bargaining unit of the employer's last
> offer of settlement for approval or rejection in
> a secret ballot. The failure or refusal of either
> party to agree to any procedure suggested by the
> Director shall not be deemed a violation of any
> duty or obligation imposed by this Act."

Last Offer Ballot

Some management representatives will insist that a Federal
mediator compel the union to "comply with the law" and submit the company's last offer to secret ballot vote by the
union membership. This insistence, apart from its wisdom
as good bargaining strategy, is often based on a misconcep-
tion of the law.

As indicated by the quoted statutory language, the mediator,
as a representative of the Director of the Service, has the
duty to induce the parties to seek methods other than mediation of settling the dispute but--

(a)   the method suggested must be voluntarily accepted by
      the parties;

(b)   if either or both fail or refuse to accept such pro-
      cedure, they cannot be charged with any violation of
      the Act.

If the suggested procedure is the submission of the last
offer to a secret ballot, the first difficulty is that the
union is free to accept or reject it and there are no legal
sanctions which could compel acceptance of the suggestion.

The decision as to acceptance or rejection of the last offer ballot procedure by a union representative is based
often on very practical considerations. Bear in mind that
the suggestion would only be made after the union representative and the negotiating committee have rejected the employer's last offer as being unresponsive to the demands
of the union membership. The judgment of the union negotiators as to the acceptability of the last offer may or may
not have solid foundation in fact. The important thing is
that the union negotiators have taken a position before the
company negotiators. If they feel that the offer has any
possibility of being accepted, they will not agree to submit it since they would be placed in a poor light in future
negotiations because of the doubt as to whether they are
truly reflective of the desires of the membership. If the
union negotiators feel that the offer will be rejected,
then they may readily agree. A rejection will strengthen
their bargaining position and if the employer desires a
prompt settlement he must start from the plateau of his
last offer and substantially improve it.

There are further difficulties. The statute makes no provision for a neutral supervision of the conduct and count of
the secret ballot. The union is well within its statutory
rights to insist that it and it alone will arrange, conduct,
and count the balloting.

It is interesting to note that if the last offer ballot procedure is suggested, a union may impose conditions which
would make a company hastily reconsider its insistence on
it. In a recent dispute involving one of the major manufacturing companies in the nation, the company urged the
union to submit its last offer to the membership on the
ground that it felt reasonably certain that its employees
would recognize the soundness and fairness of its offer and
accept it overwhelmingly. The union stated that it was perfectly willing to do so--in fact would even consent to have
an outside agency supervise and conduct the secret ballot
and it would abide by the result. It stated, however, that
since the company's suggestion called into question whether
the union was faithfully mirroring the desires of the employees, the ballot should also include the union's last
demands so that the employees could choose between both.
Of course, the union stated, it would expect the company
to agree that it also would be bound by the results of the
balloting. The company reconsidered its request.

There is difficulty, too, as to what is a final offer. If
final refers to point of time, there is no problem. However, if final connotes an end position, the concept becomes fluid. What may be a final offer at one point of
negotiations may become merely a preliminary or intermediate offer later as the exigencies of the bargaining change.

Arbitration - Fact-Finding - Public Relations Problems

On the eve of an inevitable strike, the mediator should be
particularly sensitive to the attempts by each party to
embark on the strike in the most favorable public relations
position.

Apart from public appeals through the press, the parties
may suggest procedures for the settlement of the dispute
even though they know in advance of the suggestions that
they are unacceptable to the other party. In most cases,
these suggested procedures, such as arbitration, fact-
finding, and the like, are advanced solely for public
relations reasons.

The mediator is faced with a problem when one of the parties
requests that he be the vehicle of transmission. While he
certainly has a duty to induce the parties to voluntarily
seek other means of settling the dispute without resort to
strike or lock-out, and such "other means" encompasses arbitration and fact-finding, he may become the unwitting tool
of one of the parties and thereby destroy his future effectiveness. It is not the mediator's function to enhance the
public relations position of one party at the expense of the
other.

The better mediation practice would appear to be for the
mediator, in response to his statutory duty, to explore the
alternate procedures with each party separately to see if
they present any hope of achievement. This practice will
disclose the practicality or futility of urging their adoption at a joint meeting. If one of the parties insists
that it be broached at a joint meeting, the counsel of wisdom dictates that the mediator, in turn, insist that the
moving party make it his offer and present it directly at
the joint bargaining session.

There is, of course, the larger question as to the efficacy
of the force of public opinion in the average labor dispute.
Whether, in such cases, the efforts to marshall public opinion into fruitful and persuasive channels are worthwhile,
can be the subject of a rather extensive research project.

Timing Request For Extension Or
Suggesting Alternates To Strike

When the mediator should advance his request for an extension or his suggestion for an alternate to the strike, is
often a delicate and crucial question on the eve of the
threatened strike. If the request is made too early, the
mediator loses the advantage of the build-up of the political and economic pressures on the eve of the stoppage which
compel the parties to face up to the reality of the situation. If he delays too long, he may find that strike preparations have gone too far to abort the walkout.

While the timing of a request for an extension is a matter
of the judgment of the mediator, most experienced mediators
prefer to gamble against the possibility that strike preparations cannot be reversed. They will withhold their request until they are persuaded that the deadline pressures
are insufficient to achieve agreement in the time remaining.

They feel that if they approach the union at the start of
the deadline date meeting for an extension and it and, subsequently, the company accept, both parties will relax their
efforts to seek alternatives or accommodations to the issues
remaining in dispute. Most persons shy away from facing up
to a hard decision as long as it does not have to be made
until some time in the future.

Frequency Of Meetings During Strike

There are two theories on the frequency of mediation meetings after a strike has been called:

     A. Let it run awhile - Most effective mediation can
be accomplished where the parties have felt the economic
pinch of a strike (loss of a paycheck or potential loss of
customers). Parties will then be conditioned to be more
receptive to a mediator's suggestion.

     B. Problems created or growing out of a strike in-
crease with the time lapse and often overshadow the issues
which caused the strike.   Therefore, mediation efforts
should be intensified as soon as a strike is called.

The second theory is the one experience has proven to be
the sounder approach. Some of the problems arising out of
a strike are related to replacements, picket line violence,
and strike settlement provisions.

The problem of replacements is particularly highlighted in
times of a surplus labor market. It is often one of the
main causes of a protracted strike. If the strike was
caused by the unfair labor practice of the employer, this
is not an issue. If, however, the strike is an economic
one, the problem, in most cases, can be acute.

In many cases, by hiring replacements, companies can achieve
75% to 80% of their pre-strike production. In such situations, companies have promised the replacements permanent
jobs and will resist any attempt by the union to have the
replacements discharged to make room for returning strikers.

Often, despite the admonitions of their union representative,
tempers flare on the picket line. This is particularly true
when either some employees who have abandoned the strike or
replacements attempt to cross the picket line. Strikers,
feeling that their jobs are being threatened, will do every-

thing possible to discourage those crossing their lines and attempting to enter the plant. Injuries and arrests may follow. As a result, the company may insist that it will not rehire any employees who engaged in such activities. The union may argue that the situation was deliberately created by the company by attempting to operate by hiring replacements to break the strike. This issue, which did not exist prior to the strike, may become one of the main stumbling blocks to agreement if the strike is prolonged.

Mediators, in prolonged strikes, have witnessed situations where the issues which caused the strike are settled but a return to work is delayed because of quarrels over the provisions of a strike settlement agreement. A few of these problems are:

If one party has filed unfair labor practice charges with the National Labor Relations Board, should the settlement be conditioned on the withdrawal of such charges?

Should the time of the strike be counted as time worked for vacation purposes?

Should the time of the strike be counted as time worked for retirement credits?

To what extent does an agreement that there be no reprisals inhibit a union from disciplining one of its members for his activities during a strike?

On return to work, should it be staggered, all back at the same time; if staggered, any time limitation on the company?

If the company has advanced insurance premiums during the strike, should the strike settlement agreement spell out methods of employees reimbursing the company?

There is a larger question as to whether a strike settlement agreement, even though physically separated from the collective bargaining contract, is a part of it and a condition to the validity of the main contract.

CHAPTER XXV
GRIEVANCE MEDIATION

There have been questions raised as to whether a mediation step could or should be included in a collective bargaining agreement as either the step prior to arbitration or in lieu of arbitration in the grievance procedure. A number of contracts contain such provisions.

An examination of State mediation acts fails to disclose any expressed statutory prohibition on State mediators serving grievance disputes. As far as the Federal service is concerned, prior to the passage of the Labor-Management Relations Act, there were no limitations on providing mediation assistance in grievance disputes.

Since arbitration as the terminal point of the grievance procedure had not attained its present-day acceptability, mediation was often found to be an acceptable alternative. In other contracts, provision was made for the intercession of a mediator prior to the submission of the dispute to arbitration.

Federal mediators, then associated with the United States Conciliation Service, in many cases encouraged the parties to include such provisions in their collective bargaining contracts and serviced them if requested to do so. The experience was uniformly good. However, with the passage of the Labor-Management Relations Act limitations were placed on the Federal service. Section 203(c) of that Act provides:

> "Final adjustment by a method agreed upon by the
> parties is hereby declared to be the desirable
> method for the settlement of grievance disputes
> arising over the application or interpretation
> of an existing collective bargaining agreement.
> The Service is directed to make its conciliation
> and mediation service available in the settlement
> of such grievance disputes only as a last resort
> and in exceptional cases."

Apart from the grumblings of one senator, that the foregoing provisions tended to shackle the Director is his mediation

efforts, the legislative history of the Act fails to shed
light on the reasons for the limitations.

The Director of the newly established Federal Mediation and
Conciliation Service, Cyrus Ching, was faced with the problem of translating the legislative direction into workable
internal policy. One of the dilemmas was the apparent contradiction in the statutory language. Section 203(c) states
that the method agreed upon by the parties for the disposition of grievances is the desirable method. Assuming that
the parties during the course of their negotiations decided
that mediation should be utilized either as a step before
or in lieu of arbitration, could the Service refuse to honor
it? Further, did the second sentence, which clearly prohib-
its the Director from interceding in grievance disputes unless it was an exceptional case or a last resort, grant him
authority to withhold mediation services despite the parties' contractual agreement?

Another problem was whether existing contracts which provided for mediation should be honored, and what would be
the Service policy with respect to future contracts.

Finally, the terms "exceptional" and "last resort" had to
be defined.

Motivated in a large measure by limitations of budget and
manpower, the Federal service adopted policies and procedures designed to carry forward the Congressional mandate.
In essence, these policies and procedures provide that when
a request is received for mediation assistance in a grievance dispute, a determination is first made by the Regional
Director as to whether the dispute falls into the category
of an exceptional or last resort case. If it does not, the
Service assigns a mediator to the case for certain limited
purposes. The mediator so assigned will normally urge the
parties to utilize the grievance or arbitration procedures
of their collective bargaining contract. If their contract
does not provide adequate procedures, he will assist the
parties in structuring a procedure for the purpose of settling the immediate issue in dispute. He will endeavor to
avoid discussion of the merits of the grievance and concentrate instead on a method of adjustment. If the grievance
falls into the category of exceptional or last resort, the
mediator will be instructed to address himself to the merits of the particular grievance and assist the parties to
resolve it.

Further, mediators were instructed to discourage parties
from inserting into their contracts provisions for mediation as part of the grievance procedure.

In 1982, the Federal Mediation and Conciliation Service further clarified its position with respect to the mediation
of grievance disputes. It refined its interpretation of
Section 203(d). If no adequate facility or proceudre is
available which can prevent a disruption of production, it
may offer mediation assistance if the dispute is of special
importance because of its impact on Government contracts,
defense production, inter-State commerce, or the general
health, safety and welfare of the community or public either
locally or nationally.

The internal procedures remained essentially the same as
when first interpreted by the Service in 1947 in that the
ultimate decision of whether a dispute meets the criteria
of "exceptional" and "last resort" was formerly vested in
the Assistant Regional Director but now in the District
Director.

While any other approach from the standpoint of administration of the policy appears to be impracticable, experience
has indicated that the then Regional Directors or now District Directors have narrowed or expanded the interpretation of "exceptional" and "last resort" in direct proportion
to the size of the plant involved, the mediators' caseloads,
and the pressures the parties could generate on the decision
maker.

There are some who would quarrel with the Federal Mediation
and Conciliation Service's interpretation of the statutory
provision. They claim that the 1947 interpretation was
largely based on a feeling that any other approach would
trigger off demands for mediation assistance which would
seriously strain or exceed its available manpower. The fear
was not based on experience but on guesswork as to the probable impact of a contrary interpretation.

These students of labor relations urge that it is just as
logical to give prime consideration to the first sentence
of the Section as the second. They argue that mediation
assistance should be provided where the parties have voluntarily embodied a provision in their collective bargaining
contract evoking mediation as the step before the submission of the dispute to arbitration. If that is the method

agreed upon by the parties, is there not a quasi legislative mandate on the Service to assist in this "desirable method" of settling grievances?

There appears to be some validity to these arguments. There are many grievances which if exposed to the mediation process can be adjusted. Prior to the entrance of the mediator, the parties have been exposed merely to adversarial reactions to the resolution of the grievance. The impact of the intercession and opinion of the neutral will, as so often happens in other dispute cases, cast new light on the problem and point to alternatives which both parties are seeking.

Professors Goldberg and Brett, of Northwestern University, experiments in the bituminous coal mining industry have demonstrated that grievance mediation can be a successful tool for the resolution of grievance disputes. They used three different procedures: (a) mutual consent--grievances mediated only if both parties agree, (b) demand of one party sufficient to trigger mediation of the grievance, and (c) "everything goes"--unless excluded by mutual consent, all grievances are submitted to mediation. One hundred and fifty three grievances were mediated during the experimental period. Of these, 135 were resolved without resort to arbitration--or 89%.[1]

As Eva Robbins, in speaking of grievance mediation, stated in her excellent "Guide for Labor Mediators":

> "It offers, as does preventive mediation, the
> opportunity to correct situations in the admin-
> istration of the collective bargaining agreement
> not contemplated by the parties when they nego-
> tiated the agreement, without destroying it."

Professor Mollie Bowers, in Volume 3 of the Federal Service Labor Relations Review, echoed Eva Robbins' statement, stating:

> "The attributes of grievance mediation...are
> its effectiveness in achieving settlements and
> the cost and time that can be saved if a resolu-
> tion is reached without resorting to arbitration."

William Simkin, former Director of the Federal Mediation and Conciliation Service, in his book Mediation and Dynamics

Of Collective Bargaining (p. 300) acknowledges that mediation may be one of the productive arrangements that can help
reduce growing dissatisfaction with grievance arbitration.

Some of the statutes relating to the public sector make
provision for mediation assistance before either arbitration or fact-finding, especially in interest disputes. The
experience, on the whole, under such provisions has been
uniformly good. Whenever the entire dispute has not been
adjusted through mediation, mediation has succeeded in substantially narrowing the issues to be submitted to the
final step.

With the increased criticism of the expense and delays of
arbitration, a number of commentators have urged a wider
acceptance of the concept of grievance mediation. They insist that it has a greater chance for resolving conflicts
than arbitration since the parties are more flexible than
when they are committed to arbitration.

Certainly the concept of mediation of grievances before
arbitration is worthy of further experimentation.

Grievance Mediation and Arbitration

In the field of arbitration, Sam Kagel, a most distinguished arbitrator, was one of the pioneers of the concept of
"med-arb." Under the med-arb approach the parties select
a neutral and empower him to first utilize mediation techniques to resolve some or all of the issues and, if necessary, act as arbitrator for all issues not resolved through
his mediation efforts.

Unlike mediation where the fairness of the final agreement
is the responsibility of the parties, in med-arb the neutral must consider the fairness of the final result. The
one big advantage of med-arb is that through his mediation
efforts, the neutral can explore the true aims of the parties and thus be able to fashion an award which is realistic and liveable.

A few arbitrators, particularly those with mediation experience, without labeling it as a med-arb approach, have
informally explored the possibility of a mediated solution
prior to arbitration. If there is an objection to this
approach or if tried and failed, the arbitrator then proceeds to arbitrate the grievance.

One of the criticisms of the med-arb approach in grievance
cases is that if the same individual acts as mediator and
arbitrator, he may run the risk of destroying his neutrality. If, as in a formal med-arb procedure, it is founded
on the agreement of the parties, there can be no danger of
lost acceptability. If it is an informal approach, then
the risk is in direct proportion to the skill of the individual.

One of the variations of this technique has been the media-
tion-fact-finding approach through a tripartite device. The
"neutral" or "public member" during executive sessions can
indicate to the "advocate" members of the panel some of his
preliminary reactions to the unresolved issues and then
having the advocate seek to induce his own party to find
solutions within the peripheries outined by the neutral.

This technique has led to mediated solutions in many cases.
In others it has led to a substantial narrowing of the issues so that very few issues remain for fact-finding. Not
having been placed in a position of advocate, the third party has maintained his neutrality and is in an excellent position to find the facts.

Once we accept the concept that fact-finding, arbitration,
and mediation are not mutually exclusionary terms but complement each other, then there is no limitation on variations which can be adopted. Mentioning but one--fact-find-
ing to precede mediation. Under this approach, a fact-finder can delineate the problems and make findings of fact on
the unresolved issues. The mediator can then intercede and
assist the parties to reach agreement within the peripheries
of the findings. An analysis of the old Steelworkers Human
Relations Committee approach indicates that one of its main
thrusts was to do exactly that through the collective bargaining process rather than mediation.

NOTES

1. Proceedings of the Thirty Fifth Annual Meeting of the Industrial Relations Research Association, p. 256.

CHAPTER XXVI

RELATIONS WITH PRESS— PUBLIC OFFICIALS
CITIZENS COMMITTEES

Announcing Tentative Agreements

While management negotiators are presumed to have full
authority to conclude an agreement, in the average case,
the union committee must bring any tentative settlement
to the membership for ratification. Sometimes, the ratification can be accomplished by a vote of an executive
board or council.

When the tentative agreement has been reached, it is quite
important that the terms of the settlement not be disclosed
until it is presented by the union negotiating committee to
the membership at a ratification meeting. Premature disclosure in many cases can bring about a rejection of the
settlement. Those satisfied with the agreement will feel
that there is no necessity to attend the meeting and absent
themselves, while those opposed will attend and vote against
it.

To guard against premature disclosure, when the tentative
agreement has been reached, the parties usually agree that
the only public statement be made by the mediator. In making the public announcement, the mediator must be careful
not to disclose the terms. Further, the mediator must always be conscious of his subordinate role when a settlement
is reached. The parties must get the credit for settling
the dispute--not the mediator. The mediator's announcement
may be somewhat as follows:

> "I am pleased to announce that a tentative agree-
> ment on all the outstanding issues in dispute has
> been reached. The parties have agreed not to dis-
> close the terms of the settlement pending the un-
> ion committee's report to the membership at a
> ratification meeting to be held on_____at_____.
> Both parties are to be congratulated for their un-
> tiring efforts to reach this agreement. Both put
> aside their self interests for the welfare of the
> employees and the community. The management nego-
> tiating team was headed by Mr._____.

Mr._____was the chairman of the union
negotiating team. He was assisted by Business
Representative Mr._____."

News Blackout

If a dispute, especially if it involves a protracted strike,
becomes of public concern because of its impact on the economy of a community, the local and, in some cases, the national media will cover the story.

Experience has taught that if the parties freely use the
media to castigate each other for the lack of progress in
the negotiations, the task of the mediator becomes exceed-
ingly difficult. In these situations, the parties are more
interested in protecting their public image by charges and
countercharges than resolving the issues in dispute. Under
these circumstances, the mediator should point out to the
parties the self-defeating aspects of bargaining through
the media and urge them to agree to a news blackout. Under
this arrangement, the parties agree that the only public
statements about the negotiations will be made by the mediator. Further, each party agrees that if one party desires
to be relieved of the blackout agreement, it would advise
the mediator and the other party of its intent before making any press statement.

If the parties accept the mediator's suggestion, the mediator, before the conclusion of each meeting, should write
out the statement he intends to make and clear it with both
parties jointly before meeting with the representatives of
the media. Such statements need not be too specific but
convey the impression of continuing efforts being made by
the parties in trying to resolve the dispute. In meeting
with the press, the mediator should first advise them that
by agreement the parties would not have any statements and
that the only statement will be made by him. The statement
can be somewhat as follows:

"The parties have met since_____o'clock this
morning. They have engaged in intensive bargaining on a number of key issues. While no
agreement was reached, the discussions were
constructive in giving them a better understanding of each other's position. We plan
to reconvene at_____o'clock tomorrow morning.
I am not at liberty to comment further on any
specific issues."

No Comment

Mediators should avoid a flat no comment position to the media. They should remember that the representatives of the media have a job to do especially if they are physically covering the meetings. Their superiors will find it difficult to understand why their representatives failed to get any newsworthy item after spending an entire day at the scene of the negotiations. If they cannot get a comment from the mediator, they will extract one from one of the parties and thus defeat the whole purpose of keeping the details of the negotiations secret.

If the parties are completely stalemated so that, in the mediator's judgment, it would be best not to schedule another meeting for awhile, the mediator should avoid the public appearance of a breakup by announcing a continuation of mediation efforts even though no joint meeting is scheduled. He can accomplish this by announcing that, while he is not scheduling a joint meeting at this time, he is going to meet with each side separately to explore some ideas he has for resolving some of the issues in dispute.

An exception to this is the situation where the mediator desires to create pressure on one or both parties who he feels are adhering to an unrealistic position. In such cases, he can advise the media that the parties are deadlocked on key issues and consequently he is adjourning the meeting sine die. This is particularly effective in cases of a protracted stoppage.

In strike cases, the mediator has to exercise judgment as to the frequency of meetings. If he schedules frequent meetings when the parties are still far apart, he may raise false hopes among the strikers that a settlement is at hand. When it fails to materialize, the consequent let down may cause tempers to flare. If he permits too great a time lapse between meetings, he may be unwittingly creating a situation where new issues will be interjected into the negotiations, such as picket line violence, hiring of replacements, etc.

Order of Priority - No Scoops

One sure way for a mediator to invite future grief for himself is to give a news item exclusively to one reporter when several are covering the negotiations. In a word, do not

become a party to a "scoop." Those embarrassed by it will
long remember.

At the first mediation session, reporters may request the
mediator to give them background information about the negotiations. Some of these inquiries can be anticipated if
the mediator has ready written background statements to be
distributed to all reporters covering the particular negotiations. Such statements should include such items as
names of company and union; names and titles of principal
negotiators for each party; the number of employees in the
bargaining unit; description of products manufactured by
the company; expiration date of the collective bargaining
agreement; and a generalized description of the principal
issues in dispute.

During the mediation meetings, some reporters may request
the mediator to characterize the status of negotiations on
an "off-record basis." The purpose of their request is to
assure that the stories they file accurately reflect the
progress of the negotiations. They would not want to give
an optimistic tone to their reports if none was warranted.
Whether the mediator should cooperate depends on his past
experience and relationship with the reporters. In many
large cities, newspapers have reporters whose principal assignment is to cover all significant labor disputes. These
reporters are experienced in the fragility of labor negotiations and aware of the impact an erroneous news item may
have. With such reporters, the mediator has some latitude
in deciding what information he can give, being careful,
however, not to breach confidentiality.

In smaller communities, for obvious economic reasons, reporters are given general assignments and handle comparatively few labor disputes. In such cases, unless the mediator has a personal relationship with the reporter, he
should exercise more caution as to what information he
should release.

In a few cases, reporters from the wire services, newspapers, and television all may be physically covering a
particular negotiation. In other situations, some reporters may be physically present while others may be covering
the dispute by telephone. In either case, any announcement by the mediator should be given first to the newspaper reporters. They have a deadline within which they
must get their stories into their offices. If they miss

the deadline their story becomes stale news. The announcement should then be given to the wire services which can
choose their own time as to when to transmit the story to
their subscribers. Lastly, to the radio and television reporters. They have the greatest flexibility. If the story
is important enough they need not await the regular news
programs but it can be used as a bulletin interrupting regularly scheduled programs.

If the mediator has a written statement to make, he should
have sufficient copies for all the reporters present. The
better procedure is for the mediator to hand the copies to
the reporters and advise them that he will answer questions
after they had the opportunity to read it. A less desirable
method is to give each reporter a copy of the statement and
then read it. An unsatisfactory procedure is to first read
the statement and then give copies to the reporters.

Where there are several reporters present at the site of the
negotiations, the mediator should arrange to have a room
available for them. He should obtain a commitment from the
parties that they will go to the "press room" at the conclusion of each meeting even though it is only to advise the
press that they have no comment. This procedure avoids
having reporters buttonholing the participants on their way
to rest rooms or lunch.

Relationship With Elected Public Officials

There are some disputes which, because of their economic
impact on a community, city, or State, attract the attention
of elected public officials while a mediator is actively
participating in the negotiations. In such situations, problems arise as to the proper role for each so that their
combined efforts will make the maximum contribution to the
resolution of the dispute. When referring to elected public officials, we are not speaking of State labor commissioners or State or local mediators but to governors, members of the legislatures, mayors, council members and the
like.

Some mediators take the position that such interventions
hamper their mediation efforts and they should ignore or
actively oppose any attempt by elected public officials to
intervene in a dispute they are handling. Some mediators
state "they (public officials) are just publicity hounds
and should stay out of the cases we are handling."

Such an attitude is completely unrealistic. Elected officials are necessarily political creatures. Their tenure
depends on their responsiveness to the expressed feelings
of the people and the community they have been elected to
serve. If a labor dispute results in a threatened stoppage
or a prolonged strike which may or is affecting the economic
well-being of a large segment of people residing in the city
or State, then their elected official has a responsibility
to take some steps to try to avoid the economic dislocation
caused by the labor conflict. His political life depends
on it. He can hardly respond that the matter is being handled by a Federal or State mediator and therefore he is doing nothing about it. His constituency expects some display
of concern and, often, some overt, affirmative action.

Mediators should not sulk or cry "foul" when such elected
officials intervene, but rather accept the fact that they
have no choice and direct their energies to finding means
of cooperating and at the same time directing the officials'
efforts so they complement the mediator's and affirmatively
contribute to the final solution of the dispute.

Most public officials recognize their own lack of expertise
in the mediation of labor disputes and welcome the assistance of our mediators. Further, as stated before, they are
political creatures and they must necessarily avoid antagonizing either industry or labor in their community. Each
represents a political bloc whose good-will is essential to
their political advancement.

Many of these public officials are satisfied with a conference with the mediator followed by a public announcement of
their concern and urging both parties to intensify their
efforts to seek a solution to the dispute. If a public
statement is made, the mediator can supplement it assuring
the elected official of his cooperation and promising to
keep him closely advised on the developments.

Experienced mediators should be able to anticipate the intervention of public officials. There are certain types
of disputes that will inevitably involve elected public
officials. Typical of such disputes are those involving
public transportation; public utilities; negotiations affecting the major industry of a State or local community;
disputes involving the milk and fuel industries; public
sector negotiations; and those affecting newspapers or
other public media of communications.

Mediators who are assigned to these cases can avoid many
subsequent problems if they initiate a meeting with the
appropriate public official on the basis that the mediator
wishes to alert him to the situation and bring him up-to-
date on developments. This normally results in a press announced meeting between the mediator and the public official--
a briefing by the mediator and an assurance of keeping the
official fully advised--and a press conference follows in
which the official decries the situation and expresses his
concern. The public official, through this device, is able
to satisfy his constituency of his interest in the dispute
and his personal attention to it. Further moves on his
part normally are not required.

However, there are cases where a public official will attempt to intervene. When this occurs, there are several
situations which may arise.

The mediator may be advised that a representative of the
elected public official desires to attend the next meeting
to be scheduled by the mediator. The mediator should advise the parties of the receipt of the request and ascertain
if they have any objections. He should also advise that if
they agree to the representative's presence, they should be
aware that their deliberations may not be confidential since
he would not have any control over the actions of such representative.

If one or both parties object, he should so advise the representative and deny his request. If only one party objects,
the mediator should avoid identifying it. If there is no
objection, the mediator should permit the representative to
attend. If the representative does attend, the mediator
should cooperate with him but always bearing in mind that
it is the mediator's meeting and that the mediator's sole
function is to assist the parties to resolve their differences and not to enhance the political posture of any elected official.

If the mediator is invited to attend a meeting of the disputants scheduled by an elected official in his office, it
may be difficult for the mediator to refuse, particularly
if he is stationed in the same area.

In a few States, there are provisions for the appointment of
a "fix blame" panel when a protracted dispute occurs. The
panel may request the mediator assigned to the case to brief

it on the background of the dispute and the positions of
the parties. The request may even be accompanied by an
assurance that the mediator's information will be held
confidential.

The better part of wisdom dictates that the mediator should
refuse to attend despite such assurance. If he is subpoenaed, he should appear and refuse to make any statement concerning the negotiations on the ground of confidentiality.

A number of years ago, a "fix blame" panel was appointed and
the mediator was requested to appear before it on an "off-
record" basis. The mediator did appear and his remarks
tended to throw the onus on the union for the prolongation
of the strike. Despite the panel's assurance of confidentiality, the mediator's remarks soon were made known to the
union. As a result, the mediator's neutrality was destroyed
and many years elapsed before the union welcomed any other
mediator in its negotiations.

Particularly during a protracted strike, a committee of
citizens may be formed primarily to bring home to the parties the concerns of the community. Such committees usually meet with both parties, separately or jointly, and try
to induce them to intensify their efforts to bring the dispute to a speedy end. Such committees are usually short
lived. The mediator should, within the limits of confidentiality, cooperate with the committees as long as their
efforts are not at cross purposes to his own.

Some committees, failing to persuade the parties to immediately resolve their differences, feel that they owe the
community a public statement as to their findings. In a
protracted strike in southern New England, a citizens' committee was formed. After vainly attempting to settle the
dispute, they decided to purchase a full page ad in the
local newspaper. The text of the ad, by implication and
tone, accused the company of intransigency on several key
issues. The committee invited the mediator to be one of
the signatories in the ad. The mediator, pleading agency
regulations, politely declined.

CHAPTER XXVII
MEDIATION IN HEALTH CARE INDUSTRY

The private health care business in the United States is one of our largest industries and most geographically dispersed with over five million employees at over 40,000 facilities throughout the country. These figures do not include Government facilities operated by a unit of the State, municipal, or Federal Government; nor do the figures include persons employed in producing health care equipment or pharmaceuticals. As a component of the growing service industry, the health care business accounts for 10% of the gross national product, and it continues to grow.

In spite of its size and labor intensity, the health care industry lacked a national labor policy before 1974. Prior to that year, health care labor-management relations were a patchwork of State, local, and Federal regulation or, more typically, no regulation at all. Government operated facilities were covered by public employee regulation in those States that had such laws. Proprietary hospitals and nursing homes were covered as private sector employers by the National Labor Relations Act. The nonprofit or charitable portion of the industry was covered in diverse ways under State law in 12 States; but the majority of these facilities were specifically excluded by Section 2(2) of the NLRA in 1947.

This was all changed on July 26, 1974, when President Nixon, in one of his last official acts, signed Public Law 93-360 amending the NLRA and ending the exclusion of health care employees from its protection.[1] The passage of the amendment was preceded by extensive Congressional hearings, and active lobbying by labor unions and the health care industry. The provisions of the amendment are a product of that intense debate. The amendment did more than extend coverage to the health care industry--it made special provisions for the industry based on its unique nature.

Provisions Of The Health Care Amendment

Because of the unique nature of health care, the Congressional hearings and debate focused on the concerns of the industry and the public health concerns of the nation. The

provisions finally adopted reflect these concerns by encouraging early negotiation and by discouraging strikes
with special impasse provisions. The following are the
major impasse provisions:

1. Notice Requirements - The amendment requires a 90-
day notice to the other party by the party desiring to reopen negotiation. A 60-day notice to FMCS is required. This
is in contrast with 30- and 90-day notices required of all
others under the Act. In the case of initial contracts,
the union is required to give a 30-day notice to the Federal Mediation and Conciliation Service.

2. Strike Notice - A ten-day notice of intent to
strike is required by the amendment. This was accomplished
by the new language in the Unfair Labor Practice Section at
8(g):

> "A labor organization before engaging in any
> strike, picketing, or other concerted refusal
> to work at any health care institution shall,
> not less than ten days prior to such action,
> notify the institution in writing and the FMCS
> of that intention..."[2]

This ten-day notice can only be given after the two earlier
notice requirements have been met.

3. Mandatory Mediation - The amendment institutes mandatory mediation by requiring that FMCS assign a mediator to
all health care cases once the 60-day notice (30 days on initial agreements) is received. Further, it requires that mediation services be provided, and that the parties participate in the mediation process. In non-health care cases,
the Service has always had discretion in assigning mediators
and in providing mediation. The parties in non-health care
cases have always had the option of participating in proffered mediation.

4. Board of Inquiry - In addition to mediation assistance, the impasse procedure also empowers FMCS to use a
Board of Inquiry. Section 213(a) provides:

> "If, in the opinion of the Director of the
> Federal Mediation and Conciliation Service,
> a threatened or actual strike or lock-out
> affecting a health care institution will, if

permitted to occur or to continue, substantially
interrupt the delivery of health care in the locality concerned, the Director may further assist
in the resolution of the impasse by establishing
within 30 days after the notice to the FMCS...an
impartial Board of Inquiry to investigate the
issues involved in the dispute and make a written
report thereon to the parties within 15 days after
the establishment of such a board. The written
report shall contain the findings of fact together
with the Board's recommendations for settling the
dispute with the objective of achieving a prompt,
peaceful and just settlement of the dispute."[3]

Early Experience With Mediation

In spite of the requirement in the amendment for mandatory
mediation, the Service has not provided mediation in every
health care case. However, the Service does assign a mediator in every situation in which a notice is received.
This is not done in non-health care cases because the
Service exercises discretion in the use of its limited
resources.

The Service uses the designation of "active or joint meeting case" to identify cases in which a mediator has conducted at least one formal mediation session with the parties.
Cases in which settlement is reached by the parties without
any mediation meetings are designated "inactive cases." In
health care cases, over half are joint meeting cases. In
all non-health care cases, the percentage of active cases
is much less than half. While more mediation is being provided in health care cases, mandatory mediation is not being
provided.

Mediators and the Service have very wisely chosen not to
take literally the language of the amendment on mandatory
mediation. They have, instead, recognized that most health
care negotiations result in settlement without a work stoppage and without mediation. To identify those cases where
mediation is needed, the assigned mediator monitors the
case by periodic phone calls to the negotiators so that
intervention is possible at a propitious time.

The ten-day strike notice to the Service makes is possible
for the mediator to offer mediation assistance when a real
deadline is near and the parties have already conducted

serious bargaining on their own. The 30-day notice requirement on negotiations for initial contracts has had a similar
advantage of focusing mediation at the stage in the process
when it is most likely to be needed. (There is no such requirement in non-health care cases.)

Since the Board of Inquiry process was new to the Service,
there were concerns and questions within the Service about
how the Board of Inquiry process would interface with me-
diation--the primary process of the Service. Should the
Board of Inquiry process be fashioned to accommodate mediation, or the reverse? Should the mediator and fact-finder
work together, share information, and strategy? Should the
two processes be discrete? Would there be the normal problems of healthy competition between the two neutrals over
who was going to settle the case?

These and other questions could not be answered in the ab-
stract; they would be answered only through experience in
handling cases.

During the first year under the amendment, the Service established a Health Care Industry Labor-Management Advisory
Committee composed of 14 members--seven representing the
major labor organizations in the industry and seven representing various segments of the industry. The Service
sought the advice of this group on the implementation of
the amendment and the unique features of the industry.[4]

Third-Party Payers

One of the unique features of the health care industry that
has presented a problem to collective bargaining and mediation is the existence of third-party payers.

The revenue in the health care industry is derived from the
patient, the patient's insurance, charitable donations, and
the contributions of government--State, local, and Federal.
The government(s) and the insurance companies are third-
party payers.

When a labor agreement is settled, costs of labor increase.
These increased costs to the institution, in many cases,
must be borne by the third-party payer. Since this is the
case, most management negotiators will not agree to increased costs until they have gotten an assurance from one
or more third-party payer that they will increase their

revenue to the institution. In most negotiations, third-party payers are not willing to participate directly in the labor negotiations, but their presence is felt by everyone at the bargaining table.

Third-party payers are not willing to increase their contribution to the institution until they are persuaded that they must. What transpires at the bargaining table is, in part, what influences the third-party payers.

The increasing costs of health care, which have been more pronounced than in other industries, have been very troublesome for the third-party payers and collective bargaining. For the mediator who is accustomed to dealing persuasively and directly with negotiators, the third-party payers are particularly difficult since they are not present but their influence is.

Early Experiences With Boards of Inquiry

The Board of Inquiry process involves one or more fact-finders conducting a hearing with the disputing parties to determine the issues and facts in dispute, and fact-finders issuing a written report which recommends a basis for settlement. These recommendations are not binding on the parties. The Board of Inquiry process and mediation are certainly not incompatible--mediation can precede and/or follow the Board of Inquiry process.

During the first year under the amendment, the Service appointed more Boards of Inquiry than during any subsequent year. Between October 11, 1974, when the first Board of Inquiry was appointed, and one year later, 54 Boards of Inquiry were appointed. 30% of all Boards of Inquiry ever appointed were appointed during that first year. No Boards of Inquiry have been appointed since June 1, 1983. See the chart below.

Chart Number One

Boards of Inquiry Appointed by FMCS

Year Ending	Number of BOI's
10-75	54
10-76	37
10-77	10

Year Ending	Number of BOI's
10-78	21
10-79	11
10-80	6
10-81	20
10-82	2
10-83	14
10-84	0
Total	175

Source: Arbitration Office, FMCS

The experience gained during that first year by the Service and the parties showed that less Boards of Inquiry were better for several reasons:

First, the concern about work stoppages was very high following congressional hearings and the passage of the amendment. The Service wanted to do everything possible to avoid strikes, and to avoid criticism of the Service's administration of the amendment. Therefore, the Service used the process provided by the Congress in a good faith effort to see if it would produce the result the Congress intended.

Secondly, the Service wanted to gain some experience with this new procedure, to observe how the parties reacted to it, to see how the mandatory mediation and the Board of Inquiry worked together, and to see how effective the various time limits would be.

Thirdly, the notice time limits and the deadline for the appointment of a Board of Inquiry proved not to be supportive of bargaining between the parties. Since the Service must appoint a Board of Inquiry, if one is to be appointed, within 30 days of the receipt of the 60-day notice of the parties, the appointment must be made 30 or more days before the expiration of the old agreement. In cases where the parties give a very early notice, the appointment would be even further from the expiration date. In many cases, if not most cases, no serious bargaining has taken place before the Board of Inquiry is operating. A Board of Inquiry in such situations is of no help, and it may be counter productive.

In a study conducted by the Service two years after the amendment, the labor and management negotiators, as well as the mediators and fact-finders, agreed that the time limits on the Board of Inquiry procedures were a major difficulty in making it an effective process. These participants felt that the Board of Inquiry procedure should be an option at any time during the mediation process, rather than tied to a rigid time frame.[5]

Fourthly, the Service came to realize that the impact on the bargaining was as important a criteria in the decision to appoint a Board of Inquiry as the impact of a possible work stoppage on "the delivery of health care in the locality concerned..."[6] The experience of the Service in collective bargaining and the study cited above contributed to this conclusion.

Negotiations in the health care industry are like those in other industries--serious bargaining does not occur until a real deadline is in sight. And until serious bargaining has reduced the number of issues and helped to identify priorities, neither mediation nor a Board of Inquiry can be helpful. A Board of Inquiry faced with too many issues and unclear priorities cannot fashion recommendations that will move the parties closer to settle their differences. If the Board of Inquiry cannot do that, the Service concluded it was of little value to the process of settling disputes.

Joint Stipulation Agreement

Based on the problems with Boards of Inquiry during the early years and the several court interpretations which further reduced flexibility with the time limits, the Service developed an innovative alternative to the Board of Inquiry. Former FMCS Director Horvitz explained it this way:

> The FMCS "developed the technique of using a joint stipulation agreement between the parties by which they authorize the Director of the FMCS to appoint a fact-finder at a later date, such as, at the end of the contract period if no agreement is reached, or when a ten-day strike notification is served by a union. Normally, such a fact-finder would operate under the same procedure as would a BOI, unless the parties and the FMCS agreed otherwise."[7]

The following procedure is used in obtaining a stipulation:
A mediator armed with authority to solicit a joint stipulation would discuss with the parties the impasse procedures
in the amendment, and the current state of their negotiations. In many cases, the parties can be persuaded to sign
the stipulation which would be used only if the parties cannot reach agreement on their own or with mediation assistance. In effect, the availability of the stipulation is an
additional effort by the mediator to make the process responsive to the needs of the parties; that is, it extends
the period for bargaining by the parties before a fact-
finder would enter the case, and it assures that fact-finding can be available when it will be most effective.

As the use of the stipulation has grown, the use of the Board
of Inquiry has declined. The Service is now reaching the
point where the appointment of a Board of Inquiry is the
exception. In the first eleven months of 1984, no Boards
of Inquiry were appointed by the Service. This is in spite
of the fact that two major health care strikes occurred
during that period.[8]

Other Adaptations of the Procedure

Three other improvements have been made upon the statutory
process in response to the parties' needs for more custom-
fit processes. The Service developed a practice of allowing the parties to suggest potential fact-finders for the
Board of Inquiry. The Service gives consideration to appointing fact-finders from a jointly submitted list from
the parties.

Service rules now allow deferral of the Board of Inquiry
procedure to a fact-finding procedure adopted by the parties. The parties' fact-finding procedure must meet four
requirements:

1. It must be invoked at a specific time.

2. A fixed method for selecting the fact-finder must
be agreed upon.

3. Their procedure must preclude a strike, lock-out,
or changes in the conditions before and during the fact-
finding, and for a period of seven days after the fact-
finding report is received.

4. Their procedure must require a written report by the fact-finder including a finding of facts and recommendations for settlement. The report must be given to the parties and the Service.

If the parties want to use their own fact-finding procedure, they must have it agreed upon before the date when the Service must make a decision to appoint a Board of Inquiry.

Since some State laws prior to the amendment used binding interest arbitration in health care, this type of arbitration is not unusual in that industry. For that reason, the Service has included in its regulations standards for deferring to an interest arbitration procedure agreed to by the parties. The following are the standards:

1. The procedure must exclude strikes, lock-outs, or changes in conditions during the negotiation and arbitration.

2. The arbitrator's award must be final and binding upon the parties.

3. A fixed method for selecting the arbitrator must be agreed upon.

4. A written award must be required by the procedure.

Evaluation

Twenty years ago, the health care industry was a low pay industry, without many unions and with many casual workers in the non-professional ranks. It was an industry which had few, if any, work stoppages. All of this has changed in the past ten years.

Today, this industry is much like other segments of the private sector in terms of pay, turnover, and unionization. Even strikes are being taken in stride. Health care managers now anticipate strikes and prepare for them with contingency plans and cooperation with other institutions. Books and articles have been written on dealing with a health care strike.[9]

Conclusion

After ten years of experience in the health care industry
under the amendment, collective bargaining in the industry
is increasing like collective bargaining in other segments
of the private sector. Most negotiations result in agreements without a strike, and many without mediation. In
most other cases, mediation or a procedure developed by
the parties produces a settlement. In a limited number
of cases, a Board of Inquiry, or its progeny based on a
stipulation, is used in conjunction with mediation to
achieve settlement.

NOTES

1. See Health Care Amendment in Appendix.

2. Ibid.

3. Ibid.

4. James F. Scearce and Lucretia Dewey Tanner, "Health Care Bargaining: The FMCS Experience," Labor Law Journal, Vol. 27, No. 7, July 1976, pp. 387-398.

5. Impact of the 1974 Health Care Amendment to the NLRA on Collective Bargaining in the Health Care Industry, A study by the Federal Mediation and Conciliation Service with funds from the U.S. Department of Labor, p. 473, 1979.

6. See Health Care Amendment in Appendix.

7. Wayne L. Horvitz, "The FMCS and the Peaceful Resolution of Disputes," in Health Care Law, edited by Michael Shepard and Edward Doudera, AUPHA Press: Washington, D.C., 1981, p. 148.

8. A 46-day strike involving 52,000 employees, 30 hospitals, 15 nursing homes, and 18,000 patients, ended on August 29, 1984, in New York City. Earlier that summer, the largest nurses' strike in U.S. history occurred in the Twin City area of Minnesota. Six thousand nurses struck 15 out of 33 hospitals in the area for 35 days.

9. Norman Metzger, Joseph M. Ferentino and Kenneth F. Kruger, When Health Care Employees Strike: A Guide for Planning and Action, Asper Publications, Inc.: Rockville, Md., 1984, p. 345.

CHAPTER XXVIII

PREVENTIVE MEDIATION

Definition

Preventive mediation was defined by Cyrus Ching, the first Director of the Federal Mediation and Conciliation Service, as

> "seek(ing) to improve human relations in industrial life in order that collective bargaining might be practiced in an atmosphere most favorable to peaceful settlement of disputes..."[1]

Preventive mediation was not formalized or emphasized until the creation of the Federal Mediation and Conciliation Service in 1947. However, during the existence of the U.S. Conciliation Service, the predecessor to the FMCS, mediators conducted some early forms of preventive mediation.

U.S. Conciliation Service

Under the administration of the first Director of the U.S. Conciliation Service, the mediation function was permitted to evolve on a case-by-case basis. The mediators were directed to do whatever necessary and possible to aid the parties in resolving their differences. In carrying out this responsibility, mediators often performed preventive mediation through suggesting procedures to eliminate unresolved grievances, consulting, providing informal training, and forming joint labor-management committees.

Typical of this was the second case handled by the Secretary of Labor--Erie Forge Company strike in 1913. The Secretary, upon receiving a joint request for help, assigned the Assistant Secretary of Labor to act as mediator. Soon after entering the negotiations, the mediator learned that the strike was caused by an accumulation of unresolved grievances caused by continuing friction between the foreman and the workers. There were no appeals from the decisions of the foreman. The mediator suggested the establishment of a grievance procedure with successive appellate steps terminating with the company president. His suggestion was adopted and the strike was settled.[2]

Preventive mediation was publicly acknowledged for the first
time in 1923 by the Secretary of Labor. In his report to
Congress, in referring to the Division of Conciliation, the
Secretary wrote:

> "Somewhat obscurred by its other activities, yet
> by no means unimportant, is the service rendered
> by the division in making suggestions to manufac-
> turers for the betterment of their individual re-
> lations. For example, a conciliator who had par-
> ticipated in the adjustment of a dispute was sub-
> sequently called upon to work out a plan of shop
> commitee representation."[3]

Even though the need for a "force of broad gauge technical
experts"[4] was recognized by the Secretary of Labor as early
as 1921, no such group was created until almost two decades
later.

With the growth of labor relations during the Roosevelt era,
the Service created a technical division to provide labor
and management with assistance in job evaluation, incentive
systems, work load measurement, time and motion studies, and
other new and evolving processes. The expanding industrial-
ization made skills in these processes crucial to peaceful
labor relations.

Since the parties lack these skills and these processes
were the source of many disputes, the Service decided to
provide technical assistance from a neutral and impartial
point of view. The Service recruited employees for the
new technical division based on technical expertise and
not mediation skills. Organizationally, these technicians
operated separately from the mediation staff.

Over 90% of the technical division's work involved grievances and problems arising under a labor agreement. In
many cases, the technical assistance involved conducting
studies or assisting the parties to conduct studies which
then became the basis for negotiations between the parties. In many of these situations, they acted as pure
fact-finders. Given the lack of experience of both labor
and management, much of the technical assistance had a
training dimension, however informal.

The technical division was the first formal program of preventive mediation or technical assistance offered by any
mediation agency.

By the mid-1940's, the USCS mediators were providing more
formal training to labor and management.   This was designed to help labor and management understand and carry
out their responsibilities under the provisions of their
labor agreement. During the USCS's final years, the mediators increasingly used the formation of joint labor-management committees to assist the parties in problem solving
and improving their relationship.

Federal Mediation and Conciliation Service

With the creation of the FMCS in 1947, all employees of the
USCS were transferred to the FMCS, and the technical division was eliminated along with most grievance mediation.

Cyrus Ching, the first Director of the new FMCS, began talking almost immediately about the need for a formal program,
in addition to dispute mediation, to improve the climate of
labor relations. In seeking a descriptive name for the program, he chose "preventive" mediation, equating it to preventive medicine. Justification for the program was found
not only in the fact that it was a traditional part of the
mediator's function, but also in the spirit and letter of
the Act which spoke of the Service's obligation to provide
assistance in the formulation of contract provisions or
procedures to prevent controversies in the future.[5] Under
Ching's directorship, preventive mediation became a recognized part of the mediator's responsibilities.

In the first annual report to the Congress, the FMCS Director wrote:

> "These activities have consisted mainly in search-
> ing out and analyzing situations which threaten
> peaceful industrial relations in their communities
> or areas and devising procedures and plans or for-
> mulating suggestions which have tended to remove
> impediments to good labor relations and promote
> the possibility of the parties reaching agreement
> on the occasion of the next contract reopening."[6]

For several years under the new FMCS, the preventive mediation program was intentionally vague and experimental to
allow the mediators and the regional directors to experiment
and thus determine which types of preventive mediation worked best under which circumstances. A series of staff discussions in the field and the national office sought a concensus on what the program should be. The annual reports

for several years reported on specific cases in which successful results had occurred.

By 1951, four types of preventive mediation could be identified: (1) creating joint labor-management committees, (2)
establishing liaison between top level management and high
level union officials, (3) cooperating with industrial relations institutes at colleges and universities, and (4)
conducting grievance clinics or training.[7] These basic
types have persisted since that time with some modifications and changes in emphasis.

The introduction of audio-visual training materials in 1952
started a trend toward a major emphasis on the training
category of preventive mediation. This emphasis persists
yet today within the FMCS.

In the 1960's under the directorship of William E. Simkin,
great emphasis was put on the use of joint labor-management
committees to study common problems, to improve communication, and to improve the parties' relationship. This was
long before the present-day emphasis on labor-management
cooperation. The Service's emphasis on labor-management
committees during that period met with much success, as did
several highly publicized examples in steel and meat-pack-
ing. This form of preventive mediation is probably the
most similar to dispute mediation, since it requires the
mediator to direct discussion, identify problems, and work
jointly with labor and management.

During the directorship of William Usery, a comprehensive
new form of preventive mediation was introduced. It was
called Relations by Objectives (RBO).

Also during the Usery period the name preventive mediation
was dropped and the name technical assistance has been used
ever since. (In this chapter, preventive mediation will
continue to be used.)

Over the years, new training materials were purchased or
developed for labor-management training, such as: 16mm
films, slides, projectors, case studies, study guides, and
handout materials. In the later 1970's, an entirely new
labor-management training program was developed for the
mediators' use.

Through the years, the basic purposes of preventive mediation have remained the same--to assist labor and management
in improving their relationship and/or to solve their most
difficult problems during the term of their labor agreement.
As such, preventive mediation continues to be an important
and appropriate role for the industrial relations peacemaker.

The How And What Of
Preventive Mediation[8]

When a mediator is conducting dispute mediation, he is in
an ideal position to assess the quality of the labor-management relationship. As he deals with the issues in dispute,
the mediator gets an insight into the relationship that gave
rise to those issues. As time permits, during the dispute or
later, the mediator can test and verify his impressions by
in-depth private discussions with each party.

Some of the danger signals of a poor relationship that the
mediator is alert to are:

1. An excessive number of grievances.

2. Many grievances plugging one step in the
    grievance procedure.

3. An excessive number of requests for grievance
    arbitration.

4. Wild-cat strikes.

5. Long and bitter strikes each time the agree-
    ment is renegotiated.

6. Layoffs and technological changes.

7. Poor communication between the parties.

8. Lack of trust.

9. Rejection of tentative agreements by the
    union membership.

10. Frequent or recent change of leadership on
    either side.

Once the mediator is alerted to a troubled relationship, he will, if his schedule permits, attempt to check out his impressions with the parties. In the ideal situation, this will result in the parties' jointly diagnosing their problem--determining its location and seriousness. It is only at this point that solutions can be considered.

However, where a poor relationship exists, it is frequently difficult to get the parties to jointly diagnose their problem. Here the mediator will work separately with the parties to diagnose the problem, and then attempt to get an agreement on working through the problem. This is a test of the mediator's persuasive skills and persistence.

There are two problems here that must be recognized: (1) there are problems that are not solvable through preventive mediation; and (2) there are problems that one or both parties do not want solved. The mediator who is serious about his responsibility in preventive mediation concludes that he has one of these situations only after making his best effort.

In addition to learning of opportunities for preventive mediation through dispute mediation, mediators also learn of poor labor-management relations through: (1) professional and community contacts in organizations, such as the Industrial Relations Research Association; and (2) referrals and recommendations from parties who have benefitted from earlier preventive mediation programs.

Types Of Preventive Mediation

Once the parties' problem has been diagnosed, the appropriate preventive mediation remedy can be determined. The various types of preventive mediation are:

1. <u>Joint Labor-Management Training</u>[9] - This most commonly used type of preventive mediation is directed to the persons most involved in the day-to-day implementation and application of the labor agreement--the first-line supervisor and the union steward. If these individuals, at this most crucial interface of the labor-management relationship, do not understand their responsibility or communicate effectively, the relationship throughout the organization is affected.

Joint labor-management training addresses both of these
problems: (1) It instructs the participants on their responsibilities and it helps them develop their skills in
communications and grievance handling. This is accomplished through lecture, short film presentations, and directed
discussion. (2) By having labor and management representatives together in the same session, the human relationship
is enhanced. By sharing a common experience in role playing exercises and discussion, these adversaries can begin
to set aside their stereotyped images of each other and see
their commonalities as people and employees of the organization. In this atmosphere, trust, understanding, and good-
will can grow and carry over into the work place.

The typical joint labor-management training program consists of six sessions of two hours duration with 20 participants equally divided between labor and management.
Usually, sessions are held one per week during working
hours near the work site. These details and the topics
to be covered are arranged by the mediator in discussions
with both parties.

     2. Labor-Management Committees - This type of preven-
tive mediation is probably the oldest. The first Labor-
Management Committees (LMCs) were formed during World War I.
The U.S. Conciliation Service used and promoted them; FMCS
has placed great emphasis on them.

Most mediators are very comfortable with LMCs because they
are very similar to dispute mediation. In an LMC, representatives of labor and management meet to solve common
problems--very much as they do in contract negotiations.
LMCs function during the term of a contract on questions,
problems, and issues that arise during the contract. LMCs
should exclude from their agenda those issues that are covered by the parties' grievance procedure, or those normally
handled in contract negotiations.

Any other imaginable topic of mutual interest can be handled by an LMC. Some have a very narrow focus: safety,
drug abuse, or productivity improvement. Others have a
very broad mandate: problem solving, anticipating problems, improving communication.

Mediators frequently suggest the creation of an LMC during
contract negotiations to remove a difficult problem from
the bargaining table. Difficult issues, such as health

insurance cost containment, a new or revised pension plan,
an incentive system, require extensive study and delibera-
tion. Since negotiations do not lend themselves to study
and reflection, these issues are most appropriate to the
LMC approach. LMCs have also been suggested to handle routine problems like absenteeism, tardiness, turnover, poor
workmanship, and high scrap rates; or difficult problems
such as plant closing and automation.

Some LMCs in large organizations have been formed to coordinate other forms of labor-management cooperation like
quality circles, employee involvement programs, and qual-
ity-of-work-live programs. LMCs have also been used to
sponsor and coordinate joint labor-management training.

Mediators have also been involved in setting up LMCs at the
community and industry level. Community or area LMCs bring
together labor and management in a community to promote
their common interest in peaceful relations, a growing industrial base, and low unemployment. The majority of community LMCs in the country were started with the help of an
FMCS mediator.

Industry LMCs bring together labor and management from an
industry to promote their common interest. Some of these
committees are local and regional; others are national in
scope. Many of these involve portions of the building and
construction industry.

Most mediators who have formed LMCs find it necessary to
help the parties in suggesting the participants on the
committee, developing an agenda, establishing a schedule,
writing rules or bylaws, and serving as the chairman of
the first few meetings. Once the parties have successfully
participated in several meetings, most mediators will suggest that the parties select co-chairmen who can alternate
in chairing the meetings.

The strong commitment of FMCS to the use of LMCs as a form
of preventive mediation is illustrated by the fact that
during the last several years FMCS mediators have started
over 300 LMCs each year.

    3. Consultation by the Mediator - This category of
preventive mediation has great flexibility to deal with a
variety of problems in labor-management relations. The
mediator as a consultant uses his expertise to assist the

parties on an as-needed basis limited only by the time the
mediator has available. As a consultant, the mediator provides information, makes suggestions, connects the parties
to other resources, and facilitates improvements in the
parties' relationship. Some examples will illustrate:

(a) A union and a management representative have been
having difficulty with the cost of arbitration and delays
in getting an arbitration hearing. The mediator helps the
parties consider various alternatives, and then assists them
in setting up their own permanent panel of arbitrators.

(b) A company which has been introducing new equipment
into its plant is experiencing too high a level of turnover.
The union is concerned as well. After a meeting with the
mediator in which the problem and alternatives are considered, the mediator arranges for a university professor to
discuss with the parties an employee attitude survey and
a training program.

(c) A remote plant and an independent local union are
experiencing difficulty implementing a recent agreement on
health care coverage. The mediator discovers that their
agreement was vague and incomplete. He provides them with
some written background information on health care insurance. After they have studied this, he meets with them
again to determine what else is needed. He then arranges
for an official from the State department of insurance to
consult with the parties.

Mediators also consult with universities and colleges in
planning and conducting labor-management conferences.
These conferences, usually co-sponsored by FMCS and a university, feature speakers and workshops on current topics
in labor relations. Many such conferences have become an
annual event providing an ideal setting for labor and management to expand their common interests and increase the
likelihood of better relations--outcomes consistent with
the role of the mediator.

4. Relations by Objectives (RBO) - This, the newest
type of preventive mediation, was introduced in 1975 as a
method for providing assistance in extremely poor labor-
management relationships--ones, for example, in which the
parties have not been able to renegotiate a new contract
without a lengthy and bitter strike.

The RBO format uses concepts from training, organizational development and goal setting to move a labor and a management group through an examination of their problems to the setting of mutually developed goals. The process is usually conducted in a three-day meeting away from the work site with three mediators acting as facilitators. Because of the labor intensity of the RBO, the Service limits the number it will conduct. RBOs represent less than one percent of the preventive mediation case load each year.

The impressions of mediators who have conducted RBOs, the reaction of participants, and several studies indicate very impressive results from this innovative form of preventive mediation.[10]

FMCS Grant Program

The Labor-Management Cooperation Act of 1978, for the first time in the history of the FMCS, gives the Service grant-making authority. This Act, which was not funded until 1981, directed the Service to award funds:

> "to provide assistance in the establishment and operation of plant, area and industry-wide labor-management committees which (a) have been organized jointly by employers and labor organizations representing employees in that plant, area or industry; and (b) are established for the purpose of improving labor-management relations, job security, organizational effectiveness, enhancing economic development or involving workers in decisions affecting their jobs including communication with respect to subjects of mutual interest and concern."[11]

All of the statutory language quoted above could be applied to what FMCS mediators have been doing for years in their preventive mediation work with labor-management committees. The new law added grant funds to the mediator "staff time" that the Service had been investing in labor-management committees.

Initially, the Service was concerned that the availability of funds would complicate the mediator's relationship with parties seeking funds. To avoid this problem, a separate office was created to handle the grant program completely independent from the mediator functions.

Since 1981, the Service has awarded three million dollars
to forty labor-management committees in both the public and
private sectors. The grants have included area committees,
industry committees, and in-plant committees.

NOTES

1. First Annual Report, Federal Mediation and Conciliation Service, June 30, 1948, p. 2

2. Annual Report of the Secretary of Labor and Report of Bureaus, 1913, p. 15.

3. Annual Report of the Secretary of Labor, 1923.

4. Ninth Annual Report of the Secretary of Labor,
June 30, 1921, p. 14.

5. See Labor-Management Relations Act, Section 201(c),
in Appendix.

6. First Annual Report of FMCS, 1948, p. 18.

7. Cyrus S. Ching, Review and Reflection: A Half
Century in Labor Relations, New York: B.C. Forbes & Sons
Publishing Co., 1953, pp. 83-86.

8. Portions of this section are based on John R. Stepp
and Jerome T. Barrett, "Helping Labor and Management See and
Solve Problems," Monthly Labor Review, Vol. 105, No. 9,
September 1982.

9. Jerome T. Barrett, An Historic and Descriptive
Study of the Joint Labor-Management Training Program of
the Federal Mediation and Conciliation Service, A Dissertation at George Washington University, March 1984, p. 199.

10. Anthony V. Sinicropi et al, Evaluation of the
FMCS's Technical Assistance Program in Labor-Management
Relations by Objectives (RBO), Unpublished FMCS 1978.

Denise T. Hoyer, Relations by Objectives: An
Experimental Program of Management-Union Conflict Resolution, Ph.D. Dissertation, University of Michigan, 1982.

Richard J. La Fleur, "Relations by Objectives:
A Model for Joint Labor-Management Conflict Resolution,"
An unpublished Master's paper, Cleveland State University,
December 1982.

11. See the Labor-Management Cooperation Act of 1978
in Appendix.

CHAPTER XXIX
ETHICAL CONSIDERATIONS IN MEDIATION [1]

The mediator operates in a unique work environment. He maintains a precarious high-wire perch with labor's trust securing one end of this life-line and management's the other. Beyond holding his balance in this environment, he seeks a mutual resolution to the parties' dispute. His acceptability to the parties plays a major role in this process. For the successful mediator, thus, trust is both an end and a means. In his relationship with the parties, trust is what he seeks; in resolving the dispute, trust is his most powerful ally. The trust he seeks is not only in his mediatory abilities, but in his integrity.

Given his nearly mandatory need for trust in his integrity, the mediator faces extreme ethical choices. At one extreme, he risks losing effectiveness if he brings his own "pure" standards to the bargaining table; at the other, he risks losing credibility if he allows each set of parties to determine the ethical framework of the negotiations.

As a pragmatic problem solver, the mediator recognizes the folly of the puritanical extreme; it just won't work. But as a professional, he must reject the alternative view with equal haste. Like doctors and (to a lesser extent) lawyers, the mediator represents a profession with certain accepted standards by which his work can be judged. The "Code of Professional Conduct for Mediators," adopted in 1964 by the Association of Labor Mediation Agencies (ALMA) and by FMCS, sets forth standards of conduct and defines the responsibilities of mediators to the parties, other mediators, their agency, their profession, the public, and the mediation process.[2] A "Code of Professional Responsibility" was adopted by the Society of Professionals in Dispute Resolution (SPIDR) in 1982.[3]

Both Codes recognize the need for a mediator to maintain a high standard of moral conduct in his mediation efforts. The Code of Professional Conduct says:

> "Since mediation is essentially a voluntary
> process, the acceptability of the mediator by

the parties as a person of integrity, objectivity
and fairness is absolutely essential to the effective performance of the duties of a mediator...Any
improper conduct or professional shortcomings...
reflect not only on the individual mediator but on
his employer."[4]

The language of both Codes, like the creeds of other professionals, is sufficiently vague to allow individual interpretations in practice. The not-too-surprising fact is
that mediators find themselves at neither ethical extreme
but somewhere in the middle. For not only--in working between the two extremes--does the mediator seek to avoid
sin; he must also practice virtue.

Ethical conflicts for the mediator can be divided into six
general areas:

1. Conflicts of Interest

a. Former Affiliations:

        One of the clearest situations of potential con-
flict of interest arises when a mediator is currently, or
has been a member of the union which is a party to the negotiations. Similarly, a potential conflict exists when
the mediator has been either a former employee of or has an
interest in the company involved in his mediation effort.
In such situations, it is incumbent on the mediator to make
a prompt and full disclosure to the parties. If he senses
a reluctance by either party to his continued involvement,
the mediator should withdraw from the case and request his
agency to assign another mediator.

b. Proffers of Gifts or Gratuities

        A potential conflict of interest also exists where
there is a proffer of a gift or gratuity. The following
three actual cases illustrate the potential conflicts of interest that permeate all proffers, overt or subtle, of gifts
or gratuities to the mediator.

Shortly after being transferred to a new location, a mediator handled a case with a union official who, in the course
of the mediation effort, inquired about the mediator's family and new home. Nothing unusual happened during the mediation. A week after the case was settled, a new tandem

bicycle was delivered to the mediator's home addressed to
his six-year old twin daughters. The daughters were de-
lighted with the bicycle, and wanted very much to keep it.
The mediator returned the bicycle to the union official with
a note explaining that he was not able to accept such a gift.
The mediator subsequently learned from several other mediators, who had worked in that city, that this union official
typically used a gift to test the new mediator's integrity
in a conflict of interest situation.

During the course of two days of mediation at a plywood manufacturer, a mediator mentioned his plans to build a recreation room in his basement. Near the end of negotiations,
when the mediator was convinced that the employer had been
persuaded to put its best offer on the table, the mediator
persuaded the union committee to accept the offer and recommend it to the membership. Several days after the union had
ratified the agreement, ten sheets of plywood were delivered
to the mediator's home. Although the plywood was the manufacturer's brand, no one had seen the delivery truck, nor
was there a bill of lading or other indications of who had
sent the plywood. The mediator returned the plywood to the
manufacturer. To have accepted it, if subsequently discovered by the union committee, would have created suspicion
of his honesty in urging acceptance of the company's offer.
It also might have created an impression for the company
that the mediator's judgment could be swayed by a gift. The
wisdom of the mediator's decision, apart from the ethical
consideration which prompted it, was brought home when the
mediator remembered that one member of the union bargaining
committee worked on the company loading dock.

Following a sixteen-hour mediation session, the mediator
and the parties were leaving the office building together
at one a.m. Outside the building, the parties said good
night and dispersed toward their cars. The spokesman from
the union and the mediator walked together since their cars
happened to be in the same parking lot. As they walked,
the union representative expressed his appreciation to the
mediator for being willing to work so hard and so late in
the parties' interest, on this occasion and others. As they
approached the spokesman's car, he said he wanted to give
the mediator an expression of his appreciation. He then
opened the trunk of his car and removed a quart of whiskey
from a full case. When he offered it to the mediator, the
mediator politely declined, explaining that he could not
accept something of value from either of the parties. The
spokesman hesitated for a moment and then said he would sell

the bottle to the mediator for one dollar. The mediator
accepted the gift.

This presents a close question. The proffered gift was undoubtedly an expression of gratitude. If the 16-hour session resulted in settlement, in view of the relatively small
real value of the gift, a refusal might damage his future
relationship with the union representative. If, however,
the entire case was offered at that price, a polite but
firm refusal would be best. The real value would have prohibited the acceptance. If the negotiations were incomplete, then it would be improper for the mediator to accept
even one bottle. Acceptance would deem him an ingrate if,
during the subsequent mediation effort, he found it necessary to be forceful with the union.

Some rules-of-thumb that mediators have used in gift and
gratuity situations:

(1) Offers of gifts and gratuities run the gamut of
imagination--a drink, a meal, a small token product, a
discount on a large product, an expensive personal gift.
The mediator, when deciding the propriety of accepting or
rejecting, should resolve all doubts on the side of caution. His immediate reaction should be a polite but firm
"no."

(2) The mediator should have a ready explanation for
refusing an offer. Many mediators, after expressing their
appreciation for the thoughtfulness, indicate that they have
made it a practice not to accept anything for merely doing
their job.

(3) The appearance of a conflict of interest can be as
damaging as the reality. The damage can affect the mediator's reputation with the giver as well as the other party.
If the mediator gets an opportunity to explain it, he is
already in trouble.

(4) The compromise of a mediator's reputation will not
come labeled "bribe." It will be much more subtle. The
mediator must be alert to the implications and perceptions.
It is true that the damage is in the eye of the beholder.

(5) Although it not literally true, the mediator should
view all situations as if the burden is on the mediator to
demonstrate to anyone that no conflict exists.

Formal conflict of interest complaints involving mediators are seldom made. This may be related more to the parties' control over acceptance of any specific mediator rather than an absence of conflicts of interest.

2. Techniques Used To Mediate

Most ethical questions on the techniques used to mediate are essentially a question of "means and ends." If the mediator believes that his primary function is to achieve settlement, then anything he does to achieve settlement is appropriate. However, if the mediator believes that his primary function is to assist the viability of the collective bargaining relationship, then he will do nothing that will adversely impact on the collective bargaining relationship.

This can be illustrated with the question of telling a lie to achieve an agreement. (Violating a confidence could be used also.) The issue here is not the exaggeration or misstatement which the listener assumes to be, or recognizes as, the rhetoric of negotiations. Hard core lying or intentional misleading is the issue.

For example, a mediator, having learned in confidence the final position of management on a particular issue, uses a separate meeting with the union to vigorously persuade them to reveal their final position. The union heatedly demands to know if the mediator knows the company's final position. A mediator who believes settlement is his primary function might easily deny that knowledge on the basis that it may interfere with the momentum toward a settlement that is close at hand.

Such an action by the mediator is not only ethically questionable, it is ultimately counter-productive and unnecessary. Once a settlement is reached, the individual members of labor and management live together back at the work site. When they rehash the mediation experience, this lack of candor on the part of the mediator can easily be discovered with consequent disillusionment about the settlement and suspicion of mediation. In this situation, there was no need to lie. The mediator could have easily explained his inability to answer such a question by pointing out that he had received confidential information from both parties which he is bound not to reveal to the other party or anyone else.

The handling of the confidential positions of the parties
poses another ethical issue on mediator techniques. For
example, in a separate session with each of the parties,
the mediator learns that the union's rock bottom position
is lower than the best offer the employer is prepared to
make. If the mediator reveals either party's position to
the other side, he will have caused a costly impact on the
outcome for the party whose position he revealed.

Some mediators confronted with this situation will inform
both parties that they are very close together, and suggest
that they proceed to exchange incremental offers to probe
each other's position. Other mediators, after informing
the parties that they are close together, will withdraw
from the negotiations and allow the parties to conclude the
negotiations in direct bargaining.

A significant imbalance of power between labor and management can pose another ethical issue in mediator techniques.
The parties' power may be related to bargaining experience,
the skills of the spokesman, the availability of resources
and information, or economic strength. Generally, the economic strength of the parties, in the U.S. industrial relations system, determines the outcome of the negotiation and
mediation. This is a factor which the mediator has little
influence upon--nor should he. On the other aspects of
power, the mediator can exercise some influence. The ethical question is "should he?"

Several factors influence the answer to this question: (1)
negotiations and mediations function best when the parties
have approximately equal power; (2) the neutrality of the
mediator should be maintained in practice as well as in
principle; (3) the mediator should not negotiate or act as
a broker for either side; (4) if one party is so weak relative to the other, no agreement is possible.

Based on these factors, most mediators will help the weaker
side only to the extent that no agreement is possible without it. The following case will illustrate: In mediation,
the company spokesman was an attorney. Since the union, a
weak independent local, could not afford an attorney, an
inexperienced member from the plant was serving as their
spokesman. In an effort to dissuade the union from pressing
its key issue, the attorney cast coubt on the legality of
the union's position by deliberately misstating the NLRB decisions on the subject. In this circumstance, the mediator

felt it was his duty to state his opinion of the relevant
NLRB decisions which directly contradicted the attorney.

3.   Psychological Needs Of The Mediator[5]

There are some other ethical problems involving techniques
used by a mediator that are related to the mediator's personal and professional needs for recognition. These problems are essentially a balancing of the mediator's personal
needs with the needs of the parties. The following situations will illustrate:

(a) Over the course of several negotiations, it is apparent that the parties are depending upon mediation rather
than their own resources to reach settlement. What is at
issue here is the mediator's responsibility to wean the parties away from their dependence upon mediation and to help
them become jointly self-reliant and responsible. The mediator may be tempted to focus only on his need to feel
involved and helpful to parties with whom he has worked
repeatedly.

(b) Some disputes will automatically get extensive media coverage; others can be handled to get coverage. There
are cases in which the type and extent of media coverage
can be harmful to the resolution of the dispute. There is
an ethical question here for the mediator who wants media
coverage for his own needs when such coverage may be counter-productive to the immediate resolution of the dispute.

(c) One very useful mediation technique is developing
an idea and selling it to the parties in such a way that the
parties believe that the idea is their own. This can be a
very self-effacing experience for the mediator. At some
points in a mediator's career because of his own need for
recognition, he may find this extremely difficult to do and
will be tempted to exact from the parties some recognition
that the idea or series of ideas that were crucial to settlement were actually his brainchild.

Each of these situations requires the mediator to have a
personal maturity and insight into his own needs so that
the needs of the parties are always paramount.

4.   Judging The Appropriateness Of A Settlement

The ethical question involved in the mediator's judging
the appropriateness of a settlement is basically one of

public versus private interest. For example, if the mediator believes that the labor agreement is the parties' private business, he will conclude that the parties may agree
to anything they wish without the mediator's imposing his
judgment on the legality or fairness of their agreement.
However, if the mediator believes that the labor agreement
should be fair and consistent with public policy, he will
conclude that he may not allow the parties to make an agreement which is unfair or contrary to public policy.

All mediators have an understandable reluctance to be viewed as enforcers of law or regulation because such a function
would diminish their acceptability to the parties and the
parties' willingness to take them into their confidence.

For example, if the parties are knowingly in the process of
agreeing to an illegal "hot cargo" clause and the mediator
challenges them, they are not likely to continue a confidential working relationship with him. But "hot cargo" clauses
are a clear and well established point of law. Since many
parts of the labor law are not so clear and well established,
the mediator in many cases will be less than sure of what is
precisely illegal. The equal employment opportunity requirements, for example, are regularly being modified and refined
by courts and the EEOC.

Therefore, most mediators avoid both the hazard of being enforcers and of making misstatements on the current state of
the law by cautiously suggesting to the spokesmen, probably
in separate sessions, that they may want to check with their
legal counsel before finalizing an agreement on a particular
point.

5.   Exemption From Subpoenas

Since the mediator is given much information in confidence,
he may, on occasion, get information from a party which
would be of interest to investigative agencies such as the
NLRB, IRS, or FBI. On matters of labor relations, the mediator is by law and regulation exempted from subpoenas
which would require his testimony in court or in an arbitration.[6]

On criminal matters, he could probably be subpoenaed and required to testify even to confidential matters with the same
problems of conscience that a priest/confessor has with information from a penitent, or a journalist has in protecting

a news source. Even volunteering information to appropriate authorities on criminal acts would present the mediator
with the same problem of conscience that the priest or journalist has. The possibility of a mediator's finding himself
in a situation involving criminal conduct during his mediation effort is rather remote. But it has happened.

6. The Mediator And Government Guidelines

A more relevant judgment problem for the mediator is his
role in governmental efforts to reduce inflation by wage-
price controls or wage-price guidelines. Most mediators
dislike wage-price controls because the review and approval
of negotiated agreements by a Government agency interferes
with free collective bargaining. However, if the parties
make an agreement that exceeds the known control limits,
most mediators will warn them of the futility of their actions. If the parties persist, however, most mediators will
let matters take their course with the enforcement agency.

Wage-price guidelines present a lesser but similar problem
as wage-price controls for the mediator.

The 1962 wage-price guidelines of the Council of Economic
Advisers became increasingly complex the longer they were
in effect. Since these guidelines were promulgated as Government policy, the Federal mediator had an obligation as
a Government representative to respect them. At the same
time, the mediator had to perform his mediation duties of
assisting the parties reach agreement.

The FMCS established a policy to assist the mediators when
confronting conflicts with the guidelines. The policy required mediators to be sufficiently informed about the
guidelines to advise the parties on the clear cases, or to
suggest sources of advice in difficult cases. Further, the
policy directed that in no event should a mediator act as a
reporter to another Government agency. The latter was based
on the principle that, if mediators act as policemen reporting real or possible violations, it would destroy the confidential character of their relationship with the parties.

Summary

In this chapter, the ethical considerations in mediation
have been discussed, and suggestions have been made on how
mediators might handle these problems. Ethical problems

are indigenous to the mediator's job. The mediator's
unique work environment demands acceptability with both
labor and management; it limits his power to his own persuasive abilities; it exposes him to confidential information. It places him in the almost impossible position of
trying to protect the public interest when confronted with
seemingly contradictory public policies. All of these create unique ethical pressures and problems for the mediator.

NOTES

1. Much of this chapter is based on "Ethics and the Federal Mediator," by Jerome T. Barrett, in <u>Annual Meeting Proceedings of The Society of Professionals in Dispute Resolution</u>: New York City, October 1977, pp. 81-86.

2. See The Code of Professional Conduct for Mediators in Appendix.

3. See The Code of Professional Responsibility in Appendix.

4. See The Code of Professional Conduct for Mediators in Appendix.

5. For a more extensive discussion of the topic, see Jerome T. Barrett, "The Psychology of a Mediator: A Third-Party's Psychic Balance Sheet," <u>Society of Professionals in Dispute Resolution Occasional Paper No. 83-1</u>, March 1983, pp. 1-8.

6. See Chapter XII, CONFIDENTIALITY.

CHAPTER XXX
NON– LABOR RELATIONS USE OF MEDIATION[1]

Historically, the resolution of disputes or disagreements
has been handled in ways as varied as the aggression of
fighting, violence, and wars; or as the passivity of giving in, flight, and surrender. In more civilized settings,
more civilized methods have developed--litigation, arbitration, negotiations, and mediation. In litigation and arbitration, a third party is empowered to decide the issue in
dispute. Negotiation has the advantages of allowing the
parties to fully participate in developing a solution with
which they can live. Mediation is a blend of the advantages of the other three with none of the disadvantages.
It brings the advantage of the objective third party, and
leaves the decision on the outcome with those who must live
with it.

From the mid-1960's to mid-1970's, a growing awareness
of individual human rights was spawned by the civil rights
movement, the Vietnam War protest, and the rising expectations of women, the aged, students, gays, and others. The
assertive methods used by many of these groups exceeded
society's capacity to resolve these issues using traditional methods. The courts, the most traditional dispute re-
solvers, were overcrowded, and poorly suited to resolve basic human problems. The demand for better methods for resolving disputes increasingly looked to the methods that
were routinely used in labor-management relations--collec-
tive bargaining, negotiations, mediation, and arbitration.
As a key player in labor-management dispute settlement, the
Federal Mediation and Conciliation Service was a logical
resource for protestors, institutions, and governments to
turn for help.

The Simkin Administration

Prior to William Simkin's becoming Director of FMCS in 1961,
the Service had not worked beyond its legislative mandate
in labor-management relations. The emergence of public employee unionism in the 60's changed this.

Although the Service lacked legislative authority to handle
disputes between public employees and their employer, no

other organization was available in most instances to provide assistance (cf Chapters IV and V). However, because
of public pressure and the urgent requests of the parties,
the Service began providing mediation on a case-by-case
basis. Since many of these public employee disputes in
large cities had civil rights aspects to them, the Service
was drawn further afield from its usual work.

In 1964, the Congress determined that civil rights disputes
should be mediated. The Civil Rights Act of 1964 created
two new agencies:

    1. The Community Relations Service was to provide me-
diation "assistance to communities and persons therein in
resolving disputes, disagreements, or difficulties relating
to discriminating practices based on race, color, national
origin which impairs the rights of persons..."

    2. The Equal Employment Opportunity Commission was to
use mediation and conciliation in the enforcement of the
equal employment law.

To the extent that there was any discussion within or outside the Serivce about an increased role for the Service
beyond labor-management relations, it was confined to questions about the role of preventive mediation in labor relations, and the application of mediation to State and local
public employee disputes.

The Counts Administration

J. Curtis Counts became FMCS Director in 1969 in the first
Nixon administration. This period marked a continuing increase in public employee mediation by the Service, and a
decline in the number of preventive mediation cases.

The Usery and Scearce Administrations

Bill Usery became Director during the second Nixon administration in July 1973 in what was to become a major growth
period for the Service. By strongly urging an expanded role
for the Service, Usery was able to convince the Administration and the Congress to increase the staff and budget. The
total staff grew from 425 at the end of 1972 to 570 in 1976.

Usery's expanded role for the Service was underscored by his
creation of the Office of Technical Services in the National

Office. This office coordinated and promoted technical assistance cases, conducted an improved professional development program for the mediators, provided a technical information and research function to assist the field mediator,
and experimented with new uses of mediation. During the
four years of its existence, the office was the focal point
of an increasing amount of non-labor relations work within
the Service.

In early 1974, Usery convened a three-day meeting of all
Service managers to discuss the role of the Service. The
major result was the adoption of a five-part Mission Statement. While four parts specifically referred to labor-management relations, the fifth part envisioned an expanded
role in these words: "Developing the art, science, and
practice of dispute resolution."[2] This Mission Statement
remains in effect today.

During the oil crisis in 1974, Director Usery personally became involved in some non-labor relations disputes with the
independent truckers and oil companies, and with the independent gas station operators and the oil companies.

Hopi-Navajo Dispute

Probably the most outstanding example of non-labor mediation
in which the Service was ever involved was instigated by
Congress in a 1974 statute which directed the Service to
mediate a 100-year old land dispute between the Hopi and
Navajo Indian tribes in Arizona. The Service retained former Director Bill Simkin, then a resident of Arizona, and
provided him with a mediator assistant.

Geographically, the largest reservation in the U.S., covering two and half million acres in northeastern Arizona, the
Hopi-Navajo reservation was created by an Executive Order
in 1882. Following years of dispute over land use by the
two tribes--in which every traditional dispute resolving
procedure was used with only partial and temporary settle-
ment--the Congress directed that mediation be attempted.
Five hundred thousand dollars was appropriated to finance
the mediation, and 50 million was made available to other
Federal agencies to help implement the settlement by relocation of fences, villages, families, burial grounds, and
monuments. The mediation effort was to take six months.
If settlement was not fully achieved at that point, the
mediator was to make a report and recommendations to the
Federal District Court.

After months of work by the mediator team, supported by an administrative team and supplied with information from other Government agencies, agreement was reached in principle on many issues--the mediators estimated that 85% of the issues had been resolved. The mediators submitted their report and recommendations to the Federal Judge who, after hearing evidence from the tribes, adopted the recommendations and ordered them enforced.

Since many questions remained on the implementation, the Judge and the tribes requested that the mediation effort continue. For the next year, Simkin continued to help the parties on an as-needed basis.

The success of this mediation effort was universally praised by the Court, the tribes, the Bureau of Indian Affairs, the Department of Interior, and the media. The length of the dispute, the "sacred" nature of some issues, the uniqueness of the Indian culture and habits, plus the numerous prior efforts to settle the dispute, all contributed to the difficult task of mediation. But unlike the earlier efforts-- treaties, litigation, court orders, executive orders, and Acts of Congress which produced answers to narrow questions--mediation allowed the parties to deal with their needs and desires and, in that way, to develop solutions with which they could live.

Home Owners' Warranty

Another very extensive project started during the Usery period involved the Home Owners' Warranty (HOW) program of the National Association of Home Builders. The HOW program was started in 1973 as a method of resolving disputes that arose between a home builder and a home buyer. The program, provided under a warranty, utilized mediation and arbitration to resolve disputes. Before HOW was created, the National Builders' Association came to the Service for advice and assistance.

The Service provided extensive discussion and suggestions on how the program might work, help in preparing and conducting training throughout the country, and technical advice once the program was operating to the HOW conciliators who encountered mediation problems. During 1973 and 1974, the Service conducted more than 20 training programs which in most cases were co-sponsored by FMCS and HOW to give the program credibility.

In 1976, when the Federal Trade Commission (FTC) issued
rules on warranties and guaranties under the newly passed
Magnuson-Moss Bill, the Service assisted HOW in getting
approval from FTC to allow HOW to operate as an experiment
under the new rules.

Assistance to HOW extended well into the Directorship of
Wayne Horvitz, and included the creation of the National
Academy of Conciliators.

Oglala Sioux Election

When Bill Usery became Secretary of Labor in the spring of
1976, his Deputy, James Scearce, became Director of FMCS.
As Deputy, Scearce had acted as the liaison for the Hopi-
Navajo mediation effort with the Bureau of Indian Affairs
and other Federal agencies in Washington.

As a result of these contacts, in 1975, the Oglala Sioux
Tribe of Pine Ridge Reservation in South Dakota contacted
Scearce to discuss their need for a neutral organization to
oversee their tribal election. After considerable discussion and an urgent request from the BIA, the Service agreed
to help.

The prior election had been highly contested during and after the election. The reservation is geographically the
second largest in the U.S. with 12,000 tribal members and
3,500 non-Indians. Twenty-one polling places were needed to
cover the two million acres. The Service's role was to oversee the election conducted by the tribal election board.
This role included developing the election rules and procedures, training the election judges and observers, and providing a trained election advisor for each polling place at
the primary and general elections. These advisors were FMCS
mediators and retired persons from the Department of Labor
and the National Labor Relations Board who were selected by
and worked under the direction of the Service.

Both elections were held without major problems during
January 1976.

The Oglala election and the Hopi-Navajo mediation are two
of very few non-labor cases which have been well documented.
A complete report on the election was prepared in February
1976.[3]

Helping Federal Agencies

A number of Federal agencies requested and received assistance from the Service during the Usery/Scearce period. The
following are illustrative:

    1. Community Relations Service (CRS) - The CRS is a
branch of the Justice Department charged with mediating
civil rights disputes. FMCS helped CRS develop position
descriptions for their mediators, conducted a number of
training sessions for their mediators, developed an internship program, and arranged for liaison between field
mediators of the two agencies in cases involving civil
rights and labor relations.

    2. Federal Bureau of Investigation (FBI) - The FBI
training facility in Quantico, Virginia, conducts training
for State and local police officers. The Service critiqued
training sessions and materials on domestic disputes and
hostage taking. The Service also helped develop non-violent
responses to these explosive situations.

    3. Department of Commerce (DOC) - The Service assisted
the Science and Technology Division of DOC in developing a
dispute settlement system to resolve disputes over voluntary
standards in manufactured products.

    4. Law Enforcemnet Assistance Administrtion (LEAA)
and Equal Employment Opportunity Commission (EEOC) - The
Service provided mediation training to the staff of both
agencies.

The Washington Lab

During much of the Usery/Scearce period, the Office of Technical Assistance responded to the many opportunities in the
Washington, D.C., area to provide assistance in non-labor
relations disputes. This was a mutually beneficial arrange-
ment--the recipient got help, and the Service got the opportunity to experiment and learn about the application of its
skills to new areas of conflict.

Some examples of these activities were:

    1. Mediating a racial dispute beteeen Black and White
firefighters in the D.C. Fire Department.

2. Setting up a dispute settlement procedure between landlords and tenants in D.C., and mediating several cases to help get the system working.

3. Mediating a racial dispute between the custodians and teachers in the Arlington County schools.

4. Training the staff of the Montgomery County Maryland Consumer Compliant Office in negotiation and mediation skills.

The Horvitz Administration

Wayne Horvitz became Director of FMCS in April 1977 during the Carter Administration. He was acquainted with non-labor-management mediation, having spent two years as a consultant to the National Center for Dispute Settlement in the late 1960's.

Age Discrimination Mediation

During the Horvitz tenure, the first continuing use of FMCS mediators in non-labor-management cases began with age discrimination disputes. Under the Age Discrimination Act of 1975, age discrimination is prohibited in programs and activities which receive Federal funds. The enforcement of the Act was assigned to the Secretary of Health, Education, and Welfare (HEW). Following months of discussion and planning, FMCS and HEW developed a system for handling these cases that featured mediation. The uniqueness of the system for both FMCS and civil rights cases was emphasized by Secretary Califano in a speech on Aging:

> "We propose, for the first time in the history
> of civil rights enforcement, to enlist the Fed-
> eral Mediation and Conciliation Service to re-
> view claims of discrimination and resolve them,
> within no more than 60 to 90 days. No other
> civil rights program in our government employs
> such a process of third-party mediation. But
> perhaps, in time, everyone of our civil rights
> programs should feature such a mediation process."[4]

FMCS used this program to attempt several innovations in recruiting, selection, training, and evaluations. In one half of the geographic regions of FMCS, the cases were mediated by specially trained FMCS mediators who continued

to handle their normal labor-management case load. In the
other regions, individuals were selected to mediate these
cases on an as-needed basis. These persons, called Community Conciliators, were recruited through various community
based mediation centers.

During the first eighteen months of the program, the Service handled a total of 94 cases with 55% requiring no further action after the mediation.[5]

In January 1983, because of the decline in the labor-management case load, the Service terminated the Community Conciliators and now handles all age discrimination cases with
regular staff mediators.

Helping Other Federal Agencies

The Horvitz period was characterized by an increase in the
amount of non-labor-management work done by the Service.
The following will illustrate:

    1. Federal Highway Administration (FHA) - The Office
of Environmental Planning of FHA within the Department of
Transportation, contacted FMCS in the spring of 1979 to
discuss their need for training in negotiation skills. The
employees of FHA and their State counterparts were involved
in the condemnation of property and the exercise of eminent
domain in the construction of highways. These employees
are primarily engineers with skill in areas other than human relations. The FHA, dissatisfied with the reaction
these employees were getting from the public, was seeking
a quick-fix training package. After discussions over several months, an agreement was reached between the two agencies providing for (a) travel by two mediators to learn more
about environmental disputes and the work of the trainees,
and (b) several week-long training programs by FMCS covering
a variety of dispute resolving methods such as negotiating,
prioritizing, concensus building, and problem solving. Much
of this training went well beyond the training FMCS conducted for its own mediators.[6]

    2. Other Training Programs - The Service received re-
quests for training assistance from a number of agencies
which had concluded that their programs would be helped by
having a staff more skilled in conflict resolution. Some
agencies that the Service was able to respond to were: the
Veterans Reemployment Office of the Department of Labor;

the Office of Civil Rights in the Department of Health and Human Services; and the Department of Housing and Urban Development.

3. Consultation and Systems Development - A number of requests were received from agencies seeking advice and suggestions on how to systematically deal with conflicts. Staff time limited the number of requests which FMSS could satisfy. Help was given to the following: Division of Standards and Regulations of the Environmental Protection Agency; Environmental Office of the Department of Energy; Council on Environmental Quality in the Executive Office of the President.

Non-Federal Agency Work

Although the emphasis during the Horvitz period was on helping Federal agencies, some assistance was given to others. The following are illustrative:

1. National Academy of Conciliators (NAC) - In 1979, FMCS and Home Owners Warranty (HOW) cooperated in the creation of NAC to assume responsibility for administering the HOW program and provide other dispute settlement services. In the next two years, the Service gave extensive assistance to NAC in developing its staff. NAC today has served over thirty clients in dispute settlement work; it continues to increase its role and impact on new areas of dispute settlement.

2. Family/Divorce Mediation - The Family Mediation Association--a nationwide organization of lawyers, psychologists, marriage counselors, social workers, and clergy-- utilized a very formal and structured form of mediation. At the request of some FMA members, FMCS undertook some cooperative training and consultation. Several four-day training programs were conducted with FMCS playing a major role and providing meeting facilities. Some modifications of their formal approach to mediation resulted from these programs and dialogues.

3. Alaska Environment - The Attorney General of Alaska requested FMCS assistance in developing a dispute settlement system for land use problems. A new State law required local governments to clear their land use plans with the Alaska Coastal Management Council. The Council wanted to adopt a dispute settlement system that could resolve disputes between local plans, natives, and the land/resources developer.

An Assistant Attorney General met with FMCS in Washington, D.C., to discuss a system that would include Service participation. A mediator travelled to Alaska to meet the Council and to discuss the system and the FMCS's role in it. The Council adopted the system which designated FMCS to select and assign mediators as disputes arise.

4. National Association of Social Workers - FMCS was asked to serve in an advisory capacity on a project funded by the Department of Education which would attempt to use mediation in conflicts arising under a law requiring the mainstreaming of handicapped children. The Service provided advice and suggestions, and shared instructional materials and training strategies with the program director.

Moffett Period

All involvement with non-labor work was stopped, except age discrimination mediation, because of budget cuts in 1981 and 1982. All the national office staff involved in this work were either dismissed or transferred to the field.

McMurray Administration

Kay McMurray became FMCS Director in July 1982 under budget and staff limits similar to the Moffett period. The Community Conciliators in the age discrimination mediation program were dismissed.

At the policy level, McMurray officially encouraged mediators to work in the non-labor area in a Bulletin to all Regional and District Directors in December 1982.

Field Mediators in Non-Labor Area

Given the independence of the mediator's job, they are capable of doing, and some have done, a variety of things in the non-labor area. Whether they are encouraged, discouraged, or neither, some of this work continues. The mediator's involvement seems to be motivated by personal interest, opportunity, community involvement, a feeling of professional responsibility toward mediation, and/or intellectual curiosity. Their activities have included the following, listed in part in the order of increasing involvement and difficulty:

--Giving a talk about mediation

--Providing information about mediation

--Providing training

--Helping develop a dispute settlement system

--Mediating.

Listed below are specific activities that mediators reported doing in conversation with the author. Most items listed were mentioned by more than one mediator:

--Training the human rights staff of a municipal government on conflict resolution.

--Training the human rights staff of a State government
in conflict resolution.

--Training the staff of a campus mediation program.

--Training advocates for the disabled and mentally
retarded in conflict resolution.

--Training advocates for women's, Indians' and children's rights in conflict resolution.

--Training mediators for a family mediation program.

--Training law students as mediators for a court and
police department diversion program.

--Training mediators for a community mediation program.

--Mediating cases as a special master of municipal/
county court.

--Mediating cases for the U.S. Court of Appeals. (A
mediator did this on a leave of absence for six months, then
he resigned to do it full time.)

--Mediating landlord-tenant disputes.

--Consulting with a citizens' mediation team in a
violent campus dispute.

--Consulting with a newly formed community mediation program.

--Speaking to groups and conferences of non-labor relations persons about how mediation works.

--Helping set up a community mediation program.

Evaluation

Most of the FMCS work in non-labor relations has involved training others in dispute resolution and sharing the experiences it has acquired in labor mediation. To a lesser extent, the Service has provided mediation assistance and dispute settlement systems development.

Assessing the impact or effectiveness of this initiative by FMCS beyond its traditional sphere is difficult. Certainly the amount of mediation and the uses of mediation have been greatly increased during the past ten years. To the extent that FMCS has shared its expertise, it has helped this evolution in peaceful settlement of disputes. The individual FMCS mediators who have been involved have gotten personal satisfaction and new insights into the multiple applications of mediation.

NOTES

1.   This Chapter is based on a Study by Jerome T. Barrett on the same subject with a grant from the National Institute for Dispute Resolution in 1984.

2.   See FMCS Mission Statement in Appendix.

3.   Federal Mediation and Conciliation Service Report on the 1976 Primary and General Elections of the Oglala Sioux Tribe, Pine Ridge Indian Reservation, South Dakota, February 1976.

4.   Joseph A. Califano, "Remarks to the National Journal Conference on the Economics of Aging," November 30, 1978, Washington, D.C.

5.   Jerome T. Barrett and Lucretia Dewey Tanner, "The FMCS Role in Age Discrimination Complaints: New Uses of Mediation," Labor Law Journal, Vol. 32, No. 11, November 1981, pp. 745-54.

6.   Jerome T. Barrett, "Skilled are the Peacemakers," Northeast Training News, Vol. 1, No. 10, June 1980, p. 19.

CHAPTER XXXI
MINIMIZING CRISES IN COLLECTIVE BARGAINING

This chapter is devoted to exploring a number of approaches negotiators can utilize and which may minimize a crisis in their negotiations. These suggestions have evolved from thirty-three years of a mediator's observations in literally hundreds of negotiations. Like previously suggested mediation techniques, their relevancy and utilization to a particular negotiation situation ultimately lies in the good sense and judgment of the negotiator.

At the outset, it should be recognized that there are some situations where a crisis is inevitable and cannot be avoided. To cite a few examples:

1.   Either an actual or potential political fight in a labor organization representing the employees in a particular plant. Whether it is an actual or potential, the company is often the victim of the by-plays between the "ins" and the "outs." Both are jockeying for political position. Each is seeking to do that which may be momentarily popular since it may be productive of votes, rather than that which may be both responsible and responsive to the issues being negotiated.

2.   A corporate merger or consolidation, in which the acquiring company seeks conformity with its industrial relations policies.

3.   Cases where an area or industry wage and fringe pattern has been established and the company is not in an economic position to grant similar gains.

4.   Insistence by unions on coordinated bargaining in situations where the company resists any form of such bargaining.

Some of the approaches designed to minimize crises in collective bargaining are:

1.   Avoid taking an end position prematurely.

There are many issues which are brought out at the bargaining table which at first appear to be insurmountable,

but which, as negotiations proceed, can be solved by careful explorations and discussions. Many issues presented do
not reflect the true underlying problems which gave rise to
the demand. This is particularly true in a seniority area.
Professional mediators have often found that a demand for
a sweeping change in the entire seniority system was born
of several grievances which were left unsettled. Through
careful explorations, these grievances can be brought to
the surface. By correcting the grievances, the demand oftentimes becomes less formidable. If the negotiator takes
an end position prematurely in such situations and others
similar to it, a crisis will immediately develop because it
leaves the other party only one alternative--consideration
of economic action.

Remember that a cat grows whiskers so that it won't stick
its head into a place from which it cannot back out if
necessary.

    2. <u>Forestall the premature adoption of an end posi-
        tion by the other party.</u>

        If by the nature of the discussion the other party
takes an end position in front of his committee, it is then
difficult for him to retreat from it, even though circumstances may warrant a modification of his position. This
often occurs during an acrimonious exchange between the
chairmen of each party.

Such avoidances may be obtained by the judicious use of the
caucus device or by the temporary abandonment of a line of
argument which will lead inevitably to the assumption of an
end position by the other party.

    3. <u>Complete honesty in negotiations.</u>

        During the course of negotiations, experienced ne-
gotiators search out possible areas of accommodation, often
on the basis of responses to their inquiries across the bargaining table. If a negotiator consciously or unconsciously
leads his counterpart into believing that a compromise is
possible in a certain area, it is reasonable to assume that
such counterpart may structure his entire bargaining strategy around that indication. If it subsequently develops
that he was misled, a crisis will be precipitated.

4. <u>Greater use of subcommittees in negotiations</u>.

The final settlement package should be the result of the participation of all the members of the union committee. To the extent that each has a voice in the structuring of the final settlement, the possibility of the settlement being accepted is enhanced. In most negotiations, there are a number of issues such as seniority, insurance, inequities, and the like, which lend themselves to a subcommittee approach. In such instances, the use of a subcommittee will do much to minimize the possibility of a deadlock and as a consequence a crisis in the bargaining.

5. <u>Attention to resolution of local issues</u>.

Even where the economic package offered equals or exceeds the area or industry pattern, the failure to resolve local issues can precipitate a crisis and lead to an unexpected stoppage. This is especially true where the issues are deemed to be perennial nuisances.

Recently, a multiplant midwestern company offered an economic package which in most respects exceeded settlement achieved by the union in contracts with its major competitors. As a condition of its offer, the company insisted that the union committee withdraw its demands for fixed work schedules and limitations on foremen doing bargaining unit work. The union negotiators agreed and scheduled a ratification meeting supremely confident that securing approval was a mere formality. To their astonishment, the vote was seven to one to reject and a strike occurred. In ferreting out the reason, it was discovered that the two issues dropped had been urged at the three preceding negotiations and withdrawn at the last moment. The employees affected had determined that they would no longer permit the size of the economic package to submerge resolution of these daily aggravations. By marshalling a vocal dissident group around their cause, they succeeded in voting down the agreement.

An in-depth examination and, if merited, a resolution of local issues can avoid a crisis.

6. <u>Avoid "matter of principle" attitude</u>.

Often crises are created by management negotiators by their belligerent, unyielding attitude at the bargaining table. This attitude finds expression in the phrase "that is a matter of principle with us." At other times, it is manifested by an unqualified "no."

No matter how unreasonable the demand may appear, in most instances it represents a desire of the employees. Often an unreasonable demand is based on a real grievance. Companies are not normally arbitrary or unreasonable. The "no" answer was undoubtedly the result of careful thinking on the part of the management. Why not state the reasons to the employees? It will show them that their demands were treated respectfully and were not arbitrarily dismissed by their company.

As to the "matter of principle" argument, remember there are a number of things that a company is doing today which are contrary to matters of principle it stressed a few years ago. It is rather an humiliating experience to cling to a principle as long as possible, and then have to concede the point, and "violate" the principle.

7. Avoiding by negotiators of premature announcements of fixed bargaining goals.

Just as the premature announcement of a fixed wage goal can thwart the ability of a union committee to reach a peaceful accommodation of the dispute, so too can a similar position taken by a management committee.

An announcement by management that as a condition of settlement inefficient work practices be eliminated can create a crisis. Such local practices, particularly if condoned by management over a long period of time, become "sacred cows" to the employees affected and are emotionally charged. Any precondition seeking to eliminate or curtail them provides a rallying point for dissident groups. All other union contractual gains are ignored.

The most sophisticated management bargainers seek to attain such goals not by announcing prematurely a rigid position but rather by permitting them to develop during bargaining as mutual problems which should be resolved through negotiations.

8. Insistence on settlement of one issue as a
    condition precedent.

        A premature crisis in bargaining is often created
by the insistence of one side or the other on the settlement of one issue before any meaningful negotiations can
take place on the balance of the issues. While one can
appreciate that many negotiators feel that one issue is of
such paramount importance that it must be resolved before
any other issues can be meaningfully discussed, an obdurate
position on this bargaining strategy can only invoke a similar position on the part of the other party. The adherence by one party to this position is often dictated by a
fear that either the money offer or other accommodations
will submerge or weaken the issue in the final settlement.
Nevertheless, if an agreement is the goal and not economic
action, this position should be abandoned.

    9. Flexibility of bargaining teams.

        If collective bargaining is to accomplish its pur-
pose, viz. the expeditious settlement of the dispute, then
the bargaining team must have flexibility. Flexibility
does not mean surrender or compromise for the sake of compromise. It means the ability to quickly analyze problems,
suggest solutions, make counter-proposals or to explain
clearly the need or the impossibility of granting a proposal
at the time the proposals and counter-proposals are made.

Negotiators, like mediators, must be guided by a sense of
timing. There are times during the course of negotiations,
when a proposal or counter-proposal has the best chance of
acceptance. The negotiators must have the authority at that
time to "seize the moment." A delay in order to consult
with higher authority can destroy that opportunity.

    10. Minimizing crises at bargaining time during
         contract term.

        There are a number of suggestions which have been
made during the contract term which can assist the parties
to avoid a crisis at bargaining time. Each of these suggestions is centered around the central theme--a breakdown
in communications between management and its employees. To
permit rumors and unsettled grievances to become rampant is
to create the atmosphere of mistrust and frustration, which

can only lead to strained relationships. Some of the devices which have been used successfully by companies and
unions are:

a. <u>Joint explanation of contract language</u> - All too
often the negotiators in a collective bargaining contract
lose sight of the fact that, while they may know the contents of the contract and its meaning, the actual administration falls into the hands of lower line supervisors and
shop stewards. Often, no attempt is made to assure that
these individuals fully understand the meaning and application of the contract language. Several companies have very
successfully arranged for meetings, separately or jointly,
with the shop stewards and foremen. These meetings are usually co-chaired by a union representative and a representative of a labor relations division of the company. At the
meeting, the newly negotiated contract is analyzed section-
by-section and jointly explained as to how it would apply
to specific shop situations. Questions are solicited so
that a complete understanding can be achieved.

Particularly successful in this area was the program undertaken by the Lockheed Aircraft Company and the Machinists
Union. As a result of their program, there was a dramatic
drop in the number of grievances since those who were responsible for the day-to-day administration had a clear
understanding of how the contract applied in most situations. The investment in time was amply repaid.

b. <u>Interim review of contract terms</u> - The great majority of contracts are for two or more years' duration.
A number of companies and unions have established a procedure whereby two or three days are set aside in the
middle of the contract term for review of problems which
may have arisen as a result of the administration of the
contract as negotiated. The most successful approaches
have been those in which the meeting is attended by high-
level union and company representatives.

While many practitioners scoffed at the idea of a collective bargaining contract being considered a living document
subject to change during the contract term, events have
proved that this theory was not so farfetched as it first
appeared. When it becomes obvious that some provisions are
unworkable and are creating problems for both labor and management, there should be no obstacle to modifying the contract to meet the needs of both parties. It is axiomatic

in law that any contract may be modified by mutual consent
at any time. This approach does much to dissipate problems
which, if allowed to fester, will tend to bring about a crisis at the contract expiration.

     c. <u>Joint Study Committees</u> - The issues that confront
most negotiators today are highly complex and technical.
Each requires a great deal of study, and the services of
specialists and experts in a particular subject matter must
be utilized in areas such as insurance, pensions, and incentives. There is no reason in the world why the parties who
anticipate these issues should not undertake early joint
discussions. Each side can set up a subcommittee whose
function will not necessarily be to resolve the problems,
but at the very least to get agreement on the economic facts
such as costs, and to delineate the issues in dispute. This
would do much to eliminate the situation which mediators
frequently observe: the parties approach the bargaining
table at contract expiration time without a clear understanding of the full implication and cost of the demands
raised by the other side.

     d. <u>Job security changes</u> - The experience of mediators
indicates that one of the greatest causes of stoppages is
the fear, real or fancied, of loss of job security. Statistics indicate that when the issue of job security exists,
the possibility of a stoppage, and a prolonged one, is ever
present. If a company is contemplating any changes that
have an effect on the job security of its employees, is it
not the better part of wisdom for such a company to discuss
the contemplated changes with the union representative,
much in advance of the institution of such changes?

Fears of loss of job security may arise as a result of automation, mechanization, changes in the seniority practices,
consolidation of departments, removal of certain operations
from the plant or subcontracting. Normally, the decision
of the company to undertake such programs is not one reached
on the spur of the moment. A great deal of corporate planning and thought usually goes into it. The inevitable leaks
as to what the company is contemplating creates an instability in the employees' outlook even though oftentimes the
leaks result in a distorted or exaggerated fear. This is
reflected in the employees' attitudes and productivity. Is
it not just common sense for any company, when contemplating
such a drastic change to sit down with the union representatives and advise them of its plans, seeking their suggestions as to the best manner of implementation which would

result in the least dislocation? Fears can thus be quieted
and crises at the bargaining table avoided.

11. Statistics in Crisis Bargaining

Normally the introduction of a mass of statistical
data at the bargaining table seldom persuades the other
party to change his position.

Statistics are normally introduced at the bargaining table
by company representatives. Apparently they do so in the
hope that these will engender mature reflection and a sympathetic understanding of the company's position and point
up the disastrous effects of its capitulation to the out-
rageous demands of the union. Mediators truly wish such
representatives, after they have made their very carefully
prepared presentation, could accompany the mediator into the
union caucus which inevitably follows. The characteriza-
tions of the company's statistics are, to be most polite,
bucolic and picturesque.

Why this reaction? The difficulty lies in that the company
is trying to do a job under the worst possible conditions.
Bargaining time with its emotional and political by-plays
and overtones is not the time to attempt to get over the
company's story effectively. The telling of the company's
story is a year-round job and not something to be rushed
through at bargaining time to an unreceptive group.

If the circumstances make it necessary to present statistical data at the bargaining table, then it is strongly urged
that the effort be confined to comparatively simple charts
or graphs. These are much more effective than prose in fix-
ing the attention of the audience, especially when the material has been prepared in a size that permitted the entire
group to see the same material at one time.

In selecting graphs or charts to be used, select only those
which are pertinent and illustrative. The yardstick in
making a selection should be quality not quantity.

Avoid technical or accounting language. Depletion, cost
centers, accruals, variances, earned surplus, cash flow,
flexible and standard costs, etc., may be clear to account-
ants since they are words of art in that profession. To the
average layman they are confusing and without meaning. Certainly company negotiators should have the ingenuity and

capability of expressing them in more understandable terms.
The charts or graphs used should be accurate. Above all,
the effectiveness of any chart or data depends on the confidence placed in its accuracy by the other party. False or
distorted charts or data are eventually discovered and the
company's labor relations will be put back many a year. Be
accurate--be truthful.

A factual statistical presentation of the cost impact of a
union demand may be necessary in cases where the union is
continually speaking of an only 5¢ or 10¢ difference in the
wage offer and demand. 5¢ or 10¢ sounds quite small, and
indeed it may be. But in a large company the impact of 5¢
or 10¢ on the company's annual payroll may amount to well
over $500,000 per year.

The same type of presentation may be relevant where the rank
and file seeks a so-called "blue sky" demand. The presentation may place the union representatives in a better position to convince the membership of the impracticality of
attainment.

Making A Final Offer

When the company negotiators have exhausted the possible
areas of accommodations and have reached a truly final position, the manner in which such final position is presented
becomes important. They should first emphasize that it is
their final position. The final position should be clearly
detailed and then do not permit themselves to be baited into explanations or justifications of the position taken.
If they do engage in such conversation, then it leaves the
door open for "nibblers" who will seek to eke out further
concessions.

CHAPTER XXXII

PRICING WAGE AND FRINGES OFFERS AND DEMANDS

During a mediation effort, one party may direct attention
to the cost impact of a particular offer or demand. All
too often the parties will become so engrossed in their
argumentation that they lose their perspective insofar as
the financial burdens, a concession, or demand would have
on the employer involved.

Since economic demands are couched in terms of cents per
hour or one additional holiday, the union committee may
very well feel that the difference between their respective positions is infinitesimal and chide the other side
with being niggardly in their adamancy. It is quite easy
for the union to point out that the difference between
their demands and the company's position is only 2¢ or 3¢
which on the face seems trite. However, if the difference
is translated into dollar impact on annual payroll, an entirely different picture may be painted. The "trite" difference may impose on the company a $250,000 to $750,000
increase in its annual labor bill.

Similarly, the company negotiators may insist that the cost
of the union demand would impose an intolerable burden on
the company and put it at a competitive disadvantage cost-
wise. However, the union, by comparatively simple mathe-
matics, may be in a position to point out that the cited
figure is exaggerated and that the true cost is much lower.
On this basis, the union could argue that the cost could be
readily absorbed by the company without losing its competitive position in the marketplace.

General Wage Increase Offers or Demands

a.   Impact on annual payroll costs.

        The direct impact of a general wage increase on
annual payroll costs can be readily computed. Assume that
there are 5,000 employees in the bargaining unit and the wage
offer is 25¢ per hour. To determine the direct impact on
annual payroll costs, the computation would be:

Hours per employee per year =
(40 hours x 52 weeks) = 2080
2080 hours x 25¢ offered = $520.00 per
    employee per year.
$520.00 x 5,000 employees = $2,600,000
    total annual additional payroll cost.

Sometimes the base used is the scheduled work year or total
productive time which can be either 2,000 or 2,040 hours,
with vacations and holidays deducted.

It should be emphasized that this figure represents only the
direct impact. To this must be added the indirect impact a
wage increase would have on incentives, premium pay, shift
differentials, overtime, holiday and vacation pay, severance
pay, pensions, and other benefits.

   b.   Average cost of general increases for contract
        of two or more years' duration.

        The total cost of a general increase can be com-
puted either as (a) total cost, or (b) average cost during
the term of the contract.

A contract of three years' duration providing for annual increases of 30¢ the first year, 25¢ the second year, and 20¢
the third year, entails a total cost of 75¢ per hour per
employee.   To compute the average cost:

Cents		Years		
30	x	3	=	.90
25	x	2	=	.50
20	x	1	=	.20
				$1.60

        3 years ÷ $1.60 = 53 1/3¢ average cost
                              per hour per employee.

   c.   Computing cost of night shift premium.

        To determine the cost of a night shift premium or
an increase in an established night shift premium, multiply
the percentage of employees affected by the night shift premium or increase in such premium.

Assume a plant employing 500 workers of which 50 are on the night shift. To determine the cost of a 20¢ an hour shift premium:

$$\frac{50}{500} = .10$$

.10 x .20 = $.02.

Fringe Cost Computations

No attempt is made here to reach conclusions as to portion of the total wage dollar spent for fringe benefits. Most of such studies are meaningless unless the surveyor enumerates the exact items he has designated "fringes" for the purpose of his report. The term "fringes" escapes precise definition. The resultant cost figure will expand or contract in direct relationship to the broadness or narrowness of the description of "fringes" used.

To assist mediators and negotiators, we will treat only some of the more commonly accepted fringes. For collective bargaining purposes, fringe offers and demands can be expressed in terms of (a) total annual cost to the company, or (b) cents per hour per employee.

   a. <u>Cents per hour costs.</u>

         The determination of costs in terms of cents per hour presents some difficulties in that the results may differ depending on the basic formula used. There are four basic formulas--each valid--which have been used:

      (1) Cents per straight time productive hours. The productive hours would be the straight time hours minus paid time off.

      (2) Cents per straight time hours. The straight time hours would be based on the scheduled work year; e.g., 2,040 hours.

      (3) Determining cents cost by dividing the annual cost of the fringe by the total productive man-hours. Productive man-hours can be determined by adding straight time hours and overtime hours and deducting paid time off.

      (4) Cents per straight time hour based on an arbitrary figure for annual work.

The use of these basic formulae will yield the cents per hour cost of other fringes such as vacations, rest periods, wash-up time, and the like.

b. Computing cost of holidays.

(1) Total annual cost. If a contract provides for eight paid holidays and the plant employs 500 workers in the bargaining unit with an average hourly rate of $6.00, the total cost of the holidays can be computed by the following formula:

> Number of workers x average hourly rate x hours off on holidays.

Applying the formula to the example cited:

> 500 employees x $6.00 x 64 hours = $192,000 annual cost.

(2) Cost in cents per hour. The following formula would be applicable:

> Annual cost = average hours worked per year x number of employees.

Applying this formula to the above example:

$$\frac{\$192,000}{2080 \times 500} = 18¢ \text{ per hour.}$$

(3) Total annual cost per employee. To determine total annual cost per employee:

$$\frac{\text{Company Annual Cost}}{\text{Total Number of Employees}}$$

$$\frac{\$192,000}{500} = \$384.00$$

c. Computing cost of vacations.

In computing cost of vacations, one must take into account the seniority of employees and their eligibility for vacations based on such seniority.

Let us assume that a contract calls for one week of vacation after one year of service, two weeks after three years of service, three weeks after ten years of service, and four weeks after twenty years of service. Let us use as an illustration a 500-man plant with average hourly earnings of $6.00. One hundred employees have one year seniority; 300 have more than 3 years, but less than 10; 70 have 10 years, but less than 20; and 30 have 20 or more years of service. The following would be an application of the formula:

$$
\begin{array}{rcl}
100 \times 40 \times \$6.00 & = & \$\ 24{,}000 \\
300 \times 80 \times \$6.00 & = & 144{,}000 \\
70 \times 120 \times \$6.00 & = & 50{,}400 \\
30 \times 160 \times \$6.00 & = & 28{,}800 \\
\end{array}
$$

Total annual cost....$247,200

d. Computing costs of wash-up time or rest periods.

To compute the cost of wash-up time or rest periods, the following formula may be utilized:

Time off per day x average hourly rate ÷ number of hours in work day of employees who would receive the off time.

To illustrate: If two rest periods of 10 minutes each are granted to 100 employees in a plant where the average rate is $6.00 an hour and the normal work day is 8 hours:

$$\frac{20 \text{ minutes}}{60 \text{ minutes}} = .333 \quad \text{(portion of one hour represented by rest period time)}$$

$6.00 x .333 = $2.00 (cost per day per employee)

$$\frac{\$2.00}{8 \text{ hours}} = 25¢ \text{ (cost per hour per employee).}$$

If the number of employees who receive the rest period or wash-up time is less than the total number of employees in the bargaining unit to which the cost calculation applies, multiply cost per hour per employee by the percent of employees who will receive the fringe benefit.

Computation of Changes in Consumer Price Index

Changes in the Consumer Price Index are often used to adjust the salary and wage plan during the life of the contract. The first problem is what Consumer Price Index is

to be used. The Bureau of Labor Statistics publishes not
only a national index but also local indices.

There are two formulas that are used to compute the change
in the Index. One is based on percent change in the Index
from one month of one year to the same month of the next
year. The other formula involves the change in the annual
average. This could be for any convenient 12-month period.
In this method the annual average of each of the two years
is determined by adding the 12 indices and dividing by 12.
The difference in the annual average divided by 12 the average of the first year determines the percentage increase.

Pension Plans

Costing an existing or newly negotiated pension plan depends
on a number of factors and assumptions.

Pension plans have certain basic provisions covering:

1.   normal retirement
2.   early retirement
3.   retirement after 30 years
4.   vested rights
5.   joint survivorship
6.   retirees
7.   disability benefits

All of these provisions have a cost tag except in the case
of early retirement. In early retirement, the benefit is
based on an actuarial reduction; i.e., the benefit is reduced to provide the same total outlay over the remaining
years of life expectancy.

In the case of a new pension plan, the cost estimates are
made by the actuary who uses assumptions as to each of the
following items:

1.   interest or fund earnings
2.   mortality rate before and after retirement
3.   amortization period for funding the unfunded
     past service
4.   the age spread of the group
5.   the service spread of the group
6.   the proportion of women in the group
7.   the salary schedule and a salary scale for
     the future

8. the benefits proposed or the money available
    for the purchase of benefits.

There should be little dispute about most of these assumptions, except for the interest assumption. At present, a
conservative assumption would be about 7%.

Where the plan is just starting, once the assumptions are
agreed upon, then the benefits and costs become a matter of
bargaining. Many unions and management arrange for their
specialists and actuaries to meet away from the bargaining
table to see if they can agree on assumptions to be made
and the costing of the plans or programs which are being
discussed by the negotiators. In most cases, these specialists will emerge from their subcommittee meetings in complete agreement as to the economic facts and costings. They
may quarrel as to the appropriate assumptions but seldom as
to the cost implications flowing from whatever of the two
assumptions which may be adopted.

Parties and mediators should know what the experience in
the last few years has been in relation to the cost impact.
If the fund earnings exceeded the interest assumption, it
would have a significant impact on costs. Similarly, if
the average age and service are substantially different,
this, too, will have an impact on costs.

As a general guide, the operating costs of a pension plan
can be determined by the use of the following formula:

> Costs = benefits plus administrative
> expenses minus investment earnings.

If the plan is fully funded, the formula can be stated:

> Benefits plus administrative expenses equal
> contributions plus investment earnings.

The following chart can be of assistance to the practitioner
and mediator to determine the approximate cost per year per
employee for a penison plan with values varying with the average age and average seniority of the group.

The chart makes the following assumptions:

a. retirement age - 65
b. disability - full benefit after 10 years

c.   vesting - full benefits at retirement after 10
     years of service or reduced for early retirement
     on an actuarial basis
d.   interest assumption - 7%
e.   turnover - none except for death
f.   women - if they constitute the entire force -
     costs would jump 20% to 25%. This would be
     proportionately reduced if there was a smaller
     proportion of women.
g.   mortality - GA 1971, 1955 Projection
h.   amortization of past service - 30 years.

Age	$1/mo./yr. of Future Service	$1/mo./yr. of Past Service
60	4¢/hr.	$.26/hr.
55	3.1	.17
53	2.8	.15
50	2.5	.12 (1/8)
48	2.2	.10 (1/10)
45	2	.08 (1/12)
43	1.8	.07 (1/14)
40	1.6	.06 (1/16)
38	1.45	.05 (1/20)
35	1.3	.04 (1/25)
33	1.2	.037 (1/27)
30	1	.03 (1/33)

Additional Costs:

Disability - 9%
Vested Rights - 4 1/3%.
Severance - 2%
Joint Survivorship - 55 to 65: 5% for a group with
                     50% men and 50% women.

Early retirement, including full pension at age 62 and 30 and out, regardless of age: The cost depends upon the percentage of employees who chose to retire early, the age at which they retire, and the added cost over and above the actuarially reduced pension had they retired at the same age.

Example: Assume you have a provision for 30 and out with benefits at age 65 at $300 a month. If 100% of the employees terminate at age 62, and received the actuarial reduction of 6% for each year before age 65, the benefit would be $300 x 82% or $246 a month. If they were to receive $300 a month, that would be a 22% increase. If 50% of the employees chose to retire at 62, the extra cost would be 11%.

Past service liability is determined by estimating the present value of all benefits at the present or current age of each employee and subtracting the present value of future normal contributions.

Some Observations On Costing Problems In Pension Plans

Until very recently, in the majority of pension plans, the actuarial assumption on interest remained in the range of 6% to 8%. However, there have been new developments in the pension field centered about the higher rates of interest available for pension fund investment which creates problems in determining pension plan costs for older defined benefit plans.

The new developments in the pension field include the following:

1. By changing the actuary's assumption on what the fund would earn--that is, the interest assumption--costs may be substantially reduced and the annual contribution affected in a similar manner. For instance, the February 15, 1982, issue of "Pensions and Investment Age" reported that a national midwestern corporation reduced its 1981 contribution to the pension fund by $210 million and added 70 cents per share to the company earnings.

2. Many corporations have decided to invest their pension funds in part, or entirely, in either dedicated portfolios, or guaranteed insurance contracts, either of which,

depending upon the time of investment, might earn as high as 16½%.

A large petroleum company recently sold sufficient common stock in its pension portfolio to bring in $1 billion, which it immediately invested in Guaranteed Insurance Contracts (GIC) providing a return of 13%, handled by six of the largest insurance carriers in the country.

In the case of a dedicated bond portfolio, the investment people invest in bonds to cover the period of retirement on its employees--or in the case where the dedicated portfolio is designed for its retirees, for the life expectancy of its retirees. In 1981, when the bond earnings were high, rates of 16½% could be secured from Government notes alone, not to say anything about corporate bonds.

Among the corporations investing in this approach were United Brands which earned more than 15% in June 1982, and Honeywell which earned 15.6% in 1982, and which lowered its pension costs by several million dollars in 1982. Chrysler, Bethelehem, and Signa Cos this year alone sold equities for a total of $2 billion and set up dedicated bond portfolios.

        3. A large number of corporations are cancelling pension plans and introducing IRAs. In such cancellations, the savings to the companies have been large. Already, according to Government figures, corporations have received $1.7 billion back from terminated pension plans.

Incidentally, a change of assumption on interest of 1%, where the group is fairly young, say 30-35 years old with 5 or so years of service, would provide increased benefits of 20-25% with no cost increase or a cut in cost for the company of 15-20%. Where the group is older and service is longer, each approach would have smaller percentage figures, but the basic idea is still relevant.

Insurance Costs

While the cost of an insurance program is dependent on experience, sex and age mix, and other similar factors, it is often useful for the bargaining table representatives to be able to gauge quickly an approximation of the cost impact of an insurance demand or offer.

The following are suggested general "rules of thumb" which may be helpful until there is an opportunity to gather data for a more accurate costing. The following figures apply to an average group, most of whom are not very advanced in age:

1. Life Insurance:

   70¢ per month per employee for each $1000.

2. Accidental Death and Dismemberment (with double indemnity):

   5¢ to 7¢ per month per employee for each $1000.

3. Sickness and Accident Disability:

   70¢ per month for each $10 for 26 weeks.

If long-term disability is provided equal to 50% of weekly earnings minus Social Security and other programs, the cost might vary from 2% to 4% of payroll, with the 2% applying mostly to those who have disability rights under the pension program.

BIBLIOGRAPHY

This Bibliography is intended for the reader who wants to pursue further reading in a specialized area of labor-management mediation. Articles and studies are listed under topical headings. A number of older sources have been included to provide historic contrasts and comparisons since so little had been written until recently about mediation. Items published before 1970 are denoted by an X preceding the entry.

BOOKS

X Ching, Cyrus S., Review and Reflection: A Half Century of Labor Relations, New York: B.C. Forbes & Sons, 1953, p. 204.

X Douglas, Ann, Industrial Peacemaking, New York: Columbia University, 1962, p. 675.

Dunlop, John T., Dispute Resolution: Negotiation and Concensus Building, Dover, Mass.: Auburn House Publishing Company, 1984, p. 196.

Evarts, W. Richard, James L. Greenstone, Gary Kirkpatrick, and Sharon C. Leviton, Winning Through Accommodation: The Mediator's Handbook, Dubuque, Iowa: Kendall-Hunt Publishing Company, 1983, p. 151.

Gold, Charlotte and Ruth E. Lyons, Editors, Dispute Resolution Training: The State Of The Art, New York: American Arbitration Association, 1978, p. 104.

X Indix, Bernard, B. Goldstein, J. Chernick and M. Berkowitz, The Mediator: Background, Self Image and Attitudes, New Brunswick, N.J.: Institute of Management and Labor Relations, Rutgers University, 1966, p. 64.

X Jackson, Elmore, Meeting Of The Minds: A Way to Peace Through Mediation, New York: McGraw-Hill, 1952, p. 200.

Kolb, Deborah, The Mediator, Cambridge, Mass.: MIT Press, 1983, p. 230.

Kressel, Kenneth, Labor Mediation: An Exploratory Survey,
     Albany, N.Y.: Association of Labor Mediation Agencies,
     1972, p. 36.

Levin, Edward and Daniel V. DeSantis, Mediation: An Anno-
     tated Bibliography, Ithaca, N.Y.: New York State School
     of Industrial and Labor Relations, Cornell University,
     1978, p. 28.

Maggiolo, Walter A., Techniques of Mediation in Labor Dis-
     putes, Dobbs Ferry, N.Y.: Oceana Press, 1971, p. 192.

X Peters, Edward, Conciliation in Action: Principles and
     Techniques, New London, Conn.: National Foremen's
     Institute, 1952, p. 206.

X Peters, Edward, Strategy and Tactics in Labor Negotia-
     tions, New London, Conn.: National Foremen's Insti-
     tute, 1955, p. 223.

Robins, Eva with Tia Denenberg, A Guide for Labor Mediators,
     Honolulu: Industrial Relations Center, University of
     Hawaii, 1976, p. 96.

Simkin, William E., Mediation and The Dynamics of Collec-
     tive Bargaining, Washington, D.C.: Bureau of National
     Affairs, 1971, p. 410.

X Stevens, Carl M., Strategy and Collective Bargaining
     Negotiations, New York: McGraw-Hill, 1963, p. 192.

ARTICLES

Mediation In General

Barrett, Jerome T. and James F. Power, "FMCS and the Expand-
     ing Dimensions of Mediation," Vuepoints, Vol. 2, No. 1,
     Summer 1975, pp. 4-7.

X Bernstein, Irving and Edgar L. Warren, "The Mediation
     Process," Southern Economics Journal, Vol. 15, April
     1949, pp. 441-457.

X Brooks, Thomas R., "The Role of the Federal Mediator,"
     Dun's Review and Modern Industry, Vol. 85, June 1965,
     pp. 59-60.

X Brown, Leo C., "Defense of U.S. Mediation," America, 1964,
    pp. 696-697.

X Bureau of National Affairs, "Role of Mediation in Collec-
    tive Bargaining Process," Labor Relations Yearbook,
    1967, Washington, D.C.: Bureau of National Affairs,
    pp. 159-163.

Byrnes, Joseph F., "Mediator-Generated Pressure Tactics,"
    Journal of Collective Negotiations in the Public Sec-
    tor, Vol. 7, No. 2, 1978, pp. 103-109.

X Cancio, Hiram R., "Some Reflections on the Role of Media-
    tion," Labor Law Journal, Vol. 10, No. 10, October
    1959, pp. 720-23.

X Chalmers, Ellison W., "The Conciliation Process," Indus-
    trial and Labor Relations Review, Vol. 2, April 1948,
    pp. 337-350.

X Cole, David L., "Government In The Bargaining Process:
    The Role of Mediation," Annals of the American Academy
    of Political and Social Science, Vol. 333, January
    1961, pp. 43-58.

X Colvin, Howard T., "Mediation and Conciliation Under the
    Labor-Management Act of 1947," Labor Law Journal, Vol.
    1, No. 11, November 1949, pp. 89-93.

Cook, Daniel D., "Is Federal Mediation Hurting Labor-Manage-
    ment Relations?" Industry Week, Vol. 190, September 20,
    1976, pp. 17-19.

X Enarson, Harold L., "Mediation and Education," Labor Law
    Journal, Vol. 7, No. 8, August 1956, pp. 466-471.

X Feinsinger, Nathan P., "Private Mediation: Its Potential,"
    Labor Law Journal, Vol. 7, No. 8, August 1956, pp. 493-
    496.

Fuller, L. L., "Mediation: Its Forms and Functions," South-
    ern California Law Review, Vol. 44, Winter 1971, pp.
    305-339.

X Keltner, John W., "The United States Federal Mediation and
    Conciliation Service: Catalyst To Collective Bargain-
    ing," International Labour Review, Vol. 88, No. 5,
    November 1963, pp. 476-489.

X Kerr, Clark, "Industrial Conflict and Mediation," <u>American Journal of Sociology</u>, Vol. 60, November 1954, pp. 230-245.

Krislov, Joseph and John F. Mead, "Labor-Management Attitudes Toward Mediation," <u>Personnel Journal</u>, Vol. 51, February 1972, pp. 86-94.

X Liebs, Richard, "Contributions of Mediation To The Development of Mature Collective Bargaining Relationships," <u>Labor Law Journal</u>, Vol. 9, No. 10, October 1958, pp. 797-800.

X Lovell, Hugh G., "The Pressure Level In Mediation," <u>Industrial and Labor Relations Review</u>, Vol. 6, October 1952, pp. 20-30.

X Mackraz, James A., "General Role of Mediation in Collective Bargaining," <u>Labor Law Journal</u>, Vol. 11, No. 6, June 1960, pp. 453-456.

X Maggiolo, Walter A., "Mediation's Role On The Labor Scene," <u>Labor Law Journal</u>, Vol. 4, No. 9, September 1953, pp. 632-636.

McMurray, Kay, "The Federal Mediation and Conciliation Service: Serving Labor-Management Relations in the Eighties," <u>Labor Law Journal</u>, Vol. 34, No. 2, February 1983, pp. 67-71.

X Meyer, Arthur S., "Function of the Mediator in Collective Bargaining," <u>Industrial and Labor Relations Review</u>, Vol. 13, January 1960, pp. 159-165.

Newman, Harold R., "Mediator Pressures: High and Low," <u>Journal of Collective Negotiations in the Public Sector</u>, Vol. 8, No. 1, 1979, pp. 77-81.

Newman, Harold R. "Using Neutrals to Help Settle Impasses," <u>Handbook of Faculty Bargaining</u>, Eds., G.W. Angell and E.P. Kelley and Associates, San Francisco: Jossey-Bass Publishers, 1977, pp. 330-331.

X Perez, Francisco Aponte, "Evaluation of Mediation Techniques," <u>Labor Law Journal</u>, Vol. 10, No. 10, October 1959, pp. 716-720.

X Peters, Edward, "The Mediator: A Neutral, A Catalyst Or A Leader?" <u>Labor Law Journal</u>, Vol. 9, No. 10, October 1958, pp. 764-869.

X Podell, Jerome E. and William M. Knapp, "The Effect Of Mediation on the Perceived Firmness of Opponents," <u>Journal of Conflict Resolution</u>, Vol. 13, December 1969, pp. 511-520.

Pruitt, Dean G. and Douglas F. Johnson, "Mediation As An Aid to Face-Saving in Negotiations," <u>Journal of Personality and Social Psychology</u>, Vol. 14, March 1970, pp. 239-246.

X Rehmus, Charles M., "Mediation and Conciliation," <u>Labor Law Journal</u>, Vol. 4, No. 2, February 1953, pp. 141-144.

X Schlossberg, Stephen I., "Philosophy and Procedures of Labor Mediation," <u>Labor Law Journal</u>, Vol. 13, No. 10, October 1962, pp. 828-832.

Simkin, William E., "Can Mediation Work In A Control Climate?" <u>Labor Relations Yearbook</u>, 1972, Washington, D.C.: Bureau of National Affairs, 1973, pp. 86-90.

X Simkin, William E., "Code of Professional Conduct for Labor Mediators," <u>Labor Law Journal</u>, Vol. 15, No. 10, October 1964, pp. 627-631.

X Simkin, William E., "Refusal To Ratify Contracts," <u>Industrial and Labor Relations Review</u>, Vol. 21, No. 4, July 1968, pp. 518-540.

X Stevens, Carl M., "Mediation and the Role of the Neutral," in <u>Frontiers in Collective Bargaining</u>, Edited by John T. Dunlop and Neil W. Chamberlain, New York: Harper and Row, 1967, pp. 271-290.

Usery, William J., "Industrial Peacemaking: The Government's Role," <u>Perspectives in Defense Management</u>, Summer 1974, pp. 13-19.

Usery, William J., "Mediation's Stakes in Labor Reporting," <u>Editor and Publisher</u>, Vol. 108, October 1975, p. 35.

X Warren, Edgar L., "Mediation and Fact-Finding," in Industrial Conflict, Edited by Arthur Kornhauser, Robert
Dubin and Arthur M. Ross, New York: McGraw-Hill, 1954,
pp. 292-300.

Young, Oran R., "Intermediaries: Additional Thoughts On
Third Parties," Journal of Conflict Resolution, Vol.
16, March 1972, pp. 51-65.

Grievance Mediation

Bowers, Mollie H., "Grievance Mediation: Another Route to
Resolution," Personnel Journal, Vol. 59, No. 2, February 1980, pp. 132-139.

X Freund, Richard L., "Mediation of Grievances," in New York
University, Institute of Labor Relations, Proceedings
of the Nineteenth Annual Conference on Labor, Washington, D.C.: Bureau of National Affairs, 1967, pp. 333-
344.

Goldberg, Stephen B. and Jeanne M. Brett, "An Experiment in
the Mediation of Grievances," Monthly Labor Review,
Vol. 106, No. 3, March 1983, pp. 23-30.

Gregory, Gorden and Robert Rooney, "Grievance Mediation:
A Trend in the Cost-Conscious Eighties," Labor Law
Journal, Vol. 31, No. 8, August 1980, pp. 502-508.

X Handsaker, Morrison, "Grievance Arbitration and Mediated
Settlements," Labor Law Journal, Vol. 17, No. 10, October 1966, pp. 579-583.

Hoffman, Eileen B., "Mediation of Unfair Dismissal Griev-
ances: The British Example," Industrial Relations
Research Association 32nd Annual Meeting Proceedings,
December 1979, pp. 171-179.

X McPherson, William H., "Grievance Mediation Under Collective Bargaining," Industrial and Labor Relations Review, Vol. 9, No. 2, January 1956, pp. 200-212.

O'Grady, James P., Jr., "Grievance Mediation by State Agencies," Arbitration Journal, Vol. 31, No. 2, June 1976,
pp. 125-130.

Zack, Arnold M., "Mediation and Arbitration Procedures," in Handling Employee Grievances, edited by Robert H. Helms, Chicago: Public Personnel Association, 1968, pp. 31-39.

Mediation/Arbitration (Med-Arb)

Dunlap, Karen, "Mediation-Arbitration: Reactions from Rank and File," Monthly Labor Review, Vol. 96, No. 9, September 1973, pp. 65-66.

Kagel, Sam, "Combining Mediation and Arbitration," Monthly Labor Review, Vol. 96, No. 9, September 1973, pp. 62-63.

Polland, Harry, "Mediation-Arbitration: A Trade Union View," Monthly Labor Review, Vol. 96, No. 9, September 1973, pp. 63-65.

Ross, Jerome H., "The Med-Arb Process in Labor Agreement Negotiations," Society of Professionals in Dispute Resolution, Occasional Paper No. 83-1, February 1982, pp. 1-10.

Public Sector Mediation

X Abner, Willoughby, "The FMCS and Disputes in the Federal Government," Monthly Labor Review, Vol. 92, No. 5, May 1969, pp. 27-29.

Bennett, George, "New Horizons for Mediators," Personnel, Vol. 51, No. 1, January-February 1974, pp. 43-52.

X Chisholm, Allan D., "Mediating the Public Employee Dispute," Labor Law Journal, Vol. 12, No. 1, January 1961, pp. 56-61.

X Counts, J. Curtis, "How Mediation Can Help Negotiations in the Public Sector," Monthly Labor Review, Vol. 92, No. 7, July 1969, pp. 66-67.

X Davey, Harold W., "The Use of Neutrals In The Public Sector," Labor Law Journal, Vol. 20, No. 8, August 1969, pp. 529-538.

Fishgold, Herbert, "Dispute Resolution in the Public Sector," Labor Law Journal, Vol. 27, No. 12, December 1976, pp. 234-38.

Foegen, J. H., "Mediation From Initiation: Hope for Public Labor Relations," Public Personnel Review, Vol. 31, No. 1, January 1970, pp. 7-12.

Hoh, Ronald, "The Effectiveness of Mediation in Public Sector Arbitration Systems: The Iowa Experience," Arbitration Journal, Vol. 39, No. 2, June 1984, pp. 30-40.

Kochan, Thomas A. and Todd Jick, "The Public Sector Mediation Process: A Theory and Emphirical Examination," Journal of Conflict Resolution, Vol. 22, No. 2, June 1978, pp. 209-240.

Liebowitz, Jonathan S., "Public Sector Mediation: Some Observations on Techniques," Journal of Collective Negotiations in the Public Sector, Vol. 1, No. 1, February 1972, pp. 91-96.

X Moskowitz, George, "Mediation of Public Employee Disputes," Labor Law Journal, Vol. 12, No. 1, January 1961, pp. 54-56.

Odewahn, Charles A., "The Mediator in the Public Sector: A New Breed?" Labor Law Journal, Vol. 23, No. 10, October 1972, pp. 643-648.

Robins, Eva, "Some Comparisons of Mediation in the Public and Private Sectors," in Collective Bargaining in Government: Readings and Cases, edited by J. Joseph Loewenberg and Michael Moskow, Englewood Cliffs, N.J.: Prentice-Hall, 1972, pp. 323-329.

Ross, Jerome H., "Federal Mediation in the Public Sector," Monthly Labor Review, Vol. 99, No. 2, February 1976, pp. 41-45.

Standohar, Paul D., "Some Implications of Mediation for Resolution of Bargaining Impasses in Public Employment," Public Personnel Management, Vol. 2, No. 4, July-August 1973, pp. 299-304.

Stern, James L., "The Mediation of Interest Disputes by Arbitrators Under the Wisconsin Med-Arb Law for Local Government Employees," Arbitration Journal, Vol. 39, No. 2, June 1984, pp. 41-45.

Stepp, John and Robert P. Baker, "The Art of Dispute Reso-
lution--Mediation: The Mediator and Public Bargaining
Without a Statute," Proceedings of 5th Annual Meeting
of the Society of Professionals in Dispute Resolution,
October 1977, pp. 18-28.

Usery, William J., "Bargaining in the Public Sector: Problems, Progress and Prospects," Okalahoma City University Law Review, Vol.1, No. 1, Spring 1973, pp. 11-12.

Williams, William J., "The Public Service Collective Bar-
gaining Process: Toward a New Technique," Personnel
Administration and Public Personnel Review, Vol. 1,
No. 1, July-August 1972, pp. 34-37.

Zack, Arnold M., "Improving Mediation and Fact-Finding in
the Public Sector," Labor Law Journal, Vol. 21, No. 5,
May 1970, pp. 259-73.

State and Local Mediation Agencies

Kolb, Deborah M., "Roles Mediators Play: State and Federal
Practice," Industrial Relations, Vol. 20, Winter 1981,
pp. 1-17.

X Lazar, Joseph, "Concurrent Jurisdiction of Federal and
State Mediation Agencies," Labor Law Journal, Vol. 13,
No. 3, March 1962, pp. 254-261.

Liebes, Richard A., "Partisan Mediation by the Central
Labor Council," Monthly Labor Review, Vol. 96, No.
9, September 1973, pp. 55-56.

X Mead, John F. and Joseph Krislov, "Drawing Jursidictional
Lines in Mediation," Monthly Labor Review, Vol. 92, No.
4, April 1969, pp. 41-45.

X Mead, John F. and Joseph Krislov, "The Toledo Labor-Management Citizens' Committee," Labor Law Journal, Vol.
20, No. 11, November 1969, pp. 730-750.

X Northrup, Herbert F., "Mediation: The Viewpoint of the
Mediated," Labor Law Journal, Vol. 13, No. 10, October
1962, pp. 832-841.

X Pearce, C. A., "Statistics of Labor Mediation by State
Agencies," Labor Law Journal, Vol. 6, No. 8, August
1955, pp. 574-587.

X Rosenbloom, Victor H., "How Cities Keep Industrial Peace," Labor Law Journal, Vol. 3, No. 10, October 1952, pp. 663-676.

X Rosenbloom, Victor H., "The New York City Division of Labor Relations: Its Development and Place in Municipal Mediation Plans," Labor Law Journal, Vol. 3, No. 8, August 1952, pp. 528-541.

Ross, Jerome H., "Federal-State Cooperation in Labor Mediation," State Government, Vol. 49, No. 4, Autumn 1976, pp. 254-256.

X Seligson, Harry, "Analysis of Denver's Labor-Management Citizens Commission," Labor Law Journal, Vol. 6, No. 8, August 1956, pp. 482-493.

X Stark, Arthur, "Are There Too Many Mediators?" Labor Law Journal, Vol. 5, No. 1, January 1955, pp. 33-41.

X Stutz, Robert L., "Troikas, Duets and Prima Donnas in Labor Mediation," Labor Law Journal, Vol. 13, No. 10, October 1962, pp. 845-852.

X Tinning, Paul P., "Summary of State Mediation Agencies," Labor Law Journal, Vol. 17, No. 1, January 1966, pp. 9-17.

X Turnbull, John G. and Clark Kanun, "Conciliation and Mediation in Minnesota," Labor Law Journal, Vol. 3, No. 10, October 1952, pp. 677-684.

Preventive Mediation

X Bowen, Charles L., "Preventive Mediation," in Industrial Relations Research Association, Proceedings of the 21st Annual Winter Meeting, December 1968, pp. 160-164.

X Estes, Charles T., "The Place of Communications in Maintaining Labor-Management Peace," The Southern Speech Journal, Vol. XIV, No. 4, March 1949, pp. 236-245.

X "Joint Consultation Devices in Collective Bargaining," Monthly Labor Review, Vol. 88, No. 1, February 1965, p. 173.

Popular, John J., "Labor-Management Relations: U.S. Media-
    tors Try To Build Common Objectives," World of Work,
    Vol. 1, September 1976, pp. 1-3.

X Prasow, Paul, "Preventive Mediation: A Technique to
    Improve Industrial Relations," Labor Law Journal,
    Vol. 1, No. 8, August 1950, pp. 866-68.

Steiner, Robert E., "The Labor-Management Cooperation Act,"
    Personnel Journal, Vol. 60, No. 5, May 1981, pp. 344-
    346.

Stepp, John R., Robert P. Baker and Jerome T. Barrett,
    "Helping Labor and Management See and Solve Problems,"
    Monthly Labor Review, Vol. 105, No. 9, September 1982,
    pp. 15-20.

"U.S. Mediators Try A New Role," Business Week, April 21,
    1975, p. 108.

X Valtin, Rolf, "Preventive Mediation, Grievance Disputes
    and The Taft-Hartley Act," Labor Law Journal, Vol. 7,
    No. 12, December 1956, pp. 768-775.

X White, Harold and Robert J. Dyer, "How Labor and Manage-
    ment View Preventive Mediation Training," Training and
    Development Journal, Vol. 23, 1969, pp. 36-38.

Young, Harvey A., "The Causes of Industrial Peace Revisited:
    The Case for RBO," Human Resource Management, Vol. 21,
    Nos. 2-3, Summer-Fall 1982, pp. 50-57.

Dissertations And Other Studies

Barrett, Jerome T., "An Historic and Descriptive Study of
    The Joint Labor-Management Training Program of the
    Federal Mediation and Conciliation Service," A Docto-
    rial Dissertation, George Washington University, March
    1984, p. 200.

Frees, J., "Dispute Management in Labor Relations: The Me-
    diation Process," A Doctorial Dissertation, University
    of Minnesota, 1976, p. 515.

Gaudreau, George C., "The Effectiveness of Mediation and
    Arbitration of Teacher-School Board Disagreements in
    Connecticut as Perceived by the Parties Involved," A
    Dissertation, University of Connecticut, 1975, p. 158.

Gerhart, Paul and John Drotning, "A Six-State Study of Im-
    passe Procedures in the Public Sector," Washington,
    D.C.: U.S. Department of Labor, Labor Management Serv-
    ices Administration, 1980, p. 188.

Gilroy, Thomas P. and Anthony V. Sinicropi, "Dispute Set-
    tlement in the Public Sector: The State of the Art,"
    Washington, D.C.: U.S. Government Printing Office,
    1972, p. 141.

X Lovell, Hugh G., "The Mediation Process," A Doctorial
    Dissertation, Massachusetts Institute of Technology,
    1951.

McCabe, Douglas M., "Mediation and Labor-Management Rela-
    tions in the Federal Government," Washington, D.C.:
    U.S. Department of Labor, 1980, p. 592.

X Steen, Jack E., "An Analysis of the Activities of the
    Federal Mediation and Conciliation Service in the
    Metropolitan Area of Birmingham," A Doctorial Dis-
    sertation, University of Alabama, 1965, p. 219.

Mediation In Specific Industries

Burgoon, Beatrice M., "Mediation of Railroad and Airline
    Disputes," in The Railway Labor Act At 50, Edited by
    Charles M. Rehmus, U.S. Government Printing Office:
    Washington, D.C., 1976, pp. 71-95.

Cimini, Michael H., "Emergency Boards in the Airline Indus-
    try, 1936-69," Monthly Labor Review, Vol. 93, No. 7,
    July 1970, pp. 57-65.

Cimini, Michael H., "Government Intervention In Railroad
    Disputes," Monthly Labor Review, Vol. 94, No. 12,
    December 1971, pp. 27-34.

X Gamser, Howard G., "The Role of Mediation in Airline Labor
    Disputes," Journal of Air Law and Commerce, Vol., 35,
    Summer 1969, pp. 502-512.

Horvitz, Wayne, "The FMCS and the Peaceful Resolution of
    Disputes," in Health Care Law, Edited by Michael
    Shepard and Edward Doudera, Washington, D.c.: AUPHA
    Press, 1981, pp. 145-150.

X Julian, Vance, "Mediation and Labor Disputes in Missouri Public Utilities," Labor Law Journal, Vol. 1, No. 12, December 1949, pp. 185-188.

Krislov, Joseph, "Mediation Under The Railway Labor Act: A Process in Search of a Name," Labor Law Journal, Vol. 27, No. 5, May 1976, pp. 310-315.

Scearce, James and Lucretia Dewey Tanner, "Health Care Bargaining: The FMCS Experience," Labor Law Journal, Vol. 27, No. 7, July 1976, pp. 387-398.

Mediation And Psychology

Barrett, Jerome T., "The Psychology of a Mediator: A Third Party's Psychic Balance Sheet," Society of Professionals in Dispute Resolution Occasional Paper No. 83-1, March 1983, pp. 1-8.

X Hooker, Evelyn, "Psychological Aspects of the Mediation Process," Labor Law Journal, Vol. 9, No. 10, October 1958, pp. 776-79.

X Knowles, William H., "Mediation and the Psychology of Small Groups," Labor Law Journal, Vol. 9, No. 10, October 1958, pp. 780-784.

X Koven, Adolph M., "Psychological Aspects of Mediation," Labor Law Journal, Vol. 9, No. 10, October 1958, pp. 784-786.

X Paster, Irving, "Psychological Factors In Industrial Mediation," Personnel, Vol. 31, No. 2, September 1954, pp. 115-127.

X Rosen, Hjamar, "The Psychologist Looks at the Industrial Disputes," Labor Law Journal, Vol. 8, September 1957, pp. 601-604.

Qualifications, Background, And Evaluation of Mediators

X Berkowitz, Monroe, Bernard Goldstein and Bernard Indix, "The State Mediator: Background, Self-Image, and Attitudes," Industrial and Labor Relations Review, Vol. 17, No. 1, January 1964, pp. 257-275.

X Landsberger, Henry A., "The Behavior and Personality of
    the Labor Mediator: The Parties' Perceptions of Medi-
    ator Behavior," Personnel Psychology, Vol. 13, No. 3,
    Autumn 1960, pp. 329-347.

X Landsberger, Henry A., "Final Report On A Research Proj-
    ect In Mediation," Labor Law Journal, Vol. 7, No. 8,
    August 1956, pp. 501-108.

X Ludlow, Howard T., "Formal Education and Mediator Accept-
    ability," Labor Law Journal, Vol. 17, No. 10, October
    1966, pp. 598-603.

McLellan, Larkin W. and Peter E. Obermeyer, "Science or
    Art? Performance Standards for Mediators," Labor Law
    Journal, Vol. 21, No. 9, September 1970, pp. 591-196.

X Manson, Julius, "Mediators and Their Qualifications,"
    Labor Law Journal, Vol. 9, No. 10, October 1958,
    pp. 755-764.

Parker, Hyman, "Performance Standards for Mediators,"
    Labor Law Journal, Vol. 21, No. 11, November 1970,
    pp. 738-744.

Shapiro, Fred C., "Profiles: Mediator, Theodore Kheel,"
    New Yorker, Vol. 46, August 1, 1970, pp. 36-44.

X "The Men In The Middle," American Labor, Vol. 1, August
    1968, pp. 36-41.

X Weschler, Irving R., "Who Should Be A Labor Mediator?"
    Personnel, Vol. 26, No. 3, November 1949, pp. 222-226.

X Weschler, Irving R., "The Personal Factors In Labor Medi-
    ation," Personnel Psychology, Vol. 3, Summer 1950, pp.
    113-132.

Research And Mediator Training

Barrett, Jerome T., "Skilled Are The Peacemakers," North-
    east Training News, Vol. 1, No. 10, June 1980, p. 19.

Barrett, Jerome T., "The Training and Development of Fed-
    eral Mediation and Conciliation Service Mediators,"
    in Dispute Resolution Training: The State Of The Art,
    Edited by Charlotte Gold and Ruth Lyons, New York:
    American Arbitration Association, 1978, pp. 42-46.

Brett, Jeanne M., Stephen B. Goldberg and William Ury, "Mediation and Organizational Development," Industrial Relations Research Association 33rd Annual Meeting Proceedings, September 1980, pp. 195-202.

X Douglas, Ann, "What Can Research Tell Us About Mediation?" Labor Law Journal, Vol. 6, No. 8, August 1955, pp. 545-552.

X Gershenson, Maurice I., "Can We Measure the Contributions of Mediation to Collective Bargaining?" Labor Law Journal, Vol. 9, No. 10, October 1958, pp. 795-797.

Haman, David C., Arthur P. Brief and Richard Pegnetter, "Studies in Mediation and the Training of Public Sector Mediators," Journal of Collective Negotiations in the Public Sector, Vol. 7, No. 4, 1978, pp. 347-61.

Karim, Ahmad and Richard Pegnetter, "Mediator Strategies and Qualities and Mediation Effectiveness," Industrial Relations, Vol. 22, No. 1, Winter 1983, pp. 105-114.

Kuechle, David, "The Making Of A Mediator," Labour Gazelle, Vol. 74, January 1974, pp. 23-30.

Newman, Harold R., "The Training of Neutrals by the New York State Public Employment Relations Board," in Dispute Resolution Training: The State Of The Art, Edited by Charlotte Gold and Ruth Lyons, New York: American Arbitration Association, 1978, pp. 47-50.

X Rehmus, Charles M., "The Mediation of Industrial Conflict: A Note on the Literature," Journal of Conflict Resolution, Vol. 9, March 1965, pp. 118-126.

X Rose, Arnold, "Needed Research In The Mediation Of Labor Disputes," Personnel Psychology, Vol. 5, October 1952, pp. 187-200.

X Rose, Arnold and Caroline B. Rose, "Needed Research in the Mediation of Labor Disputes," International Social Science Bulletin, Vol. 6, 1954.

Zirkel, Perry A. and Gary J. Lutz, "Characteristics and Functions of Mediators: A Pilot Study," Arbitration Journal, Vol. 36, No. 2, June 1981, pp. 15-20.

APPENDIXES

LABOR-MANAGEMENT RELATIONS ACT, 1947, TITLE I

Title I - Amendment of
National Labor Relations Act

Sec. 8. (d), For the purposes of this section, to bargain collectively is the performance of the mutual obligation of the employer and the representative of the employees to meet at reasonable times and confer in good faith with respect to wages, hours, and other terms and conditions of employment, or the negotiation of an agreement, or any question arising thereunder, and the execution of a written contract incorporating any agreement reached if requested by either party, but such obligation does not compel either party to agree to a proposal or require the making of a concession: *Provided,* That where there is in effect a collective-bargaining contract covering employees in an industry affecting commerce, the duty to bargain collectively shall also mean that no party to such contract shall terminate or modify such contract unless the party desiring such termination or modification—

(1) serves a written notice upon the other party to the contract of the proposed termination or modification sixty days prior to the expiration date thereof, or in the event such contract contains no expiration date, sixty days prior to the time it is proposed to make such termination or modification;

(2) offers to meet and confer with the other party for the purpose of negotiating a new contract or a contract containing the proposed modifications;

(3) notifies the Federal Mediation and Concili-

ation Service within thirty days after such notice of the existence of a dispute, and simultaneously

therewith notifies any State or Territory agency established to mediate and conciliate disputes within the State or Territory where the dispute occurred, provided no agreement has been reached by that time; and

(4) continues in full force and effect, without resorting to strike or lock-out, all the terms and conditions of the existing contract for a period of sixty days after such notice is given or until the expiration date of such contract, whichever occurs later:

The duties imposed upon employers, employees, and labor organizations by paragraphs (2), (3), and (4) shall become inapplicable upon an intervening certification of the Board, under which the labor organization or individual, which is a party to the contract, has been superseded as or ceased to be the representative of the employees subject to the provisions of section 9(a), and the duties so imposed shall not be construed as requiring either party to discuss or agree to any modification of the terms and conditions contained in a contract for a fixed period if such modification is to become effective before such terms and conditions can be reopened under the provisions of the contract. Any employee who engages in a strike within the sixty-day period specified in this subsection shall lose his status as an employee of the employer engaged in the particular labor dispute, for the purposes of sections 8, 9, and 10 of this Act, as amended, but such loss of status for such employee shall terminate if and when he is reemployed by such employer.

APPENDIX A

LABOR-MANAGEMENT RELATIONS ACT, 1947, TITLE II

Title II - Conciliation Of Labor Disputes
    In Industries Affecting Commerce;
        National Emergencies

Sec. 201. That it is the policy of the United States
that—

(a) sound and stable industrial peace and the
advancement of the general welfare, health, and
safety of the Nation and of the best interests of
employers and employees can most satisfactorily be secured by the settlement of issues between employers and employees through the
processes of conference and collective bargaining between employers and the representatives
of their employees;

(b) the settlement of issues between employers
and employees through collective bargaining
may be advanced by making available full and
adequate governmental facilities for conciliation, mediation, and voluntary arbitration to aid
and encourage employers and the representatives of their employees to reach and maintain
agreements concerning rates of pay, hours, and
working conditions, and to make all reasonable
efforts to settle their differences by mutual
agreement reached through conferences and
collective bargaining or by such methods as may
be provided for in any applicable agreement for
the settlement of disputes; and

(c) certain controversies which arise between
parties to collective-bargaining agreements may
be avoided or minimized by making available
full and adequate governmental facilities for
furnishing assistance to employers and the representatives of their employees in formulating

for inclusion within such agreements provision for adequate notice of any proposed changes in the terms of such agreement, for the final adjustment of grievances or questions regarding the application or interpretation of such agreements, and other provisions designed to prevent the subsequent arising of such controversies.

Sec. 202. (a) There is hereby created an independent agency to be known as the Federal Mediation and Conciliation Service (herein referred to as the "Service," except that for sixty days after the date of the enactment of this Act such term shall refer to the Conciliation Service of the Department of Labor). The Service shall be under the direction of a Federal Mediation and Conciliation Director (hereinafter referred to as the "Director"), who shall be appointed by the President by and with the advice and consent of the Senate. The Director shall receive compensation at the rate of $12,000 per annum. The Director shall not engage in any other business vocation, or employment.

(b) The Director is authorized, subject to the civil-service laws, to appoint such clerical and other personnel as may be necessary for the execution of the functions of the Service, and shall fix their compensation in accordance with the Classification Act of 1923, as amended, and may, without regard to the provisions of the civil-service laws and the Classification Act of 1923, as amended, appoint and fix the compensation of such conciliators and mediators as may be necessary to carry out the functions of the Service. The Director is authorized to make such expenditures for supplies, facilities, and services as he deems necessary. Such expenditures shall be allowed and paid upon presentation of itemized vouchers therefor approved by the Director or by any employee designated by him for the purpose.

(c) The principal office of the Service shall be in the District of Columbia, but the Director may establish regional offices convenient to localities in which labor controversies are likely to arise. The Director may by order, subject to revocation at any time, delegate any authority and discretion conferred upon him by this Act to any regional director, or other officer or employee of the Service. The Director may establish suitable procedures for cooperation with State and local mediation agencies. The Director shall make an annual report in writing to Congress at the end of the fiscal year.

(d) All mediation and conciliation functions of the Secretary of Labor or the United States Conciliation Service under section 8 of the Act entitled "An Act to create a Department of Labor," approved March 4, 1913 (U.S.C., title 29, sec. 51), and all functions of the United States Conciliation Service under any other law are hereby transferred to the Federal Mediation and Conciliation Service, together with the personnel and records of the United States Conciliation Service. Such transfer shall take effect upon the sixtieth day after the date of enactment of this Act. Such transfer shall not affect any proceedings, pending before the United States Conciliation Service or any certification, order, rule, or regulation theretofore made by it or by the Secretary of Labor. The director and the Service shall not be subject in any way to the jurisdiction or authority of the Secretary of Labor or any official or division of the Department of Labor.

Functions of the Service

Sec. 203. (a) It shall be the duty of the Service, in order to prevent or minimize interruptions of the free flow of commerce growing out of labor disputes, to assist parties to labor disputes in industries affecting commerce to settle such disputes through conciliation and mediation.

(b) The Service may proffer its services in any labor dispute in any industry affecting commerce, either upon its own motion or upon the request of one or more of the parties to the dispute, whenever in its judgment such dispute threatens to cause a substantial interruption of commerce. The Director and the Service are directed to avoid attempting to mediate disputes which would have only a minor effect on interstate commerce if State or other conciliation services are available to the parties. Whenever the Service does proffer its services in any dispute, it shall be the duty of the Service promptly to put itself in communication with the parties and to use its best efforts, by mediation and conciliation, to bring them to agreement.

(c) If the Director is not able to bring the parties to agreement by conciliation within a reasonable time, he shall seek to induce the parties voluntarily to seek other means of settling the dispute without resort to strike, lock-out or other coercion, including submission to the employees in the bargaining unit of the employer's last offer of settlement for approval or rejection in a secret ballot. The failure or refusal of either party to agree to any procedure suggested by the Director shall not be deemed a violation of any duty or obligation imposed by this Act.

(d) Final adjustment by a method agreed upon by the parties is hereby declared to be the desirable method for settlement of grievance disputes arising over the application or interpretation of an existing collective-bargaining agreement. The Service is directed to make its conciliation and mediation services available in the settlement of such grievance disputes only as a last resort and in exceptional cases.

Sec. 204. (a) In order to prevent or minimize interruptions of the free flow of commerce growing out of labor disputes, employers and employees and their representatives, in any industry affecting commerce shall—

(1) exert every reasonable effort to make and maintain agreements concerning rates of pay, hours, and working conditions, including provision for adequate notice of any proposed change in the terms of such agreements;

(2) whenever a dispute arises over the terms or application of a collective-bargaining agreement and a conference is requested by a party or prospective party thereto, arrange promptly for such a conference to be held and endeavor in such conference to settle such disputes expeditiously; and

(3) in case such dispute is not settled by conference, participate fully and promptly in such meetings as may be undertaken by the Service under this Act for the purpose of aiding in a settlement of the dispute.

Sec. 205. (a) There is hereby created a National Labor-Management Panel which shall be composed of twelve members appointed by the President, six of whom shall be selected from among persons outstanding in the field of management and six of whom shall be selected from among persons outstanding in the field of labor. Each member shall hold office for a term of three years, except that any member appointed to fill a vacancy occurring prior to the expiration of the term, for which his predecessor was appointed shall be appointed for the remainder of such term, and the terms of office of the members first taking office shall expire, as designated by the President at the time of appointment, four at the end of the first year, four at the end of the second year, and four at the end of the third year after the date of appointment. Members of the panel, when serving on business of the panel, shall be paid compensation at the rate of $25 per day, and shall also be entitled to receive an allowance for actual and necessary travel and subsistence expenses while so serving away from their places of residence.

(b) It shall be the duty of the panel, at the request of the Director, to advise in the avoidance of industrial controversies and the manner in which mediation and voluntary adjustment shall be administered, particularly with reference to controversies affecting the general welfare of the country.

National Emergencies

Sec. 206. Whenever in the opinion of the President of the United States, a threatened or actual strike or lock-out affecting an entire industry or a substantial part thereof engaged in trade, commerce, transportation, transmission, or communication among the several States or with foreign nations, or engaged in the production of goods for commerce will, if permitted to occur or to continue, imperil the national health or safety, he may appoint a board of inquiry to inquire into the issues involved in the dispute and to make a written report to him within such time as he shall prescribe.

Such report shall include a statement of the facts with respect to the dispute, including each party's statement of its position but shall not contain any recommendation. The President shall file a copy of such report with the Service and shall make its contents available to the public.

Sec. 207. (a) A board of inquiry shall be composed of a chairman and such other members as the President shall determine, and shall have power to sit and act in any place within the United States and to conduct such hearings either in public or private, as it may deem necessary or proper, to ascertain the facts with respect to the causes and circumstances of the dispute.

(b) Members of a board of inquiry shall receive compensation at the rate of $50 for each day actually spent by them in the work of the board, together with necessary travel and subsistence expenses.

(c) For the purpose of any hearing or inquiry conducted by any board appointed under this title, the provisions of section 9 and 10 (relating to the attendance of witnesses and the production of books, papers, and documents) of the Federal Trade Commission Act of September 16, 1914, as amended (U.S.C. 19, title 15, secs. 49 and 50, as amended), are hereby made applicable to the powers and duties of such board.

Sec. 208. (a) Upon receiving a report from a board of inquiry the President may direct the Attorney General to petition and district court of the United States having jurisdiction of the parties to enjoin such strike or lock-out or the continuing thereof, and if the court finds that such threatened or actual strike or lock-out—

(i) affects an entire industry or a substantial part thereof engaged in trade, commerce, transportation, transmission, or communication among the several States or with foreign nations or engaged in the production of goods for commerce; and

(ii) if permitted to occur or to continue, will imperil the national health or safety, it shall have jurisdiction to enjoin any such strike or lock-out, or the continuing thereof, and to make such other orders as may be appropriate.

(b) In any case, the provisions of the Act of March 23, 1932, entitled "An Act to amend the Judicial Code and to define and limit the jurisdiction of courts sitting in equity, and for other purposes," shall not be applicable.

(c) The order or orders of the court shall be subject to review by the appropriate circuit court of appeals and by the Supreme Court upon writ of certiorari or certification as provided in sections 239 and 240 of the Judicial Code, as amended (U.S.C., Title 29, secs. 346 and 347).

Sec. 209. (a) Whenever a district court has issued an order under section 208 enjoining acts or practices which imperil or threaten to imperil the national health or safety, it shall be the duty of the parties to the labor dispute giving rise to such order to make every effort to adjust and settle their differences, with the assistance of the Service created by this Act. Neither party shall be under any duty to accept, in whole or in part, any proposal of settlement made by the Service.

(b) Upon the issuance of such order, the President shall reconvene the board of inquiry which has previously reported with respect to the dispute. At the end of a sixty-day period (unless the dispute has been settled by that time), the board of inquiry shall report to the President the current position of the parties and the efforts which have been made for settlement, and shall include a statement by each party of its position and a statement of the employer's last offer of settlement. The President shall make such report available to the public. The National Labor Relations Board, within the succeeding fifteen days shall take a secret ballot of the employees of each employer involved in the dispute on the question of whether they wish to accept the final offer of settlement made by their employer. as stated by him and shall certify the results thereof to the Attorney General within five days thereafter.

Sec. 210. Upon the certification of the results of such ballot or upon a settlement being reached, whichever happens sooner, the Attorney General shall move the court to discharge the injunction, which motion shall then be granted and the injunction discharged. When such motion is granted, the President shall submit to the Congress a full and comprehensive report of the proceedings, including the findings of the board of inquiry and the ballot taken by the National Labor Relations Board, together with such recommendations as he may see fit to make for consideration and appropriate action.

Compilation of Collective Bargaining Agreements, etc.

Sec. 211. (a) For the guidance and information of interested representatives of employers, employees, and the general public, the Bureau of Labor Statistics of the Department of Labor shall maintain a file of copies of all available collective-bargaining agreements and other available agreements and actions thereunder settling or adjusting labor disputes. Such file shall be open to inspection under appropriate conditions prescribed by the Secretary of Labor, except that no specific information submitted in confidence shall be disclosed.

(b) The Bureau of Labor Statistics in the Department of Labor is authorized to furnish upon request of the Service, or employers, employees, or their representatives, all available data and factual information which may aid in the settlement of any labor dispute, except that no specific information submitted in confidence shall be disclosed.

Exemption of Railway Labor Act

Sec. 212. The provisions of this title shall not be applicable with respect to any matter which is subject to the provisions of the Railway Labor Act, as amended from time to time.

APPENDIX B

CIVIL SERVICE REFORM ACT

Public Law 95-454 Enacted October 11, 1978
Effective January 11, 1979

FEDERAL SERVICE LABOR-MANAGEMENT RELATIONS
Findings and Statement of Purpose

(1) in order to provide the people of the United States with a competent, honest, and productive Federal work force reflective of the Nation's diversity, and to improve the quality of public service, Federal personnel management should be implemented consistent with merit system principles and free from prohibited personnel practices;

(2) the merit system principles which shall govern in the competitive service and in the executive branch of the Federal Government, should be expressly stated to furnish guidance to Federal agencies in carrying out their responsibilities in administering the public business, and prohibited personnel practices should be statutorily defined to enable Federal employees to avoid conduct which undermines the merit system principles and the integrity of the merit system;

(3) Federal employees should receive appropriate protection through increasing the authority and powers of the Merit Systems Protection Board in processing hearings and appeals affecting Federal employees;

(4) the authority and power of the Special Counsel should be increased so that the Special Counsel may investigate allegations involving prohibited personnel practices and reprisals against Federal employees for the lawful disclosure of certain information and may file complaints against agency officials and employees who engage in such conduct;

(5) the function of filling positions and other personnel functions in the competitive service and in the executive branch should be delegated in appropriate cases to the agencies to expedite processing appointments and other personnel actions, with the control of oversight of this delegation being maintained by the Office of Personnel Management to protect against prohibited personnel practices and the use of unsound management practices by the agencies;

(6) a Senior Executive Service should be established to provide the flexibility needed by agencies to recruit and retain the highly competent and qualified executives needed to provide more effective management of agencies and their functions, and the more expeditious administration of the public business;

(7) in appropriate instances, pay increases should be based on quality of performance rather than length of service;

(8) research programs and demonstration projects should be authorized to permit Federal agencies to experiment, subject to congressional oversight, with new and different personnel management concepts in controlled situations to achieve more efficient management of the Government's human resources and greater productivity in the delivery of service to the public;

(9) the training program of the Government should include retraining of employees for positions in other agencies to avoid separations during reductions in force and the loss to the Government of their knowledge and experience that these employees possess; and

(10) the right of Federal employees to organize, bargain collectively, and participate through labor organizations in decisions which affect them, with full regard for the public interest and the effective conduct of public business, should be specifically recognized in statute.

Sec. 7119 Negotiation Impasses;

(a) The Federal Mediation and Conciliation Ser-

vice shall provide services and assistance to agencies and exclusive representatives in the resolution
of negotiation impasses. The Service shall determine under what circumstances and in what manner it shall provide services and assistance.

Federal Mediation and
Conciliation Service
Office of Arbitration Services

Policies Functions and Procedures

April 15, 1979

Title 29—Labor

Chapter XII—Federal Mediation and Conciliation Service

Part 1404—Arbitration Services

This pamphlet reprints the policies and procedures of the Federal Mediation and Conciliation Service's Arbitration Services program, Part 1404, Chapter XII of Title 29 of the Code of Federal Regulations.

These policies and procedures were proposed by the Service and published in the Federal Register (43 FR 54366) on November 15, 1978. Interested persons were invited to submit comments, data, or arguments on the proposed amendments, and numerous comments were received. A final revised version of the policies and procedures was adopted by the Service on February 28, 1979, and published in the Federal Register (44 FR 13008) on March 9, 1979, with an effective date of April 15, 1979.

These regulations supersede the revision of 29 CFR 1404 of November 17, 1976.

Index

AUTHORITY: The provisions of Part 1404 issue under sec. 202, 61 Stat. 153, as amended; 29 U.S.C. 172, and interpret or apply sec. 3, 80 Stat. 250, sec. 203, 61 Stat. 153; 5 U.S.C. 552, 29 U.S.C. 173.

Subpart A: Arbitration Policy; Administration of Roster

1404.1 Scope and Authority

This chapter is issued by the Federal Mediation and Conciliation Service (FMCS) under Title II of the Labor Management Relations Act of 1947 (Public Law 80-101) as amended in 1959 (Public Law 86-257) and 1974 (Public Law 93-360). The chapter applies to all arbitrators listed on the FMCS Roster of Arbitrators, to all applicants for listing on the Roster, and to all persons or parties seeking to obtain from FMCS either names or panels of names of arbitrators listed on the Roster in connection with disputes which are to be submitted to arbitration or fact-finding.

1404.2 Policy

The labor policy of the United States is designed to promote the settlement of issues between employers and represented employees through the processes of collective bargaining and voluntary arbitration. This policy encourages the use of voluntary arbitration to resolve disputes over the interpretation or application of collective bargaining agreements. Voluntary arbitration and fact-finding in disputes and disagreements over establishment or modification of contract terms are important features of constructive labor-management relations, as alternatives to economic strife in the settlement of labor disputes.

1404.3 Administrative Responsibilities

(a) *Director.* The Director of FMCS has ultimate responsibility for all aspects of FMCS arbitration activities and is the final agency authority on all questions concerning the Roster or FMCS arbitration procedures.

(b) *Office of Arbitration Services.* The Office of Arbitration Services (OAS) maintains a Roster of Arbitrators (the "Roster"); administers Subpart C of these Regulations (Procedures for Arbitration Services); assists, promotes, and cooperates in the establishment of programs for training and developing new arbitrators; collects information and statistics concerning the arbitration function, and performs other tasks in connection with the function that may be assigned by the Director.

(c) *Arbitrator Review Board.* The Arbitrator Review Board (the "Board") shall consist of a presiding officer and such members and alternate members as the Director may appoint, and who shall serve at the Director's pleasure and may be removed at any time. The Board shall be composed entirely of full-time officers or employees of the Federal Government. The Board shall establish its own procedures for carrying out its duties.

(1) *Duties of the Board.* The Board shall:

(i) Review the qualifications of all applicants for listing on the Roster, interpreting and applying the criteria set forth in subsection 1404.5 of this part;

(ii) Review the status of all persons whose continued eligibility for listing on the Roster has been questioned under subsection 1404.5 of this part;

(iii) Make recommendations to the Director regarding acceptance or rejection of applicants for listing on the Roster, or regarding withdrawal of listing on the Roster for any of the reasons set forth herein.

Subpart B: Roster of Arbitrators; Admission and Retention

1404.4 Roster and Status of Members

(a) *The Roster.* The FMCS shall maintain a Roster of labor arbitrators consisting of persons who meet the criteria for listing contained in subsection 1404.5 of this part and whose names have not been removed from the Roster in accordance with subsection 1404.5(d).

(b) *Adherence to Standards and Requirements.* Persons listed on the Roster shall comply with the FMCS rules and regulations pertaining to arbitration and with such guidelines and procedures as may be issued by OAS pursuant to Subpart C hereof. Arbitrators are also expected to conform to the ethical standards and procedures set forth in the Code of Professional Responsibility for Arbitrators of Labor Management Disputes, as approved by the Joint Steering Committee of the National Academy of Arbitrators.

(c) *Status of Arbitrators.* Persons who are listed on the Roster and are selected or appointed to hear arbitration matters or to serve as factfinders do not become employees of the Federal Government by virtue of their selection or appointment. Following selection or appointment, the arbitrator's relationship is solely with the parties to the dispute, except that arbitrators are subject to certain reporting requirements and to standards of conduct as set forth in this Part.

(d) *Role of FMCS.* FMCS has no power to:

(1) Compel parties to arbitrate or agree to arbitration;

(2) Enforce an agreement to arbitrate:

(3) Compel parties to agree to a particular arbitrator;

(4) Influence, alter or set aside decisions of arbitrators listed on the Roster;

(5) Compel, deny or modify payment of compensation to an arbitrator.

(e) *Nominations and Panels.* On request of the parties to an agreement to arbitrate or engage in fact-finding, or where arbitration or fact-finding may be provided for by statute, OAS will provide names or panels of names without charge. Procedures for obtaining these services are contained in Subpart C. Neither the submission of a nomination or panel nor the appointment of an arbitrator constitutes a determination by FMCS that an agreement to arbitrate or enter fact-finding proceedings exists; nor does such action constitute a ruling that the matter in controversy is arbitrable under any agreement.

(f) *Rights of Persons Listed on the Roster.* No person shall have any right to be listed or to remain listed on the Roster. FMCS retains the authority and responsibility to assure that the needs of the parties using its facilities are served. To accomplish this purpose it may establish procedures for the preparation of panels or the appointment of arbitrators or factfinders which include consideration of such factors as background and experience, availability, acceptability, geographical location and the expressed preferences of the parties.

1404.5 Listing on the Roster; Criteria for Listing and Retention

Persons seeking to be listed on the Roster must complete and submit an application form which may be obtained from the Office of Arbitration Services. Upon receipt of an executed form, OAS will review the application, assure that it is complete, make such inquiries as are necessary, and submit the application to the Arbitrator Review Board. The Board will review the completed applications under the criteria set forth in subsections (a), (b) and (c) of this Section, and will forward to the Director its recommendation on each applicant. The Director makes all final decisions as to whether an applicant may be listed. Each applicant shall be notified in writing of the Director's decision and the reasons therefore.

(a) *General Criteria.* Applicants for the Roster will be

listed on the Roster upon a determination that they:

(1) Are experienced, competent and acceptable in decision-making roles in the resolution of labor relations disputes; or

(2) Have extensive experience in relevant positions in collective bargaining; and

(3) Are capable of conducting an orderly hearing, can analyze testimony and exhibits and can prepare clear and concise findings and awards within reasonable time limits.

(b) *Proof of Qualification.* The qualifications listed in (a) above are preferably demonstrated by the submission of actual arbitration awards prepared by the applicant while serving as an impartial arbitrator chosen by the parties to disputes. Equivalent experience acquired in training, internship or other development programs, or experience such as that acquired as a hearing officer or judge in labor relations controversies may also be considered by the Board.

(c) *Advocacy.*

(1) Definition. An advocate is a person who represents employers, labor organizations, or individuals as an employee, attorney or consultant, in matters of labor relations, including but not limited to the subjects of union representation and recognition matters, collective bargaining, arbitration, unfair labor practices, equal employment opportunity and other areas generally recognized as constituting labor relations. The definition includes representatives of employers or employees in individual cases or controversies involving workmen's compensation, occupational health or safety, minimum wage or other labor standards matters.

The definition of advocate also includes a person who is directly associated with an advocate in a business or professional relationship as, for example, partners or employees of a law firm.

(2) Eligibility. Except in the case of persons listed on

the Roster before November 17, 1976, no person who is an advocate, as defined above, may be listed. No person who was listed on the Roster at any time who was not an advocate when listed or who did not divulge advocacy at the time of listing may continue to be listed after becoming an advocate or after the fact of advocacy is revealed.

(d) *Duration of Listing, Retention.* Initial listing may be for a period not to exceed three years, and may be renewed thereafter for periods not to exceed two years, provided upon review that the listing is not cancelled by the Director as set forth below. Notice of cancellation may be given to the member whenever the member:

(1) No longer meets the criteria for admission;
(2) Has been repeatedly and flagrantly delinquent in submitting awards;
(3) Has refused to make reasonable and periodic reports to FMCS, as required in Subpart C, concerning activities pertaining to arbitration;
(4) Has been the subject of complaints by parties who use FMCS facilities, and the Director, after appropriate inquiry, concludes that just cause for cancellation has been shown.
(5) Is determined by the Director to be unacceptable to the parties who use FMCS arbitration facilities; the Director may base a determination of unacceptability on FMCS records showing the number of times the arbitrator's name has been proposed to the parties and the number of times it has been selected.

No listing may be cancelled without at least sixty days notice of the reasons for the proposed removal, unless the Director determines that the FMCS or the parties will be harmed by continued listing. In such cases an arbitrator's listing may be suspended without notice or delay pending final determination in accordance with these procedures. The member shall in either case have an opportunity to submit a written response showing why the listing should not be cancelled. The Director may, at his discretion, appoint a hearing officer to conduct an inquiry into the facts of any proposed cancellation and to make recommendations to the Director.

1404.6 Freedom of Choice.

Nothing contained herein should be construed to limit the rights of parties who use FMCS arbitration facilities to select jointly any arbitrator or arbitration procedure acceptable to them.

Subpart C: Procedures for Arbitration Services

1404.10 Procedures for Requesting Arbitration Panels

The Office of Arbitration Services has been delegated the responsibility for administering all requests for arbitration services under these regulations.

(a) The Service will refer a panel of arbitrators to the parties upon request. The Service prefers to act upon a joint request which should be addressed to the Federal Mediation and Conciliation Service, Washington, D.C. 20427, Attention: Office of Arbitration Services. In the event that the request is made by only one party, the Service will submit a panel; however, any submission of a panel should not be construed as anything more than compliance with a request and does not necessarily reflect the contractual requirements of the parties.

(b) The parties are urged to use the Request for Arbitration Panel form (R-43) which has been prepared by the Service and is available in quantity at all FMCS regional offices and field stations or upon request to the Federal Mediation and Conciliation Service, Office of Arbitration Services, Washington, D.C. 20427. The form R-43 is reproduced herein for the purposes of identification.

(c) A brief statement of the issues in dispute should accompany the request to enable the Service to submit the names of arbitrators qualified for the issues involved. The request should also include a current copy of the arbitration section of the collective bargaining agreement or stipulation to arbitrate.

(d) If form R-43 is not utilized, the parties may request a panel by letter which must include the names, addresses, and phone numbers of the parties, the location of the contemplated hearing, the issue in dispute, the number of names desired on the panel, the industry involved and any special qualifications of the panel or special requirement desired.

1404.11 Arbitrability

Where either party claims that a dispute is not subject

to arbitration, the Service will not decide the merits of such claim.

```
FMCS Form R-41                                                    Form Approved
Sep 1975         FEDERAL MEDIATION AND CONCILIATION SERVICE       OMB NO 33 R0007
                           WASHINGTON, D.C. 20427

                        REQUEST FOR ARBITRATION PANEL

To  Director, Arbitration Services
    Federal Mediation and Conciliation Service
    Washington, D.C. 20427                            Date _____
1.                                  (For Company)

Name of Company       _____

Name and Address      _____
  of Representative                        (NAME)
  to Receive Panel     _____
                                           (STREET)

                      _____
                                        (CITY, STATE, ZIP)
Telephone (include area code) _____

2.                                  (For Union)

Name of Union and Local No. _____

Name and Address      _____
  of Representative                        (NAME)
  to Receive Panel     _____
                                           (STREET)

                      _____
                                        (CITY, STATE, ZIP)
Telephone (include area code) _____

3   Site of Dispute  _____
                                        (CITY, STATE, ZIP)
4   Type of Issue _____
                            (DISCHARGE, HOLIDAY PAY, SICK LEAVE, ETC)
5   A panel of seven (7) names is usually provided; if you desire a different number, please indicate _____

6   Type of Industry

    ☐ Manufacturing          ☐ Federal Government      ☐ Public Utilities, Communi-
                                                          cations, Transportation
    ☐ Construction           ☐ State Government           (including trucking)

    ☐ Mining, Agriculture    ☐ Local Government         ☐ Retail, Wholesale and
      and Finance                                         Service Industries
    ☐ Other (Specify) _____

7   Special Requirements_____
            (SPECIAL ARBITRATOR QUALIFICATIONS, TIME LIMITATIONS ON HEARING OR DECISION, GEOGRAPHICAL RESTRICTIONS, ETC)

                                            _____
                                                        (COMPANY)
8   Signatures
                                            _____
                                                        (UNION)
Although the FMCS prefers to act upon a joint request of the parties, a submission will be made based on the request of a single party. However
any submission of a panel should not be construed as anything more than compliance with a request and does not reflect on the substance or
arbitrability of the issue in dispute.

Additional forms may be obtained from the Federal Mediation and Conciliation Service or any FMCS Regional Office. See list on reverse of Copy
No. 3.
             Copy No  1. Original - To Federal Mediation and Conciliation Service
```

1404.12 Nominations of Arbitrators

(a) When the parties have been unable to agree on an arbitrator, the Service will submit to the parties on request the names of seven arbitrators unless the applicable collective bargaining agreement provides for a different number, or unless the parties themselves request a different number. Together with the submission of a panel of arbitrators, the Service will furnish a biographical sketch for each member of the panel. This sketch states the background, qualifications, experience, and per diem fee established by the arbitrator. It states the existence, if any, of other fees such as cancellation, postponement, rescheduling or administrative fees.

(b) When a panel is submitted, an FMCS control case number is assigned. All future communication between the parties and the Service should refer to the case number.

(c) The Service considers many factors when selecting names for inclusion on a panel, but the agreed-upon wishes of the parties are paramount. Special qualifications of arbitrators experienced in certain issues or industries, or possessing certain backgrounds, may be identified for purposes of submitting panels to accommodate the parties. The Service may also consider such things as general acceptability, geographical location, general experience, availability, size of fee, and the need to expose new arbitrators to the selection process in preparing panels. The Service has no obligation to put an individual on any given panel, or on a minimum number of panels in any fixed period, such as a month or a year.

(1) If at any time both parties request, for valid reasons, that a name or names be omitted from a panel, such name or names will be omitted, unless they are excessive in number.

(2) If at any time both parties request that a name or names be included on a panel, such name or names will be included.

(3) If only one party requests that a name or names be omitted from a panel, or that specific individuals be added to the panel, such request shall not be honored.

(4) If the issue described in the request appears to require special technical experience or qualifications, arbitrators who possess such qualifications

will, where possible, be included on the panel submitted to the parties.

(5) In almost all cases, an arbitrator is chosen from one panel. However, if either party requests another panel, the Service shall comply with the request providing that an additional panel is permissible under the terms of the agreement or the other party so agrees. Requests for more than two panels must be accompanied by a statement of explanation and will be considered on a case-by-case basis.

1404.13 Selection and Appointment of Arbitrators

(a) The parties should notify the OAS of their selection of an arbitrator. The arbitrator, upon notification by the parties, shall notify the OAS of his selection and willingness to serve. Upon notification of the parties' selection of an arbitrator, the Service will make a formal appointment of the arbitrator.

(b) Where the contract is silent on the manner of selecting arbitrators, the parties may wish to consider one of the following methods for selection of an arbitrator from a panel:

(1) Each party alternately strikes a name from the submitted panel until one remains.

(2) Each party advises the Service of its order of preference by numbering each name on the panel and submitting the numbered list in writing to OAS. The name on the panel that has the lowest accumulated numerical number will be appointed.

(3) Informal agreement of the parties by whatever method they choose.

(c) The Service will, on joint or unilateral request of the parties, submit a panel or, when the applicable collective bargaining agreement authorizes, will make a direct appointment of an arbitrator. Submission of a panel or name signifies nothing more than compliance with a request and in no way constitutes a determination by the Service that the parties are obligated to arbitrate the dispute in question. Resolution of disputes as to the propriety of such a submission or appointment rests solely with the parties.

(d) The arbitrator, upon notification of appointment, is required to communicate with the parties immediately to arrange for preliminary matters, such as date and place of hearing.

1404.14 Conduct of Hearings

(a) All proceedings conducted by the arbitrator shall be in conformity with the contractual obligations of the parties. The arbitrator is also expected to conduct all proceedings in conformity with Section 1404.4(b). The conduct of the arbitration proceeding is under the arbitrator's jurisdiction and control and the arbitrator's decision is to be based upon the evidence and testimony presented at the hearing or otherwise incorporated in the record of the proceeding. The arbitrator may, unless prohibited by law, proceed in the absence of any party who, after due notice, fails to be present or to obtain a postponement. An award rendered in an *ex parte* proceeding of this nature must be based upon evidence presented to the arbitrator.

1404.15 Decision and Award

(a) Arbitrators are encouraged to render awards not later than 60 days from the date of the closing of the record as determined by the arbitrator, unless otherwise agreed upon by the parties or specified by law. A failure to render timely awards reflects upon the performance of an arbitrator and may lead to his removal from the FMCS roster.

(b) The parties should inform the OAS whenever a decision is unduly delayed. The arbitrator shall notify the OAS if and when the arbitrator (1) cannot schedule, hear and determine issues promptly, or; (2) learns a dispute has been settled by the parties prior to the decision.

(c) After an award has been submitted to the parties, the arbitrator is required to submit a Fee and Award Statement, form R-19, showing a breakdown of the fee and expense charges so that the Service may be in a position to review conformance with stated charges under §1404.12(a). Filing the Statement within 15 days after rendering an award is required of all arbitrators. The Statements are not used for the purpose of compelling payment of fees.

*   *   *   *   *

2. The requirement in 29 CFR 1404.°15(d) concerning the release of copies of arbitrator awards by FMCS is deleted in conformance with the discontinuance of the submission of these awards to the agency pursuant to paragraph (c) above. Accordingly, paragraph (d) is revised to read as follows:

(d) The Service encourages the publication of arbitration awards. However, the Service expects arbitrators it has nominated or appointed not to give publicity to awards they issue if objected to by one of the parties.

1404.16 Fees and Charges of Arbitrators.

(a) No administrative or filing fee is charged by the Service. The current policy of the Service permits each of its nominees or appointees to charge a per diem fee and other predetermined fees for services, the amount of which has been certified in advance to the Service. Each arbitrator's maximum per diem fee and the existence of other predetermined fees, if any, are set forth on a biographical sketch which is sent to the parties when panels are submitted and are the controlling fees. The arbitrator shall not change any fee or add charges without giving at least 30 days advance notice to the Service.

(b) In cases involving unusual amounts of time and expenses relative to pre-hearing and post-hearing administration of a particular case, an administrative charge may be made by the arbitrator.

(c) All charges other than those specified by 1404.16(a) shall be divulged to and agreement obtained by the arbitrator with the parties immediately after appointment.

(d) The Service requests that it be notified of any arbitrator's deviation from the policies expressed herein. However, the Service will not attempt to resolve any fee dispute.

1404.17 Reports and Biographical Sketches

(a) Arbitrators listed on the Roster shall execute and return all documents, forms and reports required by the Service. They shall also keep the Service informed of changes of address, telephone number, availability, and of any business of other connection or relationship which involves labor-management relations, or which creates or gives the appearance of advocacy as defined in Section 1404.4(c)(1).

(b) The Service may require each arbitrator listed on the Roster to prepare at the time of initial listing, and to revise, biographical information in accordance with a format to be provided by the Service at the time of initial listing or biennial review. Arbitrators may also request revision of biographical information at other times to reflect changes in fees, the existence of additional charges, address, experience and background, or other relevant data. The Service reserves the right to decide and approve the format and content of biographical sketches.

Federal Mediation and Conciliation Service
Office of Arbitration Services
Washington, D.C. 20427

RULES

Voluntary
Labor
Arbitration
Rules

American
Arbitration
Association

*As amended
and in effect
January 1, 1984*

Parties who use the labor arbitration services of the American Arbitration Association are being offered a new choice. For relatively uncomplicated grievances, they may agree to use streamlined procedures which provide a prompt and inexpensive method for resolving disputes. This option responds to a concern about rising costs and delays in processing grievance arbitration cases. The AAA's Streamlined Labor Arbitration Rules, by eliminating certain procedures, are intended to resolve cases within a month of the appointment of the arbitrator. Copies of the Streamlined Labor Arbitration Rules are available from any AAA Regional Office without cost.

Voluntary Labor Arbitration Rules

1. Agreement of Parties
The parties shall be deemed to have made these Rules a part of their arbitration agreement whenever, in a collective bargaining agreement or submission, they have provided for arbitration by the American Arbitration Association (hereinafter AAA) or under its Rules. These Rules shall apply in the form obtaining at the time the arbitration is initiated.

2. Name of Tribunal
Any Tribunal constituted by the parties under these Rules shall be called the Voluntary Labor Arbitration Tribunal.

3. Administrator
When parties agree to arbitrate under these Rules and an arbitration is instituted thereunder, they

thereby authorize the AAA to administer the arbitration. The authority and obligations of the Administrator are as provided in the agreement of
the parties and in these Rules.

4. Delegation of Duties
The duties of the AAA may be carried out through
such representatives or committees as the AAA
may direct.

5. National Panel of Labor Arbitrators
The AAA shall establish and maintain a National
Panel of Labor Arbitrators and shall appoint arbi-
trators therefrom, as hereinafter provided.

6. Office of Tribunal
The general office of the Labor Arbitration Tribunal is the headquarters of the AAA, which may,
however, assign the administration of an arbitration to any of its Regional Offices.

7. Initiation under an Arbitration Clause in a Collective Bargaining Agreement
Arbitration under an arbitration clause in a collec-
tive bargaining agreement under these Rules may be
initiated by either party in the following manner:

(a) By giving written notice to the other party of
intention to arbitrate (Demand), which notice shall
contain a statement setting forth the nature of the
dispute and the remedy sought, and

(b) By filing at any Regional Office of the AAA
three copies of said notice, together with a copy of
the collective bargaining agreement, or such parts
thereof as relate to the dispute, including the arbitration provisions. After the Arbitrator is appointed,
no new or different claim may be submitted except
with the consent of the Arbitrator and all other
parties.

8. Answer
The party upon whom the Demand for Arbitration is made may file an answering statement with the AAA within seven days after notice from the AAA, simultaneously sending a copy to the other party. If no answer is filed within the stated time, it will be assumed that the claim is denied. Failure to file an answer shall not operate to delay the arbitration.

9. Initiation under a Submission
Parties to any collective bargaining agreement may initiate an arbitration under these Rules by filing at any Regional Office of the AAA two copies of a written agreement to arbitrate under these Rules (Submission), signed by the parties and setting forth the nature of the dispute and the remedy sought.

10. Fixing of Locale
The parties may mutually agree upon the locale where the arbitration is to be held. If the locale is not designated in the collective bargaining agreement or Submission, and if there is a dispute as to the appropriate locale, the AAA shall have the power to determine the locale and its decision shall be binding.

11. Qualifications of Arbitrator
No person shall serve as a neutral Arbitrator in any arbitration in which he or she has any financial personal interest in the result of the arbitration, unless the parties, in writing, waive such disqualification.

12. Appointment from Panel
If the parties have not appointed an Arbitrator and have not provided any other method of appointment, the Arbitrator shall be appointed in the following manner: Immediately after the filing of the Demand or Submission, the AAA shall submit simultaneously to each party an identical list of names of persons chosen from the Labor Panel.

Each party shall have seven days from the mailing date in which to cross off any names to which it objects, number the remaining names indicating the order of preference, and return the list to the AAA. If a party does not return the list within the time specified, all persons named therein shall be deemed acceptable. From among the persons who have been approved on both lists, and in accordance with the designated order of mutual preference, the AAA shall invite the acceptance of an Arbitrator to serve. If the parties fail to agree upon any of the persons named or if those named decline or are unable to act, or if for any other reason the appointment cannot be made from the submitted lists, the Administrator shall have the power to make the appointment from other members of the Panel without the submission of any additional lists.

13. Direct Appointment by Parties

If the agreement of the parties names an Arbitrator or specifies a method of appointing an Arbitrator, that designation or method shall be followed. The notice of appointment, with the name and address of such Arbitrator, shall be filed with the AAA by the appointing party.

If the agreement specifies a period of time within which an Arbitrator shall be appointed and any party fails to make such appointment within that period, the AAA may make the appointment.

If no period of time is specified in the agreement, the AAA shall notify the parties to make the appointment and if within seven days thereafter such Arbitrator has not been so appointed, the AAA shall make the appointment.

14. Appointment of Neutral Arbitrator by Party-Appointed Arbitrators

If the parties have appointed their Arbitrators, or if either or both of them have been appointed as provided in Section 13, and have authorized such Arbitrators to appoint a neutral Arbitrator within a specified time and no appointment is made within such time or any agreed extension thereof, the AAA may appoint a neutral Arbitrator, who shall act as Chairman.

If no period of time is specified for appointment of the neutral Arbitrator and the parties do not make the appointment within seven days from the date of the appointment of the last party-appointed Arbitrator, the AAA shall appoint such neutral Arbitrator, who shall act as Chairman.

If the parties have agreed that the Arbitrators shall appoint the neutral Arbitrator from the Panel, the AAA shall furnish to the party-appointed Arbitrators, in the manner prescribed in Section 12, a list selected from the Panel, and the appointment of the neutral Arbitrator shall be made as prescribed in such Section.

15. Number of Arbitrators
If the arbitration agreement does not specify the number of Arbitrators, the dispute shall be heard and determined by one Arbitrator, unless the parties otherwise agree.

16. Notice to Arbitrator of Appointment
Notice of the appointment of the neutral Arbitrator shall be mailed to the Arbitrator by the AAA and the signed acceptance of the Arbitrator shall be filed with the AAA prior to the opening of the first hearing.

17. Disclosure by Arbitrator of Disqualification
Prior to accepting the appointment, the prospective neutral Arbitrator shall disclose any circumstances likely to create a presumption of bias or which the Arbitrator believes might disqualify him or her as

an impartial Arbitrator. Upon receipt of such information, the AAA shall immediately disclose it to the parties. If either party declines to waive the presumptive disqualification, the vacancy thus created shall be filled in accordance with the applicable provisions of these Rules.

18. Vacancies

If any Arbitrator should resign, die, withdraw, refuse, or be unable or disqualified to perform the duties of office, the AAA shall, on proof satisfactory to it, declare the office vacant. Vacancies shall be filled in the same manner as that governing the making of the original appointment, and the matter shall be reheard by the new Arbitrator.

19. Time and Place of Hearing

The Arbitrator shall fix the time and place for each hearing. At least five days prior thereto, the AAA shall mail notice of the time and place of hearing to each party, unless the parties otherwise agree.

20. Representation by Counsel

Any party may be represented at the hearing by counsel or by other authorized representative.

21. Stenographic Record

Any party may request a stenographic record by making arrangements for same through the AAA. If such transcript is agreed by the parties to be, or in appropriate cases determined by the Arbitrator to be, the official record of the proceeding, it must be made available to the Arbitrator and to the other party for inspection, at a time and place determined by the Arbitrator. The total cost of such a record shall be shared equally by those parties that order copies.

22. Attendance at Hearings

Persons having a direct interest in the arbitration are entitled to attend hearings. The Arbitrator shall have the power to require the retirement of any witness or witnesses during the testimony of other witnesses. It shall be discretionary with the Arbitrator to determine the propriety of the attendance of any other persons.

23. Adjournments
The Arbitrator for good cause shown may adjourn the hearing upon the request of a party or upon his or her own initiative, and shall adjourn when all the parties agree thereto.

24. Oaths
Before proceeding with the first hearing, each Arbitrator may take an Oath of Office, and if required by law, shall do so. The Arbitrator may require witnesses to testify under oath administered by any duly qualified person, and if required by law or requested by either party, shall do so.

25. Majority Decision
Whenever there is more than one Arbitrator, all decisions of the Arbitrators shall be by majority vote. The award shall also be made by majority vote unless the concurrence of all is expressly required.

26. Order of Proceedings
A hearing shall be opened by the filing of the Oath of the Arbitrator, where required, and by the recording of the place, time, and date of hearing, the presence of the Arbitrator and parties, and counsel, if any, and the receipt by the Arbitrator of the Demand and answer, if any, or the Submission.

Exhibits, when offered by either party, may be received in evidence by the Arbitrator. The names and addresses of all witnesses and exhibits in order received shall be made a part of the record.

The Arbitrator may vary the normal procedure under which the initiating party first presents its claim, but in any case shall afford full and equal opportunity to all parties for presentation of relevant proofs.

27. Arbitration in the Absence of a Party

Unless the law provides to the contrary, the arbitration may proceed in the absence of any party who, after due notice, fails to be present or fails to obtain an adjournment. An award shall not be made solely on the default of a party. The Arbitrator shall require the other party to submit such evidence as may be required for the making of an award.

28. Evidence

The parties may offer such evidence as they desire and shall produce such additional evidence as the Arbitrator may deem necessary to an understanding and determination of the dispute. An Arbitrator authorized by law to subpoena witnesses and documents may do so independently or upon the request of any party. The Arbitrator shall be the judge of the relevancy and materiality of the evidence offered and conformity to legal rules of evidence shall not be necessary. All evidence shall be taken in the presence of all of the Arbitrators and all of the parties except where any of the parties is absent in default or has waived its right to be present.

29. Evidence by Affidavit and Filing of Documents

The Arbitrator may receive and consider the evidence of witnesses by affidavit, giving it only such weight as seems proper after consideration of any objections made to its admission.

All documents not filed with the Arbitrator at the hearing, but which are arranged at the hearing or subsequently by agreement of the parties to be submitted, shall be filed with the AAA for transmission to the Arbitrator. All parties shall be afforded opportunity to examine such documents.

30. Inspection

Whenever the Arbitrator deems it necessary, he or she may make an inspection in connection with the subject matter of the dispute after written notice to the parties who may, if they so desire, be present at such inspection.

31. Closing of Hearings

The Arbitrator shall inquire of all parties whether they have any further proofs to offer or witnesses to be heard. Upon receiving negative replies, the Arbitrator shall declare the hearings closed and a minute thereof shall be recorded. If briefs or other documents are to be filed, the hearings shall be declared closed as of the final date set by the Arbitrator for filing with the AAA. The time limit within which the Arbitrator is required to make an award shall commence to run, in the absence of other agreement by the parties, upon the closing of the hearings.

32. Reopening of Hearings

The hearings may be reopened by the Arbitrator at will or on the motion of either party, for good cause shown, at any time before the award is made, but if the reopening of the hearings would prevent the making of the award within the specific time agreed upon by the parties in the contract out of which the controversy has arisen, the matter may not be reopened, unless both parties agree upon the extension of such time limit. When no specific date is fixed in the contract, the Arbitrator may reopen the hearings, and the Arbitrator shall have 30 days from the closing of the reopened hearings within which to make an award.

33. Waiver of Rules

Any party who proceeds with the arbitration after knowledge that any provision or requirement of these Rules has not been complied with, and who fails to state an objection thereto in writing, shall be deemed to have waived the right to object.

34. Waiver of Oral Hearings

The parties may provide, by written agreement, for the waiver of oral hearings. If the parties are unable to agree as to the procedure, the AAA shall specify a fair and equitable procedure.

35. Extensions of Time

The parties may modify any period of time by mutual agreement. The AAA for good cause may extend any period of time established by these Rules, except the time for making the award. The AAA shall notify the parties of any such extension of time and its reason therefor.

36. Serving of Notices

Each party to a Submission or other agreement which provides for arbitration under these Rules shall be deemed to have consented and shall consent that any papers, notices, or process necessary or proper for the initiation or continuation of an arbitration under these Rules and for any court action in connection therewith or the entry of judgment on an award made thereunder, may be served upon such party (a) by mail addressed to such party or its attorney at the last known address, or (b) by personal service, within or without the state wherein the arbitration is to be held.

37. Time of Award

The award shall be rendered promptly by the Arbitrator and, unless otherwise agreed by the parties or specified by the law, not later than 30 days from the date of closing the hearings, or if oral hearings have been waived, then from the date of transmitting the final statements and proofs to the Arbitrator.

38. Form of Award

The award shall be in writing and shall be signed either by the neutral Arbitrator or by a concurring majority if there be more than one Arbitrator. The parties shall advise the AAA whenever they do not require the Arbitrator to accompany the award with an opinion.

39. Award upon Settlement
If the parties settle their dispute during the course of the arbitration, the Arbitrator, upon their request, may set forth the terms of the agreed settlement in an award.

40. Delivery of Award to Parties
Parties shall accept as legal delivery of the award the placing of the award or a true copy thereof in the mail by the AAA, addressed to such party at its last known address or to its attorney, or personal service of the award, or the filing of the award in any manner which may be prescribed by law.

41. Release of Documents for Judicial Proceedings
The AAA shall, upon the written request of a party, furnish to such party, at its expense, certified facsimiles of any papers in the AAA's possession that may be required in judicial proceedings relating to the arbitration.

42. Judicial Proceedings
The AAA is not a necessary party in judicial proceedings relating to the arbitration.

43. Administrative Fee
As a not-for-profit organization, the AAA shall prescribe an administrative fee schedule to compensate it for the cost of providing administrative services. The schedule in effect at the time of filing shall be applicable.

44. Expenses
The expense of witnesses for either side shall be paid by the party producing such witnesses.

Expenses of the arbitration, other than the cost of

the stenographic record, including required travel-
ing and other expenses of the Arbitrator and of

AAA representatives, and the expenses of any witnesses or the cost of any proofs produced at the
direct request of the Arbitrator, shall be borne
equally by the parties unless they agree otherwise,
or unless the Arbitrator in the award assesses such
expenses or any part thereof against any specified
party or parties.

45. Communication with Arbitrator
There shall be no communication between the parties and a neutral Arbitrator other than at oral hearings. Any other oral or written communications
from the parties to the Arbitrator shall be directed
to the AAA for transmittal to the Arbitrator.

46. Interpretation and Application of Rules
The Arbitrator shall interpret and apply these Rules
insofar as they relate to the Arbitrator's powers
and duties. When there is more than one Arbitrator
and a difference arises among them concerning the
meaning or application of any such Rules, it shall be
decided by majority vote. If that is unobtainable,
either Arbitrator or party may refer the question
to the AAA for final decision. All other Rules shall
be interpreted and applied by the AAA.

ADMINISTRATIVE FEE SCHEDULE

Initial Administrative Fee
The initial administrative fee is $100.00 for each
party, due and payable at the time of filing. No
refund of the initial fee is made when a matter is
withdrawn or settled after the filing of the Demand
for Arbitration.

Additional Hearings
A fee of $50.00 is payable by each party for each
second and subsequent hearing which is either

clerked by the AAA or held in a hearing room provided by the AAA.

Postponement Fee
A fee of $40.00 is payable by a party causing a postponement of any scheduled hearing.

REGIONAL DIRECTORS

ATLANTA (30361) • INDIA JOHNSON •
1197 Peachtree Street, N.E. • (404) 872-3022

BOSTON (02114) • RICHARD M. REILLY •
60 Staniford Street • (617) 367-6800

CHARLOTTE (28222) •MARK SHOLANDER •
P.O. Box 220565, 3717 Latrobe Drive • (704) 366-4546

CHICAGO (60606) • LaVERNE ROLLE •
205 West Wacker Drive • (312) 346-2282

CINCINNATI (45202) • PHILIP S. THOMPSON •
2308 Carew Tower • (513) 241-8434

CLEVELAND (44115) • EARLE C. BROWN •
1127 Euclid Avenue • (216) 241-4741

DALLAS (75201) • HELMUT O. WOLFF •
1607 Main Street • (214) 748-4979

DENVER (80203) •MARK APPEL •
789 Sherman Street • (303) 831-0823

DETROIT (48226) • MARY A. BEDIKIAN •
615 Griswold Street•(313) 964-2525

GARDEN CITY, N.Y. (11530) • MARK A. RESNICK •
585 Stewart Avenue • (516) 222-1660

HARTFORD (06106) • KAREN M. BARRINGTON •
2 Hartford Square West • (203) 278-5000

LOS ANGELES (90020) •JERROLD L. MURASE •
443 Shatto Place • (213) 383-6516

MIAMI (33129) • RENE GRAFALS •
2250 S.W. 3rd Avenue • (305) 854-1616

MINNEAPOLIS (55402) • JAMES R. DEYE •
510 Foshay Tower • (612) 332-6545

NEW JERSEY (SOMERSET 08873) • RICHARD NAIMARK •
1 Executive Drive • (201) 560-9560

NEW YORK (10020) • GEORGE H. FRIEDMAN •
140 West 51st Street • (212) 484-4150

PHILADELPHIA (19102) •ARTHUR R. MEHR •
1520 Locust Street • (215) 732-5260

PHOENIX (85012) •DEBORAH A. KRELL •
77 East Columbus • (602) 234-0950

PITTSBURGH (15222) • JOHN F. SCHANO •
221 Gateway Four • (412) 261-3617

SAN DIEGO (92101) • SHELAGH A. HURLEY •
530 Broadway • (619) 239-3051

SAN FRANCISCO (94108) • CHARLES A. COOPER •
445 Bush Street • (415) 981-3901

SEATTLE (98104) • NEAL M. BLACKER •
811 First Avenue • (206) 622-6435

SYRACUSE (13202) • DEBORAH A. BROWN •
720 State Tower Building • (315) 472-5483

WASHINGTON, D.C. (20036) • GARYLEE COX •
1730 Rhode Island Avenue, N.W. • (202) 296-8510

WHITE PLAINS, N.Y. (10601) • MARION J. ZINMAN •
34 South Broadway • (914) 946-1119

AMERICAN ARBITRATION ASSOCIATION
NEW YORK (10020) •140 West 51st Street
(212) 484-4000

AAA-6-20M-12/83

APPENDIX E

RULES AND REGULATIONS OF THE
FEDERAL LABOR RELATIONS AUTHORITY

SUBCHAPTER C—FEDERAL LABOR RELATIONS AUTHORITY AND GENERAL COUNSEL OF THE FEDERAL LABOR RELATIONS AUTHORITY

PART 2420—PURPOSE AND SCOPE

§ 2420.1 Purpose and scope.

The regulations contained in this subchapter are designed to implement the provisions of chapter 71 of title 5 of the United States Code. They prescribe the procedures, basic principles or criteria under which the Federal Labor Relations Authority or the Gen-

(5 U.S.C. 7134)

[45 FR 3497, Jan. 17, 1980]

eral Counsel of the Federal Labor Relations Authority, as applicable, will:

(a) Determine the appropriateness of units for labor organization representation under 5 U.S.C. 7112;

(b) Supervise or conduct elections to determine whether a labor organization has been selected as an exclusive representative by a majority of the employees in an appropriate unit and otherwise administer the provisions of 5 U.S.C. 7111 relating to the according of exclusive recognition to labor organizations;

(c) Resolve issues relating to the granting of national consultation rights under 5 U.S.C. 7113;

(d) Resolve issues relating to determining compelling need for agency rules and regulations under 5 U.S.C. 7117(b);

(e) Resolve issues relating to the duty to bargain in good faith under 5 U.S.C. 7117(c);

(f) Resolve issues relating to the granting of consultation rights with respect to conditions of employment under 5 U.S.C. 7117(d);

(g) Conduct hearings and resolve complaints of unfair labor practices under 5 U.S.C. 7118;

(h) Resolve exceptions to arbitrators' awards under 5 U.S.C. 7122; and

(i) Take such other actions as are necessary and appropriate effectively to administer the provisions of chapter 71 of title 5 of the United States Code.

PART 2421—MEANING OF TERMS AS USED IN THIS SUBCHAPTER

AUTHORITY: 5 U.S.C. 7134.

SOURCE: 45 FR 3497, Jan. 17, 1980, unless otherwise noted.

§ 2421.1 Federal Service Labor-Management Relations Statute.

The term "Federal Service Labor-Management Relations Statute" means chapter 71 of title 5 of the United States Code.

§ 2421.2 Terms defined in 5 U.S.C. 7103(a); General Counsel; Assistant Secretary.

(a) The terms "person," "employee," "agency," "labor organization," "dues," "Authority," "Panel," "collective bargaining agreement," "grievance," "supervisor," "management official," "collective bargaining," "confidential employee," "conditions of employment," "professional employee," "exclusive representative," "firefighter," and "United States," as used herein shall have the meanings set forth in 5 U.S.C. 7103(a).

(b) The term "General Counsel" means the General Counsel of the Authority.

(c) The term "Assistant Secretary" means the Assistant Secretary of Labor for Labor-Management Relations.

§ 2421.3 National consultation rights; consultation rights on Government-wide rules or regulations; exclusive recognition; unfair labor practices.

(a) "National consultation rights" has the meaning as set forth in 5 U.S.C. 7113;

(b) "Consultation rights on Government-wide rules or regulations" has the meaning as set forth in 5 U.S.C. 7117(d);

(c) "Exclusive recognition" has the meaning as set forth in 5 U.S.C. 7111; and

(d) "Unfair labor practices" has the meaning as set forth in 5 U.S.C. 7116.

§ 2421.4 Activity.

"Activity" means any facility, organizational entity, or geographical subdivision or combination thereof, of any agency.

§ 2421.5 Primary national subdivision.

"Primary national subdivision" of an agency means a first-level organizational segment which has functions national in scope that are implemented in field activities.

§ 2421.6 Regional Director.

"Regional Director" means the Director of a region of the Authority with geographical boundaries as fixed by the Authority.

§ 2421.7 Executive Director.

"Executive Director" means the Executive Director of the Authority.

§ 2421.8 Hearing Officer.

"Hearing Officer" means the individual designated to conduct a hearing involving a question concerning the appropriateness of a unit or such other matters as may be assigned.

§ 2421.9   Administrative Law Judge.

"Administrative Law Judge" means the Chief Administrative Law Judge or any Administrative Law Judge designated by the Chief Administrative Law Judge to conduct a hearing in cases under 5 U.S.C. 7116, and such other matters as may be assigned.

§ 2421.10   Chief Administrative Law Judge.

"Chief Administrative Law Judge" means the Chief Administrative Law Judge of the Authority.

§ 2421.11   Party.

"Party" means (a) any person: (1) Filing a charge, petition, or request; (2) named in a charge, complaint, petition, or request; (3) whose intervention in a proceeding has been permitted or directed by the Authority; (4) who participated as a party (i) in a matter that was decided by an agency head under 5 U.S.C. 7117, or (ii) in a matter where the award of an arbitrator was issued; and (b) the General Counsel, or the General Counsel's designated representative, in appropriate proceedings.

§ 2421.12   Intervenor.

"Intervenor" means a party in a proceeding whose intervention has been permitted or directed by the Authority, its agents or representatives.

§ 2421.13   Certification.

"Certification" means the determination by the Authority, its agents or representatives, of the results of an election, or the results of a petition to consolidate existing exclusively recognized units.

§ 2421.14   Appropriate unit.

"Appropriate unit" means that grouping of employees found to be appropriate for purposes of exclusive recognition under 5 U.S.C. 7111, and for purposes of allotments to representatives under 5 U.S.C. 7115(c), and consistent with the provisions of 5 U.S.C. 7112.

§ 2421.15   Secret ballot.

"Secret ballot" means the expression by ballot, voting machine or otherwise,

but in no event by proxy, of a choice with respect to any election or vote taken upon any matter, which is cast in such a manner that the person expressing such choice cannot be identified with the choice expressed, except in that instance in which any determinative challenged ballot is opened.

§ 2421.16   Showing of interest.

"Showing of interest" means evidence of membership in a labor organization; employees' signed and dated authorization cards or petitions authorizing a labor organization to represent them for purposes of exclusive recognition; allotment of dues forms executed by an employee and the labor organization's authorized official; current dues records; an existing or recently expired agreement; current exclusive recognition or certification; employees' signed and dated petitions or cards indicating that they no longer desire to be represented for the purposes of exclusive recognition by the currently recognized or certified labor organization; employees' signed and dated petitions or cards indicating a desire that an election be held on a proposed consolidation of units; or other evidence approved by the Authority.

§ 2421.17   Regular and substantially equivalent employment.

"Regular and substantially equivalent employment" means employment that entails substantially the same amount of work, rate of pay, hours, working conditions, location of work, kind of work, and seniority rights, if any, of an employee prior to the cessation of employment in an agency because of any unfair labor practice under 5 U.S.C. 7116.

PART 2424—EXPEDITED REVIEW OF NEGOTIABILITY ISSUES

Subpart A—Instituting an Appeal

Sec.
2424.8 Additional submissions to the Authority.
2424.9 Hearing.
2424.10 Authority decision and order; compliance.

Subpart B—Criteria for Determining Compelling Need for Agency Rules and Regulations

2424.11 Illustrative criteria

AUTHORITY: 5 U.S.C. 7134.

SOURCE: 45 FR 3511, Jan. 17, 1980, unless otherwise noted.

Subpart A—Instituting an Appeal

§ 2424.1 Conditions governing review.

The Authority will consider a negotiability issue under the conditions prescribed by 5 U.S.C. 7117 (b) and (c), namely: If an agency involved in collective bargaining with an exclusive representative alleges that the duty to bargain in good faith does not extend to any matter proposed to be bargained because, as proposed, the matter is inconsistent with law, rule or regulation, the exclusive representative may appeal the allegation to the Authority when—

(a) It disagrees with the agency's allegation that the matter as proposed to be bargained is inconsistent with any Federal law or any Government-wide rule or regulation; or

(b) It alleges, with regard to any agency rule or regulation asserted by the agency as a bar to negotiations on the matter, as proposed, that:

(1) The rule or regulation violates applicable law, or rule or regulation of appropriate authority outside the agency;

(2) The rule or regulation was not issued by the agency or by any primary national subdivision of the agency, or otherwise is not applicable to bar negotiations with the exclusive representative, under 5 U.S.C. 7117(a)(3); or

(3) No compelling need exists for the rule or regulation to bar negotiations on the matter, as proposed, because the rule or regulation does not meet the criteria established in Subpart B of this part.

§ 2424.2 Who may file a petition.

A petition for review of a negotiability issue may be filed by an exclusive representative which is a party to the negotiations.

§ 2424.3 Time limits for filing.

The time limit for filing a petition for review is fifteen (15) days after the date the agency's allegation that the duty to bargain in good faith does not extend to the matter proposed to be bargained is served on the exclusive representative. The exclusive representative shall request such allegation in writing and the agency shall make the allegation in writing and serve a copy on the exclusive representative: *Provided, however,* That review of a negotiability issue may be requested by an exclusive representative under this subpart without a prior written allegation by the agency if the agency has not served such allegation upon the exclusive representative within ten (10) days after the date of the receipt by any agency bargaining representative at the negotiations of a written request for such allegation.

§ 2424.4 Content of petition; service.

(a) A petition for review shall be dated and shall contain the following:

(1) A statement setting forth the express language of the proposal sought to be negotiated as submitted to the agency;

(2) An explicit statement of the meaning attributed to the proposal by the exclusive representative;

(3) A copy of all pertinent material, including the agency's allegation in writing that the matter, as proposed, is not within the duty to bargain in good faith, and other relevant documentary material; and

(4) Notification by the petitioning labor organization whether the negotiability issue is also involved in an unfair labor practice charge filed by such labor organization under Part 2423 of this subchapter and pending before the General Counsel.

(b) A copy of the petition including all attachments thereto shall be served on the agency head and on the principal agency bargaining representative at the negotiations.

[45 FR 3511, Jan. 17, 1980, as amended at 46 FR 40674, Aug. 11, 1981]

§ 2424.5 Selection of the unfair labor practice procedure or the negotiability procedure.

Where a labor organization files an unfair labor practice charge pursuant to Part 2423 of this subchapter which involves a negotiability issue, and the labor organization also files pursuant to this part a petition for review of the same negotiability issue, the Authority and the General Counsel ordinarily will not process the unfair labor practice charge and the petition for review simultaneously. Under such circumstances, the labor organization must select under which procedure to proceed. Upon selection of one procedure, further action under the other procedure will ordinarily be suspended. Such selection must be made regardless of whether the unfair labor practice charge or the petition for review of a negotiability issue is filed first. Notification of this selection must be made in writing at the time that both procedures have been invoked, and must be served on the Authority, the appropriate Regional Director and all parties to both the unfair labor practice case and the negotiability case. Cases which solely involve an agency's allegation that the duty to bargain in good faith does not extend to the matter proposed to be bargained and which do not involve actual or contemplated changes in conditions of employment may only be filed under this part.

§ 2424.6 Position of the agency; time limits for filing; service.

(a) Within thirty (30) days after the date of the receipt by the head of an agency of a copy of a petition for review of a negotiability issue the agency shall file a statement—

(1) Withdrawing the allegation that the duty to bargain in good faith does not extend to the matter proposed to be negotiated; or

(2) Setting forth in full its position on any matters relevant to the petition which it wishes the Authority to consider in reaching its decision, including a full and detailed statement of its reasons supporting the allega-

tion. The statement shall cite the section of any law, rule or regulation relied upon as a basis for the allegation and shall contain a copy of any internal agency rule or regulation so relied upon.

(b) A copy of the agency's statement of position, including all attachments thereto shall be served on the exclusive representative.

[45 FR 3511, Jan. 17, 1980; 45 FR 8933, Feb. 11, 1980]

§ 2424.7 Response of the exclusive representative; time limits for filing; service.

(a) Within fifteen (15) days after the date of the receipt by an exclusive representative of a copy of an agency's statement of position the exclusive representative shall file a full and detailed response stating its position and reasons for:

(1) Disagreeing with the agency's allegation that the matter, as proposed to be negotiated, is inconsistent with any Federal law or Government-wide rule or regulation; or

(2) Alleging that the agency's rules or regulations violate applicable law, or rule or regulation or appropriate authority outside the agency; that the rules or regulations were not issued by the agency or by any primary national subdivision of the agency, or otherwise are not applicable to bar negotiations under 5 U.S.C. 7117(a)(3); or that no compelling need exists for the rules or regulations to bar negotiations.

(b) The response shall cite the particular section of any law, rule or regulation alleged to be violated by the agency's rules or regulations; or shall explain the grounds for contending the agency rules or regulations are not applicable to bar negotiations under 5 U.S.C. 7117(a)(3), or fail to meet the criteria established in Subpart B of this part or were not issued at the agency headquarters level or at the level of a primary national subdivision.

(c) A copy of the response of the exclusive representative including all attachments thereto shall be served on the agency head and on the agency's representative of record in the proceeding before the Authority.

[45 FR 3511, Jan. 17, 1980; 45 FR 8933, Feb. 11, 1980]

§ 2424.8   Additional submissions to the Authority.

The Authority will not consider any submission filed by any party, whether supplemental or responsive in nature, other than those authorized under §§ 2424.2 through 2424.7 unless such submission is requested by the Authority; or unless, upon written request by any party, a copy of which is served on all other parties, the Authority in its discretion grants permission to file such submission.

§ 2424.9   Hearing.

A hearing may be held, in the discretion of the Authority, before a determination is made under 5 U.S.C. 7117(b) or (c). If a hearing is held, it shall be expedited to the extent practicable and shall not include the General Counsel as a party.

§ 2424.10   Authority decision and order; compliance

(a) Subject to the requirements of this subpart the Authority shall expedite proceedings under this part to the extent practicable and shall issue to the exclusive representative and to the agency a written decision on the allegation and specific reasons therefor at the earliest practicable date.

(b) If the Authority finds that the duty to bargain extends to the matter proposed to be bargained, the decision of the Authority shall include an order that the agency shall upon request (or as otherwise agreed to by the parties) bargain concerning such matter. If the Authority finds that the duty to bargain does not extend to the matter proposed to be negotiated, the Authority shall so state and issue an order dismissing the petition for review of the negotiability issue. If the Authority finds that the duty to bargain extends to the matter proposed to be bargained only at the election of the agency, the Authority shall so state and issue an order dismissing the petition for review of the negotiability issue.

(c) When an order is issued as provided in paragraph (b) of this section, the agency or exclusive representative shall report to the appropriate Regional Director within a specified period failure to comply with an order

that the agency shall upon request (or as otherwise agreed to by the parties) bargain concerning the disputed matter. If the Authority finds such a failure to comply with its order, the Authority shall take whatever action it deems necessary, including enforcement under 5 U.S.C. 7123(b).

[45 FR 48576, July 21, 1980; 45 FR 49905, July 28, 1980; 46 FR 12191, Feb. 13, 1981]

Subpart B—Criteria for Determining Compelling Need for Agency Rules and Regulations

§ 2424.11   Illustrative criteria.

A compelling need exists for an agency rule or regulation concerning any condition of employment when the agency demonstrates that the rule or regulation meets one or more of the following illustrative criteria:

(a) The rule or regulation is essential, as distinguished from helpful or desirable, to the accomplishment of the mission or the execution of functions of the agency or primary national subdivision in a manner which is consistent with the requirements of an effective and efficient government.

(b) The rule or regulation is necessary to insure the maintenance of basic merit principles.

(c) The rule or regulation implements a mandate to the agency or primary national subdivision under law or other outside authority, which implementation is essentially nondiscretionary in nature.

PART 2425—REVIEW OF ARBITRATION AWARDS

Sec.
2425.1   Who may file an exception; time limits for filing; opposition; service.
2425.2   Content of exception.
2425.3   Grounds for review.
2425.4   Authority decision.

AUTHORITY: 5 U.S.C. 7134.

SOURCE: 45 FR 3513, Jan. 17, 1980, unless otherwise noted.

§ 2425.1   Who may file an exception; time limits for filing; opposition; service.

(a) Either party to arbitration under the provisions of chapter 71 of title 5 of the United States Code may file an exception to an arbitrator's award rendered pursuant to the arbitration.

(b) The time limit for filing an exception to an arbitration award is thirty (30) days beginning on and including the date of the award.

(c) An opposition to the exception may be filed by a party within thirty (30) days after the date of service of the exception.

(d) A copy of the exception and any opposition shall be served on the other party.

[45 FR 3513, Jan. 17, 1980, as amended at 46 FR 40675, Aug. 11, 1981]

§ 2425.2 Content of exception.

An exception must be a dated, self-contained document which sets forth in full:

(a) A statement of the grounds on which review is requested;

(b) Evidence or rulings bearing on the issues before the Authority;

(c) Arguments in support of the stated grounds, together with specific reference to the pertinent documents and citations of authorities; and

(d) A legible copy of the award of the arbitrator and legible copies of other pertinent documents.

§ 2425.3 Grounds for review.

(a) The Authority will review an arbitrator's award to which an exception has been filed to determine if the award is deficient—

(1) Because it is contrary to any law, rule or regulation; or

(2) On other grounds similar to those applied by Federal courts in private sector labor-management relations.

(b) The Authority will not consider an exception with respect to an award relating to:

(1) An action based on unacceptable performance covered under 5 U.S.C. 4303;

(2) A removal, suspension for more than fourteen (14) days, reduction in grade, reduction in pay, or furlough of thirty (30) days or less covered under 5 U.S.C. 7512; or

(3) Matters similar to those covered under 5 U.S.C. 4303 and 5 U.S.C. 7512 which arise under other personnel systems.

§ 2425.4 Authority decision.

The Authority shall issue its decision and order taking such action and making such recommendations concerning the award as it considers necessary, consistent with applicable laws, rules, or regulations.

PART 2426—NATIONAL CONSULTATION RIGHTS AND CONSULTATION RIGHTS ON GOVERNMENT-WIDE RULES OR REGULATIONS

Subpart A—National Consultation Rights

Sec.
2426.1 Requesting; granting; criteria.
2426.2 Requests; petition and procedures for determination of eligibility for national consultation rights.
2426.3 Obligation to consult.

Subpart B—Consultation Rights on Government-wide Rules or Regulations

2426.11 Requesting; granting; criteria.
2426.12 Requests; petition and procedures for determination of eligibility for consultation rights on Government-wide rules or regulations.
2426.13 Obligation to consult.

AUTHORITY: 5 U.S.C. 7134.

SOURCE: 45 FR 3513, Jan. 17, 1980, unless otherwise noted.

Subpart A—National Consultation Rights

§ 2426.1 Requesting; granting; criteria.

(a) An agency shall accord national consultation rights to a labor organization that:

(1) Requests national consultation rights at the agency level; and

(2) Holds exclusive recognition for either:

(i) Ten percent (10%) or more of the total number of civilian personnel employed by the agency and the non-appropriated fund Federal instrumentalities under its jurisdiction, excluding foreign nationals; or

(ii) 3,500 or more employees of the agency.

(b) An agency's primary national subdivision which has authority to formulate conditions of employment shall accord national consultation rights to a labor organization that:

(1) Requests national consultation rights at the primary national subdivision level; and

(2) Holds exclusive recognition for either:

(i) Ten percent (10%) or more of the total number of civilian personnel employed by the primary national subdivision and the non-appropriated fund Federal instrumentalities under its jurisdiction, excluding foreign nationals; or

(ii) 3,500 or more employees of the primary national subdivision.

(c) In determining whether a labor organization meets the requirements as prescribed in paragraphs (a)(2) and (b)(2) of this section, the following will not be counted:

(1) At the agency level, employees represented by the labor organization under national exclusive recognition granted at the agency level.

(2) At the primary national subdivision level, employees represented by the labor organization under national exclusive recognition granted at the agency level or at that primary national subdivision level.

(d) An agency or a primary national subdivision of an agency shall not grant national consultation rights to any labor organization that does not meet the criteria prescribed in paragraphs (a), (b) and (c) of this section.

§ 2426.2 Requests; petition and procedures for determination of eligibility for national consultation rights.

(a) Requests by labor organizations for national consultation rights shall be submitted in writing to the headquarters of the agency or the agency's primary national subdivision, as appropriate, which headquarters shall have fifteen (15) days from the date of service of such request to respond thereto in writing.

(b) Issues relating to a labor organization's eligibility for, or continuation of, national consultation rights shall be referred to the Authority for determination as follows:

(1) A petition for determination of the eligibility of a labor organization for national consultation rights under criteria set forth in § 2426.1 may be filed by a labor organization.

(2) A petition for determination of eligibility for national consultation rights shall be submitted on a form prescribed by the Authority and shall set forth the following information:

(i) Name and affiliation, if any, of the petitioner and its address and telephone number;

(ii) A statement that the petitioner has submitted to the agency or the primary national subdivision and to the Assistant Secretary a roster of its officers and representatives, a copy of its constitution and bylaws, and a statement of its objectives;

(iii) A declaration by the person signing the petition, under the penalties of the Criminal Code (18 U.S.C. 1001), that its contents are true and correct to the best of such person's knowledge and belief;

(iv) The signature of the petitioner's representative, including such person's title and telephone number;

(v) The name, address, and telephone number of the agency or primary national subdivision in which the petitioner seeks to obtain or retain national consultation rights, and the persons to contact and their titles, if known;

(vi) A showing that petitioner holds adequate exclusive recognition as required by § 2426.1; and

(vii) A statement as appropriate: (A) That such showing has been made to and rejected by the agency or primary national subdivision, together with a statement of the reasons for rejection, if any, offered by that agency or primary national subdivision;

(B) That the agency or primary national subdivision has served notice of its intent to terminate existing national consultation rights, together with a statement of the reasons for termination; or

(C) That the agency or primary national subdivision has failed to respond in writing to a request for national consultation rights made under § 2426.2(a) within fifteen (15) days after the date the request is served on the agency or primary national subdivision.

(3) The following regulations govern petitions filed under this section:

(i) A petition for determination of eligibility for national consultation rights shall be filed with the Regional Director for the region wherein the headquarters of the agency or the agency's primary national subdivision is located.

(ii) An original and four (4) copies of a petition shall be filed, together with a statement of any other relevant facts and of all correspondence.

(iii) Copies of the petition together with the attachments referred to in paragraph (b)(3)(ii) of this section shall be served by the petitioner on all known interested parties, and a written statement of such service shall be filed with the Regional Director.

(iv) A petition shall be filed within thirty (30) days after the service of written notice by the agency or primary national subdivision of its refusal to accord national consultation rights pursuant to a request under § 2426.2(a) or its intention to terminate existing national consultation rights. If an agency or a primary national subdivision fails to respond in writing to a request for national consultation rights made under § 2426.2(a) within fifteen (15) days after the date the request is served on the agency or primary national subdivision, a petition shall be filed within thirty (30) days after the expiration of such fifteen (15) day period.

(v) If an agency or primary national subdivision wishes to terminate national consultation rights, notice of its intention to do so shall include a statement of its reasons and shall be served not less than thirty (30) days prior to the intended termination date. A labor organization, after receiving such notice, may file a petition within the time period prescribed herein, and thereby cause to be stayed further action by the agency or primary national subdivision pending disposition of the petition. If no petition has been filed within the provided time period, an agency or primary national subdivision may terminate national consultation rights.

(vi) Within fifteen (15) days after the receipt of a copy of the petition, the agency or primary national subdivision shall file a response thereto with the Regional Director raising any matter which is relevant to the petition.

(vii) The Regional Director shall make such investigation as the Regional Director deems necessary and thereafter shall issue and serve on the parties a report and findings with respect to the eligibility for national consultation rights. A party may obtain a review of such report and findings pursuant to § 2422.6(d) of this subchapter: *Provided, however,* That a determination by the Regional Director to issue a notice of hearing shall not be subject to review by the Authority. The Regional Director, if appropriate, may cause a notice of hearing to be issued to all interested parties where substantial factual issues exist warranting a hearing. Hearings shall be conducted and decisions issued by Administrative Law Judges and exceptions and related submissions filed with the Authority in accordance with §§ 2423.14 through 2423.28 of this subchapter excluding § 2423.18, with the following exceptions:

(A) The Administrative Law Judge may not make conclusions as to remedial action to be taken or notices to be posted as provided under § 2423.26(a), and

(B) Reference to "charge, complaint" in § 2423.26(b) shall be read as "petition, notice of hearing," respectively. After considering the Administrative Law Judge's decision, the record and any exceptions and related submissions filed by the parties, the Authority shall issue its decision and order as provided under § 2423.29(a) of this subchapter.

§ 2426.3   Obligation to consult.

(a) When a labor organization has been accorded national consultation rights, the agency or the primary national subdivision which has granted those rights shall, through appropriate officials, furnish designated representatives of the labor organization:

(1) Reasonable notice of any proposed substantive change in conditions of employment; and

(2) Reasonable time to present its views and recommendations regarding the change.

(b) If a labor organization presents any views or recommendations regarding any proposed substantive change in conditions of employment to an agency or a primary national subdivision, that agency or primary national subdivision shall:

(1) Consider the views or recommendations before taking final action on any matter with respect to which the views or recommendations are presented; and

(2) Provide the labor organization a written statement of the reasons for taking the final action.

(c) Nothing in this subpart shall be construed to limit the right of any agency or exclusive representative to engage in collective bargaining.

Subpart B—Consultation Rights on Government-wide Rules or Regulations

§ 2426.11   Requesting; granting; criteria.

(a) An agency shall accord consultation rights on Government-wide rules or regulations to a labor organization that:

(1) Requests consultation rights on Government-wide rules or regulations from an agency; and

(2) Holds exclusive recognition for 3,500 or more employees.

(b) An agency shall not grant consultation rights on Government-wide rules or regulations to any labor organization that does not meet the criteria prescribed in paragraph (a) of this section.

§ 2426.12   Requests; petition and procedures for determination of eligibility for consultation rights on Government-wide rules or regulations.

(a) Requests by labor organizations for consultation rights on Government-wide rules or regulations shall be submitted in writing to the headquarters of the agency, which headquarters shall have fifteen (15) days from the date of service of such request to respond thereto in writing.

(b) Issues relating to a labor organization's eligibility for, or continuation of, consultation rights on Government-wide rules or regulations shall be referred to the Authority for determination as follows:

(1) A petition for determination of the eligibility of a labor organization for consultation rights under criteria set forth in § 2426.11 may be filed by a labor organization.

(2) A petition for determination of eligibility for consultation rights shall be submitted on a form prescribed by the Authority and shall set forth the following information:

(i) Name and affiliation, if any, of the petitioner and its address and telephone number;

(ii) A statement that the petitioner has submitted to the agency and to the Assistant Secretary a roster of its officers and representatives, a copy of its constitution and bylaws, and a statement of its objectives;

(iii) A declaration by the person signing the petition, under the penalties of the Criminal Code (18 U.S.C. 1001), that its contents are true and correct to the best of such person's knowledge and belief;

(iv) The signature of the petitioner's representative, including such person's title and telephone number;

(v) The name, address, and telephone number of the agency in which the petitioner seeks to obtain or retain consultation rights on Government-wide rules or regulations, and the persons to contact and their titles, if known;

(vi) A showing that petitioner meets the criteria as required by § 2426.11; and

(vii) A statement, as appropriate:

(A) That such showing has been made to and rejected by the agency, together with a statement of the reasons for rejection, if any, offered by that agency;

(B) That the agency has served notice of its intent to terminate existing consultation rights on Government-wide rules or regulations, together with a statement of the reasons for termination; or

(C) That the agency has failed to respond in writing to a request for consultation rights on Government-wide rules or regulations made under § 2426.12(a) within fifteen (15) days after the date the request is served on the agency.

(3) The following regulations govern petitions filed under this section:

(i) A petition for determination of eligibility for consultation rights on

Government-wide rules or regulations shall be filed with the Regional Director for the region wherein the headquarters of the agency is located.

(ii) An original and four (4) copies of a petition shall be filed, together with a statement of any other relevant facts and of all correspondence.

(iii) Copies of the petition together with the attachments referred to in paragraph (b)(3)(ii) of this section shall be served by the petitioner on the agency, and a written statement of such service shall be filed with the Regional Director.

(iv) A petition shall be filed within thirty (30) days after the service of written notice by the agency of its refusal to accord consultation rights on Government-wide rules or regulations pursuant to a request under § 2426.12(a) or its intention to terminate such existing consultation rights. If an agency fails to respond in writing to a request for consultation rights on Government-wide rules or regulations made under § 2426.12(a) within fifteen (15) days after the date the request is served on the agency, a petition shall be filed within thirty (30) days after the expiration of such fifteen (15) day period.

(v) If an agency wishes to terminate consultation rights on Government-wide rules or regulations, notice of its intention to do so shall be served not less than thirty (30) days prior to the intended termination date. A labor organization, after receiving such notice, may file a petition within the time period prescribed herein, and thereby cause to be stayed further action by the agency pending disposition of the petition. If no petition has been filed within the provided time period, an agency may terminate such consultation rights.

(vi) Within fifteen (15) days after the receipt of a copy of the petition, the agency shall file a response thereto with the Regional Director raising any matter which is relevant to the petition.

(vii) The Regional Director shall make such investigation as the Regional Director deems necessary and thereafter shall issue and serve on the parties a report and findings with respect to the eligibility for consultation rights. A party may obtain a review of such report and findings pursuant to § 2422.6(d) of this subchapter: *Provided, however,* That a determination by the Regional Director to issue a notice of hearing shall not be subject to review by the Authority. The Regional Director, if appropriate, may cause a notice of hearing to be issued where substantial factual issues exist warranting a hearing. Hearings shall be conducted and decisions issued by Administrative Law Judges and exceptions and related submissions filed with the Authority in accordance with §§ 2423.14 through 2423.28 of this subchapter, excluding § 2423.18, with the following exceptions:

(A) The Administrative Law Judge may not make conclusions as to remedial action to be taken or notices to be posted as provided under § 2423.26(a); and

(B) Reference to "charge, complaint" in § 2423.26(b) shall be read as "petition, notice of hearing," respectively. After considering the Administrative Law Judge's decision, the record and any exceptions and related submissions filed by the parties, the Authority shall issue a decision and order as provided under § 2423.29(a) of this subchapter.

§ 2426.13   Obligation to consult.

(a) When a labor organization has been accorded consultation rights on Government-wide rules or regulations, the agency which has granted those rights shall, through appropriate officials, furnish designated representatives of the labor organization:

(1) Reasonable notice of any proposed Government-wide rule or regulation issued by the agency affecting any substantive change in any condition of employment; and

(2) Reasonable time to present its views and recommendations regarding the change.

(b) If a labor organization presents any views or recommendations regarding any proposed substantive change in any condition of employment to an agency, that agency shall:

(1) Consider the views or recommendations before taking final action on any matter with respect to which the

views or recommendations are presented; and

(2) Provide the labor organization a written statement of the reasons for taking the final action.

PART 2427—GENERAL STATEMENTS OF POLICY OR GUIDANCE

Sec.
2427.1 Scope.
2427.2 Requests for general statements of policy or guidance.
2427.3 Content of request.
2427.4 Submissions from interested parties.
2427.5 Standards governing issuance of general statements of policy or guidance.

AUTHORITY: 5 U.S.C. 7134.

SOURCE: 45 FR 3516, Jan. 17, 1980, unless otherwise noted.

§ 2427.1 Scope.

This part sets forth procedures under which requests may be submitted to the Authority seeking the issuance of general statements of policy or guidance under 5 U.S.C. 7105(a)(1).

§ 2427.2 Requests for general statements of policy or guidance.

(a) The head of an agency (or designee), the national president of a labor organization (or designee), or the president of a labor organization not affiliated with a national organization (or designee) may separately or jointly ask the Authority for a general statement of policy or guidance. The head of any lawful association not qualified as a labor organization may also ask the Authority for such a statement provided the request is not in conflict with the provisions of chapter 71 of title 5 of the United States Code or other law.

(b) The Authority ordinarily will not consider a request related to any matter pending before the Authority, General Counsel, Panel or Assistant Secretary.

§ 2427.3 Content of request.

(a) A request for a general statement of policy or guidance shall be in writing and must contain:

(1) A concise statement of the question with respect to which a general statement of policy or guidance is re-quested together with background information necessary to an understanding of the question;

(2) A statement of the standards under § 2427.5 upon which the request is based;

(3) A full and detailed statement of the position or positions of the requesting party or parties;

(4) Identification of any cases or other proceedings known to bear on the question which are pending under chapter 71 of title 5 of the United States Code; and

(5) Identification of other known interested parties.

(b) A copy of each document also shall be served on all known interested parties, including the General Counsel, the Panel, the Federal Mediation and Conciliation Service, and the Assistant Secretary, where appropriate.

§ 2427.4 Submissions from interested parties.

Prior to issuance of a general statement of policy or guidance the Authority, as it deems appropriate, will afford an opportunity to interested parties to express their views orally or in writing.

§ 2427.5 Standards governing issuance of general statements of policy or guidance.

In deciding whether to issue a general statement of policy or guidance, the Authority shall consider:

(a) Whether the question presented can more appropriately be resolved by other means;

(b) Where other means are available, whether an Authority statement would prevent the proliferation of cases involving the same or similar question;

(c) Whether the resolution of the question presented would have general applicability under the Federal Service Labor-Management Relations Statute;

(d) Whether the question currently confronts parties in the context of a labor-management relationship;

(e) Whether the question is presented jointly by the parties involved; and

(f) Whether the issuance by the Authority of a general statement of policy or guidance on the question would promote constructive and cooperative labor-management relationships in the Federal service and would otherwise promote the purposes of the Federal Service Labor-Management Relations Statute.

PART 2428—ENFORCEMENT OF ASSISTANT SECRETARY STANDARDS OF CONDUCT DECISIONS AND ORDERS

Sec.
2428.1 Scope.
2428.2 Petitions for enforcement.
2428.3 Authority decision.

AUTHORITY: 5 U.S.C. 7134.

SOURCE: 45 FR 3516, Jan. 17, 1980, unless otherwise noted.

§ 2428.1 Scope.

This part sets forth procedures under which the Authority, pursuant to 5 U.S.C. 7105(a)(2)(I), will enforce decisions and orders of the Assistant Secretary in standards of conduct matters arising under 5 U.S.C. 7120.

§ 2428.2 Petitions for enforcement.

(a) The Assistant Secretary may petition the Authority to enforce any Assistant Secretary decision and order in a standards of conduct case arising under 5 U.S.C. 7120. The Assistant Secretary shall transfer to the Authority the record in the case, including a copy of the transcript if any, exhibits, briefs, and other documents filed with the Assistant Secretary. A copy of the petition for enforcement shall be served on the labor organization against which such order applies.

(b) An opposition to Authority enforcement of any such Assistant Secretary decision and order may be filed by the labor organization against which such order applies twenty (20) days from the date of service of the petition, unless the Authority, upon good cause shown by the Assistant Secretary, sets a shorter time for filing such opposition. A copy of the opposition to enforcement shall be served on the Assistant Secretary.

§ 2428.3 Authority decision.

(a) A decision and order of the Assistant Secretary shall be enforced unless it is arbitrary and capricious or based upon manifest disregard of the law.

(b) The Authority shall issue its decision on the case enforcing, enforcing as modified, refusing to enforce, or remanding the decision and order of the Assistant Secretary.

PART 2429—MISCELLANEOUS AND GENERAL REQUIREMENTS

Subpart A—Miscellaneous

Sec.
2429.1 Transfer of cases to the Authority.
2429.2 Transfer and consolidation of cases.
2429.3 Transfer of record.
2429.4 Referral of policy questions to the Authority.
2429.5 Matters not previously presented; official notice.
2429.6 Oral argument.
2429.7 Subpenas.
2429.8 Stay of arbitration award; requests.
2429.9 Amicus curiae.
2429.10 Advisory opinions.
2429.11 Interlocutory appeals.
2429.12 Service of process and papers by the Authority.
2429.13 Official time.
2429.14 Witness fees.
2429.15 Authority requests for advisory opinions.
2429.16 General remedial authority.
2429.17 Reconsideration.

Subpart B—General Requirements

2429.21 Computation of time for filing papers.
2429.22 Additional time after service by mail.
2429.23 Extension; waiver.
2429.24 Place and method of filing; acknowledgement.
2429.25 Number of copies and paper size.
2429.26 Other documents.
2429.27 Service; statement of service.
2429.28 Petitions for amendment of regulations.

AUTHORITY: 5 U.S.C. 7134.

SOURCE: 45 FR 3516, Jan. 17, 1980, unless otherwise noted.

Subpart A—Miscellaneous

§ 2429.1 Transfer of cases to the Authority.

(a) In any representation case under Part 2422 of this subchapter in which the Regional Director determines, based upon a stipulation by the parties, that no material issue of fact exists, the Regional Director may transfer the case to the Authority; and the Authority may decide the case on the basis of the formal documents alone. Briefs in the case must be filed with the Authority within thirty (30) days from the date of the Regional Director's order transferring the case to the Authority. In any unfair labor practice case under Part 2423 of this subchapter in which, after the issuance of a complaint, the Regional Director determines, based upon a stipulation by the parties, that no material issue of fact exists, the Regional Director may upon agreement of all parties transfer the case to the Authority; and the Authority may decide the case on the basis of the formal documents alone. Briefs in the case must be filed with the Authority within thirty (30) days from the date of the Regional Director's order transferring the case to the Authority. The Authority may also remand any such case to the Regional Director for further processing. Orders of transfer and remand shall be served on all parties.

(b) In any case under Parts 2422 and 2423 of this subchapter in which it appears to the Regional Director that the proceedings raise questions which should be decided by the Authority, the Regional Director may, at any time, issue an order transferring the case to the Authority for decision or other appropriate action. Such an order shall be served on the parties.

[45 FR 3516, Jan. 17, 1980; 45 FR 8933, Feb. 11, 1980, as amended at 46 FR 40675, Aug. 11, 1981]

§ 2429.2 Transfer and consolidation of cases.

In any matter arising pursuant to Parts 2422 and 2423 of this subchapter, whenever it appears necessary in order to effectuate the purposes of the Federal Service Labor-Management Relations Statute or to avoid unnecessary costs or delay, Regional Directors may consolidate cases within their own region or may transfer such cases to any other region, for the purpose of investigation or consolidation with any proceedings which

may have been instituted in, or transferred to, such region.

§ 2429.3 Transfer of record.

In any case under Part 2425 of this subchapter, upon request by the Authority, the parties jointly shall transfer the record in the case, including a copy of the transcript, if any, exhibits, briefs and other documents filed with the arbitrator, to the Authority.

§ 2429.4 Referral of policy questions to the Authority.

Notwithstanding the procedures set forth in this subchapter, the General Counsel, the Assistant Secretary, or the Panel may refer for review and decision or general ruling by the Authority any case involving a major policy issue that arises in a proceeding before any of them. Any such referral shall be in writing and a copy of such referral shall be served on all parties to the proceeding. Before decision or general ruling, the Authority shall obtain the views of the parties and other interested persons, orally or in writing, as it deems necessary and appropriate.

§ 2429.5 Matters not previously presented; official notice.

The Authority will not consider evidence offered by a party, or any issue, which was not presented in the proceedings before the Regional Director, Hearing Officer, Administrative Law Judge, or arbitrator. The Authority may, however, take official notice of such matters as would be proper.

§ 2429.6 Oral argument.

The Authority or the General Counsel, in their discretion, may request or permit oral argument in any matter arising under this subchapter under such circumstances and conditions as they deem appropriate.

§ 2429.7 Subpenas.

(a) Any member of the Authority, the General Counsel, any Administrative Law Judge appointed by the Authority under 5 U.S.C. 3105, and any Regional Director, Hearing Officer, or other employee of the Authority designated by the Authority may issue subpenas requiring the attendance and testimony of witnesses and the production of documentary or other evidence. However, no subpena shall be issued under this section which requires the disclosure of intramanagement guidance, advice, counsel, or training within an agency or between an agency and the Office of Personnel Management.

(b) Where the parties are in agreement that the appearance of witnesses or the production of documents is necessary, and such witnesses agree to appear, no such subpena need be sought.

(c) A request for a subpena by any person, as defined in 5 U.S.C. 7103(a)(1), shall be in writing and filed with the Regional Director, in proceedings arising under Parts 2422 and 2423 of this subchapter, or filed with the Authority, in proceedings arising under Parts 2424 and 2425 of this subchapter, not less than fifteen (15) days prior to the opening of a hearing, or with the appropriate presiding official(s) during the hearing.

(d) All requests shall name and identify the witnesses or documents sought, and state the reasons therefor. The Authority, General Counsel, Administrative Law Judge, Regional Director, Hearing Officer, or any other employee of the Authority designated by the Authority, as appropriate, shall grant the request upon the determination that the testimony or documents appear to be necessary to the matters under investigation and the request describes with sufficient particularity the documents sought. Service of an approved subpena is the responsibility of the party on whose behalf the subpena was issued. The subpena shall show on its face the name and address of the party on whose behalf the subpena was issued.

(e) Any person served with a subpena who does not intend to comply, shall, within five (5) days after the date of service of the subpena upon such person, petition in writing to revoke the subpena. A copy of any petition to revoke a subpena shall be served on the party on whose behalf the subpena was issued. Such petition to revoke, if made prior to the hearing, and a written statement of service, shall be filed with the Regional Direc-

tor, who may refer the petition to the Authority, General Counsel, Administrative Law Judge, Hearing Officer, or any other employee of the Authority designated by the Authority, as appropriate, for ruling. A petition to revoke a subpena filed during the hearing, and a written statement of service, shall be filed with the appropriate presiding official(s). The Regional Director, or the appropriate presiding official(s) will, as a matter of course, cause a copy of the petition to revoke to be served on the party on whose behalf the subpena was issued, but shall not be deemed to assume responsibility for such service. The Authority, General Counsel, Administrative Law Judge, Regional Director, Hearing Officer, or any other employee of the Authority designated by the Authority, as appropriate, shall revoke the subpena if the evidence the production of which is required does not relate to any matter under investigation or in question in the proceedings, or the subpena does not describe with sufficient particularity the evidence the production of which is required, or if for any other reason sufficient in law the subpena is invalid. The Authority, General Counsel, Administrative Law Judge, Regional Director, Hearing Officer, or any other employee of the Authority designated by the Authority, as appropriate, shall make a simple statement of procedural or other ground for the ruling on the petition to revoke. The petition to revoke, any answer thereto, and any ruling thereon shall not become part of the official record except upon the request of the party aggrieved by the ruling.

(f) Upon the failure of any person to comply with a subpena issued, upon the request of the party on whose behalf the subpena was issued, the General Counsel shall, on behalf of such party, institute proceedings in the appropriate district court for the enforcement thereof, unless, in the judgment of the General Counsel, the enforcement of such subpena would be inconsistent with law and the policies of the Federal Service Labor-Management Relations Statute. The General Counsel shall not be deemed thereby to have assumed responsibility for the effective prosecution of the same before the court thereafter.

§ 2429.8 Stay of arbitration award; requests.

(a) A request for a stay shall be entertained only in conjunction with and as a part of an exception to an arbitrator's award filed under Part 2425 of this subchapter. The filing of an exception shall not itself operate as a stay of the award involved in the proceedings.

(b) A timely request for a stay of an arbitrator's award to which an exception has been filed shall operate as a temporary stay of the award. Such temporary stay shall be deemed effective from the date of the award and shall remain in effect until the Authority issues its decision and order on the exception, or the Authority or its designee otherwise acts with respect to the request for the stay.

(c) A request for a stay of an arbitrator's award will be granted only where it appears, based upon the facts and circumstances presented, that:

(1) There is a strong likelihood of success on the merits of the appeal; and

(2) A careful balancing of all the equities, including the public interest, warrants issuance of a stay.

§ 2429.9 Amicus curiae.

Upon petition of an interested person, a copy of which petition shall be served on the parties, and as the Authority deems appropriate, the Authority may grant permission for the presentation of written and/or oral argument at any stage of the proceedings by an amicus curiae and the parties shall be notified of such action by the Authority.

§ 2429.10 Advisory opinions.

The Authority and the General Counsel will not issue advisory opinions.

§ 2429.11 Interlocutory appeals.

The Authority and the General Counsel ordinarily will not consider interlocutory appeals.

§ 2429.12 Service of process and papers by the Authority.

(a) *Methods of service.* Notices of hearings, reports and findings, decisions of Administrative Law Judges, complaints, written rulings on motions, decisions and orders, and all other papers required by this subchapter to be issued by the Authority, the General Counsel, Regional Directors, Hearing Officers and Administrative Law Judges, shall be served personally or by certified mail or by telegraph.

(b) *Upon whom served.* All papers required to be served under paragraph (a) of this section shall be served upon all counsel of record or other designated representative(s) of parties, and upon parties not so represented. Service upon such counsel or representative shall constitute service upon the party, but a copy also shall be transmitted to the party.

(c) *Proof of service.* Proof of service shall be the verified return by the individual serving the papers setting forth the manner of such service, the return post office receipt, or the return telegraph receipt. When service is by mail, the date of service shall be the day when the matter served is deposited in the United States mail.

§ 2429.13 Official time.

If the participation of any employee in any phase of any proceeding before the Authority, including the investigation of unfair labor practice charges and representation petitions and the participation in hearings and representation elections, is deemed necessary by the Authority, the General Counsel, any Administrative Law Judge, Regional Director, Hearing Officer, or other agent of the Authority designated by the Authority, such employee shall be granted official time for such participation, including necessary travel time, as occurs during the employee's regular work hours and when the employee would otherwise be in a work or paid leave status. In addition, necessary transportation and per diem expenses shall be paid by the employing activity or agency.

§ 2429.14 Witness fees.

(a) Witnesses (whether appearing voluntarily, or under a subpena) shall be paid the fee and mileage allowances which are paid subpenaed witnesses in the courts of the United States: *Provided*, That any witness who is employed by the Federal Government shall not be entitled to receive witness fees in addition to compensation received pursuant to § 2429.13.

(b) Witness fees and mileage allowances shall be paid by the party at whose instance the witnesses appear, except when the witness receives compensation pursuant to § 2429.13.

§ 2429.15 Authority requests for advisory opinions.

(a) Whenever the Authority, pursuant to 5 U.S.C. 7105(i) requests an advisory opinion from the Director of the Office of Personnel Management concerning the proper interpretation of rules, regulations, or policy directives issued by that Office in connection with any matter before the Authority, a copy of such request, and any response thereto, shall be served upon the parties in the matter.

(b) The parties shall have fifteen (15) days from the date of service of a copy of the response of the Office of Personnel Management to file with the Authority comments on that response which the parties wish the Authority to consider before reaching a decision in the matter. Such comments shall be in writing and copies shall be served upon the other parties in the matter and upon the Office of Personnel Management.

§ 2429.16 General remedial authority.

The Authority shall take any actions which are necessary and appropriate to administer effectively the provisions of chapter 71 of title 5 of the United States Code.

§ 2429.17 Reconsideration.

After a final decision or order of the Authority has been issued, a party to the proceeding before the Authority who can establish in its moving papers extraordinary circumstances for so doing, may move for reconsideration of such final decision or order. The motion shall be filed within ten (10) days after service of the Authority's decision or order. A motion for reconsideration shall state with particularity the extraordinary circumstances claimed and shall be supported by appropriate citations. The filing and pendency of a motion under this provision shall not operate to stay the effectiveness of the action of the Authority, unless so ordered by the Authority. A motion for reconsideration need not be filed in order to exhaust administrative remedies.

[46 FR 40675, Aug. 11, 1981]

Subpart B—General Requirements

§ 2429.21 Computation of time for filing papers.

In computing any period of time prescribed by or allowed by this subchapter, except in agreement bar situations described in § 2422.3 (c) and (d) of this subchapter, and except as to the filing of exceptions to an arbitrator's award under § 2425.1 of this subchapter, the day of the act, event, or default from or after which the designated period of time begins to run, shall not be included. The last day of the period so computed is to be included unless it is a Saturday, Sunday, or a Federal legal holiday in which event the period shall run until the end of the next day which is neither a Saturday, Sunday, or a Federal legal holiday: *Provided, however,* In agreement bar situations described in § 2422.3 (c) and (d), if the sixtieth (60th) day prior to the expiration date of an agreement falls on Saturday, Sunday, or a Federal legal holiday, a petition, to be timely, must be received by the close of business of the last official workday preceding the sixtieth (60th) day. When the period of time prescribed or allowed is seven (7) days or less, intermediate Saturdays, Sundays, and Federal legal holidays shall be excluded from the computations. When this subchapter requires the filing of any paper, such document must be received by the Authority or the officer or agent designated to receive such matter before the close of business on the last day of the time limit, if any, for such filing or extension of time that may have been granted.

§ 2429.22   Additional time after service by mail.

Whenever a party has the right or is required to do some act pursuant to this subchapter within a prescribed period after service of a notice or other paper upon such party, and the notice or paper is served on such party by mail, five (5) days shall be added to the prescribed period: *Provided, however,* That five (5) days shall not be added in any instance where an extension of time has been granted.

[46 FR 40675, Aug. 11, 1981]

§ 2429.23   Extension; waiver.

(a) Except as provided in paragraph (d) of this section, the Authority or General Counsel, or their designated representatives, as appropriate, may extend any time limit provided in this subchapter for good cause shown, and shall notify the parties of any such extension. Requests for extensions of time shall be filed in writing no later than five (5) days before the established time limit for filing, shall state the position of the other parties on the request for extension, and shall be served on the other parties.

(b) Except as provided in paragraph (d) of this section, the Authority or General Counsel, or their designated representatives, as appropriate, may waive any expired time limit in this subchapter in extraordinary circumstances. Request for a waiver of time limits shall state the position of the other parties and shall be served on the other parties.

(c) The time limits established in this subchapter may not be extended or waived in any manner other than that described in this subchapter.

(d) Time limits established in 5 U.S.C. 7117(c)(2) and 7122(b) may not be extended or waived under this section.

[45 FR 3516, Jan. 17, 1980, as amended at 46 FR 40675, Aug. 11, 1981]

§ 2429.24   Place and method of filing; acknowledgement.

(a) A document submitted to the Authority pursuant to this subchapter shall be filed with the Authority at the address set forth in the Appendix.

(b) A document submitted to the General Counsel pursuant to this subchapter shall be filed with the General Counsel at the address set forth in the Appendix.

(c) A document submitted to a Regional Director pursuant to this subchapter shall be filed with the appropriate regional office, as set forth in the Appendix.

(d) A document submitted to an Administrative Law Judge pursuant to this subchapter shall be filed with the appropriate Administrative Law Judge, as set forth in the Appendix.

(e) All documents filed pursuant to paragraphs (a), (b), (c) and (d) of this section shall be filed by certified mail or in person.

(f) All matters filed under paragraphs (a), (b), (c) and (d) of this section shall be printed, typed, or otherwise legibly duplicated: Carbon copies of typewritten matter will be accepted if they are clearly legible.

(g) Documents in any proceedings under this subchapter, including correspondence, shall show the title of the proceeding and the case number, if any.

(h) The original of each document required to be filed under this subchapter shall be signed by the party or by an attorney or representative of record for the party, or by an officer of the party, and shall contain the address and telephone number of the person signing it.

(i) A return postal receipt may serve as acknowledgement of receipt by the Authority, General Counsel, Administrative Law Judge, Regional Director, or Hearing Officer, as appropriate. The receiving officer will otherwise acknowledge receipt of documents filed only when the filing party so requests and includes an extra copy of the document or its transmittal letter which the receiving office will date stamp upon receipt and return. If return is to be made by mail, the filing party shall include a self-addressed, stamped envelope for the purpose.

§ 2429.25   Number of copies and paper size.

Unless otherwise provided by the Authority or the General Counsel, or their designated representatives, as appropriate, or under this subchapter, and with the exception of any prescribed forms, any document or paper filed with the Authority, General Counsel, Administrative Law Judge, Regional Director, or Hearing Officer, as appropriate, under this subchapter, together with any enclosure filed therewith, shall be submitted on 8½ x 11 inch size paper in an original and four (4) legible copies. A clean copy capable of being used as an original for purposes such as further reproduction may be substituted for the original.

[47 FR 55379, Dec. 9, 1982]

§ 2429.26   Other documents.

(a) The Authority or the General Counsel, or their designated representatives, as appropriate, may in their discretion grant leave to file other documents as they deem appropriate.

(b) A copy of such other documents shall be served on the other parties.

§ 2429.27   Service; statement of service.

(a) Except as provided in § 2423.10(c) and (d), any party filing a document as provided in this subchapter is responsible for serving a copy upon all counsel of record or other designated representative(s) of parties, upon parties not so represented, and upon any interested person who has been granted permission by the Authority pursuant to § 2429.9 to present written and/or oral argument as amicus curiae. Service upon such counsel or representative shall constitute service upon the party, but a copy also shall be transmitted to the party.

(b) Service of any document or paper under this subchapter, by any party, including documents and papers served by one party on another, shall be made by certified mail or in person. A return post office receipt or other written receipt executed by the party or person served shall be proof of service.

(c) A signed and dated statement of service shall be submitted at the time of filing. The statement of service shall include the names of the parties and persons served, their addresses, the date of service, the nature of the document served, and the manner in which service was made.

(d) The date of service or date served shall be the day when the matter served is deposited in the U.S. mail or is delivered in person.

§ 2429.28   Petitions for amendment of regulations.

Any interested person may petition the Authority or General Counsel in writing for amendments to any portion of these regulations. Such petition shall identify the portion of the regulations involved and provide the specific language of the proposed amendment together with a statement of grounds in support of such petition.

APPENDIX F

SUBCHAPTER D—FEDERAL SERVICE IMPASSES PANEL

PART 2470—GENERAL

Subpart A—Purpose

Sec.
2470.1 Purpose.

Subpart B—Definitions

2470.2 Definitions.

Subpart A—Purpose

§ 2470.1 Purpose.

The regulations contained in this subchapter are intended to implement the provisions of section 7119 of title 5 of the United States Code. They prescribe procedures and methods which the Federal Service Impasses Panel may utilize in the resolution of negotiation impasses when voluntary arrangements, including the services of the Federal Mediation and Conciliation Service or any other third-party mediation, fail to resolve the disputes.

(5 U.S.C. 7119, 7134)
[45 FR 3520, Jan. 17, 1980]

Subpart B—Definitions

§ 2470.2 Definitions.

(a) The terms "agency," "labor organization," and "conditions of employment" as used herein shall have the meaning set forth in 5 U.S.C. 7103(a).

(b) The term "Executive Director" means the Executive Director of the Panel.

(c) The terms "designated representative" or "designee" of the Panel means a Panel member, a staff member, or other individual designated by the Panel to act on its behalf.

(d) The term "hearing" means a factfinding hearing, arbitration hearing, or any other hearing procedure deemed necessary to accomplish the purposes of 5 U.S.C. 7119.

(e) The term "impasse" means that point in the negotiation of conditions of employment at which the parties are unable to reach agreement, notwithstanding their efforts to do so by direct negotiations and by the use of mediation or other voluntary arrangements for settlement.

(f) The term "Panel" means the Federal Service Impasses Panel described in 5 U.S.C. 7119(c) or a quorum thereof.

(g) The term "party" means the agency or the labor organization participating in the negotiation of conditions of employment.

(h) The term "quorum" means three (3) or more members of the Panel.

(i) The term "voluntary arrangements" means any method adopted by the parties for the purpose of assisting them in their resolution of a negotiation dispute which is not inconsistent with the provisions of 5 U.S.C. 7119.

(5 U.S.C. 7119, 7134)
[45 FR 3520, Jan. 17, 1980]

PART 2471—PROCEDURES OF THE PANEL

Sec.
2471.1 Request for Panel consideration; request for Panel approval of binding arbitration.
2471.2 Request form.
2471.3 Content of request.
2471.4 Where to file.
2471.5 Copies and service.
2471.6 Investigation of request; Panel recommendation and assistance; approval of binding arbitration.
2471.7 Preliminary hearing procedures.
2471.8 Conduct of hearing and prehearing conference.
2471.9 Report and recommendations.
2471.10 Duties of each party following receipt of recommendations.
2471.11 Final action by the Panel.
2471.12 Inconsistent labor agreement provisions.

AUTHORITY: 5 U.S.C. 7119, 7134.

SOURCE: 45 FR 3520, Jan. 17, 1980, unless otherwise noted.

§ 2471.1 Request for Panel consideration; request for Panel approval of binding arbitration.

If voluntary arrangements, including the services of the Federal Mediation and Conciliation Service or any other third-party mediation, fail to resolve a negotiation impasse:

(a) Either party, or the parties jointly, may request the Panel to consider the matter by filing a request as hereinafter provided; or the Panel may, pursuant to 5 U.S.C. 7119(c)(1), undertake consideration of the matter upon request of (i) the Federal Mediation and Conciliation Service, or (ii) the Executive Director; or

(b) The parties may jointly request the Panel to approve any procedure, which they have agreed to adopt, for binding arbitration of the negotiation impasse by filing a request as hereinafter provided.

§ 2471.2   Request form.

A form has been prepared for use by the parties in filing a request with the Panel for consideration of an impasse or approval of a binding arbitration procedure. Copies are available from the Office of the Executive Director, Suite 209, 1730 K Street, NW., Washington, D.C. 20006.

§ 2471.3   Content of request.

(a) A request from a party or parties to the Panel for consideration of an impasse must be in writing and include the following information:

(1) Identification of the parties and individuals authorized to act on their behalf;

(2) Statement of issues at impasse and the summary positions of the initiating party or parties with respect to those issues; and

(3) Number, length, and dates of negotiation and mediation sessions held, including the nature and extent of all other voluntary arrangements utilized.

(b) A request for approval of a binding arbitration procedure must be in writing, jointly filed by the parties, and include the following information about the pending impasse:

(1) Identification of the parties and individuals authorized to act on their behalf;

(2) Brief description of the impasse including the issues to be submitted to the arbitrator;

(3) Number, length, and dates of negotiation and mediation sessions held, including the nature and extent of all other voluntary arrangements utilized;

(4) Statement that the proposals to be submitted to the arbitrator contain no questions concerning the duty to bargain; and

(5) Statement of the arbitration procedures to be used, including the type of arbitration, the method of selecting the arbitrator, and the arrangement for paying for the proceedings or, in the alternative, those provisions of the parties' labor agreement which contain this information.

§ 2471.4   Where to file.

Requests to the Panel provided for in this part, and inquiries or correspondence on the status of impasses or other related matters, should be directed to the Executive Director, Federal Service Impasses Panel, Suite 209, 1730 K Street, NW., Washington, D.C. 20006.

§ 2471.5   Copies and service.

Any party submitting a request for Panel consideration of an impasse or request for approval of a binding arbitration procedure and any party submitting a response to such requests shall file an original and one copy with the Panel, shall serve a copy promptly on the other party to the dispute and on any mediation service which may have been utilized, and shall file a statement of such service with the Executive Director. When the Panel acts on a request from the Federal Mediation and Conciliation Service or acts on a request from the Executive Director, it will notify the parties to the dispute and any mediation service which may have been utilized.

§ 2471.6   Investigation of request; Panel recommendation and assistance; approval of binding arbitration.

(a) Upon receipt of a request for consideration of an impasse, the Panel or its designee will promptly conduct an investigation, consulting when necessary with the parties and with any mediation service utilized. After due consideration, the Panel shall either:

(1) Decline to assert jurisdiction in the event that it finds that no impasse exists or that there is other good cause for not asserting jurisdiction, in whole or in part, and so advise the parties in writing, stating its reasons; or

(2) Recommend to the parties procedures, including but not limited to arbitration, for the resolution of the impasse and/or assist them in resolving the impasse through whatever methods and procedures the Panel considers appropriate.

(b) Upon receipt of a request for approval of a binding arbitration procedure, the Panel or its designee will promptly conduct an investigation, consulting when necessary with the parties and with any mediation service utilized. After due consideration, the Panel shall either approve or disapprove the request; provided, however, that when the request is made pursuant to an agreed-upon procedure for arbitration contained in an applicable, previously negotiated agreement, the Panel may use an expedited procedure and promptly approve or disapprove the request, normally within five (5) workdays.

§ 2471.7 Preliminary hearing procedures.

When the Panel determines that a hearing is necessary under § 2471.6, it will:

(a) Appoint one or more of its designees to conduct such hearing; and

(b) Issue and serve upon each of the parties a notice of hearing and a notice of prehearing conference, if any. The notice will state (1) the names of the parties to the dispute; (2) the date, time, place, type, and purpose of the hearing; (3) the date, time, place, and purpose of the prehearing conference, if any; (4) the name of the designated representative appointed by the Panel; and (5) the issues to be resolved.

§ 2471.8 Conduct of hearing and prehearing conference.

(a) A designated representative of the Panel, when so appointed to conduct a hearing, shall have the authority on behalf of the Panel to:

(1) Administer oaths, take the testimony or deposition of any person under oath, receive other evidence, and issue subpenas;

(2) Conduct the hearing in open, or in closed session at the discretion of the designated representative for good cause shown;

(3) Rule on motions and requests for appearance of witnesses and the production of records;

(4) Designate the date on which posthearing briefs, if any, shall be submitted (An original and one (1) copy of each brief, accompanied by a statement of service, shall be submitted to the designated representative of the Panel with a copy to the other party.); and

(5) Determine all procedural matters concerning the hearing, including the length of sessions, conduct of persons in attendance, recesses, continuances, and adjournments; and take any other appropriate procedural action which, in the judgment of the designated representative, will promote the purpose and objectives of the hearing.

(b) A prehearing conference may be conducted by the designated representative of the Panel in order to:

(1) Inform the parties of the purpose of the hearing and the procedures under which it will take place;

(2) Explore the possibilities of obtaining stipulations of fact;

(3) Clarify the positions of the parties with respect to the issues to be heard; and

(4) Discuss any other relevant matters which will assist the parties in the resolution of the dispute.

(c) An official reporter shall make the only official transcript of a hearing. Copies of the official transcript may be examined and copied at the Office of the Executive Director in accordance with Part 2411 of this chapter.

§ 2471.9 Report and recommendations.

(a) When a report is issued after a hearing conducted pursuant to §§ 2471.7 and 2471.8, it normally shall be in writing and, when authorized by the Panel, shall contain recommendations.

(b) A report of the designated representative containing recommendations shall be submitted to the parties, with two (2) copies to the Executive Director, within a period normally not to exceed thirty (30) calendar days after receipt of the transcript or briefs, if any.

(c) A report of the designated representative not containing recommendations shall be submitted to the Panel with a copy to each party within a period normally not to exceed thirty (30) calendar days after receipt of the transcript or briefs, if any. The Panel shall then take whatever action it may consider appropriate or necessary to resolve the impasse.

§ 2471.10 Duties of each party following receipt of recommendations.

(a) Within thirty (30) calendar days after receipt of a report containing recommendations of the Panel or its designated representative, each party shall, after conferring with the other, either:

(1) Accept the recommendations and so notify the Executive Director; or

(2) Reach a settlement of all unresolved issues and submit a written settlement statement to the Executive Director; or

(3) Submit a written statement to the Executive Director setting forth the reasons for not accepting the recommendations and for not reaching a settlement of all unresolved issues.

(b) A reasonable extension of time may be authorized by the Executive Director for good cause shown when requested in writing by either party prior to the expiration of the time limits.

(c) All papers submitted to the Executive Director under this section shall be filed in duplicate, along with a statement of service showing that a copy has been served on the other party to the dispute.

§ 2471.11 Final action by the Panel.

(a) If the parties do not arrive at a settlement as a result of or during actions taken under §§ 2471.6(a)(2), 2471.7, 2471.8, 2471.9, and 2471.10, the Panel may take whatever action is necessary and not inconsistent with 5 U.S.C. chapter 71 to resolve the impasse, including but not limited to, methods and procedures which the Panel considers appropriate, such as directing the parties to accept a factfinder's recommendations, ordering binding arbitration conducted according to whatever procedure the Panel deems suitable, and rendering a binding decision.

(b) In preparation for taking such final action, the Panel may hold hearings, administer oaths, take the testimony or deposition of any person under oath, and issue subpenas as provided in 5 U.S.C. 7132, or it may appoint or designate one or more individuals pursuant to 5 U.S.C. 7119(c)(4) to excercise such authority on its behalf.

(c) When the exercise of authority under this section requires the holding of a hearing, the procedure contained in § 2471.8 shall apply.

(d) Notice of any final action of the Panel shall be promptly served upon the parties, and the action shall be binding on such parties during the term of the agreement, unless they agree otherwise.

(e) Within thirty (30) calendar days after receipt of such notice of final action by the Panel, each party shall send to the Executive Director of the Panel evidence of compliance with the decision.

(f) All papers submitted to the Executive Director under this section shall be filed in duplicate, along with a statement of service showing that a copy has been served on the other party to the dispute.

§ 2471.12 Inconsistent labor agreement provisions.

Any provisions of the parties' labor agreements relating to impasse resolution which are inconsistent with the provisions of either 5 U.S.C. 7119 or the procedures of the Panel shall be deemed to be superseded, unless such provisions are permitted under 5 U.S.C. 7135.

APPENDIX G

CODE OF PROFESSIONAL CONDUCT
FOR LABOR MEDIATORS

Preamble

The practice of mediation is a profession with ethical responsibilities and duties. Those who engage in the practice
of mediation must be dedicated to the principles of free and
responsible collective bargaining. They must be aware that
their duties and obligations relate to the parties who engage in collective bargaining, to every other mediator, to
the agencies which administer the practice of mediation, and
to the general public.

Recognition is given to the varying statutory duties and
responsibilities of the city, State, and Federal agencies.
This code, however, is not intended in any way to define or
adjust any of these duties and responsibilities, nor is it
intended to define when and in what situations mediators
from more than one agency should participate. It is, rather,
a personal code relating to the conduct of the individual
mediator.

This code is intended to establish principles applicable to
all professional mediators employed by city, State, or Federal agencies or to mediators privately retained by parties.

The Responsibility Of The Mediator
To The Parties

The primary responsibility for the resolution of a labor
dispute rests upon the parties themselves. The mediator at
all times should recognize that the agreements reached in
collective bargaining are voluntarily made by the parties.
It is the mediator's responsibility to assist the parties
in reaching a settlement.

It is desirable that agreement be reached by collective bargaining without mediation assistance. However, public policy and applicable statutes recognize that mediation is the
appropriate form of governmental participation in cases
where it is required. Whether and when a mediator should
intercede will normally be influenced by the desires of the

parties. Intercession by a mediator on his own motion
should be limited to exceptional cases.

The mediator must not consider himself limited to keeping
peace at the bargaining table. His role should be one of
being a resource upon which the parties may draw and, when
appropriate, he should be prepared to provide both procedural and substantive suggestions and alternatives which
will assist the parties in successful negotiations.

Since mediation is essentially a voluntary process, the
acceptability of the mediator by the parties as a person
of integrity, objectivity, and fairness is absolutely essential to the effective performance of the duties of the
mediator. The manner in which the mediator carries out his
professional duties and responsibilities will measure his
usefulness as a mediator. The quality of his character as
well as his intellectual, emotional, social, and technical
attributes will reveal themselves by the conduct of the
mediator and his oral and written communications with the
parties, other mediators, and the public.

The Responsibility Of The Mediator
Toward Other Mediators

A mediator should not enter any dispute which is being
mediated by another mediator or mediators without first
conferring with the person or persons conducting such mediation. The mediator should not intercede in a dispute
merely because another mediator may also be participating.
Conversely, it should not be assumed that the lack of mediation participation by one mediator indicates a need for
participation by another mediator.

In those situations where more than one mediator is participating in a particular case, each mediator has a responsibility to keep the other informed of developments
which are essential to a cooperative effort, and should
extend every possible courtesy to his fellow mediator.

The mediator should carefully avoid any appearance of disagreement with or criticism of his fellow mediator. Discussions as to what positions and actions mediators should
take in particular cases should be carried on solely between or among the mediators.

The Responsibility Of The Mediator
Toward His Agency And His Profession

Agencies responsible for providing mediation assistance to
parties engaged in collective bargaining are a part of Government. The mediator must recognize that, as such, he is
part of Government. The mediator should constantly bear in
mind that he and his work are not judged solely on an individual basis but that he is also judged as a representative
of his agency. Any improper conduct or professional short-
coming, therefore, reflects not only on the individual mediator, but upon his employer and, as such, jeopardizes the
effectiveness of his agency, other governmental agencies,
and the acceptability of the mediation process.

The mediator should not use his position for private gain
or advantage, nor should he engage in any employment, activity, or enterprise which will conflict with his work as
a mediator, nor should he accept any money or thing of value
for the performance of his duties--other than his regular
salary--or incur obligations to any party which might interfere with the impartial performance of his duties.

The Responsibility Of The Mediator
Toward The Public

Collective bargaining is in essence a private, voluntary
process. The primary purpose of mediation is to assist the
parties to achieve a settlement. Such assistance does not
abrogate the rights of the parties to resort to economic
and legal sanctions. However, the mediation process may include a responsibility to assert the interest of the public
that a particular dispute be settled; that a work stoppage
be ended; and that normal operations be resumed. It should
be understood, however, that the mediator does not regulate
or control any of the content of a collective bargaining
agreement.

It is conceivable that a mediator might find it necessary
to withdraw from a negotiation, if it is patently clear
that the parties intend to use his presence as implied
Government sanction for an agreement obviously contrary
to public policy.

It is recognized that labor disputes are settled at the
bargaining table; however, the mediator may release appropriate information with due regard (1) to the desires of

the parties, (2) to whether that information will assist or impede the settlement of the dispute, and (3) to the needs of an informed public.

Publicity shall not be used by a mediator to enhance his own position or that of his agency. Where two or more mediators are mediating a dispute, public information should be handled through a mutually agreeable procedure.

The Responsibility Of The Mediator
Toward The Mediation Process

Collective bargaining is an established institution in our economic way of life. The practice of mediation required the development of alternatives which the parties will voluntarily accept as a basis for settling their problems. Improper pressures which jeopardize voluntary action by the parties should not be a part of mediation.

Since the status, experience, and ability of the mediator lend weight to his suggestions and recommendations, he should evaluate carefully the effect of his suggestions and recommendations and accept full responsibility for their honesty and merit.

The mediator has a continuing responsibility to study industrial relations to improve his skills and upgrade his abilities.

Suggestions by individual mediators or agencies to parties, which give the implication that transfer of a case from one mediation "forum" to another will produce better results, are unprofessional and are to be condemned.

Confidential information acquired by the mediator should not be disclosed to others for any purpose, or in a legal proceeding or be used directly or indirectly for the personal benefit or profit of the mediator.

Bargaining positions, proposals, or suggestions given to the mediator in confidence during the course of bargaining for his sole information, should not be disclosed to another party without first securing permission from the party or person who gave it to him.

APPENDIX H

CODE OF PROFESSIONAL RESPONSIBILITY
FOR MEMBERS OF
THE SOCIETY OF PROFESSIONALS IN DISPUTE RESOLUTION

Introduction

The Society of Professionals in Dispute Resolution (SPIDR)
is an organization for individuals who are interested in
the resolution of disputes and controversies between persons and organizations, or either or both, in American and
Canadian society whose disparate interests lead to impasses
or potential impasses.

During recent years there has been an increasing need for
neutrals in many areas of societal relationships. Such
areas include, but are not limited to, labor relations,
insurance, landlord/tenant, seller/buyer, health care,
court litigation, prisons, environment, race, education.

Regular members of SPIDR have had significant experience in
dispute resolution in one or more areas. Associate membership is open to persons with less experience, or who are
interested, in the discipline of dispute resolution.

The members of SPIDR are dedicated to the voluntary resolution of disputes and controversies. This includes the resolution of disputes and controversies which have already
been submitted to legal statutory procedures.

To the extent that disputes and controversies are resolved
without the necessity of court or administrative agency
procedures, or the completion thereof, or by direct action,
the public is served.

SPIDR members should subscribe to the purposes set forth in
the SPIDR by-laws and to the principles enunciated in this
Code.

The Neutral Role

The non-judicial neutral role is divided into three parts:
arbitration, fact-finding, and mediation. While the three

procedures are well defined, the same individual may serve
in more than one role. However, except as required or authorized by statute or Government rule, a neutral should
not change from one role to another without the consent of
both or all parties.

Codes of Responsibility Applicable to Neutrals

A non-judicial neutral serving as a decision maker (arbitrator, fact-finder, panel member) may be compared to a
judge of a law court or administrative agency. Such neutral should consider himself or herself subject to the
same standards of behavior as are part-time judges under
the American Bar Association Code of Judicial Conduct.
Full-time neutrals should be familiar with the principles
of the American Bar Association Code of Judicial Ethics,
and conform to the Code as far as applicable.

Mediators assist parties at impasse, in controversy, or
holding differing opinions or positions, to resolve their
controversy.

The Code of Professional Responsibility for Arbitrators of
Labor-Management Disputes, adopted by the National Academy
of Arbitrators, the American Arbitration Association, and
the Federal Mediation and Conciliation Service, is applicable to neutrals serving as decision makers in other relationships.

Standards of Conduct for Neutrals

Both decision makers and mediators must be persons of integrity and competence. Objectivity is required for both.
A successful neutral must be able to receive and evaluate
evidence and argument and, after presentations have been
made, reach a conclusion based on the facts and (if relevant) law presented.

The roles of decision maker and mediator differ to the extent that a decision maker must render a decision based on
evidence and (if relevant) law. A mediator does not have
the responsibility to arrive at a decision, but must use
the information received and (if relevant) law to persuade
parties in controversy to resolve their differences.

Although a mediator is not barred from expressing an opinion on the merits of a controversy, he/she should exercise

caution in so doing. Generally, each party to a dispute is
persuaded of the merits of its (his/her) respective position. A mediator may lose his/her ability to persuade by
telling the parties in a dispute of his/her evaluation of
the merits of the parties' positions, unless requested to
do so. While evaluation is not a breach of ethics, per se,
it could be a breach if a mediator presents an evaluation
to the parties jointly and in so doing reveals confidential information which he/she has not been authorized to
disclose.

CONFIDENTIALITY   APPENDIX I

PART 1401 - PUBLIC INFORMATION

Subpart A - Information in Response
to Subpoenas

Authority: Sec. 202, 61 Stat. 153, as amended; 29 U.S.C.
172; Pub. L. 90-23, 81 Stat. 54-56 as amended by Pub. L.
93-502, 88 Stat. 1561-1565 (5 U.S.C. 552).

Source: 40 FR 8169, Feb. 26, 1975, unless otherwise noted.

Subpart A

§1401.1 Purpose and scope.

This subpart contains the regulations of the Service concerning procedures to be followed when a subpoena, order,
or other demand of a court or other authority is issued for
the production or disclosure of (a) any material contained
in the files of the Service; (b) any information relating

to material contained in the files of the Service; or (c) any information or material acquired by any person as a part of the performance of his official duties or because of his official status, while such person was an employee of the Service.

§1401.2 Production of records or testimony by FMCS employees.

(a) Public policy and the successful effectuation of the Federal Mediation and Conciliation Service's mission require that commissioners and employees maintain a reputation for impartiality and integrity. Labor and management or other interested parties participating in mediation efforts must have the assurance and confidence that information disclosed to commissioners and other employees of the Service will not subsequently be divulged, voluntarily or because of compulsion, unless authorized by the Director of the Service.

(b) No officer, employee, or other person officially connected in any capacity with the Service, currently or formerly shall, in response to a subpoena, subpoena duces tecum, or other judicial or administrative order, produce any material contained in the files of the Service, disclose any information acquired as part of the performance of his official duties or because of his official status, or testify on behalf of any party to any matter pending in any judicial, arbitral or administrative proceedings, without the prior approval of the Director.

§1401.3 Procedure in the event of a demand for production, disclosure, or testimony.

(a) Any request for records of the Service, whether it be by letter, by subpoena duces tecum, or by any other written demand, shall be handled pursuant to the procedures established in Subpart B of this part, and shall comply with the rules governing public disclosure.

(b) Whenever any subpoena or subpoena duces tecum calling for production of records or testimony as described above shall have been served upon any officer, employee, or other person as noted in §1401.2(b), he will, unless notified otherwise to appear in answer thereto, and unless otherwise expressly directed by the Director, respectfully decline to produce or present such records or to give such testimony,

by reason of the prohibitions of this section, and shall
state that the production of the record(s) involved will
be handled by the procedures established in this part.

Subpart B

§1401.20 Purpose and scope.

This subpart contains the regulations of the Federal Mediation and Conciliation Service providing for public access
to information from records of the Service. These regulations implement the Freedom of Information Act, 5 U.S.C.
552, as amended by Pub. L. 93-502, and the policy of the
FMCS to disseminate information on matters of interest to
the public and to disclose to members of the public on request such information contained in records in its custody
insofar as is compatible with the discharge of its responsibilities and the principle of confidentiality of dispute
resolution by third-party neutrals, consistent with applicable law.

§1401.21 Information policy.

(a) Except for matters specifically excluded by subsection
552(b) of Title 5, United States Code, or other applicable
statute, all documents and records maintained by this agency
or within the custody thereof shall be available to the public upon request filed in accordance with these regulations.
To the extent permitted by other laws, the Service also will
make available records which it is authorized to withhold
under 5 U.S.C. 552(b) whenever it determines that such disclosure is in the public interest.

(b) Any document released for inspection under the provisions of this part may be manually copied by the requesting
party. The Service shall provide facilities for copying
such documents at reasonable times during normal working
hours so long as it does not interfere with the efficient
operation of the agency.

(c) The Service will also publish and maintain a current
index, revised quarterly, providing identifying information
for the public as to statements of policy and interpretation
adopted by the agency and still in force but not published
in the Federal Register, and administrative staff manuals
and instructions to staff that affect a member of the public. The Service will also maintain on file all material

published by the Service in the Federal Register and currently in effect.

(d) Records or documents prepared by the Service for routine public distribution, e.g., pamphlets, speeches, and
educational or training materials, shall be furnished free
of charge upon request to the Office of Information, Federal Mediation and Conciliation Service, 14th Street and
Constitution Avenue, N.W., Washington, D.C. 20427, as long
as the supply lasts. The provisions of §1401.36 shall not
be applicable to such requests except when the supply of
such material is exhausted and it is necessary to reproduce
individual copies upon specific request.

(e) All existing FMCS records are subject to routine de-
struction according to standard record retention schedules.

§1401.22 Partial disclosure of records.

If a record contains both disclosable and nondisclosable
information, the nondisclosable information will be deleted
and the remaining record will be disclosed unless the two
are so inextricably intertwined that it is not feasible to
separate them or release of the disclosable information
would compromise or impinge upon the nondisclosable portion
of the record.

§1401.23 Preparation of new records.

(a) The Freedom of Information Act and the provisions of
this part apply only to existing records that are resonably
described in a request filed with the Federal Mediation and
Conciliation Service pursuant to the procedures established
in §§1401.31-1401.34.

(b) The Director may, in his discretion, prepare new records in order to respond to a request for information when
he concludes that it is in the public interest and promotes
the objectives of the Labor-Management Relations Act, 1947,
as amended.

§1401.24 Notices of dispute are disclosable.

Written notices of disputes received by the Service pursuant
to sections 8(d)(3), 8(d)(A), and 8(d)(B) of the Labor-Management Relations Act, 1947, as amended, are not exempt from
disclosure. Parties at interest have the right to receive

certified copies of any such notice of dispute upon written request to the regional director of the region in which the notice is filed.

§1401.30 Applicability of procedures.

Requests for inspection or copying of information from records in the custody of the FMCS which are reasonably identifiable and available under the provisions of this part shall be made and acted upon as provided in the following sections of this subpart. The prescribed procedure shall be followed in all cases where access is sought to official records pursuant to the provisions of the Freedom of Information Act, except with respect to records for which a less formal disclosure procedure is provided specifically in this part.

§1401.31 Filing a request for records.

(a) Any person who desires to inspect or copy any record covered by this part shall submit a written request to that effect to the appropriate office of FMCS which has custody of the record. Standard forms for making a request are not required.

(1) If the records are kept in Washington, D.C., the request shall be directed to the Director of the office, as specified in paragraph (b).

(2) If the records are kept in a field office, the request shall be directed to the office of the Regional Director of the region within which the field office maintains custody of such records, as specified in paragraph (c).

(3) If the person making the request does not know where the record is located, he may direct his request to the Director of Administration, FMCS, listed in paragraph (b), below.

(b) The Washington, D.C., offices of FMCS referred to in paragraph (a)(1) of this section, located at 14th Street and Constitution Avenue, N.W., Washington, D.C. 20427, are as follows:

(1) Office of the National Director (202) 961-3501.
(2) Office of the General Counsel (202) 961-3714
(3) Office of Mediation Services (202) 961-3505.

(4) Office of Arbitration Services (202) 961-3513.
(5) Office of Administration (202) 961-3566.
(6) Office of Technical Services (202) 961-3553.
(7) Office of Information (202) 961-3518.

(c) The Regional Directors' offices referred to in paragraph (a)(2) of this section are:

Region 1 - Room 2937, Federal Building, 26 Federal Plaza,
           New York, N.Y. 10007; (202) 264-1000.
Region 2 - Room 401, Mall Building, Fourth and Chestnut
           Streets, Philadelphia, Pa. 19106; (215) 597-7680.
Region 3 - Suite 400, 1422 West Peachtree Street, S.W.,
           Atlanta, Ga. 30309; (404) 526-2473.
Region 4 - Room 1525, Superior Building, 815 Superior Ave-
           nue, N.E., Cleveland, Ohio 44114; (216) 522-4800.
Region 5 - Room 1402, Everett McKinley Dirksen Building,
           219 S. Dearborn Street, Chicago, Illinois 60604;
           (312) 353-7350.
Region 6 - Room 3266, Federal Building, 1520 Market Street,
           St. Louis, Mo. 63103; (314) 622-4591.
Region 7 - Room 13471, New Federal Office Building, 450 Gold-
           en Gate Avenue, P.O. Box 36007, San Francisco,
           Calif. 94102; (415) 556-4670.

§1401.32 Description of information requested.

(a) Each request should reasonably describe the records
being sought, in a way that they can be identified and located. A request should include all pertinent details that
will help identify the records sought.

(b) If the description is insufficient, the officer processing the request will so notify the person making the
request and indicate the additional information needed.
Every reasonable effort shall be made to assist in the
identification and location of the records sought.

§1401.33 Logging of written requests.

(a) All requests for records should be clearly and prominently identified as a request for information under the
Freedom of Information Act, and if submitted by mail or
otherwise submitted in an envelope or other cover, should
be clearly and prominently identified as such on the envelope or other cover.

(b) Upon receipt of a request for records, the officer processing the request shall enter it in a public log. The log shall state the date and time received, the name and address of the person making the request, the nature of the records requested, the action taken on the request, and the date of the determination letter sent pursuant to §1401.34 (b) and (d), the date(s) any records are subsequently furnished, the number of staff hours and grade levels of persons who spent time responding to the request, and the payment requested and received.

§1401.34 Time for processing requests.

(a) All time limitations established pursuant to this section shall begin as of the time at which a request for records is logged in by the officer processing the request pursuant to §1401.33(b). An oral request for records shall not begin any time requirement. A written request for records sent to an office of FMCS other than the one having authority to grant or deny access to the records shall be redirected immediately to the appropriate officer for processing, and the time shall begin upon its being logged in there in accordance with §1401.33(b).

(b) The officer passing upon the request for records shall, within ten (10) working days following receipt of the request, respond in writing to the requester, determining whether, or the extent to which, the agency shall comply with the request.

(1) If all of the records requested have been located and a final determination has been made with respect to disclosure of all of the records requested, the response shall so state.

(2) If all of the records have not been located or a final determination has not been made with respect to disclosure of all the records requested, the response shall state the extent to which the records involved shall be disclosed pursuant to the rules established in this part.

(3) If the request is expected to involve an assessed fee in excess of $50.00, the response shall specify or estimate the fee involved and shall require prepayment before the records are made available.

(4) Whenever possible, the response relating to a request for records that involves a fee of less than $50.00, shall be accompanied by the requested records. Where this is not possible, the records shall be forwarded as soon as possible thereafter, consistent with other obligations of the agency.

(c) In the following circumstances, the time for passing upon the request may be extended for up to an additional 10 working days by written notice to the person making the request, setting forth the reasons for such extension and the time within which a determination is expected to be made:

(1) The need to search for and collect the requested records from field facilities or other establishments that are separate from the office processing the request;

(2) The need to search for, collect and appropriately examine a voluminous amount of separate and distinct records which are demanded in a single request; or

(3) The need for consultation, which shall be conducted with all practicable speed, with another agency having a substantial interest in the determination of the request or among two or more components of the agency having substantial subject matter interest therein.

(d) If any request for records is denied in whole or in part, the response required by paragraph (b) of this section shall notify the requester of the denial. Such denial shall specify the reason therefor and also advise that the denial may be appealed to the Office of Deputy National Director of the agency as specified in 1401.35.

§1401.35 Appeals from denials of request.

(a) Whenever any request for records is denied, a written appeal may be filed with the Deputy National Director, FMCS, Washington, D.C. 20427, within 30 days after requester receives notification that the request has been denied or after the requester receives any records being made available, in the event of partial denial. The appeal shall state the grounds for appeal, including any supporting statements or arguments.

(b) Final action on the appeal shall be taken within 20 working days from the time of receipt of the appeal. Where novel and complicated questions have been raised or unusual difficulties have been encountered, the Deputy National Director may extend the time for final action up to an additional 10 days, depending upon whether there had been an extension pursuant to §1401.34(c) at the initial stage. In such cases, the applicant shall be notified in writing of the reasons for the extension of time and the approximate date on which a final response will be forthcoming.

(c) If on appeal the denial of the request for records is upheld in whole or in part, the Deputy National Director shall notify the applicant of the reasons therefor, and shall advise the requester of the provisions for judicial review under 5 U.S.C. 552(a)(4) and (6).

§1401.36 Fees--duplication cost and search.

(a) Unless waived in accordance with paragraph (d) of this section, the following schedule of fees shall be imposed for the production and copying of any record pursuant to this part:

(1) Copy of records. Twenty ($0.20) cents per copy per page.
(2) Clerical searches. $1.25 for each one-quarter hour or fraction thereof spent in excess of the first quarter hour in searching for or producing a requested record, including time spent copying any record.
(3) Nonclerical searches. $3.50 for each one-quarter hour spent by professional or managerial personnel searching for or producing a requested record, including time spent copying any record.
(4) Certification or authentication of records. $2.00 per certification or authentication.
(5) Forwarding material to destination. Postage, insurance, and special fees will be charged on an actual cost basis.

(b) Rules of construction: In providing the foregoing fee schedule pursuant to the provisions of 5 U.S.C. 552(a)(3), it is the intent of this section to apply 29 U.S.C. 9(b) and the user charge statute (31 U.S.C. 483(a)) to cover those situations where the agency is performing for a requester services which are not required under the Freedom of Information Act.

(c) No fee shall be charged if a record requested is not found or for any record that is exempt from disclosure.

(d) The officer processing the request for records may, in his discretion, waive or reduce fees otherwise applicable under paragraph (a) of this section for services in producing and copying record information under the following circumstances:

(1) Where inability to pay is demonstrated and it is clear that a significant public interest would be served by providing the service free of charge.

(2) Where it is in the public interest because furnishing the information can be considered primarily as benefiting the general public.

(3) In making a determination of the broad public interest involved, the officer shall weigh the agency resources involved against the likely benefit to the public.

(e) Payment of fees: Payment shall be made by check or money order payable to "Federal Mediation and Conciliation Service," and shall be sent to the Director of the Office of Administration, FMCS, 14th and Constitution Avenue, N.W., Washington, D.C. 20427.

§1401.37 Annual report.

(a) The Office of National Director shall annually, within 60 days following the close of each calendar year, prepare a report covering each of the categories of records to be maintained in accordance with 5 U.S.C. 552(d) for such calendar year and shall forthwith submit the same to the Speaker of the House of Representatives and the President of the Senate for referral to the appropriate committees of the Congress.

APPENDIX J

FMCS FORM F-7
REVISED 8/84

NOTICE TO MEDIATION AGENCIES

FORM APPROVED
OMB NO. 3-078-0061

MAIL TO:

NOTICE PROCESSING UNIT
FEDERAL MEDIATION AND CONCILIATION SERVICE
2100 K STREET, N.W.
WASHINGTON, D.C. 20427

AND

THE STATE OR TERRITORIAL MEDIATION AGENCY

You are hereby notified that written notice of proposed termination or modification of the existing collective bargaining contract was served upon the other party to this contract and that no agreement has been reached.

IF THIS IS A HEALTH CARE INDUSTRY NOTICE PLEASE INDICATE (MARK "X")

① ☐ INITIAL CONTRACT ☐ EXISTING CONTRACT

(MARK ONE "X") AND GIVE APPROPRIATE: MO. DAY YR.

☐ CONTRACT EXPIRATION DATE ___/___/___

② ☐ CONTRACT REOPENER DATE ___/___/___

③ NAME OF EMPLOYER OR EMPLOYER ASSOCIATION/ORGANIZATION (IF MORE THAN ONE, SUBMIT NAMES AND ADDRESSES ON AN ATTACHED LIST)

④ ADDRESS OF EMPLOYER/ASSOCIATION
NO. STREET CITY STATE ZIP

⑤ EMPLOYER OFFICIAL TO CONTACT

⑥ (AREA CODE) PHONE NUMBER

⑦ NAME OF INTERNATIONAL UNION OR PARENT BODY

⑧ NAME AND NO. OF LOCAL (IF NOT A LOCAL, GIVE NAME AND NUMBER, IF ANY, OF THE UNION ORGANIZATION INVOLVED IN THE NEGOTIATIONS)

⑨ ADDRESS OF LOCAL UNION
NO. STREET CITY STATE ZIP

⑩ UNION OFFICIAL TO CONTACT

⑪ (AREA CODE) PHONE NUMBER

a. LOCATION OF AFFECTED ESTABLISHMENT CITY STATE

b. LOCATION OF NEGOTIATIONS (COMPLETE ONLY IF DIFFERENT FROM 12a) CITY STATE

⑬ TOTAL NUMBER EMPLOYED AT AFFECTED LOCATION(S)

⑭ NUMBER OF EMPLOYEES COVERED BY CONTRACT

⑮ INDUSTRY AND TYPE OF ESTABLISHMENT (E.G., STEEL INDUSTRY — FACTORY; FOOD INDUSTRY — RETAIL CHAIN STORE; EDUCATION — PRIVATE COLLEGE; ELECTRICAL INDUSTRY — PUBLIC UTILITY)

⑯ PRINCIPAL PRODUCT OR SERVICE

⑰ THIS NOTICE IS FILED ON BEHALF OF (MARK "X")
☐ UNION ☐ EMPLOYER

⑱ TYPE OF NEGOTIATIONS (MARK "X")

☐ SINGLE ESTABLISHMENT
☐ MULTI-PLANT
☐ AREA OR INDUSTRY WIDE
☐ OTHER (SPECIFY)

⑲ TYPE OF EMPLOYEES COVERED BY CONTRACT (MARK "X" ALL THAT APPLY)

☐ PROFESSIONAL/TECHNICAL
☐ PRODUCTION/MAINTENANCE
☐ CLERICAL
☐ OTHER (SPECIFY)

⑳ NAME AND TITLE OF OFFICIAL FILING NOTICE

㉑ SIGNATURE DATE

Receipt of this form does not constitute a request for mediation nor does it commit FMCS to offer its facilities. Receipt of this notice will not be acknowledged in writing by FMCS. FMCS does not forward copies of this notice to state or territorial mediation agencies. While the use of this form is voluntary, it will facilitate our service to respondents.

NO. 1 ORIGINAL — TO F.M.C.S.

APPENDIX K

Original Issuance
January 1982

CHAPTER 2100   -   GENERAL MEDIATION INFORMATION   2103:2

DIRECTIVE 2103 - MEDIATION OF LABOR-MANAGEMENT GRIEVANCE
                 DISPUTES

1. Introduction. This directive states the policy of the
    Service in connection with its mediation of grievance
    disputes.

2. Statutory Provisions. The Labor-Management Relations
    Act, 1947, imposes certain restrictions upon the Serv-
    ice with respect to the extent to which it may make its
    services available in labor-management grievance dis-
    putes. The Act provides as follows:

        "Section 203(d), Final Adjustment by Method
        Agreed Upon by the Parties, is hereby de-
        clared to be the desirable method for set-
        tlement of grievance disputes arising over
        the application or interpretation of an ex-
        isting collective bargaining agreement. The
        Service is directed to make its conciliation
        and mediation services available in the set-
        tlement of such grievance disputes only as a
        last resort and in exceptional cases."

3. FMCS Policy. The Service may offer its services in any
    labor-management grievance dispute of special importance
    because of the essential nature and impact on Government
    contracts or operations, defense production, interstate
    commerce, or to the economy as a whole, to related and
    involved industries, or to the general health, safety,
    and welfare of the community or the public, either lo-
    cally or nationally. The preceding is with a clear
    understanding that no other adequate facility or proce-
    dure is available which can prevent a disruption to pro-
    duction and assist in maintaining sound labor-management
    relations.

4. Definitions. The Service interprets the terms excep-
    tional, last resort, and grievance disputes as follows:

a. <u>Exceptional</u>. Of special importance because of
the essential nature of the products of the involved employing establishment to Government
contracts or operations, to defense production,
to interstate commerce, to the economy as a
whole, to related and involved industries, or
to the general health, safety, and welfare of
a community or the public, either locally or
nationally.

b. <u>Last Resort</u>. No other adequate facility or procedure is available which can prevent a disruption to production, and assist in maintaining
sound labor-management relations.

c. <u>Labor-Management Grievance Disputes</u>. Labor-management disputes arising over the application or interpretation of an existing collective bargaining
agreement. Labor-management disputes which do not
directly involve the application or interpretation
of an existing collective bargaining agreement are
not grievances within the meaning of the Act, even
though they may be designated as grievances by one
or both of the disputing parties.

5. <u>Internal Procedures</u>. On assignments for labor-management grievance dispute cases, the mediator should urge
the parties to utilize the grievance or arbitration
procedures in their collective bargaining contract, if
the contract contains such provisions. If the contract
lacks adequate procedures, the mediator should urge them
to agree upon a procedure for settling the immediate issue in dispute. If successful, the mediator should
close the case with a Final Report (FMCS Form F-3), indicating the method of settlement. However, if limited
mediation fails, the mediator shall send to his or her
Assistant Regional Director a complete written report
which will serve as a basis for classifying a dispute
as "exceptional and last resort," as well as for planning future action. After reviewing the report, the
Assistant Regional Director must decide whether to withdraw the mediator and close the case, or to amend the
assignment to authorize participation without limitation.

6. <u>Effect of Contract Provisions and Joint Agreements</u>. The
Service cannot be bound by contract provisions or joint
agreements requiring the Service to mediate labor-management grievance disputes or to perform any other act or

service except as authorized by existing law, official
regulations, and policies. It does not matter that the
parties may have agreed upon mediation by the Service
as a method for settlement of grievances. The Service
shall make its conciliation and mediation services available in the settlement of such disputes on the same basis as if the agreement did not provide for the Service
to intervene in the grievance procedure. If such a provision is proposed for inclusion in a collective bargaining agreement, the mediator must tactfully inform the
parties of the policy of the Service as outlined in
these operating procedures; and that the Service must
reserve the right to determine, in accordance with its
general policies, whether it will intervene in each
labor-management grievance dispute.

Original Issuance
January 1982

HEALTH CARE ACT

Public Law 93-360, 93rd Congress
S. 3203 - July 26, 1974

To amend the National Labor Relations Act to extend its coverage and protection to employees of nonprofit hospitals, and for other purposes.

Be it enacted by the Senate and House of Representatives of the United States of America in Congress assembled, That (a) section 2(2) of the National Labor Relations Act is amended by striking out "or any corporation or association operating a hospital, if no part of the net earnings inures to the benefit of any private shareholder or individual,".

(b) Section 2 of such Act is amended by adding at the end thereof the following new subsection:

"(14) The term 'health care institution' shall include any hospital, convalescent hospital, health maintenance organization, health clinic, nursing home, extended care facility, or other institution devoted to the care of sick, infirm, or aged person.".

(c) The last sentence of section 8(d) of such Act is amended by striking out the words "the sixty-day" and inserting in lieu thereof "any notice" and by inserting before the words "shall lose" a comma and the following: "or who engages in any strike within the appropriate period specified in subsection (g) of · this section,".

(d)(1) The last paragraph of section 8(d) of such Act is amended by adding at the end thereof the following new sentence:

"Whenever the collective bargaining involves employees of a health care institution, the provisions of this section 8(d) shall be modified as follows:

"(A) The notice of section 8(d)(1) shall be ninety days; the notice of section 8(d)(3) shall be sixty days; and the contract period of section 8(d)(4) shall be ninety days.

"(B) Where the bargaining is for an initial agreement following certification or recognition, at least thirty days' notice of the existence of a dispute shall be given by the labor organization to the agencies set forth in section 8(d)(3).

"(C) After notice is given to the Federal Mediation and Conciliation Service under either clause (A) or (B) of this sentence, the Service shall promptly communicate with the parties and use its best efforts, by mediation and conciliation, to bring them to agreement. The parties shall participate fully and promptly in such meetings as may be undertaken by the Service for the purpose of aiding in a settlement of the dispute."

(e) Section 8 of such Act is amended by adding at the end thereof the following new subsection.

"(g) A labor organization before engaging in any strike, picketing, or other concerted refusal to work at any health care institution shall, not less than ten days prior to such action, notify the institution in writing and the Federal Mediation and Conciliation Service of that intention, except that in the case of bargaining for an initial agreement following certification or recognition the notice required by this subsection shall not be given until the expiration of the period specified in clause (B) of the last sentence of section 8(d) of this Act. The notice shall state the date and time that such action will commence.

The notice, once given, may be extended by the written agreement of both parties."

Sec. 2. Title II of the Labor Management Relations Act, 1947, is amended by adding at the end thereof the following new section:

"Conciliation of Labor Disputes in the Health Care Industry

"Sec. 213. (a) If, in the opinion of the Director of the Federal Mediation and Conciliation Service a threatened or actual strike or lockout affecting a health care institution will, if permitted to occur or to continue, substantially interrupt the delivery of health care in the locality concerned, the Director may further assist in the resolution of the impasse by establishing within 30 days after the notice to the Federal Mediation and Conciliation Service under clause (A) of the last sentence of section 8(d) (which is required by clause (3) of such section 8(d)), or within 10 days after the notice under clause (B), an impartial Board of Inquiry to investigate the issues involved in the dispute and to make a written report thereon to the parties within fifteen (15) days after the establishment of such a Board. The written report shall contain the findings of fact together with the Board's recommendations for settling the dispute, with the objective of achieving a prompt, peaceful and just settlement of the dispute. Each such Board shall be composed of such number of individuals as the Director may deem desirable. No member appointed under this section shall have any interest or involvement in the health care institutions or the employee organizations involved in the dispute.

"(b)(1) Members of any board established under this section who are otherwise employed by the Federal Government shall serve without compensation but shall be reimbursed for travel, subsistence, and other necessary expenses incurred by them in carrying out its duties under this section.

"(2) Members of any board established under this section who are not subject to paragraph (1) shall receive compensation at a rate prescribed by the Director but not to exceed the daily rate prescribed for GS-18 of the General Schedule under section 5332 of title 5, United States Code, including travel for each day they are engaged in the performance of their duties under this section and shall be entitled to reimbursement for travel, subsistence, and other necessary expenses incurred by them in carrying out their duties under this section.

"(c) After the establishment of a board under subsection (a) of this section and for 15 days after any such board has issued its report, no change in the status quo in effect prior to the expiration of the contract in the case of negotiations for a contract renewal, or in effect prior to the time of the impasse in the case of an initial bargaining negotiation, except by agreement, shall be made by the parties to the controversy.

"(d) There are authorized to be appropriated such sums as may be necessary to carry out the provisions of this section."

Sec. 3. The National Labor Relations Act is amended by adding immediately after section 18 thereof the following new section:

"Individuals With Religious Convictions

"Sec. 19. Any employee of a health care institution who is a member of and adheres to established and traditional tenets or teachings of a bona fide religion, body, or sect which has historically held conscientious objections to joining or financially supporting labor organizations shall not be required to join or financially support any labor organization as a condition of employment; except that such employee may be required, in lieu of periodic dues and initiation fees, to pay sums equal to such dues and initiation fees to a nonreligious charitable fund exempt from taxation under section 501(c)(3) of the Internal Revenue Code, chosen by such employee from a list of at least three such funds, designated in a contract between such institution and a labor organization, or if the contract fails to designate such funds, then to any such fund chosen by the employee."

Sec. 4. The amendments made by this Act shall become effective on the thirtieth day after its date of enactment.

Approved July 26, 1974.

LABOR-MANAGEMENT COOPERATION ACT OF 1978

Assistance to Plant, Area, and Industrywide Labor Management Committees

Sec. 6 (a) This section may be cited as the "Labor Management Cooperation Act of 1978."

(b) It is the purpose of this section—

(1) to improve communication between representatives of labor and management;

(2) to provide workers and employers with opportunities to study and explore new and innovative joint approaches to achieving organizational effectiveness;

(3) to assist workers and employers in solving problems of mutual concern not susceptible to resolution within the collective bargaining process;

(4) to study and explore ways of eliminating potential problems which reduce the competitiveness and inhibit the economic development of the plant, area or industry;

(5) to enhance the involvement of workers in making decisions that affect their working lives;

(6) to expand and improve working relationships between workers and managers; and

(7) to encourage free collective bargaining by establishing continuing mechanisms for communication between employers and their employees through Federal assistance to the formation and operation of labor management committees.

(c) (1) Section 203 of the Labor-Management Relations Act, 1947, is amended by adding at the end thereof the following new subsection:

"(e) The Service is authorized and directed to encourage and support the establishment and operation of joint labor management activities conducted by plant, area, and industrywide committees designed to improve labor management relationships, job security and organizational effectiveness, in accordance with the provisions of section 205A.".

(2) Title II of the Labor-Management Relations Act, 1947, is amended by adding after section 205 the following new section:

"Sec. 205A. (a) (1) The Service is authorized and directed to provide assistance in the establishment and operation of plant, area and industrywide labor management committees which—

"(A) have been organized jointly by employers and labor organizations representing employees in that plant, area, or industry; and

"(B) are established for the purpose of improving labor management relationships, job security, organizational effectiveness, enhancing economic development or involving workers in decisions affecting their jobs including improving communication with respect to subjects of mutual interest and concern.

"(2) The Service is authorized and directed to enter into contracts and to make grants, where necessary or appropriate, to fulfill its responsibilities under this section.

"(b) (1) No grant may be made, no contract may be entered into and no other assistance may be provided under the provisions of this section to a plant labor management committee unless the employees in that plant are represented by a labor organization and there is in effect at that plant a collective bargaining agreement.

"(2) No grant may be made, no contract may be entered into and no other assistance may be provided under the provisions of this section to an area or industrywide labor management committee unless its participants include any labor organizations certified or recognized as the representative of the employees of an employer participating in such committee. Nothing in this clause shall prohibit participation in an area or industrywide committee by an employer whose employees are not represented by a labor organization.

"(3) No grant may be made under the provisions of this section to any labor management committee which the Service finds to have as one of its purposes the discouragement of the exercise of rights contained in section 7 of the National Labor Relations Act (29 U.S.C. 157), or the interference with collective bargaining in any plant, or industry.

"(c) The Service shall carry out the provisions of this section through an office established for that purpose.

"(d) There are authorized to be appropriated to carry out the provisions of this section $10,000,000 for the fiscal year 1979, and such sums as may be necessary thereafter.".

(d) Section 302(c) of the Labor Management Relations Act, 1947, is amended by striking the word "or" after the semicolon at the end of subparagraph (7) thereof and by inserting the following before the period at the end thereof:"; or (9) with respect to money or other things of value paid by an employer to a plant, area or industrywide labor management committee established for one or more of the purposes set forth in section 5(b) of the Labor Management Cooperation Act of 1978".

(e) Nothing in this section or the amendments made by this section shall affect the terms and conditions of any collective bargaining agreement whether in effect prior to or entered into after the date of enactment of this section.

- - -

The Labor-Management Cooperation Act of 1978 was passed by the Congress as Section 6 of the Comprehensive Employment and Training Act of 1978 (CETA). The Labor-Management Cooperation Act provides grant-making authority to the Federal Mediation and Conciliation Service.

<u>APPENDIX N</u>

<u>THE POSTAL REORGANIZATION ACT OF 1970</u>

Chapter 12 - <u>Employee-Management Agreements</u>

Sec.
1201 - Definition
1202 - Bargaining units
1203 - Recognition of labor organizations
1204 - Elections
1205 - Deductions of dues
1206 - Collective bargaining agreements
1207 - Labor disputes
1208 - Suits
1209 - Applicability of Federal labor laws.

§1201 - <u>Definition</u>

As used in this chapter, "guards" means--

    (1) maintenance guards who, on the effective date of
this chapter, are in key position KP-5 under the provisions
of former section 3514 of title 39; and

    (2) security guards, who may be employed in the Postal
Service, and whose primary duties shall include the exercise
of authority to enforce rules to protect the safety of property, mail, or persons on the premises.

§1202 - <u>Bargaining Units</u>

The National Labor Relations Board shall decide in each case
the unit appropriate for collective bargaining in the Postal
Service. The National Labor Relations Board shall not include in any bargaining unit--

    (1) any management official or supervisor;

    (2) any employee engaged in personnel work in other
than a purely nonconfidential clerical capacity;

    (3) both professional employees and employees who are

not professional employees unless a majority of such professional employees vote for inclusion in such unit; or

(4) together with other employees, any individual employed as a security guard to enforce against employees
and other persons, rules to protect property of the Postal
Service or to protect the safety of property, mail, or persons on the premises of the Postal Service; but no labor
organization shall be certified as the representative of
employees in a bargaining unit of security guards if such
organization admits to membership, or is affiliated directly or indirectly with an organization which admits to
membership, employees other than guards.

§1203 - Recognition of labor organizations

(a) The Postal Service shall accord exclusive recognition to a labor organization when the organization has
been selected by a majority of the employees in an appropriate unit as their representative.

(b) Agreements and supplements in effect on the date
of enactment of this section covering employees in the former Post Office Department shall continue to be recognized
by the Postal Service until altered or amended pursuant to
law.

(c) When a petition has been filed, in accordance with
such regulations as may be prescribed by the National Labor
Relations Board--

(1) by an employee, a group of employees, or any
    labor organization acting in their behalf,
    alleging that (A) a substantial number of
    employees wish to be represented for col-
    lective bargaining by a labor organization
    and that the Postal Service declines to
    recognize such labor organization as the
    representative; or (B) the labor organiza-
    tion which has been certified or is being
    currently recognized by the Postal Service
    as the bargaining representative is no longer
    a representative; or

(2) by the Postal Service, alleging that one or
    more labor organizations has presented to
    it a claim to be recognized as the represen-
    tative;

the National Labor Relations Board shall investigate such petition and, if it has reasonable cause to believe that a question of representation exists, shall provide for an appropriate hearing upon due notice. Such hearing may be conducted by an officer or employee of the National Labor Relations Board, who shall not make any recommendations with respect thereto. If the National Labor Relations Board finds upon the record of such hearing that such a question of representation exists, it shall direct an election by secret ballot and shall certify the results thereof.

(d) A petition filed under subsection (c)(1) of this section shall be accompanied by a statement signed by at least 30 percent of the employees in the appropriate unit stating that they desire that an election be conducted for either of the purposes set forth in such subsection.

(e) Nothing in this section shall be construed to prohibit the waiving of hearings by stipulation for the purpose of a consent election in conformity with regulations and rules of decision of the National Labor Relations Board.

§1204 - Elections

(a) All elections authorized under this chapter shall be conducted under the supervision of the National Labor Relations Board, or persons designated by it, and shall be by secret ballot. Each employee eligible to vote shall be provided the opportunity to choose the labor organization he wishes to represent him, from among those on the ballot, or "no union."

(b) In any election where none of the choices on the ballot receives a majority, a runoff shall be conducted, the ballot providing for a selection between the 2 choices receiving the largest and second largest number of valid votes cast in the election. In the event of a tie vote, additional runoff elections shall be conducted until one of the choices has received a majority of the votes.

(c) No election shall be held in any bargaining unit within which, in the preceding 12-month period, a valid election has been held.

§1205 - Deductions of dues

(a) When a labor organization holds exclusive recognition, or when an organization of personnel not subject to

collective bargaining agreements has consultation rights
under section 1004 of this title, the Postal Service shall
deduct the regular and periodic dues of the organization
from the pay of all members of the organization in the unit
of recognition if the Post Office Department or the Postal
Service has received from each employee, on whose account
such deductions are made, a written assignment which shall
be irrevocable for a period of not more than one year.

(b) Any agreement in effect immediatly prior to the
date of enactment of the Postal Reorganization Act between
the Post Office Department and any organization of postal
employees which provides for deduction by the Department of
the regular and periodic dues of the organization from the
pay of its members, shall continue in full force and effect
and the obligation for such deductions shall be assumed by
the Postal Service. No such deduction shall be made from
the pay of any employee except on his written assignment,
which shall be irrevocable for a period of not more than
one year.

§1206 - Collective bargaining agreements

(a) Collective bargaining agreements between the Postal
Service and bargaining representatives recognized under section 1203 of this title shall be effective for not less than
2 years.

(b) Collective bargaining agreements between the Postal
Service and bargaining representatives recognized under section 1203 may include any procedures for resolution by the
parties of grievances and adverse actions arising under the
agreement, including procedures culminating in binding third-
party arbitration, or the parties may adopt any such procedures by mutual agreement in the event of a dispute.

(c) The Postal Service and bargaining representatives
recognized under section 1203 may by mutual agreement adopt
procedures for the resolution of disputes or impasses arising in the negotiation of a collective bargaining agreement.

§1207 - Labor disputes

(a) If there is a collective bargaining agreement in
effect, no party to such agreement shall terminate or modify
such agreement unless the party desiring such termination or
modification serves written notice upon the other party to

the agreement of the proposed termination or modification
not less than 90 days prior to the expiration date thereof,
or not less than 90 days prior to the time it is proposed
to make such termination or modification. The party serving such notice shall notify the Federal Mediation and Conciliation Service of the existence of a dispute within 45
days of such notice, if no agreement has been reached by
that time.

(b) If the parties fail to reach agreement or to adopt
a procedure providing for a binding resolution of a dispute
by the expiration date of the agreement in effect, or the
date of the proposed termination or modification, the Director of the Federal Mediation and Conciliation Service shall
direct the establishment of a factfinding panel consisting
of 3 persons. For this purpose, he shall submit to the parties a list of not less than 15 names, from which list each
party, within 10 days, shall select 1 person. The 2 so selected shall then choose from the list a third person who
shall serve as chairman of the factfinding panel. If either
of the parties fails to select a person or if the 2 members
are unable to agree on the third person within 3 days, the
selection shall be made by the Director. The factfinding
panel shall issue after due investigation a report of its
findings, with or without recommendations, to the parties
no later than 45 days from the date the list of names is
submitted.

(c) (1) If no agreement is reached within 90 days after
the expiration of termination of the agreement or the date
on which the agreement became subject to modification under
subsection (a) of this section, or if the parties decide
upon arbitration but do not agree upon the procedures therefor, an arbitration board shall be established consisting
of 3 members, not members of the factfinding panel, 1 of whom
shall be selected by the Postal Service, 1 by the bargaining
representatives of the employees, and the third by the 2 thus
selected. If either of the parties fails to select a member,
or if the members chosen by the parties fail to agree on the
third person within 5 days after their first meeting, the
selection shall be made by the Director. If the parties do
not agree on the framing of the issues to be submitted, the
factfinding panel shall frame the issues and submit them to
the arbitration board.

(2) The arbitration board shall give the parties a full
and fair hearing including an opportunity to present evidence
in support of their claims, and an opportunity to present

their case in person, by counsel or by other representative
as they may elect. Decisions of the arbitration board shall
be conclusive and binding upon the parties. The arbitration
board shall render its decision within 45 days after its
appointment.

(3) Costs of the arbitration board and factfinding
panel shall be shared equally by the Postal Service and
the bargaining representative.

(d) In the case of a bargaining unit whose recognized
collective bargaining representative does not have an agreement with the Postal Service, if the parties fail to reach
agreement within 90 days of the commencement of collective
bargaining, a factfinding panel will be established in accordance with the terms of subsection (b) of this section,
unless the parties have previously agreed to another procedure for a binding resolution of their differences. If the
parties fail to reach agreement within 180 days of the commencement of collective bargaining, and if they have not
agreed to another procedure for binding resolution, an arbitration board shall be established to provide conclusive
and binding arbitration in accordance with the terms of subsection (c) of this section.

§1208 - Suits

(a) The courts of the United States shall have jurisdiction with respect to actions brought by the National Labor Relations Board under this chapter to the same extent
that they have jurisdiction with respect to actions under
title 29.

(b) Suits for violation of contracts between the Postal Service and a labor organization representing Postal
Service employees, or between any such labor organizations,
may be brought in any district court of the United States
having jurisdiction of the parties, without respect to the
amount in controversy.

(c) A labor organization and the Postal Service shall
be bound by the authorized acts of their agents. Any labor
organization may sue or be sued as an entity and in behalf
of the employees whom it represents in the courts of the
United States. Any money judgment against a labor organization in a district court of the United States shall be
enforcible only against the organization as an entity and

against its assets, and shall not be enforcible against any
individual member or his assets.

(d)   For the purposes of actions and proceedings by or
against labor organizations in the district courts of the
United States, district courts shall be deemed to have jurisdiction of a labor organization

(1) in the district in which such organization maintains its principal offices, or

(2) in any district in which its duly authorized officers or agents are engaged in representing or acting for
employee members.

(e)   The service of summons, subpoena, or other legal
process of any court of the United States upon an officer
or agent of a labor organization, in his capacity as such,
shall constitute service upon the labor organization.

§1209 - Applicabitliy of Federal Labor Laws

(a)   Employee-management relations shall, to the extent
not inconsistent with provisions of this title, be subject
to the provisions of subchpater II of chapter 7 of title 29.

(b)   The provisions of chapter II of title 29 shall be
applicable to labor organizations that have or are seeking
to attain recognition under section 1203 of this title, and
to such organizations' officers, agents, shop stewards,
other representatives, and members to the extent to which
such provisions would be applicable if the Postal Service
were an employer under section 402 of title 29.   In addition to the authority conferred on him under section 438 of
title 29, the Secretary of Labor shall have authority, by
regulation issued with the written concurrence of the Postal Service, to prescribe simplified reports for any such
labor organization.   The Secretary of Labor may revoke such
provision for simplified forms of any such labor organization if he determines, after such investigation as he deems
proper and after due notice and opportunity for a hearing,
that the purposes of this chapter and of chapter 11 of title
29 would be served thereby.

(c)   Each employee of the Postal Service shall have the
right, freely and without fear of penalty or reprisal, to
form, join, and assist a labor organization or to refrain

from any such activity, and each employee shall be protected in the exercise of this right.

Labor Agreements

Sec. 10.   (a)   As soon as practicable after the enactment of this Act, the Postmaster General and the labor organizations which as of the effective date of this section hold national exclusive recognition rights granted by the Post Office De-partment, shall negotiate an agreement or agreements cover-ing wages, hours, and working conditions of the employees represented by such labor organizations. The parties shall commence bargaining for such agreement or agreements not later than 30 days following delivery of a written request therefor by a labor organization to the Postmaster General or by the Postmaster General to a labor organization. Any agreement made pursuant to this section shall continue in force after the commencement of operations of the United States Postal Service in the same manner and to the same extent as if entered into between the Postal Service and recognized collective bargaining representatives under chapter 12 of title 39, United States Code.

(b)   Any agreement negotiated under this section shall establish a new wage schedule whereunder postal employees will reach the maximum pay step for their respective labor grades after not more than 8 years of satisfactory service in such grades. The agreements shall provide that where an employee had sufficient satisfactory service in the pay step he occupied on the effective date of this section to have qualified for advancement to the next highest pay step un-der the new wage schedule, had such schedule been in effect throughout the period of such service, the employee shall be advanced to such next highest step in the new schedule on the effective date of the new schedule.

(c)   An agreement made under this section shall become effective at any time after the commencement of bargaining, in accordance with the terms thereof. The Postmaster Gen-eral shall establish wages, hours, and working conditions in accordance with the terms of any agreement or agreements made under this section notwithstanding the provisions of any law other than title 39.

(d)   If the parties fail to reach agreement within 90 days of the commencement of collective bargaining, a fact-finding panel will be established in accordance with the terms of section 1207(b) of title 39, United States Code, unless the parties have previously agreed to another procedure for a binding resolution of their differences. If the parties fail to reach agreement within 180 days of the commencement of collective bargaining, and if they have not agreed to another procedure for binding resolution, an arbitration board shall be established to provide conclusive and binding arbitration in accordance with the terms of section 1207(c) of such title.

APPENDIX O

FEDERAL MEDIATION AND CONCILIATION SERVICE

MISSION

Promoting the development of sound and stable labor-management relationships,

Preventing or minimizing work stoppages by assisting labor and management to settle their disputes through mediation,

Advocating collective bargaining, mediation, and voluntary arbitration as the preferred process for settling disputes between employers and representatives of employees,

Developing the art, science, and practice of dispute resolution,

And fostering constructive joint relationships of labor and management leaders to increase their mutual understanding and ability to resolve common problems.

INDEX